Albert Barnes

Prayers for the use of Families

Chiefly Selected from Various Authors ; with a Preliminary Essay...

Albert Barnes

Prayers for the use of Families
Chiefly Selected from Various Authors ; with a Preliminary Essay...

ISBN/EAN: 9783744781121

Printed in Europe, USA, Canada, Australia, Japan

Cover: Foto ©Lupo / pixelio.de

More available books at **www.hansebooks.com**

PRAYERS

FOR

THE USE OF FAMILIES,

WITH A

A Selection of Hymns.

PRAYERS

FOR

THE USE OF FAMILIES,

CHIEFLY SELECTED FROM VARIOUS AUTHORS; WITH A
PRELIMINARY ESSAY:

TOGETHER

With a Selection of Hymns

BY REV. ALBERT BARNES.

New Revised Edition

PHILADELPHIA:
CHARLES DESILVER; CLAXTON, REMSEN AND
HAFFELFINGER; J. B. LIPPINCOTT & CO.
BOSTON: NICHOLS & HALL.

New York: OAKLEY, MASON & CO.; A. S. BARNES & CO.; D. APPLETON & CO.—*San Francisco, Cal.:* A. L. BANCROFT & CO.—*Cincinnati:* WILSON, HINKLE & CO.; ROBERT CLARKE & CO.—*Charleston, S. C.:* J. M. GREER; EDWARD PERRY.—*Raleigh, N. C.:* WILLIAMS & LAMBETH.—*Baltimore, Md.:* CUSHINGS & BAILEY; SELBY & DULANEY.—*New Orleans, La.:* STEVENS & SEYMOUR.—*Savannah, Ga.:* J. M. COOPER & CO.—*Macon, Ga.:* J. M. BOARDMAN.—*Augusta, Ga.:* THOS. RICHARDS & SON.—*Richmond, Va.:* WOODHOUSE & PARHAM.

1871.

Entered, according to the Act of Congress, in the year 1849, by
THOMAS, COWPERTHWAIT & CO.
in the Clerk's Office of the District Court of the United States, for the Eastern District of Pennsylvania.

STEREOTYPED BY J. FAGAN.
CRISSY AND MARKLEY, PRINTERS.

ADVERTISEMENT.

The following Selection of Prayers and Hymns, has been made for the aid of those heads of families who believe family devotion to be a duty, but who are deterred from it by diffidence, or by supposed want of ability. In the Preliminary Essay I have endeavoured to show the importance of the duty, and to meet the usual excuses made for neglecting it. One of these excuses is the plea of the want of ability. To meet that, as far as lies in my power, has been the main design of this selection. In meeting it, free use has been made of all the helps to family devotion within my reach. Alterations have been made where they were deemed to be desirable, and especially made to render the prayers as simple and direct as possible. A few additions have been made to adapt them to our times, and especially to Sunday Schools, and to the great efforts of Christian benevolence to fill the earth with the gospel.

These additions are indicated at the beginning and the end by a small asterisk. And as *praise* may be made a most important and interesting part of family devotion, a selection of Hymns has been added especially adapted to this design. As no such selections came within my reach, I have made this from various authors, and in the best manner that I was able, with the helps to which I have had access. The Selection has been made from the "Church Psalmody," by Messrs. Mason and Green; from the General Assembly's Psalms and Hymns; the "Village Hymns;" "Sacred Lyrics," by Mr. Beman; Dr. Dwight's Psalms and Hymns; and Hymns by Dr. Alexander. The book is committed to the blessing of God, with the prayer that it may be one of the aids by which the great ends of the family organization may be secured; and a means by which the worship of God may be extended and perpetuated amidst the families of this land. A. B.

PHILADELPHIA, January, 1850.

CONTENTS.

PRELIMINARY ESSAY ..Page 13

Morning and Evening Prayers.

First week	50
Second week	88
Third week	122
Fourth week	156
Fifth week	188

Prayers and Thanksgivings for Particular Occasions.

Last Evening of the Old Year	216
First morning of the New Year	219
For Christmas Day (Morning)	223
For Christmas Day (Evening)	225
For a Sacrament Sabbath (Morning)	228
For a Sacrament Sabbath (Evening)	230
Fast Day (Morning)	233
(Evening)	236
In Time of Pestilence	239
For Rain	239
For Fair Weather	240
Under Family Affliction	241
For a Sick Child	245
Under Dangerous Sickness	246
For One Dying	248
The Evening after a Funeral	249
Mourning for the Loss of Relatives and Friends	251

The Seasons—

Spring	253
Summer	254
Autumn	254
Winter	255
For a Day of Thanksgiving (Morning)	256
For a Day of Thanksgiving (Evening)	258
Thanksgiving for Rain after a Drought	261
For Fair Weather after Rain	261
For a Good Harvest	261
For the Restoration of Plenty	262
For a Safe Return from a Journey	263
For Recovery from Sickness	263
Prayers at Table	264

INDEX TO THE HYMNS.

Morning Hymns	269
Evening Hymns	277
Saturday Night	285
Morning or Evening	286
Family Religion	288
Sabbath Morning	293
Sabbath Evening	300
For the Beginning of the Year	303
The Close of the Year	305
The Seasons	307
The Spread of the Gospel	315
Early Piety	323
Miscellaneous	328
The Holy Scriptures	337
Afflictions and Death	340
Time and Eternity	346
The Judgment	349
Heaven	352

INDEX OF FIRST LINES.

A

Again the Lord of life and light .... Page	297
All hail, the great Immanuel's name	321
Am I a soldier of the cross..................................	330
And must this body die	350
And now, my soul, another year	305
Another day is past...	279
Another six day's work is done............................	295
Author of good, to thee we turn	291
Awake, my drowsy soul......................................	273
Awake, my soul, and with the sun........................	270
Awake, our drowsy souls....................................	297

B

Begone, my worldly cares, away..........................	285
Behold, the morning sun....................................	339
Blest are the sons of peace..................................	290
Blest be the tie that binds...................................	289
Blest morning, whose first dawning rays	299

C

Children, to your Creator, God............................	324
Cease, ye mourners, cease to languish	340
Come, dearest Lord, and bless this day	296
Come, Holy Spirit, heavenly Dove	333
Come, let us anew...	304
Come, let us join with sweet accord.....................	296
Come, let us now forget our mirth.......................	325

D

Day of Judgment — day of wonders.....................	351
Dread Sovereign, let my evening song	277

E

Eternal God! I bless thy name............................	303
Eternity is just at hand......................................	349

(viii)

F

Father, by saints on earth ador'd 282
Father of all, thy care we bless 288
Frequent the day of God returns 300
From all that dwell below the skies 323
From earliest dawn of life 324
From Greenland's icy mountains 318

G

God of the morning, at thy voice 270
God of my life, my morning song 270
God of our fathers, by whose hand 291
God of our lives, thy various praise 306
Glory to thee, my God, this night 287
Great God! my early vows to thee 247
Great God, to thee my evening song 278
Great God! this sacred day of thine 296
Great God, we sing thy mighty hand 305
Great God, whose universal sway 319
Great God, I own thy sentence just 349
Great God, at thy command 309
Great Saviour, let thy power divine 319
Great Sun of Righteousness, arise 319
Guide me, O thou great Jehovah 329

H

Hail, happy day! thou day of holy rest 295
Hail, sacred truth! whose piercing rays 337
Hark! the voice of love and mercy 332
Hark! that shout of rapturous joy 351
Hear what the voice from heaven proclaims 341
Heav'n is the land where troubles cease 354
Hosanna, with a cheerful sound 287
How bless'd the righteous when he dies 340
How blest is our brother bereft 342
How pleasant 'tis to see 291
How pleasing is the voice 307
How precious, Lord, thy sacred word 338
How shall the young secure their hearts 339
How short and hasty is our life 346
How soft the words my Saviour speaks 327
How still and peaceful is the grave 307
How vain are all things here below 336
How vain is all beneath the skies! 359

1*

INDEX TO FIRST LINES.

I

I long to behold him arrayed	357
I love thy kingdom, Lord	321
I love to steal awhile away	302
I send the joys of earth away	333
In all my vast concerns with Thee	284
Indulgent God, whose bounteous care	279
Indulgent Father, by whose care	280
In mercy, Lord, remember me	281
Inspirer and Hearer of prayer	284
In this calm impressive hour	299
Is there a time when moments flow	301

J

Jerusalem! my happy home	356
Jesus shall reign where'er the sun	320
Jesus, lover of my soul	334

L

Let all the earth their voices raise	320
Let Zion praise the mighty God	313
Life is the time to serve the Lord	347
Lo! he comes, with clouds descending	350
Lo! what an entertaining sight	290
Lord, in the morning thou shalt hear	293
Lord, thou wilt hear me when I pray	285

M

My few revolving years	306
My God, how endless is thy love	286
My God, accept my early vows	288
My son, know thou the Lord	325

N

Now from labour and from care	281
Now in the heat of youthful blood	323
Now the shades of night are gone	267

O

O'er the gloomy hills of darkness	317
O for a closer walk with God	336
O for the death of those	345
O for a sweet, inspiring ray	353
O happy soul, that lives on high	359

INDEX TO FIRST LINES.

O Lord, how many are my foes	Page 272
O Lord, another day is flown	283
Oh where shall rest be found	352
Oh, when shall Afric's sable sons	316
Once more, my soul, the rising day	269
Once more my eyes behold the day	247
On God the race of man depends	312
On thee, each morning, O my God	287
On wings of faith, mount up, my soul, and rise	360
Oppress'd with guilt, and full of fears	338

P

Pleasing spring again is here	310

R

Religion is the chief concern	326
Rise, my soul, and stretch thy wings	334

S

Safely through another week	286
Salvation, O the joyful sound	330
Saviour, breathe an evening blessing	282
Saviour, visit thy plantation	315
Shine on our souls, eternal God	348
Show pity, Lord; O Lord, forgive	331
Sing to the Lord, exalt him high	313
Softly now the light of day	280
Soon as the morning rays appear	293
Sovereign of worlds above	315
Sovereign of worlds above	322
Sovereign of worlds! display thy power	317
Stern winter throws his icy chains	311
Stretch'd on the cross the Saviour dies	331
Sweet is the scene when Christians die	345
Sweet is the time of spring	309

T

That awful day will surely come	352
That once lov'd form, now cold and dead	341
The day is past and gone	280
Thee we adore, Eternal Name	347
The flow'ry spring, at God's command	308
The grave is now a favour'd spot	342
The Lord is good, the heavenly King	312
The night shall hear me raise my song	283
There is an hour of hallowed peace	353

There is a land of pure delight.................Page	355
There is an hour of peaceful rest	356
The time is short! Sinners beware....................	346
The winter is over and gone..........................	310
Thine earthly Sabbaths, Lord, we love	301
Thou, gracious Lord, art my defence	272
Thou, Lord, through every changing scene.............	292
Thou that dost my life prolong	271
Thrice happy souls, who, born of heaven	257
Thus far the Lord has led me on	277
'Tis finish'd, the conflict is past.....................	343
To-morrow, Lord, is thine	348
To praise the ever-bounteous Lord	311
'Twas by an order from the Lord.....................	337
'Twas for my sins, my dearest Lord..................	331

W

Wake the song of Jubilee............................	322
We lift our hearts to thee	237
Welcome, sweet day of rest	294
Welcome, delightful morn	294
We've no abiding city here	357
What are these in bright array	358
When bending o'er the brink of life..................	341
When blooming youth is snatch'd away...............	344
When I can read my title clear......................	354
When I survey the wond'rous cross..................	329
When, on the third auspicious day	300
When verdure clothes the fertile vale	308
While in the tender years of youth	324
While with ceaseless course the sun..................	304
Whilst thee I seek, protecting Power.................	328
Who but thou, Almighty Spirit	317
Why do we mourn departing friends.................	344
With humble heart and tongue	327
With songs and honours sounding loud	314

Y

Ye lovely bands of blooming youth	326
Yes, we trust the day is breaking....................	335

PRELIMINARY ESSAY

ON

FAMILY PRAYER.

TO PARENTS:

I wish, in this Preliminary Essay, to make a candid appeal to parents on the duty of family prayer. In doing this, I shall assume but one thing as a conceded point—a thing which may commonly, at least, be assumed without danger of error. It is, that you feel a deep interest in the welfare of your children; and are willing to make use of any proper means to promote their happiness. This point I assume, because the God of nature has so constituted us, that as a great universal rule parents will love their children; and because no small part of their exertions are called forth with express, and almost sole reference to their present and future bliss. You who are parents, will instantly run over in your minds, many most tender and affecting scenes of watchfulness, care, anxiety, sleeplessness, and toil, to provide for their wants, alleviate their pains, defend them from danger, and train them for future respectability and happiness. The tenderest emotions in your bosoms now, relate to them. Your deepest interest is to see them virtuous, amiable, happy. You would run to their relief in danger, and deny yourself of ease to alleviate their pains in sickness. Your brightest visions of future bliss in this world are connected with their welfare. The loveliest view in the future, is when they stand forth, pure and happy, in bold relief,—single, or in lovely groups. The chief solace in the prospect of your future trials; in the anticipated days of feebleness and pain, and in the imbecility and weariness of advancing age; is that a son will live to bless you by his toil, or to cheer your last days by his virtues; or that a daughter, lovely and tender, shall come around your bed, and mingle her tears with yours, and catch your last breath, and with a gentle hand close your eyes as you sink into the long sleep of death. I wish to show you that family prayer will be one of the most important helps in meeting your wishes in regard to your children. And in doing this, I invite your attention, in the

1st place, to the design of the family organization. God might have fitted up a world of independent individuals, bound by no common sympathies; cheered by no common joys; impelled by no common wants. All that is tender in parental and filial affection; all that is mild, bland, peaceful in love; and all that is sympathetic in sorrow, and in joy; might have been denied us. Solitary beings, we might have wept alone, rejoiced alone, thought alone, died alone. The sun might have shed his beams around our lonely rambles, and not a mortal have felt an interest in our bliss or wo. Man might have lived unbenefited by the experience of his ancestors; and with none to shed a tear around the bed of moss on which he would recline in disease, and where unwept he would die. But this is not the way which he has chosen. He has made the race one great brotherhood—and we feel *some* interest at least, in the obscurest man that seeks a shelter beneath a rock, or that finds a home in a tent, or in a cave. "I am a man, and I regard nothing pertaining to man as unimportant to me"—was the language of an ancient dramatist, and a heathen theatre rang with plaudits at the noble sentiment. This great brotherhood God has broken up into communities of nations, and clans, and tribes, and families, and neighbourhoods; each with its own set of sympathies; with peculiar interests; with peculiar resources. One design is, to divide our sorrows by sympathetic emotions. Another, to double our joys by imparting them to others who sympathize with us. Sorrow hath not half its pangs when you can mingle your tears with those of a friend; and joy has not diffused half its blessings until *your* joy has lighted up the countenance of a father, or touched the sympathies of a brother or a sister.

This organization will be seen at once to be eminently adapted to religion. On no subject have we so many sympathies as in the great business pertaining to our eternal welfare. I look on a family circle. What tender feelings! what mutual love! what common joys! what united sorrows! The blow that strikes one member, reaches all. The joy that lights up one countenance, diffuses its blessings over all. Together they bend over a sick member; together they rejoice at his recovery; or together they bow their heads and weep, and go sad to his grave. They are plunged into the same apostacy. They are together under the fearful visitations of that malady which has travelled down from Paradise lost. They are going to a common tomb; and over the circle shines the same sunbeams of hope; and the same balm of Gilead, and the same great Physician may diffuse health, peace and salvation there. Cheered with the hopes of the same immortality, they may travel to the tomb; and the joy in religion that beams from a father's eye, may be reflected from the happy faces of beloved sons and daughters. The whole organization is clearly one of the most profound and wise in this world, to deepen, extend, and perpetuate the principles of the Christian religion. Of this any one may be satisfied who will for a moment compare the facilities of deepening and prolonging the feelings of religion under all the advantages of the family sympathy, compared with what it would and must be if the earth were tenanted by isolated and independent individuals. God designed the organization with reference to all that is pure, and lovely in man; and *in fact* he has at all times made the family organization one of the most important facilities for extending, and perpetuating religious feeling.

The question now arises, whether the full benefits of this organization can be accomplished without the aid of family devotion? In answer to this, you will see at once, that the neglect of religion *as a family*, will be to break in upon the whole design of the organization, so far as religion is concerned, and to throw every member upon his own individual strength and responsibilities. That is, to separate religion from all other things, and deny it the aid which is rendered to every other object which you wish to promote—the aid derived from the sympathies of the domestic alliance, and the endearments of the family circle. You call in this aid when you wish to promote other commendable designs—when you would prompt to industry, to learning, to morals, to esteem; and you withhold this aid in the greatest and most important matter that can ever press on the attention of your sons and daughters, and make their religion to be a cold, isolated, independent matter, in which they receive no sympathy from you; and where they are rudely put back from all the tender sympathies which divide their sorrows, and joys, in all their other interests. We all know the power of alliance and confederation. It is the way in which good and evil ever have been, and ever must be, propagated in this world. Solitary, undivided efforts avail little, and from the nature of the case must avail little. This is understood by all men. He who wishes to rouse his countrymen to arms, does it by an appeal to the social principle, and seeks confederated talents and valour. Individual and unorganized efforts would do little in the day when men struggle for freedom. Hence they seek to pour on the battle field combined talent, and organized and compacted energy. So in great deeds of evil. The drunkard, the profligate, the infidel, the pirate, seeks alliance and desires confederation in the enormous deeds of guilt which are contemplated and planned. In the same way, if religion is to be spread, it must be by the same alliance and confederation. It must be by bringing combined powers to act on combined ills and dangers. It is designed to be done by calling in all the aid of the family confederation; by appealing to all the authority and venerableness of a father; the tender love of a mother; the silken cords which bind sons and daughters in common love, and in common hopes. This is clearly one great design of the organization. Religion brings one of the most obvious and plain appeals which can ever be made to the family sympathies. It has more that is adapted to the family compact; more that carries forward the tender family sympathies; and more that will consolidate and cement the alliance, than any other subject that can be presented to the little community.—Yet to secure this, it is clear that it must be primary and prominent in the family doings. It must occupy a place that shall be obvious and often seen. It must be often presented; and the strength and tenderness of the family emotions must be often brought to bear upon it. I shall attempt to show that this can never be done without family prayer. Indeed, it is almost so clear as not to admit of argument. The force of the organization—the power of all the sympathies in the family, *cannot* be made to bear on it, except by daily acts, in which the whole community shall bow with united feelings before the God of grace.

II. I proceed to remark, 2dly, that family worship is one of the most direct and obvious means of meeting the evils to which the family is exposed. The design of the family organization is well understood—at least all parents have *some* great ends which they are endeavouring to reach by it. Whatever these ends may be, it will be assumed that they contemplate education, restraint, guidance, defence from danger, preparation for future years. You regard your children as exposed to dangers; subject to passions which demand control; liable to headlong and dangerous propensities, which need, in the earliest years, to be met and restrained. The world is setting in upon them even in very early life, like a mist from the ocean, with a full tide of influences, which you desire to resist. You know there are a thousand opinions and habits among men from which you would gladly restrain your children. Pious you may not be; but you would be willing to see *them* walking in the paths of wisdom. You know that there are vices to which they are exposed; and they may meet with companions which would ruin them; and that they will soon be beyond your control; and you would throw around them a panoply which should shield them from evil. You seek that the influence of a father and mother may be prolonged, and live even when you may lie in the grave. You would give to yourself a kind of omnipresent influence, that your example and precepts at least may speak when *they* are away from you, or when your tongue may no more be able to give utterance to the precepts of experience, or to the tenderness of parental love.

Now contemplate for a moment the influences from the world, against which a parent would guard.

There is, at first, the influence of *formed* plans and employments. The schemes of yesterday travel over the night watches, and meet them in the morning. They are still under the influence of the world which they met yesterday. Their schemes may not be complete. The world which they saw before they retired to rest; the opinions which they heard; the temptations which they met, shall put forth new power in the freshness of the morning. The charm has not been dissolved by the slumbers of the night. The forming habits have not been crushed, or even slept, while they have sought repose. The influence of the world which you feared yesterday, will meet them again in the morning. The enemy that made advances, did not lose his hold or even slumber while they reposed. The ever sleepless foe is strengthening his power, riveting the chains, and making his prisoner sure. Can there be any way so likely to break in upon this influence, as by a solemn presentation in the morning, to the God of grace; to bring in the parental power, and suffer *them* to see that *you* are influenced by better things; and to bring down all the sacredness of the religious feeling to arrest and annihilate this malignant influence?

A second influence from the world, results from your own plans, and views, which they see from day to day, and with which they are becoming increasingly informed and familiar. They see what engrosses *your* thoughts. They know what is in *your* heart. You are encompassing them with a set of influences in your family, and plans, which is each day determining *their* views of the relative value of objects. If religion has no place—no obvious, seen, and prominent place, in those plans, they will understand it; and they will learn what to think of it. Let the pleasures of living be all; or the gains of traffic be all; or adorning be all; or the first and last energies in your house, and your conversation be to grasp the world, and your children will be among the first of mortals to comprehend your whole character. Other men may learn it slowly. Your children will learn it at once. And to-day shall deepen the lesson of yesterday, and to-morrow shall write it with the pen of a diamond on their hearts. Can there be any way of meeting this influence so direct, and decided, as by a solemn presentation of them to God, in the morning and evening; and by thus leaving on them the deep fixed impression, that though engaged of necessity in the world, yet that you are not unmindful of better things, and that your *first* and *last* thoughts are given unto God? This act will shed a new influence over all your doings. It will teach the child that your worldly plans are not primary, or all. It will satisfy him that your toils for gain are the result of necessity, and duty; not of idolatrous choice. It will show that religion is the deep voluntary preference of your soul; excited not by selfishness and interest, but by love and a conviction of its truth and importance; and though your ardour in worldly achievement should be little varied, yet all your efforts will assume to their view a new direction, and put on a new aspect.

A third influence which your children are to meet, that needs a guardian power, is that which proceeds from other men, and other families — from the nameless attractions and seductions, that go forth each day from the world. Of this you can know nothing definite. Your family go forth to encounter you know not what. You know not what new and untried scenes of temptation they shall meet before the shades of evening descend around them. You know not what new baits and allurements the world shall present, when they are away from the watchful parental eye. You know not how attractive some form of evil shall appear to them—how it shall appeal to youthful passion or dance in delightful vision before the mind just awake to the sentiments of pleasure, vanity or ambition. Long since *you* passed through such scenes, and *you* know their power. You felt their danger, and you would guard your children from the seductive influence. To *you* of riper years, and wisdom, there may be no danger. To *them* all is fresh, attractive, lovely, like the first light of a morning, without mists or pestilential vapours. They know not the dangers; and are slow to learn. Still further, you little know what *companions* they may meet with, before the evening. The spendthrift, the profligate, the infidel — the young man, profane, flippant, confident, polished yet dissolute; or the aged man skilled in the cunning of unbelief, and knowing each avenue to the youthful heart, may meet him, and in a moment undo the slow work of parental instruction of many years.

Now I submit it to you, whether there can be any so effectual safeguard against this, as family devotion? I do not affirm that it will be infallible. But I ask whether any influence can be formed so *likely* to shield from these dangers, as the solemnity of an invocation of the presence and blessing of God, and the expectation of a similar solemn presentation in the evening. *It is a kind of familiarizing the mind in early life, to the judgment seat of God.* It is a species of arraignment there each day to suffer *His* all-seeing eye to rest on each thought and deed. That God hears prayer: and that God is every where. To him, it is as easy to guard your child when away from your roof, as when the eye of the earthly father is upon him. That God will see each temptation; mark each alluring influence; go before each child in the hour of danger; and restrain the power of the tempter. He can impress parental precept on the soul; and when the theatre, or the tavern, or the gambling place allures, the power of God unseen, can freshen in his memory the precepts of a father, and recall the expressed wishes and the pleadings of a mother. All the influences in this world are under his control; nor can there be any way so effectual of meeting them as to secure the favour of that God who can give them a direction to virtue and to heaven. Greatly do I wonder, that in a world of temptations like this, and at a period of life so exposed as that of childhood and youth, any parent *dare* suffer his children to go forth into the allurements of a city, or a wicked world, without having once asked the Father of mercies to take them beneath his protecting care, and to defend them from the ills that may bring ruin into their souls; and wo, deep and inconsolable, into your own bosom. And much do I marvel, that any parent can send them forth upon the ocean of life—amid the billows that break around the frail bark, and never seek for them the protection of that God who rides upon that ocean. And I wonder much that you can fail to implore the help of Him, who when your eye shall sleep in death, and the child shall walk over your unconscious grave, can stretch forth a hand more mighty than yours, and speak with a voice more tender than yours, to save him from the ways of ruin and despair. And much do I wonder also, that there is rest to your pillow, when you have offered no sacrifice of praise to God for preserving mercy, and sought no protection from Him whose eye never slumbers nor sleeps.

III. I remark, thirdly, that the *direct* influence of dovotion in obtaining the ends of the family organization, may be, and should be incalculably great. I mean the influence in all those great interests which you are endeavouring to secure. One of these is family government—a thing, which to be efficient, must be mild, steady, consistent, firm. There are two ways of governing a family. One is with the rod of a tyrant, and the rage of the furies; by cold, unfeeling statute, and never-ending reproof; by passion, and fire, and wrath. The other is by love, and tenderness, and discipline, administered with calmness, and yet with a faithful hand—by calling into exercise all that is tender in the social affections—all the budding and blossoming ingenuousness of the child—by the aid of conscience and of reason—and by severity only when other means fail; and then suffering the feelings of the *father* to be seen, at the same time that the firmness of the *ruler* shows itself to the child. The one is modelled on the plan which tyrants choose; the other is the plan of God. The one shuts God out of view; the other is like him, and borrows its features from the Divinity. And this one truth is established, and will yet be better known—that the model of a proper domestic administration is God in his moral government—and is a bringing down the great principles on which *he* acts, to bear on the smaller community over which presides an earthly father. Now I think I am warranted in affirming, that no father will be likely to embody these principles and express them, without prayer. They are not to be possessed without it. No man can understand the principles, on which God governs men, without that familiarity with him, which results from prayer. No man can keep this great plan before him, without that close and pressing converse and contact with God, which exists in solemn devotion. And on a father's own spirit, there will be no so happy restraint as that imposed by family intercession. Anger and passion, ill become the bosom of the man who has just been engaged in a solemn presentation of his family to the God of love. And wrath, and anger, flee away, when we know that soon we are to bend together before a common altar.

Besides, there is no way so direct, of giving authority and sanction to your commands, as by family devotion. Whatever will increase the venerableness of the paternal character, will, of course, impress his laws with additional sanctions, and power. Now, it is clear to my mind, that there can be no way of doing this so effective, as by connecting the image of a father in the mind of a child, with the sacredness of religion. Let him be regarded by them as the venerable priest of the family, to bow before the altar, and speak their wants into the ears of God—the converser with the Deity—the invoker of heaven's blessings on the community—the venerable organ through whom the sought blessings of heaven will descend on them, and a sanction is given to his laws and opinions, which you will gain in no other mode. It is not easy to treat the man with disrespect, who is known often to approach the throne of grace;—sacred by such an approach—and who is known to approach that throne only to obtain heaven's blessings on us. At all times, the ministers of religion have been regarded with respect, and there is no way so effectual of securing esteem in your family, as by suffering it to be *seen* daily, that you are a friend of God—a converser with the Deity—and that you are invested not only with the character of a father, but with the additional venerableness of being the priest of the family, and presenting their wants and feelings to the King of kings.

Thus, too, by your example, you shall correct and adjust their views of the world. More effectually than by any lessons, you shall teach them *your* sense of the value of earthly objects. Time, gold, pleasure, cannot be esteemed to be all, when the first and the last thoughts of the day are given to God. Nor can your children, in advancing years, go forth so easily to the undivided pursuit of gain and pleasure, when they know that a father and a mother, at the altar, have expressed *their* views of the value of these things. It will check the wantonness of worldly pursuits; it will come into the pleasures of the ball-room and the theatre, with a chilling influence on all those delights, if the thought then crosses the bosom of the son or daughter that at this late hour, parental feelings are expressed at the family altar, and a father and mother bow before God, to implore his blessing on thoughtless sons and daughters. "I should be there," will be the instinctive language of the heart; "my place is not amid these scenes of vanity, when a parent seeks God; and these scenes can afford no permanent joy, against whose malignant influence a parent prays, and to guard me from which a parent now implores the protection of the eye and arm of God." Such prayers are often heard. And even while it is fresh breathing from the lips of pious parentage, the serious thought, the painful misgiving of the child in the place of pleasure, may be already an answer to prayer, and the purpose may even then be forming to forsake forever such scenes, and seek peace and joy in the endearments of the fireside and of home. Let me add, too, that such amusements find their support, with few — few exceptions, from the children of families who never pray; and this devotion in all our habitations, would at once close our theatres, and no small part of the haunts of vice and ruin.

You will pass, also, into scenes of affliction. You will go down into a dark valley, and turbid waters shall roll at your feet, and a sunless sky shall be over your head. A son, a daughter, may die. Calamity may strip away your property; and slander may asperse your name; and the waves of trouble may roll high and mighty over your habitation. Your pillow may give you no rest; and the deep calamity may spread weeping and wo through all your house. In such scenes who is he that is to be calm? Who to stand like Mount Atlas, "when storms and tempests thunder on its brow, and oceans break their billows at its feet" unmoved? Who to allay the swelling tide of grief, and be a counsellor and an example there? Who to wipe away the tears from the weeping eyes of children, and pour, under God, consolation there? Who but the father at the family altar—the venerable guide and friend of the little community—he whose heart may bleed like others—for he felt the stroke more keenly than all, when his son or daughter died; but who still can gather the weeping group before God, and calmly say, "not our will but thine, O God, be done?" And if he cannot do this; if he be first in agony, and a stranger to consolation, and shall murmur at the stroke, and refuse to be comforted, who knows not the effect on the family? Grief will deepen and prolong its reign, and sorrow there shall have no comforter. Yet how shall this be done? Who does not see that the habit of daily seeking God, of acknowledging him in all the ways of the family, is the only mode of meeting this grief, and soothing these bitter pains of life? Family devotion shall change the storm to peace, and open a pathway through all these clouds; and beyond the region of these muttering thunders, in that upper sky, the splendours of an eternal day are still seen, and it shall be felt that *there* is peace.

I add here, one other remark. There are times when your children think—deeply think, of the subject of religion. They inquire what they must do to be saved. They are pressed with the great truths of eternity, and they desire to know the path that leads to immortality. Every parent knows that such thoughts are right; and that their *first* days are their *best* days, to attend to the concerns of the soul. And few are the parents who would not express a desire that these serious thoughts should ripen into the settled peace and purity of the Christian. They are the sweet openings of the buds of spring, the putting forth of lovely flowers, and may be nurtured to produce a rich harvest of piety. How shall this be done? what will be the most effectual deepener and promoter of these feelings? It is clear that if the object of the parent was to secure the ascendency of these feelings, no way could be found so effectual as daily religion in the family. Let the child see that his seriousness has the countenance of a father and mother—that it falls in with their views, and accords with their most deep desires—that to cherish these feelings would be to pour balm into their bosoms, and to fill their lips with praise—that there is an altar for the morning and evening sacrifice to deepen them, and there is no earthly influence that could be so effectual to ripen these feelings into the love of God. It seems to be a power expressly organized to accomplish this great work on the soul of the child. And on the other hand, let there be no family altar, and no sacrifice of praise in the habitation, and it is easy to see what is to be the result on the mind of a child anxious about his eternal welfare. True, he feels, and deeply feels. He prays, he trembles, he weeps. He lifts the eye to heaven in a state of deep anxiety, and waits for a guide to conduct him to the Saviour of men. The world to him is losing its charms. Temptation is shorn of its power. Fashion, wealth, and splendour, are dimmed of their lustre, and the spirit pants for immortality—for brighter peace,—more perennial joys than this world can give. What is demanded then to fill the whole soul with peace? What but the family altar—the deep seriousness of religion there—the pleading father, the bending circle, seeking for common salvation? And if there be no such altar, how cold and chill all that influence in a family! If the world be all, and fashion only has its seat there, or wealth is the grand object, or a mother's lips invite to the theatre or the ball-room, and never speak of prayer; and a father's hand guides only to scenes of gain or ambition, who can fail to see the result? How soon all seriousness shall disappear! How soon the Spirit of God shall be grieved! How soon a new current will be given to the affections, and the Son of God be shut from the view, and the Prince of darkness establish again his broken and enfeebled reign. Stronger fetters shall bind the captive to the chariot of the dark monarch of despair; and all the influence of a family be imparted to prolong his empire over the soul. And if to this we add what *may*, and does often exist, in a family without prayer, cold and cutting remarks about religion; perversion of its doctrines and duties; derision of the work of God in saving man; apparent respect, but real sarcasm, the work is done, and the enemy of man has gained his object. The most sad narrative, perhaps, that could be penned in this world, would be the history of families who have thus stifled the serious thoughts of children, and driven back by neglect or derision, the Son of God advancing to take possession of the human heart. For the wealth of the Indies, I would not come into the secret of such families; nor hazard the loss and ruin which might accrue to my children in days of seriousness, by the neglect of family prayer. There *are* times when the neglect of this plain and obvious duty, may seal the character of a child, and mark his course forever onward in the ways of sin and of hell.

IV. My fourth argument on this subject will be derived from the fact, that without family prayer, *there will be no religious teaching in a family that will be effectual.* This proposition I maintain by the following considerations. 1. The duty of family worship is one of the most obvious that strikes a child; and especially if an attempt is made to instruct that child in the principles of religion. Other duties he may not so readily understand; but this is one which is plain and apparent. He sees it; and sees it clearly. There is something so unnatural in constantly receiving benefits without acknowledging them; in being protected, and provided for, from day to day, and week to week, and year to year, without any recognition of the kind unseen hand that does it, that the mind even of a child cannot but be struck with it. If *he* who experiences a father's and mother's tenderness from year to year, should by no act express his sense of obligation, he would be conscious of something exceedingly ungrateful, and unamiable in his character. And he cannot but feel that something of the same kind must attach itself to his father and mother. Especially is this the case, if you attempt to teach him religion, to show him the duty of thanksgiving to yourself, or to God; and to set before him the evil of ingratitude. Vile, and mean, and odious, he may easily be made to see ingratitude to be. His natural honesty, and ingenuousness, may easily be excited to indignation and scorn at the base feelings of the recipient of favours, who repays them with thoughtlessness and unconcern. But are you not, in doing this, teaching him to frame an argument against yourself? 'If to be ungrateful be a trait of character so unlovely, then why is it that no gratitude is expressed to God, amid the many mercies of my father's house? How are *his* teachings about the evil of ingratitude in *me*, to be reconciled with entire amiableness in *his* deportment toward God? And if *he* can live from year to year, and exercise no gratitude to his great Benefactor, then why is *my* character to be esteemed so unlovely if I imitate his example, and receive the kindness of *my* father with cold reserve; or as entitled to few expressions of thankfulness?' And is not this the same as to *teach* ingratitude on a large scale, and make it the prominent lesson in the house, that blessings may be received to *any amount* from a benefactor, and yet no guilt be incurred by forgetting the giver, and rioting on his beneficence without one grateful emotion?

2. Prayer is one of the prime duties of religion. There can be no religion without it. You cannot teach your children *any* of the precepts of religion, without making *this* one of them. Perhaps the first lesson which you will of necessity teach, will be that it is their duty to pray. Yet how can you consistently teach this lesson without setting them the example? If prayer is of so much moment, then why should not he who inculcates the lesson, exemplify it also in his family? And what will be the effect of this *teaching*, if in the family he observes that you are a stranger to devotion? Can it be possible to teach the precepts, or the duties of religion, unless it be done in connexion with making them **prominent** and constant, in the arrangements of the

household? It will be remembered that on no other subject do you make such an experiment. You wish to inculcate the lessons pertaining to business, or the mechanic arts. You wish to train up the child to habits of industry, frugality, and order. You wish to inculcate on him the lessons of economy, or the value of polite intercourse, or of accomplishment. You have but one way of doing it. It is by example—by making these things prominent—by making them stand forth in all your domestic arrangements, so that your views cannot *but* be seen and apprehended. By making *your* conception of their value manifest to the child, you hope that he will be brought to feel as you feel, and be trained up so as to be an ornament to your name and family. Religion, you attempt to teach on a different principle—to acquaint him with the theory, not the practice; to express with the lips what the heart feels not; and to suffer the language to teach one thing, which is as regularly denied by the life. Now what is this but to take religion from all its proper connexions, and to make it a cold, distant, unmeaning thing? If I wished to tell a man how he could effectually disgust a child with a subject, it would be to teach it as he does nothing else: to take it out of all the ordinary relations of human things, and proclaim with his lips what is known never to be practised in his life.

3. Your example, without family prayer, will neutralize all the instructions of religion. If religion is of so much importance as you would endeavour to persuade him, then the child will ask, at once, 'Why does not my father exemplify it? If the world is a trifle, and eternity be all, as he tells me, then why do I see his first and last thoughts given to that world? Why all his time engrossed in the counting room, the office, or the ways of pleasure or ambition? Why is not a portion of that time given to that which is pronounced to be of such transcendent value? And if the world be so full of temptations, and trials, why does he not implore for me the blessing of that God, who I am told, can encompass

me, and shield me from danger? Is it my father's belief that that God affords protection unasked, and that he would not desire to be invoked to grant that defence and protection which circumstances of danger and trial demand? And can that be of so much moment which is suffered to be broken in upon by the veriest trifle, and excluded by any project of pleasure or gain?'

4. I appeal then to *the facts* in the case. I appeal to those parents who neglect family prayer, whether, in fact, they do not neglect the religious training of their children, as a matter of regular, sober, faithful arrangement. Does such instruction come in, in any way, as a part of the family organization? Is it not a fact that you see the inconsistency of *attempting* it without family prayer, and that rather than do the one, you choose also to neglect the other? And if so, then I put the matter on this broad ground, and urge the duty of family worship, by all the importance of the religious training. If it be so, that, if the one is neglected, the other will be, then I appeal to you by all the solemnity of their eternal interests —by a reference to their religious character in this life, and their eternal doom in the life to come, and ask you whether you *dare* to do a thing which, in its results, is to shut religion from your family, and preclude all parental religious training in your household? That parent who can coolly take a step like that, is advancing to meet an account which I humbly pray to God I may never be called to render in the day of judgment.

And this sad neglect has given rise to an abuse of one of the noblest institutions of this age—I mean the Sunday School. The parent who is unwilling to teach his children for himself, or to pray with them at home, finds a salvo to his conscience by devolving the task on others. Neglecting his own duty, he attempts to put the onerous burden on others; and to find peace in the conviction that *they* will do that which he is conscious he is neglecting.—In regard to this, I make two remarks. One is, that the Sunday School teacher is not, and will not be, and cannot be, responsible for *your* neglect of duty. A burden—if to teach and pray for your own children be a burden, has been laid on you by a higher authority than any human power; and there is no device, by which you can free yourself from the obligation. *God most High*, has clothed you with responsibility, that of training up your children in the nurture and admonition of the Lord;—that of exerting the influence of a parent to prepare them for usefulness, and for heaven. And that is no enviable feeling which attempts to flee from the responsibility, and devolve its duties on others. Besides, the Sunday School teacher has a responsibility of his own, quite enough for any human being to endure. After *you* have done your duty, still *his* work is as arduous as any mortal would willingly undertake. It is unkindness to your children, and to such a teacher, to *ask* him to bear your responsibilities. It cannot be done. He will not stand at the judgment bar in your place; nor will he meet there the doom which awaits parental neglect in the family. The other remark is this. It is, that one of the prominent effects of the instructions in the Sunday School, is to teach the duty of family devotion. That is a lesson soon learned. And your children return to you from those nurseries of piety, often deeply feeling, and greatly grieved, that their father's house is a place where no God is acknowledged, and where mercies are ever descending without any returns of praise. Each Sabbath shall deepen this lesson. And you are not to wonder if the lips of children should sometimes tenderly ask you why so plain a duty is neglected; or if they throw their arms around your necks, and intreat you to acknowledge the God of all your mercies in your habitation. I regard the Sunday School as one of the means prompting to family prayer, and not the least of its blessings do I esteem it to be, that it throws an influence back upon your families, and makes your children pleaders for God, and prompters to duty, in the business of family religion.

But while the duty of family prayer appears thus manifest and clear, while every parent would probably admit that he can see the propriety of the duty, and that most important benefits would result from its observance, yet it has so happened that there is not probably any single duty against which so many objections are urged as this. To what this fact is owing, it is not now necessary to inquire. It may be remarked, however, that the fact of the existence of so many objections, is no small confirmation of the strength of the arguments in favour of family prayer. Men do not commonly invent and urge objections where a duty is not strongly and plausibly pressed. The amount of objection will be in proportion to the strength and frequency with which the argument is urged. When that occurs daily, as in the case of family devotion, where the duty is palpable and obvious, and yet from any cause there is an unwillingness to engage in it, then it is necessary that there should be some excuse always at hand, and sufficiently plausible to turn aside, at least for the present, the force of the argument. It is of importance to notice these objections.

The first and most plausible is, that the duty of family prayer is not expressly enjoined in the Scriptures. This I admit—and having frankly made the admission, let us advance to ascertain, if possible, the precise shape which this subject assumes in the sacred volume. This will be seen by the following observations:—1. One design of law, and especially of laws pertaining to morals, is to give general statutes, or injunctions, applicable to all the cases which may occur. It is not to specify *each case*, in which business there could be no end—but to advance general principles that can be readily understood, and applicable to all the cases which may occur. That you should relieve your neighbour when he is sick, or defend his child when in danger, is not expressly commanded; but the golden rule of the Saviour will meet any number of cases of that kind which may happen. To legislate about *each* particular case would be endless. The general rule to do to others as you would wish them to do to you, is easy and easily applied to all the instances which may exist. 2. It is not the manner of the Scriptures to *command* a thing which was already in existence, and which it was supposed would be performed if there were right feeling. Thus, that men should love their children, and provide for them, was assumed without express statute, because the very organization of the family relation supposed it, and it was secured by a more ancient law than by any express statute. 3. The whole subject of prayer was left substantially in this manner. There is no injunction to prayer at all in the Scriptures, until the world was three thousand years old, nor until eight hundred years after the calling of Abraham.* Ps. cxxii. 6; Jer. xxix. 7. Yet during this time, the subject of prayer is not unfrequently mentioned; and the *fact* is recorded that men *did* call on God. Gen. xxiv. 63; Job xv. 4; xvi. 17, 15; xxiii. 26. 4. There is not in the Scriptures any injunction to *any* particular kind of prayer. Thus when secret prayer is mentioned, it is not as a command, but as a thing which *was* practised, and which it was assumed *would be* practised. All that was needed in the case, was to *regulate the manner* of its performance. Matt. vi. 5, 6. The same is true of public worship. The general command to *pray* is given; the fact is recorded that the church *did* pray; and regulations are suggested about the proper way of performing it. Is it not to be presumed, that the subject of family prayer would be left in the same manner? 5. There are injunctions respecting prayer, which imply the duty of family prayer as well as any other. Thus the command, Eph. vi. 18. Praying always (Gr. in every time — or at all times) with *all prayer* — that is, with all kinds of prayer, or offering it on all proper occasions. 1 Tim. ii. 8. I will that men pray *every where*. Phil. iv. 6. *In every thing* by prayer and supplication, with thanksgiving let your requests be made known before God. 1 Pet. iv. 7. Be ye therefore sober and *watch unto prayer*. Now if a question should arise

---

* Dr. Dwight.

what kind of prayer was contemplated in these places, on the principle of the objector it would be impossible to determine; or rather the tendency of his objection is to nullify the whole precept. He objects that the commands do not imply the duty of family prayer. They do not distinctly *specify* it, and therefore it is not a part of the injunction. For the same reason *I* may object that *secret* prayer is not commanded here, and as it is not specified, it cannot be intended. A third person, with the same reason and propriety, shall remark that *social* and *public* prayer are not commanded, and he feels released from that. What is this but to trifle with the Scriptures, and to make them unmeaning? If the command to pray with *all* prayer does not imply *family* prayer, it implies nothing and means nothing. 6. The duty of family worship—and I may assume that there will be no worship without prayer—is often mentioned with approbation, and so mentioned as to show that it is acceptable to God. Thus of Abraham. I know that he will command his children, and his household after him, that they shall keep the way of the Lord, to do justice and judgment. Gen. xviii. 19. Thus said Joshua. As for me, and my house, we will serve the Lord. Josh. xxiv. 15. Thus Job offered *daily* worship in his house—by offering daily sacrifices to obtain the blessing of God, and to turn away the divine indignation from his sons. Job i. 4. And thus also our Saviour with his apostles, and the apostles after his ascension, offered united prayer; expressed their common wants, and commended themselves to the common paternal guidance of God. That beautiful model of all proper supplication—the Lord's prayer—implies in its very structure that it is to be used daily, and in some community like a family. It is to be a *daily* supplication—" give us *this day* our daily bread." It is to be used not by an individual, but by a community. "Our Father," not *my* Father—which art in heaven. "Give us this day"—"forgive us our trespasses"—"lead us not into temptation"—"deliver us from evil." Yet there is no community that can use this but a family; none that are together each day, and none where the prayer would be so *directly* adapted to the wants of the petitioners, as in a household dependent on God, bowing down before him in the morning to ask the supply of their returning wants, and to implore protection and defence in the various trials to which the household would be exposed. "What a live coal," says Dr. Hunter, "is applied to devotion, when the solitary *my* Father and *my* God, is changed into the social *our* Father, and *our* God!" 7. God has expressly declared his abhorrence of the neglect of family devotion. It is given as a characteristic of those who know not God, that they call not on his name, and as classifying them with the heathen world. Jer. x. 25. "Pour out thy fury upon the heathen that know thee not, *and upon the families that call not on thy name.*" 8. I would only add here, that to a parent it would seem that there was no duty that less required an authoritative injunction from heaven. I would not sit down here to an inquiry into the nature of abstract statute and law. I would not look for iron enactments, and Gothic and terrific mandates here. A parent's *love* for his children, prompts him to do *all that is possible* for their welfare. For them he toils, he denies himself, he watches around their beds of pain. What is there which a mother or a father will not sacrifice for the welfare of their children? How freely do health, and property, and rest, go to promote their peace, and train them for usefulness and felicity! And who, when a child is sick, asks for an iron statute, to learn whether he shall send for a physician? Who, when the storm howls, or the flames rage, looks for inexorable law to know whether he shall stretch out his arms to aid? Why is it not so, we ask, in regard to all the great helps and blessings that may establish their virtue and promote their welfare here, or prepare them for glory hereafter? You, and your children, rise from beds of repose, protected by the hand of God. The blessings of his providence crown your board, and fill your houses with rejoicing. Protected by an unseen arm, raised by unseen power, and blessed by an invisible hand, what inexorable law is demanded to induce you, with them, to express thanksgiving to your great Benefactor? You go forth to the duties of the day. You know not its temptations, its toils, its dangers. No eye can see what unexpected occurrence may meet you—what dangers may assail—what temptations may lie in your path. Who can crown your goings with blessings but God? Who can watch over them but his unseen and never slumbering eye? And do we look for statutes to *bind* us to seek his blessing and ask his protecting care? The shades of evening come around you. Again protected, defended, shielded, you come into the family circle. Peace is there, and health, and cheerfulness, and plenty. Do I need a *formal* law when I go into such an abode, and say, here the goodness of God should be acknowledged; here it is appropriate that heaven's Eternal King should listen to the voice of praise, and the watchfulness of that eye that never slumbers nor sleeps, should be invoked? Your children go into—what? a world of peace, and friendship, of virtue, and of joy? O no. They tread a vale of sorrow. You have given them existence in a dwelling of temptation and of danger. Foes, deadly, and malignant, are in their path. The most fragrant bower may be the residence of the serpent, beguiling to destroy. The most lovely glade, the fairest path, and most charming stream, may be the residence of foes that shall attack their peace, or endanger their souls. They will be in peril—they will be allured, beguiled. Other lips than yours will attempt to influence them; and the guilty and the voluptuous may seek to make them their prey. They will weep. They will feel—yes, deeply feel, that they are in a cold, unfriendly, guilty world. They will be laid on beds of pain; will pant, will struggle, will expire. But one eye can mark their dangers or their pains, when you are dead. Far away from them in the cold grave, your eye will have lost its power to pity, and your hands their strength to relieve. Say, parent—father, mother, do we need the formality of *law*, the sternness of *command*, to tell us we MUST seek the blessing of God on our family? Is it not the instinctive feeling of every father, "*May* I bend before the God of heaven; and *will* his ear be open: and *can* I have the assurance that he is ready and willing to defend my children?" Cast the eye onward. What shall be the doom of your children beyond the grave? Whither shall they wander in that undiscovered world? Shall they repose forever in the arms of heaven's King, or shall they be vagrants and outcasts, excluded from the place of mercy and of peace, and driven away with the polluted and the lost forever! On whom is dependent their eternal doom? On that Being who is to be invoked by prayer. Who alone can save them from being cast down into hell? None but that Almighty God, whose blessing you never ask for your children, whose protecting care you never seek.

Now I would only ask of any parent, to look at his children with a parent's feeling, and remember they go to a world of dangers, and woes; to inevitable scenes of sorrow and of death; to an illimitable eternity; and to remember that none but the arm of Jehovah can shield them; and then to contemplate his household as *practically heathen*, where no God is adored; no voice of prayer is heard; no song of praise is offered; no hands are stretched out to the heavens to save your beloved sons and daughters! We are here tempted to ask, can there be such scenes? Certainly we do ask, can there be such a scene among the friends of God, and among parents, feeling that they are professedly devoted to the service of the Most High? If I speak to such an one, I address you as a Christian father, as a dying man, and beseech you that this night the God of heaven may be invoked in your abode, and that your dwelling become consecrated as the dwelling-place of the Most High.

2. A second objection is want of time. This objection scarce deserves a serious answer; and yet it is one of the most frequent that is made. I reply to it—1. That the objection is one which *may* be turned to account, and

do good, if you ever establish family worship. The great fault of devotion in families is, that it is too tedious, monotonous, and long—that it becomes wearisome and disgusting. It will be well if you can enter on it with all the advantage of the objection so often urged, and with the hope that you will feel the propriety of being short. 2. I reply, make your devotions in the family as short as you please. I am not pleading for *long* services. I am pleading *for the thing itself*. And assuredly it would not greatly impede the more important business of making money, or enjoying the world, to give five minutes or three minutes to God. 3. Is this objection ever urged by those who are conscientious about this thing, and who feel that time was given them for some valuable purpose? Is it urged by those who have actually engaged with interest in this duty, and who love it? From *them* should come the objection, if from any quarter; and it is not fair for an objector to *presume* that *he*, of all men, is conscientious about his time; and that those who offer prayer in their families are the idle, and the prodigal. An investigation on this subject might show that all conscience is not on the side of the objector, and that the acknowledgment of God interferes with no man's welfare; and that there *may* be a conscientious appropriation of time, even among those who regard family devotion as a pleasure and a duty. To such objectors I respectfully submit whether no time is spent in unnecessary sleep; whether the toilet claims no time that God *might* claim; and whether no time is spent in unprofitable reading or remark, on which God might have a claim on the head of the family. I feel that I am *letting down* this subject by noticing this objection. It requires some self-denial to meet the reasonings of men, who suppose that God is an aggressor, and an usurper; that the Eternal King is violating all the laws of property, and is rudely intruding, when he claims a jurisdiction over your hours, or moments; and that for God, your Creator, to demand even a few moments of human life, is to come in as an unbidden and unwelcome guest into your family; and is such an act of trespass on a man's castle, as to demand the deliberate purpose of a father to exclude him each day from the domain. I add in the language of Barrow, "Do we take devotion itself to be no business, or a business of no consideration? Do we conceit, when we pay God his debts, or discharge our duty toward him, when we crave his mercy, when we solicit the main concernments of our souls, that we are idle, or misemployed? that we lavish our time, and lose our pains? What other affairs can we have of greater moment, or necessity, than this? Can there be any interest more close, and weighty, than this, of promoting for our own souls eternal health and happiness? Is not this indeed the great work—*the only necessary matter*—in comparison with which, all other occupations are trifling? What are the great businesses of this world? What but scraping for pelf, compassing designs of ambition, courting the respect and favour of men, gratifying sinful curiosity, and carnal humour? Shall these images, these shadows of business, suppress or crowd out devotion?—that which procureth wealth inestimable, pleasure infinitely satisfactory, and honour incomparably noble: above all that this earth can afford? Is it not, beside, no such indispensable business, but rather some base dotage on lucre, some inveigling bait of pleasure, that crosseth our devotion? Is it not often a complimental visit, an appointment to tattle, a wild ramble in vice or folly, that so deeply urgeth us to put off our duty? Nay, is it not commonly sloth, rather than activity, an averseness from this, rather than inclination to any other employment, which diverts us from our prayers? Is it not the true reason why we pray so seldom, not because we are very busy, *but because we are extremely idle:* so idle, that we cannot willingly take the pains to withdraw our affections from sensible things, to reduce our wandering thoughts, to compose our hearts to right frames, to bend our untoward inclinations to a compliance with our duty? Do we not betake ourselves to other conversations and commerces, merely for *re-*

fuge, shunning this intercourse with God, and with our selves."

3. A third objection arises from *diffidence*. This demands a more respectful consideration. And yet there is scarcely any thing in which men are more liable to err. I shall assume the strongest case. It is that where a father is naturally timid, and retiring. Where he finds it difficult to express himself, clearly and fluently, on any subject. Where he has arrived to a somewhat advanced period of life, and his family have grown up around him. Where he even apprehends opposition, or ridicule, from his companion or children. In such a case, is it the duty of the father to establish the worship of God in his family? I reply, 1. You can speak to your children about other matters, you can address *them* on any topic; why can you not, in their presence, address God? Does it require more talent, more learning, more eloquence? The simplest language, and the humblest petitions, are those which will be most acceptable to him. 2. Every parent must feel that it is no creditable thing for him to be afraid of his children, when called to do his duty. To *fear them*, is to throw disorder into all family government; and to fear them more than God, is more. It is to throw "shadows, clouds, and darkness," on all his piety. How can a man be a Christian, when he trembles more at the fear of his children, than he does at the presence of God; and when he regards *their* opinion as of more consequence than the judgment of heaven? This was not the spirit of the apostles and martyrs, who faced the world, and defied tyrants on their thrones, and feared not racks and flames rather than to depart from the will of heaven. 3. All duty demands self-denial. He who expects to reach the heavens by sailing on the bosom of a calm and unruffled stream, will find yet that he has greatly mistaken the nature of piety. And especially is this the case where duty has been long neglected. Then, to return is always difficult. Fear and shame will always plead for a longer indulgence. The man will be diffident just in proportion to the extent of his sin, and to

the amount of influence that will be opposed to his return. The world will oppose him, perhaps deride and persecute him. But it is not reserved to this time to know what is to be done in such a case. It is long since made known. Duty is imperious. It yields nothing. And Christianity demands that whatever shame, or ridicule, or persecution, be to be encountered, it be cheerfully met and borne, even on the rack or in the flames. You will never be a Christian without self-denial. That matter is put beyond debate. 4. On this subject there is a most solemn and fearful declaration of Jesus Christ. He that is ashamed of me and of my words before men, of him shall the Son of man be ashamed before his Father, and the holy angels. 5. You are probably mistaken about your family. Suffer me to ask, what reason have you to suppose that they will regard an attempt to pray, with disapprobation, or derision? Have they thus ever met an attempt to do your duty? Have you made the experiment? Have you seen any indications that *your* attempt to obey God would meet with opposition? Then it is time that the authority of a father should be exercised, and attended by all the sanctions and pleadings of religion. If you have so long neglected to do your duty, so long neglected their religious training, that they begin to deride the religion of the Son of God, then no time is to be lost in meeting this influence, and showing them *your* sense of the value of the Christian religion, and the importance of being prepared to die. But you have not estimated aright the feelings of your children. Long since they have wondered that a father acknowledges no God in his habitation; and perhaps this may have been the burden of their secret prayers that the God of heaven might be honoured in their father's house. It is not common, in this land, at least, that a family is disposed to deride a father for a serious attempt to do his duty.—I will add here, that all these difficulties vanish when a man commences the duty in earnest. Mountains at once dwindle to mole-hills. What was formidable in appearance, becomes easy in the reality;

and delight comes in where you expected dismay and alarm. I appeal to your own experience in other things. How often have you found that all your difficulties have vanished when you have seriously resolved to do your duty! So you would find it in family prayer.

4. A fourth objection is want of ability to pray to edification. To this I answer, 1. It is not talent or eloquence that is required in addressing God. It is a humble and contrite heart. 2. You can speak before your family on other subjects with propriety. You make no plea of want of ability when you express your desires to them. Why urge this plea about expressing *their* and *your* desires to God? 3. You have as much ability in this case as the publican had. It was not eloquence or learning in him that received the commendation of the Son of God. 4. There is scarcely any thing in which *pride* is more apparent; and none in which it is more abominable, than in the excuses about prayer. If it were not for their fellow sinners, men could pray. Alone, they are never known to urge the plea of want of ability. And this is saying that they have more respect for their fellow men than they have for God. And this is the same as to say, if they were not proud they would find no difficulty in devotion. When an objection can be reduced to *this* condition, there it is proper to leave it. 5. All this difficulty can be avoided by availing yourself of forms of prayer. If the objection be sincere, that is a full answer to it, and you should commence at once. Such forms are not forbidden in the New Testament, and as if to meet this whole difficulty, and with an *expressed* design to teach his disciples *how* to pray, Christ left that inimitably beautiful model which is known as his. *That*, you can at least use in your family. And whatever may be the abstract opinion about the comparative value of forms of prayer, yet there will be no question, I apprehend, that it is better to use a form, than not to pray at all.

5. There is but one other difficulty that I think it important to notice; and that is one that demands the

utmost tenderness and kindness in the reply. It relates to the duty of a mother, and especially of a widowed mother; and the question is whether such a mother should lead a family advancing in years to the throne of Grace. The duty of a mother, where the father is *opposed* to it, is manifestly clear. It is not to assume authority, or to demand the privilege as a right, of conducting herself the devotions of the family. In retirement with her children, however, she may, and should, supplicate the blessing of God on them and him. When, however, he is unwilling to perform the duty himself, but willing that *she* should conduct the devotions of the house, there can be no violation of propriety in her maintaining family devotion. The more difficult question pertains to the widow. Let us look at this. On this, then, I remark, 1. She is obviously the very person who needs the aid of family prayer. God has taken away the head and earthly father in his mysterious dealings—he whose it was to conduct your devotions—and why should you not look to him who is your Father and Comforter in heaven? The benefit of the counsels of the earthly parent is withdrawn. You need the counsel of a higher Being; and why should you not seek it? You feel now more and more your dependence on God, and why should you not express it? 2. You especially need all this aid, in the business of governing and directing your children. They have lost their father's counsel, his example, his authority. On your feebler arm now all is dependent. It is yours to guide, to counsel, to govern. In this you need all the aid which can be obtained. What so direct and mighty as to call in the aid of religion—amid your sighs and tears to beseech the God of mercy to take you beneath his kind paternal care? It is not easy for children to treat with disrespect a praying, widowed mother. This is the very time, and occasion, for seeking the God of grace, and his ear will not be heavy to hear, nor his arm short to help her, that comes and pleads day and night before his throne, his own oft-repeated promises to the widow and the fatherless. 3. There is no scene on earth, it seems to me, so lovely as that of a bereaved family, thus pouring its sorrows into the ears of God, and seeking repose on his bosom. And in that family—that widowed and fatherless family where this is wanting, there is a chasm which no adorning, no amiableness, no intelligence can fill. God should be acknowledged there. It is the very place where there should be an altar. And if all places of worship should be broken up; if all our assemblies should be dissolved; if the fires of devotion every where else should grow dim, or expire, yet they should be seen to shed their pure beams on the abode of the widow, and to diffuse light and joy in the otherwise sad dwelling-place of the fatherless. 4. The plea of want of ability should not be urged there. It is proper to use forms of prayer; and the widow comes to her duty under the advantage of more cheering promises made to her in the Scriptures, than are made to any other class of the human family.

It is proper, before we close, to make a few remarks on the *way* in which family devotion should be performed. As *general* remarks on a subject like this do no good, I shall specify a few particulars.

1. Prayer should be *short*. A family cannot be brought to attend with interest to a prayer that shall much, if any, exceed five minutes in length. It is better to fall short of that than to exceed it. The tendency of long prayers is to disgust and weary, and to train them up to dread, and to hate the whole business of family devotion.

2. Prayer should be *simple* and *plain*. The Lord's prayer is on this subject an inimitable model of devotion. It is unsurpassed in simplicity, and it is one of the first things that a child can be made to understand. A family will soon be disgusted with that which is above their comprehension; and the only way to interest children in such devotions is to frame them so that they can understand them and feel an interest in them.

3. It should be *direct*. There should be some object to be prayed for. It should be commonly limited to a

few topics, and those should be presented in the most simple way possible. The practice of praying for every body and every thing, in every prayer, has a direct tendency to destroy all the effects of devotion. *Historical* prayers — prayers beginning with the creation of man, and tracing all his history to the times of the millennium, repeated from one day to another, soon disgust and weary any audience, and soonest of all, a family. Till men learn to concentrate their feelings, and have really some *object* for which they wish to pray — an object in which they feel *some* interest, the business of praying will be dull, monotonous, disgusting.

4. Prayer should be *solemn*. It should not be a matter of form. Nor should it be in an affected tone, or mock solemnity. Few audiences understand the *real nature* of such prayers, sooner than a family. The God whom you worship is not an idol. Your wants are not fictions. Your sins are real. The dangers of your children are mighty and pressing. Your relation to God and eternity, is not a cold formality. It has every thing to thrill, to pierce, to awe, to overwhelm. And coldness, and spiritual death, become any place better than the family altar. Let the snows of Greenland, and the ice of the northern seas, be in any other place of devotion, rather than on that where you plead with God for the guidance and salvation of your sons and daughters.

5. Prayer should be *regular*. It is not the business of the sabbath merely; nor of scenes of affliction merely; nor a matter to be attended to when you are not otherwise employed. It is to be the real *business* of the family — a part of its systematic organization, and employment. Without this its interest will expire. When I plead with you that God be acknowledged in your family, I plead that it may enter into your plans, that religion is to be a prominent part of the design for which you live.

6. Family prayer should obviously be connected with instruction, and especially with the perusal of the Holy

Scriptures. Its interest may also be heightened, and its great ends furthered, by making it the occasion of celebrating the praises of God, by psalms and hymns I add—

7. That it should be the offering *of the family.* I deem this remark of more importance than any one which I have made. When I say that it should be the offering of the family, I mean that it should enter into the *plan*, and the arrangement, that children, and servants, should be present at the time of devotion. I make the observation, because it is so easy to forget that our servants are a part of the family, or that they have any sympathies in common with us. Whoever looks into the epistles of Paul, will see that the religious treatment of servants occupies a large place in his instructions to the churches. It is clear, that proper religious attention will not be shown to them, unless it is made a matter of conscience with you to admit them to the privileges of family prayer. They are a part of your family. They are under your care. Their religious instruction is to be subject to your control. And it is perfectly manifest that their attachment to you, their fidelity, their good conduct, can be in no way so effectually secured as to admit them to the privileges of the Christian, and share with them the hopes of the mercy of heaven, and the favour of God. If you wish to secure their attachment, show them that you are interested in their religious welfare. If you wish to bind them to your family, admit them to the privileges of that religion, where there is neither Jew nor Greek, neither bond nor free; but where Christ is all and in all. These great interests you have in common. The hopes of heaven may be theirs, as well as yours. And rank, and wealth, and the relation of master, afford no passport to the favour of God, and confer no elevation before the throne of grace. Besides, there is no so effectual way of producing humility, kindness, and fidelity, among servants, as by imbuing them with a knowledge of that religion which recognises their condition, teaches them their

duty, and makes them prayerful and conscientious. Before the throne of God masters and servants should bow in common. They will soon stand at a common bar of judgment. And it is well even for the rich and the powerful, to feel every day, that in the great interests of human existence, wealth and splendour confer no prerogatives; and that those poor, dependent, and ignorant, have spirits precious as our own, and that it is ours to attempt to raise them up to the blessings of redemption, and that there is no respect of persons with God.

The same remarks are applicable to your children The evil of disorganized families results from irregularity in their attendance on family devotion. Indulge them in sleep; or suffer them to be absent amid the scenes of gaiety, fashion, splendour, or dissipation, at the regular times of devotion, and it is not difficult to foresee what will be the character of your sons and daughters. Deeds of wickedness are commonly literally deeds of darkness; and more than half the evils inflicted on a community, result from the want of power or inclination of parents to restrain, and bind to proper hours, and times, the headlong, and daring propensities of children. That parent, in my view, greatly fails in his duty, and is pointing thorns for a future pillow, who suffers his children to be absent from his view at the proper seasons of devotion. Summon them to your side, and present them before God; and there, if any where, they are safe.

In conclusion, I remark, that there is not on earth a scene more interesting than a family thus bending before the God of heaven. A collection of dependent beings, with tender feelings, with lively sympathies, with common hopes, fears, joys, blending their bliss, and their woes together, and presenting them all to the King of kings, and the Great Father of all the families of mankind. There is not on earth a man more to be venerated, or that will be more venerated, than the father who thus ministers at the family altar. No other man, like that father, so reaches all the sources of human action, or so gently controls the powers yielding in their first years, and following the direction of his moulding hand, that are soon to control all that is tender and sacred in the interests of the church and state. No Solon or Lycurgus is laying the foundation of codes of laws so deep, or taking so fast a hold on all that is to affect the present or future destiny of man. We love, therefore, to look at such venerable locks; and to contemplate these ministers of God which stand between the rising generation—feeble, helpless, and exposed to a thousand perils—and the Eternal Parent of all. They stand between the past and the coming age—remnants of the one, and lights to the other; binding the past with that which is to come; living lights of experience to guide the footsteps of the ignorant and erring; to illuminate the coming generation—to obtain for it blessings by counsel and prayer, and then to die. And if the earth contains, amid its desolations, one spot of green on which the eye of God reposes with pleasure, it is the collected group, with the eye of the father raised to heaven, and the voice of faith and prayer commending the little worshippers to the protecting care of Him who never slumbers nor sleeps.

The inimitable language of Burns, on this subject, is not fiction. In hundreds of families you might witness all that is pure and sublime in the scene contemplated by the Scottish bard.

> "They chant their artless notes in simple guise:
> They tune their hearts, by far the noblest aim:
> Perhaps *Dundee's* wild warbling measures rise
> Or plaintive *Martyrs*, worthy of the name:
> Or noble *Elgin* beats the heav'nward flame,
> The sweetest far of *Scotia's* holy lays:
> Compar'd with these, Italian trills are tame;
> The tickl'd ears no heart-felt raptures raise;
> Nae unison hae they with our Creator's praise.
>
> "The priest-like father reads the sacred page,
> How *Abram* was the *friend of God* on high;
> Or *Moses* bade eternal warfare wage
> With *Amalek's* ungracious progeny;
> Or how the *royal bard* did groaning lie

Beneath the stroke of Heaven's avenging ire;
Or *Job's* pathetic plaint, and wailing cry;
Or rapt *Isaiah's* wild, seraphic fire;
Or other holy seers that tune the sacred lyre.

" Perhaps the *Christian volume* is the theme,
How guiltless blood for guilty man was shed;
How *He*, who bore in heaven the second name,
Had not on earth whereon to lay his head:
How his first followers and servants sped;
The precepts sage they wrote to many a land;
How *he* who lone in *Patmos* banished,
Saw in the sun a mighty angel stand;
And heard great *Bab'lon's* doom pronounc'd by Heaven's command.

" Then kneeling down, to Heaven's Eternal King,
The *saint*, the *father*, and the *husband* prays;
Hope " springs exulting on triumphant wing,"*
That *thus* they all shall meet in future days;
There ever bask in uncreated rays,
No more to sigh, or shed the bitter tear,
Together hymning their *Creator's* praise,
In such society, yet still more dear;
While circling time moves round in an eternal sphere."

* Pope's Windsor Forest.

FAMILY PRAYERS.

FIRST WEEK.

SABBATH MORNING. *Jay*

O Thou King eternal, immortal, invisible, dwelling in the light which no man can approach unto, and whom no eye hath seen, or can see. Thou art incomprehensible, and the highest archangel can never find thee out unto perfection. Yet thou hast been pleased to reveal thyself to man; and by means of thy word, we behold thee in every character and relation that can suit our necessities, or encourage our hope. Thy throne is in the heavens, and thy kingdom ruleth over all; and all nations before thee are as nothing; yet thou condescendest to regard the things that are done in the earth; and thou despisest not the prayer even of the destitute. Thou art exalted above all blessing and praise: our goodness extendeth not to thee—but unless thine be extended to us, we are undone forever. Without thee we can do nothing; we *are* nothing. In thee we live, and move, and have our being. The way of man is not in himself; it is not in man that walketh to direct his steps. We are poor and dependent; but as thou art able, so thou art willing, to take the charge of us; and here we are, the living to praise thee; and to acknowledge that goodness and mercy have followed us all the days of our lives.

We bless thee, that thou hast regarded our souls, as well as our bodies; and no less provided for our future interests, than our present. When there was no eye to pity us, thou didst remember us in our low estate; and when there was no arm to rescue, thou wast pleased to lay help on one that is mighty; and thou hast sent thy own Son into the world, not to condemn the world, but that the world through him might be saved. To him may we turn our hearts, and find in him the wisdom, righteousness, sanctification, and redemption, which, as perishing sinners, we need. In all our approaches to thee, may we have boldness, and access, with confidence, by the faith of him. May we know that he has borne our griefs, and carried our sorrows; and be able to rejoice in him as our sacrifice, our sympathising friend, our almighty helper, and our lovely example. May we drink into his spirit. May we transcribe the excellencies of his character into our own. May we place our feet in the very prints of his steps; and follow him till we shall be perfectly like him, and see him as he is.

We desire to acknowledge thee in the dispensations of thy providence; and to own thy agency in all the events that befall us, whether pleasing or painful. Thou hast a right to govern us; and thou knowest what will best advance our welfare. May we commit our way unto the Lord, and be able to say at thy footstool, in unfeigned submission, Here I am, let him do what seemeth him good. If darkness veils thy dealings with us, may we trust and not be afraid; believing that what we know not now, we shall know hereafter; and that the development of thy conduct will issue in perfect satisfaction and praise.

We bless thee for the institutions of religion, in the use of which thou hast promised to draw near to those that draw near to thee. We rejoice in another of the days of the Son of man; may we call off our minds from the cares of the world, and attend upon the Lord without distraction. Quicken and elevate our souls, that rising above the formality of devotion, we may come even to thy seat, and enjoy a little of the blessedness of those that have entered thy temple above, and are singing the song of Moses and the Lamb. We are about to assemble in the house of prayer—pour upon us the spirit of grace and of supplication; and rank us in the number of those who hunger and thirst after righteousness. We are going to the house of praise—awaken in us every grateful and cheerful emotion, and may we speak to ourselves in psalms and hymns, and spiritual songs, singing, and making melody in our hearts unto the Lord. We are repairing to the house of instruction—enable us to receive the kingdom of God as a little child. Teach us of thy ways. Lead us into all truth. And let us be neither barren nor unfruitful in the knowledge of our Lord and Saviour Jesus Christ.

For this purpose, let thy presence go with us; and let thy word come to us; not in word only, but in power, and in the Holy Ghost, and in much assurance. Bless all the churches of the faithful; and the ministers of the everlasting gospel, of every name, and of every nation. Clothe the priests with salvation; and let thy saints shout aloud for joy. May our country prosper in all her lawful interests, both domestic and foreign. Bless the chief magistrate of our nation, and all that are in authority; may they rule in thy fear, and be guided by thy counsel; and may the people lead quiet and peaceable lives in all godliness and honesty. Make us glad according to the days wherein thou hast afflicted us, and the years wherein we have seen evil. Let thy work appear unto thy servants, and thy glory unto their children, and let the beauty of the Lord our God be upon us; establish thou the work of our hand upon us, yea, the work of our hand, establish thou it.

And we especially invoke thy blessing, O Lord, to attend this day all the instructions imparted in Sabbath schools and Bible classes. We pray that thou wilt be graciously pleased to grant the influences of the Holy Spirit, that that instruction may be impressed deeply on the heart and may produce abundant fruit in the life. Give grace, Almighty God, to those who are teachers in those schools; that they may be deeply impressed with their responsibility; that they may be themselves thy children; and that they may engage in their work with an earnest desire to benefit those entrusted to their charge. May their minds be enlightened that they may understand thy holy word. May they see clearly the great plan of redeeming mercy. May they be enabled to present thy truth simply, clearly, with affection, and with prayer. May the sacred Spirit—the Comforter—be given them, to guide them into all truth. And do thou be pleased to bless all children in those schools. Preside over them and give to them thy Holy Spirit. Grant to them tender, teachable minds. May they learn the paths of wisdom, and delight in instruction. May their hearts be given to the Saviour in their early years. May they come to him, who, when on earth, said, Suffer little children and forbid them not to come unto me, for of such is the kingdom of Heaven. Take, O blessed Saviour, those lambs of the flock into thine arms, and guide them by thine unerring counsel. Defend them from the perils and temptations of life, and conduct thou them to the joys of thine everlasting kingdom. [May our own children be trained up in the knowledge of thy name; and whatever instruction in accordance with thy word may be imparted to them in the family, the Sunday school, or the sanctuary, we pray that it may be attended with thy blessing, and be the means of fitting them for the duties of this life, and for the joys of thine eternal kingdom.]

These mercies, and all we need, we humbly ask in the name of thy Son, Jesus Christ, our most gracious Lord and Redeemer. *Amen.*

SABBATH EVENING. *Jay;*

It is a good thing to give thanks unto the Lord, and to sing praises unto thy name, O Most High, to show forth thy loving-kindness in the morning, and thy faithfulness every night.

We this evening acknowledge the blessings, not only of another day, but of another Sabbath. We bless thee that the Sabbath was made for man, and that thou hast hallowed such a portion of our time, for purposes so important, but which, alas, we are prone to neglect. Thus thou art affording us opportunities to retire and to learn, among all the cares of life, that one thing is needful; and to hear the inquiry, what is a man profited, if he should gain the whole world and lose his own soul. Thus we have moments of leisure, in which we can more fully investigate our character; examine our condition; and ask, for what purpose we entered this mortal stage, and what will become of us when these scenes close.

We thank thee that the lines are fallen to us in pleasant places, and that we have a goodly heritage: so that we can add to private meditation and devotion, the public ordinances of religion; and can sit under our own vine and fig-tree, none daring to make us afraid. We bless thee, that we have not only the Scriptures, but the ministry of the gospel; and have this day not only read, but heard the words of eternal life.

But, O God, the effects we experience while waiting upon thee, though delightful, often prove like the morning cloud, and early dew. Before the lapse of a single day, we are compelled to complain, My soul cleaveth unto the dust; and to pray, Quicken thou me according to thy word. Render therefore the impressions made upon us, deep and durable: keep these things for ever in the imagination of the hearts of thy people; and let thy word *dwell* in us richly, in all *wisdom*.

May the instructions we receive, attend us in every part of our life, and regulate, and excite us in the discharge of all our relative duties, so that whether we are husbands or wives, parents or children, masters or servants, we may adorn the doctrine of God our Saviour in all things. May we be satisfied with no knowledge, no belief, no professions, no feelings in religion—while our hearts are void of thy love, and we are strangers to that grace which bringeth salvation, and teacheth us to deny ungodliness and worldly lusts, and to live soberly, righteously, and godly in the present world.

We take shame to ourselves, not only for our open violations of thy law; but for our secret faults, our omissions of duty, our unprofitable attendance on the means of grace, our carnality in worshipping thee; and all the sins of our holy things. Our iniquities are increased over our head, and our trespass is gone up into the very heavens — and there he is gone also, who is our Advocate with the Father, and the Propitiation for our sins. Behold his hands and his feet: and hear, O hear, the voice of the blood of sprinkling, that speaketh better things than that of Abel.

Pity those who have this day been deprived of the public means of grace by sickness or infirmity. Let them know that thou art not confined to temples made with hands: be with them in trouble; and give them their vineyards from thence, and the valley of Achor for a door of hope.

And remember the millions who were never favoured with the advantages we enjoy, and would be grateful for the crumbs that fall from our table. But they never smiled when a sabbath appeared. They never heard the name of Jesus. They feel guilt, but know nothing of the blood that cleanseth from all sin; they feel depravity, but know nothing of the renewing of the Holy Ghost. No one proclaims among them the balm of Gilead; and the physician there. O, send out thy light and thy truth. Let thy way be known on earth; thy saving health among all nations.

We now commit ourselves, with all our connexions, into thy hands. Guard us through the defenceless hours of sleep, from every evil to which we are exposed. If, as life is always uncertain, it should please thee to call us hence this night — may we awaken in glory, and be forever with the Lord: or if thou shouldst continue us in being — may we rise in health and comfort, to pay thee the homage of a grateful heart, in a course of cheerful obedience.

In thy favour is life—Do thou bless us, and we shall be blessed—safe from every evil, and sure of every good.

And prepare us at length for the rest that remains for thy people; in which we shall join the general assembly and church of the first born, in ascribing blessing and honour, and glory, and power, to him that sitteth upon the throne, and to the Lamb, for ever and ever. *Amen.*

MONDAY MORNING.*   *Jay.*

O Thou, who hast characterized thyself as the hearer of prayer, unto thee shall all flesh come: and that we may come with acceptance and success, we come in the name of the great intercessor, Jesus Christ, the righteous—and thou Eternal Spirit of grace and supplication, do thou make intercession for us, by making intercession in us, according to the will of God.

Bless the services in which we were engaged on the past day. Let a savour of divine things be left on our spirits, and be diffused in our conversation. Let those around us take knowledge of us, that we have been with Jesus; and may our profiting appear unto all men. May our light shine before men. May we be *manifestly* the disciples of Christ. May we put on, as the elect of God, holy and beloved, bowels of mercies, kindness, humbleness of mind, meekness, long suffering, forgiving one another. May we be followers of God, as dear children: may we be perfect, as our Father, who is in heaven, is perfect.

We confess and bewail, not only our deficiencies, but our backslidings also. O, recall us to thyself; enable us to feel our first love, and to do our first works. Yea, may we forget the things that are behind, and reach forth unto those that are before. May we not only have life,

---

* The first Monday in the month is observed, by most Christian denominations, as a monthly concert of prayer for the spread of the gospel throughout the world.

but may we have it more abundantly; and not only be fruitful, but bear much fruit.

May our improvements correspond with our privileges; and our practice with our knowledge. May our wills always bow to the decisions of our judgments; may we choose what we approve, and never condemn ourselves in the things that we allow.

May all our churches continue steadfastly in the apostles' doctrine, and in fellowship, and in breaking of bread, and in prayer; and may the Lord add daily to their number, such as shall be saved.

May the dead hear the voice of the Son of God, and live. May those who are asking the way to Zion, with their faces thitherward, find a teacher that will say to them, This is the way, walk ye in it, when they turn to the right hand, and when they turn to the left. Let the rich be poor in spirit; and the poor be made rich in faith, and heirs of the kingdom which thou hast promised to them that love thee. Let the ignorant be enlightened; and let those that are wise, become fools, that they may be wise.

*We acknowledge thee, O most merciful God, as the Father of all flesh. Thou hast made of one blood all the nations of men, to dwell on the face of all the earth; and hast fixed the bounds of their habitation. Thou upholdest all in being; providest for their wants; causest thy sun to rise on the evil and on the good, and sendest rain on the just and on the unjust. We rejoice, O our Father, and thank thee for thy goodness to all men. We praise thee that thou hast had mercy on the human family, and hast provided a plan of salvation, adapted to the wants of all mankind. And we bless thee for all thy promises in relation to the spread, and final triumph of the gospel of thy dear Son, that the heathen shall be given to him for his inheritance, and the ends of the earth for his possession—that the desert shall bud and bloom as the rose, and the wilderness and solitary place shall be glad.

Be pleased, O Lord, to look down in mercy, on all who shall this day assemble to supplicate thy blessing on a fallen world. Give to thy people a spirit of grace and supplication. May they approach thy throne with humble hearts; with true faith; with earnest desires, that thy kingdom may come, and thy will be done on earth as it is done in heaven. May they approach thee, feeling that they plead for the salvation of a dying world; and give thee no rest until the righteousness of Zion go forth as brightness, and her salvation as a lamp that burneth. Do thou graciously hear and answer their supplications. Look in mercy upon a ruined world. Pity the nations that are sitting in the region and shadow of death; and may the sun of righteousness arise upon them with healing in his beams. May the dark places of the earth, now full of the habitations of cruelty, become the dwelling-place of righteousness, and the abodes of peace. May the ignorant be enlightened; the wretched be comforted; the oppressed go free. May thy glorious gospel shed its blessings on all the nations of the earth; and all the means now used to advance the glory of the latter day, be crowned with success.

Attend, O most merciful Father, all those who have gone to other lands, to make known the unsearchable riches of Christ. Give to them much of the spirit of thy dear Son. Give them wisdom to direct them—grace to support them in all their trials—success in all their efforts. Make them burning and shining lights among the nations. May they be kept from sin, and temptation; from despondency, and doubt; from persecution, and want. In all their trials may they stay themselves on thee, and ever have an unshaken confidence in the promises of thy holy word. Keep, by thy mighty power, all who among the heathen have been converted to the Christian faith. Preserve them from temptation and apostacy. Afford them light and strength as they need, and amid all the trials with which they may meet, may they find thee to be a present help, a refuge, and a strength. May they see more and more of the beauty of that religion which they profess, and daily rejoice more and more in hope of the glory of God.

Advance, O Lord, all the great interests of man. May the blessings of civil and religious freedom, of Christian education, and of peace, be every where enjoyed. May wars, and rumours of wars cease. May the sword be beat into a ploughshare, and the spear into a pruning hook, and nations learn war no more. Let the mild and peaceful principles of thy glorious gospel every where prevail, and the ends of the earth soon be filled with thy glory.*

We bless thee, for all thy former loving-kindnesses to this family, and pray that they may be continued to us, and sanctified to us. May the outgoings of the morning and evening of another day be made to rejoice. May we continually live under the shadow of thy wing and the influence of thy grace: and let the words of our mouth, and the meditations of our hearts, be acceptable in thy sight, O Lord, our strength and our Redeemer.

And unto Him that is able to do for us exceeding abundantly above all that we ask or think, according to the power that worketh in us, unto Him be glory in the church, by Christ Jesus, throughout all ages, world without end. *Amen.*

MONDAY EVENING. *Jay.*

Our Father, who art in heaven, we approach thee at the close of another day to render thee thanks for thy mercies, and to implore thy blessing on us and on all mankind. Thy mercies are new to us every morning, fresh every evening, repeated every moment. To thy name we give thanks for our birth in a Christian land, and for all the mercy thou hast shown us in our lives. We thank thee for thy glorious gospel, that gospel which we have so long slighted and abused, and which thou art graciously continuing to us. We would remember this night, that millions of our fellow beings are sitting in the region and shadow of death; that on them no light has risen, and none have gone to them to break to them the bread of life. Make us sensible of thy distinguishing mercy to us. May we remember that where much is given, there much will be required; and that soon we must appear at thy bar, with an assembled world, to render an account for the improvement of all our privileges.

We bless thee for a purpose of grace given us in Christ Jesus before the world began. We rejoice that in the fulness of time he assumed our nature, and became obedient unto death; even the death of the cross; and that as he was delivered for our offences, so he was raised again for our justification, and ascending up on high, entered into the holy place, as a proof of the sufficiency and acceptance of the sacrifice he offered. We rejoice that he has received the whole dispensation of the Spirit, and that in him all fulness dwells. And we bless thee for the proclamations of the gospel, which hold him forth to our view in all his grace and glory, and unsearchable riches, that we through patience and comfort of the Scriptures, might have hope.

O thou God of hope, fill us with all joy and peace, in believing thy promises and invitations, that we may abound in hope through the power of the Holy Ghost. May we esteem all things but loss for the excellency of the knowledge of Christ Jesus our Lord; and may we supremely desire to win Christ, knowing that he who hath the Son of God hath life, and shall never come into condemnation. May we prove that we are joined to the Lord, by being one spirit with him; may our sentiments, tempers, and conduct, be formed after the example which he left us; and may we never consider ourselves Christians, but as we long to be like him, and the life also of Jesus is made manifest in our mortal body. May we never love a world that crucified the Lord of glory; nor suffer those sins to live that caused him to die. May his grace, in becoming poor, that we through his poverty might be rich, make us ashamed of our selfishness; and may his love, in giving his life a ransom for us, so con-

F

strain us, as to render any services or sacrifices, for his sake, our delight.

May he never be wounded in the house of his professed friends; may we rather die than bring a reproach upon his cause. May all his followers be dear to us. May we recommend him to those that know him not, that they may seek him, with us. Let the number of those who love his salvation, daily increase; and let the accessions include every member of our household, and all our absent friends. And hasten, O Lord, the blessed hour, when all kings shall fall down before him, and all nations shall serve him — and blessed be his glorious name forever! And let the whole earth be filled with his glory.

*Be pleased, O Lord, to hear the prayers which thy people have this day offered in behalf of Zion. Grant an answer to the desires and supplications of thy people. Send out thy light and thy truth, and let all nations be illuminated with the gospel of thy grace. We commend to thee thy cause. We beseech thee to look in mercy upon the nations of the earth. We pray that thy people may be more deeply impressed with the wants and woes of man. Grant that thy people may more and more deny themselves; may feel more deeply affected in view of all the miseries and crimes of our race; and more earnestly desirous that all nations should hear thy gospel. We commend to thy care all Missionary, Tract, Bible, and Education Societies, and all the institutions of benevolence in our land, and throughout the world. May those who are called, in thy providence, to direct the charities of thy people, and to preside in the institutions of benevolence, be endowed with true wisdom, with conscientiousness, with a spirit of prayer, and with deep and expansive benevolence. May they ever feel their responsibility, and in all their deliberations be conducted to such results as shall be for the glory of thy name, and for the speedy and universal extension of the gospel among the nations of the earth. We pray that revivals of true religion in all lands may be multiplied. We beseech thee to send forth more labourers into the harvest. May all our schools and colleges be under thy fostering care, and may the young men of this land, and this generation, be imbued with the spirit of self-denial, and with a readiness to obey thy call in diffusing the blessings of civilization and Christianity among all men. May every continent and island partake of thy blessing, and every nation and tribe speedily hear in their own language the wonderful works of God. Let thy holy word be translated into all the languages of the earth, and every habitation of man be soon blessed with the inestimable treasure of the word of life.

Behold in mercy, O God, all who are oppressed. Especially look in tenderness upon benighted and injured Africa. Send to all her millions thy holy gospel, and may Christian nations soon be roused to repair her wrongs, and to send to that people, so long injured and afflicted, the healing balm of life. Put a period, we do earnestly pray thee, to the traffic in human flesh. May the eyes of men be opened to the guilt and wo of this traffic, and their hearts feel, deeply feel, for that injured people. Remember, O Lord, all the sons of Africa who are held in bondage in all lands. May that gospel, which is sent to bind up the broken-hearted, to proclaim liberty to the captives, and the opening of the prison to them that are bound, be sent to all those lands, and may the prisoner speedily go free. Especially remember all in bondage in our own land. Bless all the means that are used to promote their welfare; and soon may this land be freed from this burden, and all men here be admitted to the rights with which, by nature, thou hast endowed them. Direct to such means as may result in their freedom, in consistency with the peace and welfare of this nation; and grant that their captivity here, may yet be the means of bestowing the rich blessings of Christianity on the land of their fathers.*

We praise thee as the length of our days and the God of our mercy. In the morning we committed ourselves to thy care, and thou hast been with us in our going out and our coming in; and hast kept us in all our ways. Pardon whatever thou hast seen amiss in us through another period of our time. Accept the charge of us through the approaching night; and grant us the sleep which thou givest thy beloved; as we hope we desire it, not only as creatures, but as Christians; not only to gratify our feelings, but to renew our strength for thy service, and to fit us to glorify thee in our bodies as well as in our spirits, through our adorable Redeemer. *Amen.*

TUESDAY MORNING. *Jay.*

O Thou, whose name also is Jehovah, the Most High over all the earth, we desire to adore the perfections of thy nature, and to admire the works of thy hands. May the united displays of thy greatness, and thy goodness, impress our minds, and influence our thoughts and affections, while we approach thee.

Heaven is thy throne, and the earth is thy footstool. The universe, with all its creatures, was made by thy word, and is upholden by thy power; and thou doest according to thine own will in the army of heaven, and among the inhabitants of the earth; none can stay thy hand, or say unto thee, What doest thou?

But thou art the Father of mercies, the God of all grace, and the God of all comfort. Even we, poor, mean, dying creatures, are not beneath thy care. Thou hast been mindful of us; thou hast visited us; and thy visitation hath preserved our spirits. The lines are fallen to us in pleasant places; yea, we have a goodly heritage; we live in a land of light; we have the Scriptures in our hands, and our ears hear the joyful sound of the gospel. We know that thou hast not spared thine own Son, but delivered him up for us all. We know that he has borne our griefs, and carried our sorrows: that his blood cleanseth from all sin, and that whosoever believeth on him, shall not perish, but have everlasting life.

We come in *his* name, and make mention of his rightteousness only. We plead the obedience and sufferings of *him* who magnified the law, and made it honourable. May we be justified by his blood; and may we be saved by his life. May we be joined to the Lord, and of one spirit with him. May we deny ourselves, and take up our cross, and follow him. May the agency of thy Holy Spirit prepare us for all the dispensations of thy providence. May we be willing that the Lord should choose our inheritance for us, and determine what we shall retain or lose; what we shall suffer or enjoy.

If indulged with prosperity, may we be secured from its snares, and use its advantages as not abusing them. And may we patiently and cheerfully submit to those afflictions, which are necessary to hedge up our way when we are tempted to wander, to excite an abhorrence of sin, to wean us from the present evil world, and to make us partakers of thy holiness. In whatsoever state we are, may we be therewith content. Only assure us that thou wilt be with us in trouble, and, that at the end of the vale of tears, we shall enter Emmanuel's land, where the inhabitants no more say, I am sick; where our sun shall no more go down, nor our moon withdraw itself, but God shall be our everlasting light, and the days of our mourning shall be ended.

May our friends and relations be fellow-heirs with us of the grace of life. Let our house be the tabernacle of the righteous: let our children and servants be a seed to serve thee: and among none of those who surround this family altar, may there be weeping and wailing, and gnashing of teeth, when they shall see Abraham, and Isaac, and Jacob, in the kingdom of God, and they themselves shut out.

Lord, help us all to view our religious opportunities as talents, for which we are accountable: to remember, that our greatest danger results from our highest privileges; and to fear, lest a promise being left us of entering into thy rest, any of us should seem to come short of it.

Thou hast determined the bounds of our habitation, and by the events of thy providence, many of those in whose society we delight, are separated from us. When we are absent in body, may we be often present in spirit. We commend our absent friends and kindred to thy covenant care. May no evil tidings concerning them, wound our hearts: spare them in mercy: may we often embrace each other in circumstances of health and comfort: or if we have had our last interview on earth, may we all meet in our heavenly Father's house, and be for ever with each other, and for ever with the Lord.

In the duties of this day, be graciously pleased to be with us. Preserve us from temptations, and the allurements of the world. Defend us from danger, and prepare us for whatever may be thy will in regard to us. In all circumstances may we evince the Christian spirit: be kept from anger, and pride, and ambition; from envy, hatred, and malice, and all uncharitableness. May we be diligent in business; fervent in spirit; serving the Lord; rejoicing in hope; patient in tribulation; continuing instant in prayer; distributing to the necessity of saints; given to hospitality. May we rejoice with them who do rejoice, and weep with them who weep. Help us to provide things honest in the sight of all men; and to live peaceably with all. To the end of our lives may we be the humble and consistent followers of Jesus Christ, so that at last, through his merits, we may, with all thy people, be admitted to the joys of thy kingdom above.

And to the only wise God, our Saviour, be praise and glory everlasting. *Amen.*

TUESDAY EVENING. *Jay.*

O Thou King of Glory, we desire to approach thy divine Majesty with reverence and godly fear, and to worship thee in the beauty of holiness. Every perfection adorns thy nature, and sustains thy throne. The heavens are thine; the earth also is thine: the world is thine, and the fulness thereof. Thy power formed the universe from nothing. Thy wisdom has managed all its multiplied concerns, presiding over nations, families, and individuals, and numbering the very hairs of our head. Thy goodness is boundless; the eyes of all wait upon thee, and thou givest them their meat in due season. Thou openest thine hand, and satisfiest the desire of every living thing. How precious are the thoughts of thy mercy and grace—and so excellent is thy loving kindness, that even the children of men put their trust under the shadow of thy wing.

Thou art the blessed and happy God. O, teach us to place our happiness in thyself. May we never seek the living among the dead, nor ask with the deluded many, Who will show us any good? But, may we prize the light of thy countenance; implore the joy of thy salvation; and passing by the attractions of creatures, be able to say, Whom have I in heaven but thee, and there is none upon earth that I desire beside thee.

Thou hast been infinitely more attentive to our happiness than we ever have been, or ever can be. Thou madest man upright, and when, by voluntary transgression, we fell away from thee, thou didst not treat us with the severity or the neglect we deserved. In thy love and pity thou wast pleased to provide for us a Saviour, who bore our griefs and carried our sorrows, and put away sin by the sacrifice of himself.

Apply this redemption to our hearts, by the justification of our persons, and the sanctification of our natures. We confess our transgressions—Have mercy upon us. We are heavy laden—Give us rest. We are ignorant—Make us wise unto salvation. We are helpless—Let thy strength be made perfect in our weakness. We are poor and needy—Bless us with all the unsearchable riches of Christ. May we run and not be weary, and walk and not faint. And though perplexities, and trials, and dangers await us, yet may we travel on, unchecked and undismayed, knowing, thou hast said, I will never leave thee, nor forsake thee.

Thus far, blessed be thy name, thou hast led us on, and we have found thee faithful to thy promises. We have had our sorrows; but thou hast been a very present help in every time of trouble. We have had our fears; **but** thou hast not suffered the enemy to triumph over us. We have sometimes been on the verge of despair, and have said, I am cast out of thy sight: but we have been enabled to look again towards thy holy temple; and the shadow of death has been turned in the morning. Hitherto hath the Lord helped us. Thy vows are upon us, O God: we will render praises unto thee, for thou hast delivered our souls from death: wilt not thou deliver our feet from falling, that we may walk before God in the light of the living?

We would feel the connexions which unite us to others, and by sympathy, and prayer, and praise, make their miseries and mercies our own. We would rejoice with those that rejoice, and weep with those that weep. Provide support and employment for the poor. Make the widow's heart to sing for joy: and in thee, may the fatherless find mercy. Visit those who are on beds of sickness, and prepare them for thy pleasure; that if they live, it may be to serve thee. Bless our nation. May every department of the nation be under the control of infinite wisdom and goodness; and let righteousness and peace be the stability of our times. Do good, in thy good pleasure, unto Zion; build thou the walls of Jerusalem: and may all our churches, like the original disciples, continue steadfastly in the apostles' doctrine, and in fellowship, and in breaking of bread, and in prayers.

Protect and refresh us through the night season: and then cause us to hear thy loving kindness in the morning: for in thee do we trust: cause us to know the way wherein we should go, for we lift up our souls unto thee. We implore it through the intercession of thy dear Son, and our Saviour.

And blessing, and honour, and glory, and power, be unto Him that sitteth upon the throne, and unto the Lamb, for ever and ever. *Amen.*

WEDNESDAY MORNING. *Jay.*

O Thou Most High! enable us to feel, and to express, becoming regards towards thee, as the Creator of the ends of the earth, the Preserver of men, the Governor of the universe, the Judge of all, the Saviour of sinners. Thy greatness is unsearchable, and thy goodness is infinite. It is because thy compassions fail not, that we are not consumed. Thou hast not only prolonged our unworthy lives under numberless provocations, but thou hast afforded us every needful supply and indulgence. Thy mercies have been new every morning and every moment. Through thy good hand upon us we have been rescued from the perils of another night; our repose has been unterrified and undisturbed; sleep has refreshed our bodies, and renewed our strength; and we find ourselves surrounded, at the commencement of another day, with all our accustomed privileges.

But, O God, we can never be sufficiently thankful that we have our existence in a Christian country, and where we can hear words, by which we may be saved. O, how important, how suitable, how encouraging are the discoveries, the doctrines, the promises, the invitations of the gospel of peace! We are lost; but here is presented to us a free, full, and everlasting salvation. We are left without strength; but here we learn, that help is laid on one that is mighty. We are poor and needy; but here we behold the unsearchable riches of Christ. We are blind and ignorant; but in him are hid all the treasures of wisdom and knowledge. We thank thee, O God, for thine unspeakable gift, and we cordially accept of thy mercy extended to us, through the mediation of thy dear Son. We rejoice that he has been delivered for our offences, and raised again for our justification; and that he is now exalted at thy right hand, to be a Prince and a Saviour. We abandon every other refuge to hide in, and every other foundation to build upon, and make him our only hope, and our only confidence. And while we depend on his death, and make mention of his righteousness only, we admire his example, and desire to be conformed to his image. May we put on the Lord Jesus Christ, and increasingly resemble him, whose life was beneficence; whose soul was meekness and humility; who pleased not himself; and who, of obedience the most trying and difficult, could say, I delight to do thy will, O my God, yea, thy law is within my heart. May his glory fill our minds; may his love reign in our affections; and at his cross, and at his tomb, may we burn with ardour to live, not to ourselves, but to him that died for us and rose again.

Let the number of his followers daily increase; and may none of our friends be found among his enemies. Pour thy Spirit upon our seed, and thy blessing upon our offspring. Let our sons be as plants grown up in their youth, and our daughters as corner-stones, polished after the similitude of a palace. May our domestics be the servants of God; may they do his will from the heart; and be prepared for that world, where those who serve will be as those who are served, and all the distinctions now necessary, will be done away, and none remain, but those which arise from character. And whatever be our conditions in life, may we fill them as Christians; may we escape the snares to which they expose us; discharge the duties that grow out of their circumstances; enjoy with moderation and gratitude their advantages; and improve with decision and diligence, their opportunities and resources of usefulness. May every place, and every company, in which we are found, be benefited by us.

And whatever may be the opinion of our fellow creatures concerning us, may we be satisfied and happy, in having the testimony that we please God. We are now going forth into the concerns of another day. Take us under thy protection and influence. Guide us in all our steps. Enable us to realize thy presence and thy providence. Succeed us in all our lawful endeavours, or prepare us for disappointment; and assure us that we are in the number of those to whom all things are working together for good; and who will forever acknowledge—marvellous are thy works, Lord God Almighty, just and true are all thy ways, O thou King of saints.

We ask these mercies, sensible of our guilt and unworthiness. We come not in our own names, and we plead no merit of our own. We come in the worthy name of our Lord Jesus Christ, who died for us, and who ever lives to make intercession for us; and we desire to ascribe to him, with the Father and the Holy Spirit, all praise, power, glory, and dominion, both now and forever. *Amen.*

WEDNESDAY EVENING. *Jay.*

Our Father, who art in heaven, we desire to acknowledge thy being and agency; to adore thy perfections, and to admire the works of thy hands. Thou hast made summer and winter. Thou hast appointed the moon for seasons, and the sun knoweth his going down. The day is thine; the night also is thine: and thou makest the outgoings of the morning and the evening to rejoice. To that throne, from which none were ever sent empty away, we again approach for mercy and grace to help in time of need. Let our prayer come before thee as incense, and the lifting up of our hands as the evening sacrifice. Preserve us from formality in these exercises in which we so daily engage; and alarm our fears, lest we should provoke thee to say, In vain do they worship me.

For this purpose, enable us to realize thine all-seeing eye, to remember with *whom* we have to do, and what we have to do with him: may we deeply feel the guilt of the sins we confess, and hunger and thirst after the blessings we implore. And while we review the numberless blessings we have received from thy hands, may we be more than ever sensible of our unworthiness, that our hearts may be unfeignedly thankful, and that we may be disposed to show forth thy praise, not only with our lips, but in our lives, by giving up ourselves to thy service, and walking before thee in holiness and righteousness all our days.

He that is our God is the God of salvation, and unto God the Lord belong the issues from death. We bless thee this evening as the preserver of men. Another day has been added, by thy good providence, to the season of thy long suffering, and the time of our preparation for eternity. We lament that the design of our being placed and continued here, has been so imperfectly subserved; that in so many things we have offended, and in all, come short of the glory of God. If, where much is given, much will be required, and the servant who knew his Lord's will and did it not, shall be beaten with many stripes—if thou, Lord, should mark *our* iniquities, O Lord, who shall stand? We cannot answer thee for one of a thousand of our transgressions: the review of a single day is enough to plunge us into despair—our only relief is, that there is forgiveness with thee; and that with thee there is plenteous redemption.

But while we hope in thy mercy, we would not abuse it. We would not sin that grace may abound; or be evil, because thou art good. But since thou art good, and ready to forgive, we would the more sincerely grieve, that ever we have offended a Being, so worthy of our devotedness, and be the more concerned in future, to walk so as to please thee.

Create in us a clean heart, and renew a right spirit within us. Set a watch, O God, upon our mouth; keep the door of our lips. And in simplicity and godly sincerity, not with fleshly wisdom, but by thy grace, may we have our conversation in the world, and in the church, and in the family.

We again commend ourselves to thy care. As thou hast been through the day, our sun and our shield, be thou through the night, our shade and our defence. Undisturbed by anxieties, unalarmed by fears, undistressed by pain or indisposition, may we retire and enjoy repose. Remind us, by putting off our garments, and lying down to sleep, of putting off the body, and sleeping in the grave, the house appointed for all living. Prepare us for the night of death, the morning of the resurrection, and the day of judgment.

And all we implore is, through the mediation of Him, who bore the sins of many, and made intercession for the transgressors, to whom, with the Father, and the Holy Spirit, be endless prayers. *Amen.*

THURSDAY MORNING. *Jay.*

O LORD our God, blessed is the man whom thou choosest, and causest to approach unto thee. In thy presence there is fulness of joy, and at thy right hand there are pleasures forever more. With thee is the fountain of life, and in thy light alone can we see light.

We therefore entreat thy favour, with our whole heart. We acknowledge that we have forfeited all claims to it; and if we had no better ground of hope than our deservings, we must sink into despair. For against thee, thee only have we sinned, and done evil in thy sight, that thou mightest be justified when thou speakest, and clear when thou judgest.

But with thee there is mercy, and with thee there is plenteous redemption. We bless thee for the assurance, that thou hast sent thine own Son into the world, not to condemn the world, but that the world, through him, might be saved. We rejoice, that neither the number nor heinousness of our transgressions, is a bar to that forgiveness, which is founded on the sufferings and sacrifice of the cross. The blood of Jesus Christ, thy Son, cleanseth from all sin. Graciously absolve us from our guilt; and pronounce our discharge from all condemnation, that being justified by faith, we may have peace with God and enjoy the glorious liberty of thy children.

But, O, save us from the hope of the hypocrite, which shall perish. Never suffer us to impose upon ourselves, in any thing that relates to our eternal state. May we never suppose that we are in Christ, unless we are new creatures; or that we are born of the Spirit, unless we mind the things of the Spirit. May we never rest satisfied with any professions of belief or any outward forms or services, while the heart is not right with God. May we judge of our sincerity in religion, by our fear to offend thee; by our concern to know what thou wilt have us to do; and by our willingness to deny ourselves, and take up our cross and follow the Lamb, whithersoever he goeth.

May nothing render us forgetful of thy glory; may nothing turn us aside from thy commands; may nothing shake our confidence in thy promises. Take from us the evil heart of unbelief; the cause of all our waverings and wanderings: may we believe, that we may be established in our goings, and be always abounding in the work of the Lord.

Prepare us for whatever we have to meet with, between this morning and the grave. We know not what lies before us; but thou knowest, and thy grace can make us sufficient for every service and every suffering.

Let not our temporal occupations ever injure our spiritual concerns; or the cares of this life make us forget, or neglect, the one thing needful: may we learn the holy art of abiding with God in our callings; of being in the world without being of it; and of making every thing not only consistent with religion, but conducive to it.

May we do, and may we say nothing, by which we shall offend against the generation of thy children. May we bear the infirmities of the weak, and not please ourselves. May we restore a brother that has been overtaken in a fault, in the spirit of meekness, considering ourselves, lest we also be tempted.

Bless those who have done us good, and render sevenfold into their own bosom, and forgive those who have done us evil, and enable us to forgive them.

Bless those who are near and dear to us; may they be near and dear to thee. Bless them in their outward comforts; but above all, may their souls prosper.

Be gracious to our native land. Be mindful of our

rulers. Teach our senators wisdom; and so control the minds and hearts of those who are entrusted with the public welfare, as that they may glorify thee, and secure the best good of the people. Bless the gates of Zion, and all the dwellings of Jacob. Let thy secret reside in the families of them that fear thee; and may those that have neglected to call upon thy name, immediately adopt the resolution of Joshua, As for me and my house, we will serve the Lord.

To thy merciful providence we owe it, that we have been preserved another night. We thank thee that thou hast kept us from the pestilence that walketh in darkness, and the destruction that wasteth by noonday. We thank thee that thine eyes have been open towards us, and that no plague has come nigh our dwelling. May we realize this morning that our lives are thy gift, and that we are brought under renewed obligations to devote ourselves to thy service. With this feeling deeply engraved on our souls, with a deep and solemn conviction that all we have is thine, may we go forth to meet the various trials, dangers, and duties of the day before us. May we go forth to our work and our labour until evening, under thy merciful providence. Bless thou the work of our hands; and at the close of the day gather us together in safety and in health, to offer to thee an acceptable sacrifice of praise and thanksgiving.

This morning sacrifice, we offer in the all prevailing name of our adorable Redeemer—and unto Him that loved us, and washed us from our sins in his own blood, and hath made us kings and priests unto God, and to his Father, to him be glory and dominion, for ever and ever. Amen.

THURSDAY EVENING. *Jay.*

O God, all thy works praise thee, and thy saints bless thee. By thy mercies, we again surround this family altar, and engage in the exercises of devotion. May we worship thee, a holy God, in the beauty of holiness; and worship thee, who art a Spirit, in spirit and in truth. Such worship alone thy word requires; but such worship, thy grace alone can enable us to render. For we know, from thy word, and from our own experience we know, that without thee, we can do nothing. All our sufficiency is of thee: do thou work in us to will, and to do, of thy good pleasure.

We would call to remembrance our true character and condition before thee. We would not go about to establish our own righteousness, or seek to deny or extenuate our guilt. We are not only unprofitable servants, but condemned criminals. We confess the number and offensiveness of our transgressions, and acknowledge that we deserve to perish. But we bless thee for the everlasting consolation and good hope, through grace, which the gospel affords; for the news of a Mediator between thee and us; of a High Priest who has put away sin by the sacrifice of himself; of an Advocate with the Father, who ever lives to make intercession for us, and of a Saviour, in whom it has pleased thee, that all fulness should dwell.

Produce in us, all the feelings of those who are blessed with repentance unto life. Give us that faith by which we can be justified from all things, and have peace with God, through our Lord Jesus Christ. To the Redeemer's cross may we retreat, and there find security and relief, refreshment and delight. Assure us of an interest in thy favour, which is life; and clothe us with thine image, which is the beauty and dignity of the soul.

We bless thee for thy word, which we have been reading. May it dwell in us richly in all wisdom. May we yield a suitable attention to its various parts. May we make it, not only our song in the house of our pilgrimage, but the man of our counsel, a light unto our feet, and a lamp unto our paths. May we take it along with us, into all the concerns of life; and whether we are rich or poor, whether we are parents or children, whether we are appointed to govern or serve, may we walk by this rule, that mercy and peace may be upon us.

May we ever be willing that the Lord should choose our inheritance for us, and readily and piously accommodate ourselves to the dispensations of thy providence. May we never lean to our own understanding: may we never take a step, without asking counsel of the Lord, nor be unwilling to take one, at the intimation of thy pleasure. May we never think that thou art less wise, and righteous, and good, in a cloudy and dark day, than in a shining one; when we cannot trace thee, may we trust; and walking by faith, and not by sight, be fully persuaded, that just and right are all thy ways, O thou King of saints.

Regard those, who, under the pressure of affliction, are saying, Brethren pray for us. Be with them in trouble. Thou knowest the anxieties of thy people, lest by any of their temper or carriage in the evil day, they should injure the religion they profess: let thy grace be sufficient for them: let faith and patience have their perfect work: let them glorify thee in all their trials.

Bless all in authority over us, and so rule their hearts and strengthen their hands, that they may punish wickedness and vice, and maintain true religion and virtue.

May all those who are placed above others in condition, go before them in the profession of truth and the practice of holiness, and be examples to all inferior ranks in society.

*We now commit ourselves to thy merciful protection for this night. May we lie down to rest, at peace with thee, and with all the world. Forgive, we humbly pray thee, all the sins we may have committed this day. Whatever we have done or said amiss, do thou pardon. If in our intercourse with our friends or foes we have manifested a spirit unlike that of thy dear Son, do thou be graciously pleased to forgive it. If we have neglected our duty to the poor, or the needy; if we have failed in setting a holy example before each other; if we have had improper feelings towards thee or our fellow men, we pray thee to forgive us. Sprinkle upon us that blood which cleanseth from all sin; and take us into **thy holy care and keeping. Let no** plague come nigh our dwell**ing.** Preserve **us from** sickness and sudden death; **from alarm, and from the** devouring element; from **the** pestilence that walketh in darkness, as thou hast done from the destruction **that** wasteth at noon-day. And raise us in the morning, **fitted for all the duties** and events of another day. These **mercies, and whatever else** we need, we humbly ask **in the** name of thy dear Son, our Saviour Jesus Christ; to whom, with thee, and the Holy Ghost, be all honour and praise, both now and **for ever.*** *Amen.*

FRIDAY MORNING. *Jay.*

Our voice shalt thou hear in the morning, O Lord: in the morning will we direct our prayer unto thee, O thou Most High! How does it become **us to be** thankful! Many, during the past night, have had no place where **to lay their head.** Many, the victims of disease, have been full of tossing to and fro, until the dawning of the day; **so that** their bed has not comforted them, nor their couch eased their complaint. Many have been deprived of **rest** while watching over their connexions in pain and sorrow. How many have slept the sleep of death, and will **not wake till** the **heavens are no more!** Others, whose lives are prolonged, have risen to be surrounded with want and wo: and thousands, who have all things richly to enjoy, have risen to enjoy another day without God in the world.

And why is not this the case with us? Thou, O God, hast remembered, and distinguished, and indulged us. Bless **the** Lord, O our souls, and all that is within us bless his holy name. O magnify the Lord, and let us exalt his name *together.*

And thy mercies have been new every morning, yea, **every moment.** All our desires have not been gratified;

but it was love that denied us, when the accomplishment of our wishes would have proved our ruin or our injury; we have had our trials, but they have been few compared with our sins; they have been attended with numberless alleviations.

Thou hast often wiped away our tears; and restored peace to thy mourners. Thou hast never chastened us but for our profit; we already see the design of many of our griefs, and can say, It is good for me that I have been afflicted; and in all other cases where darkness yet clouds the dispensation, we desire to walk by faith. We believe that thou hast done all things well, and that thy work is perfect.

But, O what do we owe thee for the word of thy truth—the throne of thy grace—the Son of thy love—thy unspeakable gift; what do we owe thee, that we have any reason to hope that we are in Christ, and free from all condemnation; and that when he, who is our life, shall appear, we shall also appear with him in glory, and be forever with the Lord!

Surely, gratitude becomes us that will not evaporate in a morning acknowledgment with the lip, but such as will keep us in the fear of the Lord all the day long, and lead us to ask, What shall I render unto the Lord for all his benefits towards me? We therefore, by the mercies of God, present our bodies a living sacrifice, holy and acceptable unto thee, which is our reasonable service.

And now, O thou Author of all good, we come to thee for the grace another day will require—the grace its duties and events will require; for we know not when we leave our apartments in the morning, what a day will bring forth. But we know that we are stepping into a wicked world, and that we carry about us an evil heart: we know that without thee we can do nothing: and we know that there is nothing with which we shall have any concern in the day, however harmless in itself, but may prove an occasion of sinning and falling, unless we are kept by the power of God. We, therefore, desire to commit ourselves into thy holy keeping. Hold *thou* us up, and we shall be safe. Preserve our understandings from the subtlety of error; our affections from the love of idols; our senses from the ungovernable impressions of outward objects; our character from every stain of vice, and our profession from every appearance of evil: and may the God of peace sanctify us wholly; and may our whole spirit, soul, and body, be preserved blameless unto the coming of our Lord Jesus Christ.

May we engage in nothing on which we cannot implore thy blessing, and to which we cannot welcome thy inspection. Prosper us in our lawful undertakings, or prepare us for disappointment. Give us neither poverty nor riches. Feed us with food convenient for us, lest we be full and deny thee, and say, Who is the Lord? or lest we be poor, and steal, and take the name of our God in vain.

May every creature be good to us, being sanctified by the word of God and prayer. Teach us how to use the world as not abusing it. Enable us to improve our talents, and to redeem our time. May we walk in wisdom towards them that are without, and in kindness towards them that are within; and do good as we have opportunity unto all men, especially unto them that are of the household of faith.

And unto Him that is able to keep us from falling, and to present us faultless before the presence of his glory with exceeding joy: to the only wise God, our Saviour, be glory, and majesty, dominion, and power, both now and ever. *Amen.*

FRIDAY EVENING. *Jay.*

O God, thy command and thy promise, our duty and our privilege, induce us to avail ourselves of every opportunity of approaching the throne of thy grace. We are poor and helpless and needy. It is not in the power of men and angels to reach our cause; and afford us the blessings we so much need, and so much desire. Our only hope is in the name of the Lord God, who made heaven and earth.

But thou art over all; and rich unto all that call upon thee; and thou Lord hast not forsaken them that seek thee. We love to reflect upon the displays of thy perfections; and to contemplate, what thou hast done for others as poor and destitute, as sinful and guilty, as we are: and to remember that thy hand is not shortened that it cannot save, nor thy ear heavy that it cannot hear.

Behold a company of guilty suppliants at thy footstool. O, thou God of all grace, work thou in us to will and to do of thy good pleasure; and vile as we are in ourselves, make us an eternal excellency, the joy of many generations. Our understandings are darkened. Our hearts are hearts of stone. Our very conscience also is defiled. Our affections are earthly and sensual. Open thou the eyes of our understanding. Give us hearts of flesh. Purify our consciences from dead works to serve the living God. Set our affections on things that are above: and as he who has called us is holy, so may we also be holy in all manner of conversation and godliness.

Deliver us from the bondage of corruption, and bring us into the glorious liberty of thy children: that being made free from sin, and become servants unto God, we may have our fruit unto holiness, and our end everlasting life.

Preserve us from all self-delusion, especially where our souls are concerned. May we never be flattered by the good opinion of our fellow-creatures, against the convictions of our own consciences; but remember, that if our hearts condemn us, God is greater than our hearts, and knoweth all things. May we never substitute mere opinions, and outward forms and ceremonies, in the room of that grace, which renews the soul and sanctifies the life. Ever keep alive in our minds the belief, that in Christ Jesus, neither circumcision availeth any thing, nor uncircumcision, but a new creature: and in the examinations of our religious state and character, may we look after that kingdom, which is not meat and drink, but righteousness, and peace, and joy in the Holy Ghost.

Inspire us with a well-grounded hope of being, one day, presented before the presence of thy glory, when we shall see thee without obscurity, approach thee without sin, serve thee without imperfection, and enjoy thee without sorrow. How remote now do we often feel from this exalted state! And how improbable does it frequently seem that we should ever attain it! We have never yet been better than a bruised reed, and a smoking flax: and thy patience alone could have borne with our imperfections and perverseness. Yet we trust the root of the matter is found in us; and we bless thee, if thy grace—by which alone we are what we are, has caused us to loathe sin, and abhor ourselves, and to hunger and thirst after righteousness, and to place our happiness in serving and enjoying thee.

And we pray, that our path may be as a shining light, that shineth more and more unto the perfect day. Complete that which is lacking in our faith. Lead us into all truth; and establish our hearts with grace. Fill our minds with the sublime and elevating objects of revelation, that worldly things may find there no room: and keep near us, all the affecting and awful motives of the gospel, that we may not be able to sin,—the view of thine all-seeing eye, a burning world, a judgment to come, and the cross of our Lord Jesus Christ.

And the Lord make us, also, to increase and abound in love, one towards another, and towards all men. Let all bitterness, and wrath, and anger, and clamour, and evil speaking, be put away from us, with all malice; and may we be kind, one towards another, tender hearted; forgiving one another, even as God, for Christ's sake, hath forgiven us.

Prepare us for all the duties and trials that lie before us. We bless thee for thy promises, which provide against every want we feel; and for every condition in which we can be found. In God will we praise his word In

God have we put our trust. We will not fear what flesh can do unto us. Thou tellest our wanderings. Put thou our tears into thy bottle. Are they not in thy book?

We commend ourselves with all our relations and friends, this evening, to thy forgiving mercy, and providential care. O Thou, that givest thy beloved sleep, indulge us with refreshing repose: or if thou holdest our eyes waking in the night, may thy song be with us, and our prayer unto the God of our life. Guide us by thy counsel, through life, and afterward receive us to glory.

And to the only wise God our Saviour, be glory, and majesty, dominion and power, for ever and ever. *Amen.*

SATURDAY MORNING. *Jay.*

O Thou King eternal, immortal, and invisible — we would adore thee, and take shame to ourselves: and though allowed to approach thy divine majesty, we would never forget the sentiments of humiliation and contrition, which become such creatures as we are. Father! we have sinned against heaven and in thy sight, and are not worthy to be called thy children: we are not worthy of the least of all thy mercies. Yea, we have merited thy displeasure; and thy righteousness would be completely acquitted in our destruction.

O, for hearts of flesh! Lord, produce in us that sensibility of soul, which will lead us to feel our vileness, to deplore our guilt, and to cast ourselves at thy feet, abhorring ourselves and repenting in dust and ashes. And impart to us that faith, which will enable us to hope in thy word, and derive strong consolation from the invitations and promises of the gospel. We are come to implore the greatest blessings the God of love can give: we are come to call thee, Abba Father; to enter thy house; to sit down at thy table; to lean on thy arm; to walk with God; but we are not come unbidden or uncalled: Thou hast called us by thy grace; and it is thy commandment that we should believe on the name of thy

Son, Jesus Christ. Lord, we assent, we submit, we depend, we apply. Since he came into the world to save sinners, we take him as *our* Saviour; and glory in him, as made to us wisdom and righteousness, sanctification and redemption.

And O, may our minds be fixed and filled with admiring thoughts of his person and offices; may our hearts be inflamed with a sense of his boundless compassion and love. By the new and living way which he has not only revealed but consecrated for us, may we come to thee; and enjoy all the advantages of a state of reconciliation and friendship with God. May the most open and familiar intercourse be maintained between thee and our souls. To thee may we commit our way and our works; and in every thing by prayer and supplication make known our requests unto God; and be thou always near, to guide us and to defend; to relieve us in trouble, and to help us in duty. And may we walk humbly with our God; wondering at the condescension, that deigns to regard our mean affairs; the patience, that bears with our manners; and the kindness, that employs so many means to advance our everlasting welfare.

We grieve to think, that a world so full of thy bounty, should be so empty of thy praise. O, that men would praise the Lord for his goodness, and for his wonderful works to the children of men. Bless the Lord, all his works, in all places of his dominion; bless the Lord, O my soul.

Again thy visitation hath preserved our spirits. Through the dark and silent watches of the night, thou hast suffered no evil to befall us, nor any plague to come nigh our dwelling. And we are not only the living to praise thee, this morning, but the distinguished, and the indulged. Many who have seen the light of the day, as well as ourselves, are encompassed with want, and pain, and wretchedness; but we have all things richly to enjoy.

Thou takest pleasure in the prosperity of thy servants; may we always take pleasure in the advancement of thy glory. Thou art never weary in doing us good; may we never grow weary in well doing. Thy mercies are new every morning; every morning, by thy mercies, may we present our bodies a living sacrifice, holy, and acceptable, which is our reasonable service.

And to the God of our salvation, the Father, the Son, and the Holy Spirit, be ascribed, the kingdom, the power, and the glory, for ever and ever. *Amen.*

SATURDAY EVENING. *Jay.*

O God, thou hast made, and thou upholdest all things by the word of thy power. Darkness is thy pavilion. Thou walkest upon the wings of the wind. All nations before thee are as nothing. One generation passeth away, and another cometh; and we are hastening back to the dust from whence we were taken. The heavens we behold will vanish away like the cloud that covers them; and the earth we tread will dissolve like a morning dream; but thou art, from everlasting to everlasting, God over all, unchangeably the same, and thy years shall not fail.

Infinitely great and glorious as thou art, we are thy offspring and thy care. Thy hands have made us and fashioned us. Thou hast watched over us with more than parental tenderness. Thou hast holden our soul in life, and not suffered our feet to be moved. Thy divine power has given us all things, not only necessary for life, but godliness. Bless the Lord, O, our souls, and forget not all his benefits; who forgiveth all our iniquities; who healeth all our diseases; who redeemeth our lives from destruction; who crowneth us with loving kindness and tender mercies; who satisfieth our mouth with good things, so that our youth is renewed like the eagles'.

We raise this evening a fresh memorial, and inscribe it to the God of our salvation. Hitherto hath the Lord helped us. We have passed, not only through another day, but through another week. The sun has not smitten us by day, nor the moon by night. We have been preserved in our going out, and coming in. But thine has been the vigilance, that turned aside the evils which threatened us. Thine have been the supplies that have nourished us. Thine the comforts that have indulged us. Thine the relations and friends that have delighted us. Thine have been the means of grace which have edified us; and thine the book, which, amidst all our enjoyments, has told us, that this is not our rest; and in all our successes, that one thing is yet needful.

Nothing can equal the number of thy mercies, but our imperfections and sins. These, O God, we would not conceal, or palliate; but confess them, with a broken heart and a contrite spirit.

In what a condition would we be this evening, were it not for the assurance that there is forgiveness with thee, that thou mayest be feared, and with thee plenteous redemption. Yet, while we hope for pardon through the blood of the cross, we pray to be clothed with humility; to be quickened in thy way; and to be more devoted to the things that belong to our everlasting peace.

How soon has the week rolled away! Its days have fled like a dream, a vapour, a shadow. So will all our days flee; so will they all appear when the end arrives. O, help us to keep that end in remembrance; and endeavour to view things now, as they will appear from the borders of the grave. May we know how frail we are, that we may be cured of the folly of delay and indecision; and so number our days, that we may apply our hearts unto wisdom.

May we call the approaching Sabbath a delight, the holy of the Lord, honourable; and may we honour thee, in not doing our own ways, nor finding our own pleasures, nor speaking our own words. May the private moments of the day, be sacred; and the social—innocent and edifying. And may we keep our foot, when we go to the house of God, and offer not the sacrifice of fools. Let us not go as they go, and sit as they sit, and hear thy words, but do them not.

Preserve us from trifling with the things of the soul and eternity, or trusting in those privileges, which unimproved, will only augment our guilt and our misery.

Thy people, the Jews, were distinguished by thy favours, above all the families of the earth; but wrath came upon them to the uttermost. The churches of Asia provoked thee to remove the candlestick out of its place; and they were left in darkness. We have awful examples still nearer. How many, who once heard and professed the gospel, have been turned by the abuse of it into apostates and infidels, blasphemers and persecutors; ten-fold more the children of hell than before; while numbers, who yet maintain the form of godliness, are too hardened to feel the power of it.

While, therefore, we go to thy house in the multitude of thy mercies, may we in thy *fear* worship towards thy holy temple; for thou art greatly to be feared in the assembly of the saints. O, let us not perish under means designed to save us. O, let not the savour of life unto life, prove to us only the savour of death unto death.

Make the place of thy feet glorious. Bring us to thy holy mountain, and if we are not made joyful in thy house of prayer, convince us, alarm us, humble us, banish the spirit of the world from our hearts, and fill us with all the fulness of God.

So we thy people, and the sheep of thy pasture, will give thee thanks forever, we will show forth thy praise throughout all generations. **Amen.**

SECOND WEEK.

SABBATH MORNING. *Jenks.*

O most blessed and gracious Lord our God, whose almighty hand has brought us out of nothing, to what we are; to see the light, and enjoy the comforts of life; and whose free grace has called us out of a state of sin and ruin, to the hope of thy heavenly glory! We bless thy name, that thou hast conducted us safe, through all states and events, and through all the trials and troubles in our lives, to see the comfortable light of this day; and that we have yet a day of grace wherein to attend to the things belonging to our peace. We bless thee that thou hast consulted the good of our souls, as well as the glory of thy name, in setting apart this day for holy uses, to engage us to a solemn attendance upon the Lord; in whose service consists all our honour and happiness. O how much higher might we have been in grace, and thy blessed favour—how much nearer to thee our God, and fitter for thy heavenly kingdom, had we rightly used, and conscientiously improved those seasons and means of grace, which thou hast been pleased to put into our hands, for the best advantage of our souls.

But we have been unkind and cruel to our own souls, as well as disobedient and rebellious against our Lord; many times frustrating the opportunities of appearing before thee; shunning and neglecting the duties of thy holy service; and even when we have set ourselves to seek thy face, it has been with such coldness, and dulness, and distraction, that thou mightest justly abhor our souls, despise our prayers, for any thing that there is in us or them, to recommend us to thy blessed favour and acceptance.

But be thou pleased to look upon us in the Son of thy

love, the Lord our peace and righteousness; and forgive us all that is past wherein we have neglected thy work, or ill-performed it, or done what is inconsistent with it. Help us, O God of our salvation, and deliver us from the burden of our guilt; and purge away all our sins for the glory of thy name; that they may not stand as a partition-wall, to hinder the desire of our souls from ascending up to thee; nor hinder the light of thy countenance from descending upon us. But let thy peace, and love, and favour shine on our souls; that we may see the felicity of thy chosen, and with joy draw water out of the wells of salvation.

O let us not rest in any forms of godliness, denying the power thereof; nor take up with the name and show, and the profession of Christianity, but be swayed with its life, and power and spirit; that the gospel of our Lord, and the graces of the good Spirit of God may shine forth in our lives, to the glory of thee our heavenly Father; and to the adorning of the doctrine of God our Saviour in all things. O gracious God, be with us, and with all the ministers and stewards of thy holy things, who are this day to speak thy word to thy people: and furnish them with abilities suitable to their great work, that they may fitly apply themselves to the capacities, and to the necessities of their several hearers. And grant, Lord, unto us, and unto all the hearers of thy holy word, humble and teachable spirits; to receive thy truth in meekness, and in the love of it, so as to profit and grow by it. O do thou remove all the hinderances to our spiritual growth and improvement, that thy word may have free course, and be glorified among us. And let us this day go forth in the strength of the Lord God; and prosper and increase with the increase of God, by thy grace and blessing accompanying our desires and endeavours; till from serving thee imperfectly here upon earth, we may attain to glorify and enjoy thee, our God, in the perfection of holiness, and in those everlasting joys and glories of thy kingdom, which thou hast prepared for them that love thee.

Attend, we beseech thee, with thy gracious help, all the endeavours that shall this day be made to promote the honour of thy holy name. Revive pure religion in all the churches of the Lord Jesus in this land, and throughout the Christian world; and graciously extend thy kingdom over other people; and bring distant nations to the knowledge of thy Son. Wherever amidst any people thy work may be commenced, wilt thou deepen and extend it. Wilt thou there this day especially bless thy truth, and upon those churches which are cold or lukewarm in thy service, wilt thou send down thy Holy Spirit, that they may awake to newness of life and that thy power may there be seen in the conversion of sinners. Do thou mercifully restrain and reform the violators of the Holy Sabbath, and give them better minds and a due regard for thy holy laws. Be merciful to the profligate and profane. May they be inclined to reverence thy holy name. And may all classes and conditions of men be brought under the influence of religion, and the time soon come when on this thy day, the offerings of the whole world, converted unto thee, shall come up on thine altars, and the entire race praise and adore thee for the riches of redeeming mercy.

And let thy grace and blessing, thy love and fellowship, thy direction and assistance, O Heavenly Father, Son and Holy Spirit, be with us and with all whom we ought to beg thy mercy for in our prayers, this day, and for evermore. *Amen.*

SABBATHDAY EVENING. *Jenks*

HOLY GOD, we are all as an unclean thing, and all our very righteousnesses are as filthy rags; nor can we ever hope to be justified in thy sight, upon account of any works or worth of our own; for by our own hearts and deeds we are reproved and condemned, and should be left speechless in thy judgment, if thou, O Lord, shouldst call us to account, according to even our best services

But we desire to take refuge and sanctuary under the shadow of our crucified Saviour; and to be found in him, not having on our own righteousness, but that which is by the faith of Jesus Christ, that all our sinful deformities may be hid from thine eyes; that thou mayest forgive us mercifully, and receive us graciously, and love us freely in the Son of thy love, in whom thou art well pleased.

Command a blessing, we pray thee, O Lord, upon the word, which this day we have heard, and upon all the means of grace that have been used for the good of our souls. It is not of him that planteth, nor of him that watereth, but of thee, our God, who giveth the increase. O be thou pleased to attend the preaching of thy word with the powerful influences of thy grace and Holy Spirit; that it may be the savour of life to our souls, and the power of God to our salvation.

*And we especially beseech of thee, Almighty Father, that thou wilt be pleased to follow with thy blessing the instructions imparted this day in Sunday schools. May the truths of thy holy word be deeply impressed on the minds of children, and may they grow up in the knowledge and love of Jesus Christ the Saviour. May those truths so influence their minds and hearts, as to guide and comfort them in all the journey of life. Grant, O Lord, that as they advance in years they may evince the benefits of the instruction received in Sabbath shools; and that this generation may be trained up devoted to thy cause, and prepared to promote thy glory, when their parents and teachers shall have descended to the tomb.

Will the God of grace be also pleased to bless all Sunday school teachers. Let their hearts be comforted by seeing thy work prosper in their hands. In their own souls may they experience the reward of their self-denials and toils; and in thine everlasting kingdom may they at last be admitted to a seat at thy right hand with thousands saved by the instrumentality of Sabbath schools.*

Supply the want of thy public ordinances, we beseech thee, by the immediate teachings of thy good Spirit, to all such as through any unavoidable impediments are kept from them; and continue to us, O gracious Lord, the light of thy gospel, and all the happy opportunities which we enjoy for our souls' advantage. And preserve us also, by thy grace, from the curse of barrenness, under all thy holy means and abundant mercies. That they may not, therefore, hereafter rise up in judgment against us, O make them now efficacious to us; and write thy laws in our hearts, and cause them to accomplish all the purposes of thy grace in our souls, and to shine forth with a convincing splendour in our lives; to make us every way such as thou wouldst have us.

And now we give thanks, as we are infinitely bound, to thee, O Lord God, our heavenly Father, for the mercies of this day; and for thy great mercy and goodness that has hitherto followed us all the days of our lives. O how wonderful is thy patience and long-suffering, that thou shouldst all day long stretch forth thy hands to a rebellious and gainsaying people! And how unwearied thy kindness and love, that we still enjoy so many comforts with our lives. Blessed be thy name, O most merciful Father, that thou hast defended us from so many dangers in our lives, which threatened to destroy us; and delivered us out of so many troubles, under which we should have sunk and perished, if thou hadst not been nigh to us, and done great things for us. We bless thee for our health and plenty, peace and liberty; for the use of our reason, limbs and senses; for the kindness of friends, and safety from our enemies; for the benefits and refreshments of society, and the success and prosperity of our affairs here in the world. But above all, we bless thee for the mercies and blessings relating to the world to come; for Jesus Christ, and all spiritual blessings in heavenly things in him tending to the salvation of our souls; for remembering us in our low estate, and sending eternal redemption to us by the hands of thy dear Son; for the light and direction of thy word;

for the teachings and strivings, the aids and consolations of thy Spirit; for all the means and helps which we have to do us good; for all thy grace wrought in us, and bestowed upon us; and for all the discoveries and hopes of eternal glory which thou hast given to us. O how infinitely indebted are we to the kindness and love of God our Saviour! O that we may ever be sensible and thankful as we ought! And with all that thou hast given us, blessed God, give us hearts filled with thy love, and lifted up in thy praise, and devoted to thy honour and service.

And help us, O Lord our God, to glorify thy name, not only in speaking to thy praise, but so entirely devoting ourselves to thy pleasure, that we may be thine in faithfulness, and in the sincerity of our hearts, even all the days of our lives.

O make us truly penitent, and humbled for all which this day we have done amiss, and make us unfeignedly thankful for all the good that we have received; and for all which thou hast, in any manner or measure, enabled us to do aright. The evil is from ourselves alone, and to us belong shame and confusion of face for it; but all the good is of thy free grace, and thy mere mercy; and to thy blessed name, O Lord our God, be all the praise and glory rendered, with the most sensible and grateful hearts, now and for evermore. *Amen.*

MONDAY MORNING. *Jenks.*

O LORD God, merciful and gracious, long suffering, and abundant in goodness and truth! Thou keepest mercy for thousands, pardonest iniquity, transgression and sin, and dost not retain thy anger forever, because thou delightest in mercy. How excellent is thy loving-kindness, O God! therefore do the sons of men put their trust under the shadow of thy wings. And therefore do we desire still to look up to that bountiful hand of thine, from whence we have received all our good things. O

Lord our God! be thou pleased to look down mercifully upon us, and be gracious and favourable to us, as thou art unto those that love thy name. O look not upon the sins of our hearts and lives; which are more than we can remember, and greater than we can express; and such as make us seem vile, even in our own eyes, and so highly guilty before thy holy Majesty, that it is of the Lord's mercies we are not consumed, because thy compassions fail not. But behold us in mercy, through the merits and mediation of thy Son our Saviour, who did no sin, and was manifested that he might take away our sins: by whom it is that we have this access to the Majesty on high, and encouragement to come into thy presence, to ask what we need.

And seeing there is in Christ Jesus an infinite fulness of all that ever we can want or wish to make us holy, and to make us most blessed eternally, O that we may all receive of his fulness grace sufficient for us; to pardon our sins and subdue our iniquities; to justify our persons, and to sanctify our souls; and to complete upon our hearts and lives that holy renovating change, which may still more and more transform us into the blessed image after which thou didst create us; and make us still more meet to be partakers of the inheritance of thy saints in light.

And teach us, O Lord our God, to use this world without abusing it, and to enjoy the things of it, without losing our part in thy love, which is better than life. Whatever we have of the world, O may we have the same with thy leave and love, sanctified to us by the word of God, and prayer; and by the right employment and improvement thereof to thy glory, who art the gracious Giver of all our good things. And whatsoever we want of the things of this life, O Lord, our heavenly Father, leave us not destitute of any of those things that accompany salvation, but adorn our souls with all such graces of thy Holy Spirit, as may enable us to adorn the doctrine of God our Saviour in all things, by such a conversation as does become it.

Help us, O gracious Lord, in the whole of our duty to thee our God; and also in the discharge of all relative duties which we owe to men, whether superiors, equals, or inferiors, all with whom we have our conversation in the world: that we may walk wisely toward them that are without, and kindly toward them that are within; and not to be justly offensive unto any; but, what in us lies, useful and beneficial to all. And thus let us pass the time of our sojourning here, in thy fear and favour, and to thy honour and glory; that at our last review thereof, thy name may have the praise, and our souls the comfort, in the hour of death, and in the great day of our Lord Jesus Christ.

Let the spirit of thy holy Sabbath go with us into the duties of this week. May we, in all our employments, have that seriousness, calmness, peace, prayerfulness, and conscientiousness, which the observance of thy holy day is fitted to produce. May thy truth be seasonably brought to our remembrance. May we be enlightened by that truth in the knowledge of our duty to thee, and to our fellow creatures. Suffer us not to become worldly minded—to be influenced inordinately, by the things of this life; or to forget that thy people are advancing to a world of eternal purity and love. Amid all our worldly employments, may we remember that our treasure should be laid up in a world where moth and rust do not corrupt, and where thieves do not break through nor steal. Amid all our perplexities and trials, may we remember that there remaineth a rest to the people of God,—and may we so live as to be prepared to enter upon that eternal Sabbath, which awaits Christians beyond the grave.

And now that thou hast renewed our lives and thy mercies to us this morning, help us, good God, to renew our desires, and resolutions, and endeavours, to live in the obedience of thy holy will, and to the honour of thy blessed name. O restrain us from the evils and follies into which we are prone to fall; and quicken us to the offices and duties which we are averse to perform. And grant that we may think and speak, and will and do, the things becoming the children of our heavenly Father; and so find the strong consolation of thy gracious acceptance in Jesus Christ our Saviour; who, when we pray, has taught us to say, Our Father, &c.

MONDAY EVENING.†   *Jenks.*

O Lord our God! thou art infinitely great, and infinitely good. Thy glory is above all our thoughts, and thy mercies are over all thy works. And above all thy mercies, have we cause to admire, and bless, and praise thee for those mercies which, in so large a measure, and especial manner, thou hast been pleased still to vouchsafe unto us, who are daily objects of thy bounty, and who continue still the living monuments of thy goodness.

Thou didst create us, O Lord, after thy own blessed image, in an holy and happy estate; but we have made ourselves vile and miserable, averse to good and prone to evil. But thou hast so far declared thy willingness to be reconciled even to thy enemies, that thou hast sent thy only Son into the world, upon the great errand of our salvation; that whosoever believe in him, should not perish in their sins, but have everlasting life, for his sake. O Lord, we believe, help our unbelief; and give us the true repentance towards God, and faith in our Lord Jesus Christ; that we may be of the number of those who do indeed repent and believe, to the saving of the soul.

And save us, O good Lord, from our sinful selves, and from the love and course of this present evil world, and from every self-destroying way which we are tempted to follow. Make us a way to escape, out of all the snares of temptation, wherewith we have been entangled and held, and hindered in running the race set before us. Make thy ways plain before us. Establish, O Lord, and strengthen and settle us; that going forth in thy strength,

---

† The second Monday in the month is extensively observed as a concert of prayer for Sunday schools.

we may do thy will to all well-pleasing; and continue in thy fear and love to our lives' end.

Which things we beg, not for ourselves alone, but also in behalf of all whom we ought to intreat thy mercy for in our prayers. O bring nigh unto thee all those that are yet afar off; and make manifest the savour of thy knowledge in every place; that such as yet sit in darkness and in the shadow of death, may come to see the light of thy truth, and the joy of thy salvation. O that every one who names the name of Christ may depart from iniquity, and so live up to their high and holy profession, that they may give no just occasion to the enemies of the Lord to blaspheme; but adorn the doctrine of God, our Saviour, in all things, and so put to silence the ignorance of foolish men by well doing.

Be gracious and favourable, O Lord, in an especial manner, to thy church. Arise, O God, and plead thy own cause, and maintain thy true, and holy religion, which thou hast so long and so wonderfully owned and asserted. O let not the enemies of thy church ever have cause to say, that they have prevailed against thy people; but let all that do espouse thy cause, and stand up for the honour and defence of thy truth, be still prevalent and prosperous in all their pious designs; and still have cause to say, the Lord be magnified, who has pleasure in the prosperity of his servants.

And on this day, set apart by many of thy people as a season of prayer for thy mercy on Sunday schools, we humbly implore thy blessing on all who are engaged in those schools as teachers, or learners. Enlighten by the Holy Spirit all teachers, that they may truly understand thy word. Make them the true friends of Jesus Christ. May they be endowed with his spirit of self-denial, patience, humility, and prayer. May they evermore copy the example of Him who, when on earth, said, Suffer little children, and forbid them not to come unto me. While engaged in instructing the rising generation, in leading others to the cross of Christ, may they themselves be interested in thy promises, and sanctified by all their efforts to promote thy glory. And grant, O gracious God, that their labours may be attended with thy blessing. Do thou send down thy Spirit on all Sunday schools, that the rising generation may grow up in the knowledge of Jesus Christ, and in preparation for great usefulness in the church, and in the state. May schools be established in all the destitute places of our land; and all the means used to enlarge and perpetuate these blessings be crowned with success. Never suffer the zeal of thy people to languish in this cause, or thy ministers to forget their obligations to use every influence in their power to promote the religious training of the rising generation. Hear and answer the prayers which this day may have been offered in behalf of Sunday schools; excite in all thy people a spirit of benevolence; and fill the earth with thy glory.

Comfort all that want the comforts which we enjoy. Remember with the favour which thou bearest to thy people, all our friends and benefactors, our kindred after the flesh, and whomsoever are dear to us, on any other account. Make them, O Lord, such as thou wouldst have them, and such as, in Christ Jesus, thou wilt mercifully accept of them, here to thy gracious favour, and hereafter to thy glorious kingdom. Forgive our enemies, and turn their hearts; and turn ours to forgive them. And direct all our ways to please thee, that thou mayest make even our enemies to be at peace with us.

Hear us, O God of the spirits of all flesh; hear us for ourselves and others; others for themselves and us: and hear the Son of thy love, the lover of our souls, for us and all the members of thy church militant here on earth, whereof Christ Jesus in heaven is the glorious head. For him and to him with thine eternal self, most holy Father, and the blessed Spirit of grace, our Guide and Comforter, be all thanks and praise, and honour, and glory, humbly and heartily rendered and ascribed of us, and all thy people, now and for evermore. *Amen.*

TUESDAY MORNING. *Jenks.*

O Lord, thou art the God whose we are, and whom we ought to serve, with all the endowments and abilities for thy service, wherewith thou hast blessed us. For thou hast laid upon us all the obligations of thy laws, and all the endearments of thy love, to be faithful in the covenant of our God, and to abound in the work of the Lord. And we desire to humble ourselves here before thee, that our lives have been so unserviceable to thee, and so full of provocation against thee; that we have lived to ourselves, more than to the Lord and Giver of our lives; and that we have served our own lusts and pleasures more than thy holy blessed will; which is the rule of all righteousness, and in the performance whereof, there is the greatest reward. O how we have disbelieved thy truths, disobeyed thy commands, disregarded thy promises and threats! and resisted and defeated all thy gracious methods to reclaim us from the evil of our ways, and to bring us over entirely to thyself.

We have sinned against thee, our God, to the infinite wrong and damage of our own souls, and by our sins we have spoiled and destroyed ourselves; but it is not in us to recover and save ourselves. In thee alone is all our help. Yea, thou hast laid help upon one that is mighty and able to save to the uttermost all that come to God through him: through whom thou hast encouraged us to come boldly to thy throne of grace; that we may obtain mercy, and find grace to help in every time of need. In him, therefore, we beg, Lord, that thou wilt be reconciled to us, and at peace with us; as a Father of mercies, and a God of consolation.

And for his sake, enable us also, we beseech thee, to demean ourselves as becomes the children of God, the redeemed of the Lord, and the followers of Jesus Christ. O put such principles of grace and holiness into our hearts, as may make us to hate all iniquity, and every false way.

And put thy Spirit within us, causing us to walk in thy statutes, and to keep thy judgments, and to do them. Not only lay thy commands upon us, but be pleased, O Lord, to enable us for the performance of every duty required of us. And so engage our hearts to thyself, that we may make it our meat and drink to do thy will; and with enarged hearts run the way of thy commands. O make our ervices acceptable to thee while we live, and our souls ready for thee when we die. And as long as we are in this world, keep us, O Lord our God, from the evil of it, and from the snares and dangers which thou knowest we are continually exposed to in it. O make our passage safe and sure, through all the changes, troubles, temptations, and various conditions of this mortal life, to the unchangeable glories and felicities of life everlasting.

Be merciful to us, good Lord, and bless us, and keep us this day, in all our ways, and in all our lawful designs and undertakings; and may we take nothing in hand, but what is warranted in thy word. O let us be in the fear of the Lord all the day long; let thy fear be ever before our eyes to restrain us from the things provoking to our God, and destructive to our souls. And let thy love abound in our hearts, and sweetly and powerfully constrain us to all faithful and cheerful obedience, acceptable in thy sight, through him that has loved and redeemed us; even the Lord our righteousness; in whose blessed name, and the words of prayer which himself has taught us, we continue praying our Father, &c.

The blessing of God Almighty, Father, Son and Holy Ghost, be with us, and with all that belong to us, this day, and for evermore. *Amen.*

TUESDAY EVENING. *Jenks.*

O LORD, thou art our gracious God, and our most merciful Father in Jesus Christ; in whose great name, and prevailing mediation, alone it is that we, who have multiplied our offences against thee, are encouraged still to present our persons, and our prayers here before thee. It is a privilege which we acknowledge ourselves utterly unworthy to enjoy, that thou shouldst admit us into thy service; yea, into fellowship with thy blessed self. We dare not appear in the presence of such a holy glorious Majesty, in our own names, or trusting in any merits or righteousness in ourselves. But we come in the name and mediation of thy dear Son, whom thou dost infinitely love above all; who has fully satisfied thy justice for our sins, and does continually intercede at thy right hand for our souls; whom thou delightest to honour in sparing, accepting, and saving poor unworthy sinners upon his account. O deliver us, most gracious Lord, for his sake, from all our transgressions; and from all, of which thou, that are greater than our hearts, knowest us to be guilty. And seal to us a pardon, in his most precious blood, which speaks better things in our behalf than we are able to do ourselves, in all our prayers.

And may the time past of our lives suffice to have lived to ourselves, and to have served our own lusts and pleasures. Grant us new and clean, humble and contrite hearts, to tremble at thy word and presence, and to hate and abandon all our foolish and sinful misdoings.

Hear us, O Lord, for ourselves, and let our supplications also ascend before thee in the behalf of all men living. Send thy word, and the means of grace to such as are yet destitute of them; and make them efficacious, and the savour of life in those that do enjoy them. Convert the unconverted, and perfect thy good work where thou hast begun it. Give a check to all profaneness, vice, and ungodliness, that presumptuous sinners may be ashamed, and the wickedness of the wicked may come to an end. O make thy church to increase and flourish, and thy servants to prevail and rejoice. Be gracious and favourable to this land, and to the head and governors thereof, and to all inferior and particular members of it. O do thou rule all our rulers, counsel all our counsellors, teach all our teachers, and turn and order all our public affairs, to the glory of thy name, to the welfare of thy church, and to the happiness of this nation. Avert from us, we beseech thee, the judgments which we feel or fear, and continue to us the blessings and comforts for our bodies, and especially the helps and advantages for our souls, which through thy favour we do enjoy. And notwithstanding all the devices of the enemies of our peace, and all the great and crying provocations of our sins, O be thou still our God, and let us be thy people.

Think thoughts of pity and compassion to all the sons and daughters of affliction. O sanctify thy fatherly corrections to them, support them under their several burdens, and in thy good time deliver them from all the pressures that are upon them. Be good to all our friends and neighbours, reward our benefactors, bless our relations with the best of thy blessings, making them near to thyself by grace, as they are to us by alliance. Preserve us from our enemies, and reconcile them both to us and to thyself. O that all the habitations of Christians may be houses of prayer, and be thou especially kind to the several families where thy blessed name is called upon. Let thy heavenly blessings, and thy saving grace, descend and rest upon us here in this family. O guide us, and keep us; make us wise and faithful in our duty, and prosperous and blessed in the issue. Fit us all for whatsoever thou shalt be pleased to call us to. O teach us how to want and how to abound; and both in a prosperous and suffering condition, secure our hearts to thyself, and make us ever to approve ourselves sincere and faithful in thy service.

And now, O Lord, be pleased to accept our evening sacrifice of praise and thanksgiving, to thee the Father of mercies, and fountain of all goodness, for the mercies of the day past, and for thy great mercy and goodness, that has hitherto followed us all the days of our lives.— For our lives have been filled with thy mercies, and thou hast abounded towards us in loving-kindness, and variety of thy sweet and comfortable blessings, pertaining to this world, and a better; passing by our innumerable sins, as if thou sawest them not, thou goest on still to oblige us with new favours. O Lord, imprint and preserve upon our hearts a lively and grateful sense and remembrance of all thy kindness unto us, that our souls may bless thee, and all that is within us may praise thy holy name.

Yea, let us give thee thanks from the heart, and praise our God, whilst we have our being. And for all thy patience with us, thy care over us, and thy continual mercy to us, blessed be thy name, O Lord God, our heavenly Father: and unto thee be all thanks, and praise, and love, and obedience, and honour, and glory, offered by us and all thine, every where, now and evermore. *Amen.*

WEDNESDAY MORNING. *Jenks.*

O Lord, the blessed God of our salvation! thou art the hope of all the ends of the earth, upon whom the eyes of all do wait: for thou givest unto all life, and breath, and all things. In thee we ever live, and move, and are; and upon thee we continually do depend for all the good that ever we have, or hope for. Still thou takest care of us, and watchest for good over us; even in our rest and sleep, when we have not so much as any thoughts of caring for ourselves; and daily thou renewest to us our lives, and thy mercies; every morning giving us new occasions still for thy praise, and our thankfulness. And thou hast given us the assurance of thy word, that if we commit our affairs to thee, and acknowledge thee in all our ways, thou wilt establish our thoughts, and direct our path. And therefore we desire, O Lord, still to put ourselves under thy gracious conduct, and thy fatherly protection; and to beg thy heavenly guidance and blessing, and assistance of thy good Spirit, to choose our inheritance for us; and to dispose of us and of all that concern us, to the glory of thy name.

O Lord, withdraw not thy tender mercies from us,

nor the comforts of thy presence, nor the assistance of thy Spirit, for our great contempt and manifold abuses of all such grace and goodness. Never punish our past sins, by giving us over to the love and power of our sins; but give us true penitent hearts for all the evils committed by us; and thy merciful discharge from all the guilt that lies upon us. And grant us, O God, the comfortable sense and apprehension of thy gracious acceptance of us, and thy merciful intentions towards us in the Son of thy love, the lover of our souls: that our souls may bless thee, and all that is within us may praise thy holy name.

And O that we may find the joy of the Lord to be our strength, to enable us to contend against our sins; especially the sins to which we are most addicted, and whereof we are in greatest danger; and to make us also more ready to every good work, and better disposed for all the duties of piety, justice, charity, and sobriety, which we owe to thee our God, to our neighbour and ourselves: that herein we may experience ourselves to have always a conscience void of offence towards God, and towards men. O help us to walk circumspectly, not as fools, but as wise; carefully redeeming the time that we have lost, and conscientiously improving all those seasons, and means of grace which thou art pleased to put into our hands, for the best profit and advantage of our souls. And while we are upon earth, O give us all things needful and convenient for our present pilgrimage; and sanctify to us all our enjoyments, and all events that now befall us; till, through the merits of thy Son, and the multitude of thy mercies, we are conducted safe to be ever with the Lord. Amidst all our other affairs in this world, O let us never forget or neglect the one thing needful; but be in greatest care so to demean ourselves every day, as may forward our comfortable accounts in the great day of thy appearing and glory.

O gracious Father! keep us, we beseech thee, this day in thy fear and favour; and help us to live to thy honour and glory. If thou guide us not, we shall run into errors; if thou preserve us not, we shall fall into dangers; O let thy good providence be our defence and security; and let thy Holy Spirit be our guide and counsellor in all our ways. And grant that we may take the ways and courses agreeable to thy will, and acceptable in thy sight, through Jesus Christ; in whose sacred name and words we close up these our imperfect requests to thee, Our Father, &c.

Let thy grace, O Lord Jesus Christ, thy love, O heavenly Father, thy comfortable fellowship, O holy blessed Spirit, be with us, and with all whom we ought to beg thy mercy for in our prayers, this day, and for evermore. *Amen.*

WEDNESDAY EVENING. *Jenks.*

O LORD, our God, thou art most high and mighty, most wise, and holy, and good! Thou art, and for ever wast, and for ever shalt continue, unspeakably blessed and glorious, above all that we are able to express or to conceive. Thou dost not need the services of men or angels to make the least addition to thy glory and bliss. Men cannot be profitable unto God; our goodness will not extend to the Lord. But in kindness and love to our souls it is, that thou art pleased to lay thy commands upon us, to wait upon thee in these duties of thy immediate service. Thou humblest thyself even to behold the things that are in heaven, to take notice of the worship of those blessed creatures above. O how wonderful is thy condescension then, to look down upon us, poor sinful worms, that dwell here in houses of clay, whose foundation is in the dust! Lord, what is man that thou takest knowledge of him, and the son of man that thou makest account of him! Thou canst not at all need us, nor any thing of ours, O blessed God; but we all stand in great and continual need of thee, our only sovereign good; in need of thy mercy and forgiveness, thy grace and guidance, thy blessing and assistance; without which we could never hope to escape the curses and miseries which are the due wages of our sins; nor ever to attain to that glory and blessedness, which are the free gifts of God in Jesus Christ.

The desire of our souls, therefore, is to thy name, O Lord, and to the remembrance of thee. Our eyes are towards thee, and all our expectation is from thee: and still we wait, and call, and depend upon thee, till thou have mercy upon us, according to our several necessities; and according to the riches of thy grace, and the multitude of thy mercies. O remember not against us our former iniquities; enter not into judgment with us, according to the desert of our sins; but according to thy mercy remember thou us. For thy goodness' sake, O Lord, blot out our transgressions as a cloud; and justify us freely by thy grace, through the redemption that is in Jesus Christ. And bless us, holy God of our salvation, in turning us from all our iniquities, and giving us grace, to repent and amend our lives according to thy holy word.

And to this end, be thou pleased to enlighten our darkened minds with the beams of thy saving truth, that we may not be unwise, but understand what the will of the Lord is—And reform our depraved wills, inclining them to a cheerful and ready compliance with all the motion of thy good Spirit. Regulate our unruly passions; purify our corrupt affections; and convert all the faculties of our souls, to be instruments of thy glory, as they have been of thy dishonour; and make our bodies fit temples for thy Holy Spirit to dwell in. Yea, sanctify us wholly, that we may, as we ought, sanctify thy blessed name.

And quicken us, O Lord, to hear thy voice while it is called to-day; that we may make haste, and not delay to keep thy commandments. O keep us frequently and affectionately mindful of the shortness of our time, the frailty of our lives, and the uncertainty of our being here in this mutable world, that so soon passeth away, and where we have no continuing city: but are strangers and sojourners with thee, as all our fathers before us were. O let the remembrance and consideration of this have such a prevailing influence upon us, as to crucify the world to us, and make us more concerned for our everlasting welfare, and more careful to improve every present enjoyment to our souls' eternal advantage; and to grow holier still as we grow older; that the days which pass over us may not leave us, without any amendment wrought upon us; but that the work of thy grace may go on successfully upon our hearts, till it has made us ripe and ready for the joys and glories of thy kingdom.

The same things also we beg in behalf of all that ought to share in our prayers. O forgive the sins, and relieve the miseries of thy poor creatures every where. Enlarge the borders of thy church, and make additions to it daily of such as shall be saved. O that all who are called Christians, may be truly Christians, both in their right believing and their holy living. Advance the interest, and extend the limits of thy Son's kingdom, and may all nations flow into it, as to their rest. Bless our land, and endue our rulers, and those who direct our public affairs, with wisdom from on high. Give our judges the spirit of discernment, and aid and countenance our magistrates in the faithful execution of their office. Make them all men fearing God, and eschewing evil.—And O that all who are called to serve at thy altar, may be blessed with skilful understandings, and compassionate hearts, and exemplary lives. Make them wise to win souls, and faithful, industrious and successful in their sacred office, as workmen that need not be ashamed. Bless and prosper all the places of learning and education; and make all this people the Lord's people; that they may all know thee from the greatest to the least; and so order their conversation aright, that they may see the salvation of God. Remember them all for good, who have been any way instruments of our good; and all that have, or would hurt us, O Lord forgive them. Give unto all that mourn in Zion, beauty for ashes, the oil of joy for mourning, and the garments of praise for the spirit of heaviness. O Lord! continue thy gracious favour to us, and thy fatherly care over us this night. As we go to rest after the labours of the day, so help us to do thy work that we may enter into that rest which remains for thy people in the close of this life. And so discharge us from our sins, and supply us still with thy grace, that we may finish our course with joy, and in the end of our lives find the greatest of all mercy, to be received into thy glory: which we beg for the all-sufficient merits of our only Redeemer; for whom, and to whom, with thee, O everlasting Father, and the Holy Ghost the Comforter, in the unity of the ever glorious Trinity, be all praise, and honour and glory ascribed of us, and of all the Israel of God, now and for evermore. *Amen.*

THURSDAY MORNING. *Jenks.*

O LORD God, that hearest prayer, and art nigh to all that call upon thee in truth, have thine ears open to a world of creatures, that continually depend upon thee! As we are moved by our own necessities, so are we encouraged by the daily experience of thy mercies still to shelter ourselves under the shadow of thy wings, and to continue our suits and supplications at the throne of thy grace. And we beg of thee, who fashioneth all the hearts of the sons of men, that thou wilt prepare our hearts to come into thy holy presence, and to call upon thy blessed name, in due and acceptable manner! O pour upon us the spirit of grace and of supplications; and let thy good Spirit help our infirmities, and teach us to pray so as shall be most agreeable to thy will, and most advantageous to our souls.

For we, who are but poor worms, and sinful dust and ashes; that have too much cause to be afraid, lest our great and manifold sins have provoked thee to hide thy face from us, and to shut up thy loving-kindness in displeasure against us, have taken upon us to speak unto thee, the Sovereign Majesty of heaven and earth. For we have done foolishly and wickedly, in not hearkening to the calls of thy word. nor yielding to the monitions of thy Spirit, to walk in the ways which thou hast set before us. Our iniquities are increased over our heads, our trespasses are grown even up to heaven, and our sins are a sore burden, too grievous and heavy for us to bear. They are infinite debts, and sad accounts; for which if thou, O Lord, shouldst enter into judgment with us, we could not answer thee one of a thousand; but must lay our hands upon our mouths, and plead nothing but guilty, having our whole dependence upon thy mercy.

O God, be merciful to us miserable sinners, for his sake, whom thou hast exalted to be a Prince and a Saviour, to give repentance to thy people, and forgiveness of their sins: be merciful to us, we pray thee, and heal our souls, that have greatly sinned against thee. O heal our backslidings, renew us to true repentance, establish our hearts in thy true fear and love, and establish our goings in thy holy ways; that we may not be so wavering and bent to backslidings, nor revolt from thee to turn to folly, after thou in mercy hast spoken peace to our souls; but may go on conquering and to conquer all the enemies of our souls, and all the hinderances of our salvation, till Satan be bruised under our feet.

O thou God of all grace! bring such thoughts to our minds, and lay such considerations home powerfully upon our hearts, as thou knowest most effectual to prevail with us, to work in us thy will, and to keep us from our iniquity within the bounds of our duty, till thou receive us into the blessed kingdom of thy glory. And, in the mean time, sanctify to us all thy dealings with us; and bless us in all our undertakings, and in all our conditions and relations. Make us humble, contented, and duly careful of our souls; following after the things now which will bring us true peace and comfort at the last.

Dispose of us, we beseech thee, our God, and of all that concerns us this day, to the glory of thy name. O keep us at all times, and in all places and companies, from the evil of sin, and from all other evils, to which the greatness of our sins does make us liable. And take thou, O heavenly Father, the gracious charge, and guidance, and government of us; and so lead us here in all our ways, with thy counsel, that hereafter thou mayest receive us into thy glory; through thy tender mercies, and our Saviour's abundant merits; in whose own words, we beg all things needful for ourselves and others, at thy hands.

Our Father, &c.

THURSDAY EVENING. *Jenks.*

O Lord, the great and glorious God, infinite in power, wisdom and goodness; the wonderful maker and preserver, ruler and disposer, of us and of all the world! thou hast created all things by thy almighty hand; sustainest and orderest all that thou hast made by thy wise and righteous providence; and thy mercy is everlasting, and over all thy works. O who is able to express or conceive the exceeding riches of that grace and goodness of the Lord, which in such plentiful measure is still descending and overflowing upon poor sinful creatures, who deserve nothing from thee but to be forsaken and abhorred by thee! This day, and every day of our lives, O Lord, have we tasted largely of thy mercy, and lived altogether still upon thy fatherly care and bounty.

But notwithstanding all thy patience and gracious dealings with us, and all the repeated pledges of thy favour and kindness to us; O how ill we have requited thy love! And what unsuitable returns have we made for all thy great and continued goodness that we have found! Beside the guilt of our inbred corruption, which hangs heavy upon us; we are amazed at the greatness and multitude of all our other sins that we have committed against the light and teachings of thy gospel, against the dictates and strivings of thy Spirit, and the love and sufferings of thy Son; against all the patience and long forbearance which thou hast exercised towards us; and against the many mercies and methods of our conversion and sanctification, wherewith from time to time, thou hast sought to make us such as thy word requires we should be. O Lord, we have given thee so great provocation that we are afraid lest thou shouldst forsake us utterly, and cause the day of thy patience to be at an end with us, and grant us no more of thy grace which we have so greatly abused, no more of thy Holy Spirit, which we have so frequently refused. And what have we now but judgment to expect from thee, O Lord, but that thy mercy rejoices over judgment! And thy word assures us that thou delightest not in the death of sinners, but rather that they should turn to thee and live. Therefore still thou leavest us these opportunities to appear before thee, to plead with our God, for the life of souls that have sinned against thee. And what have we to plead, O blessed Lord, but thy own gracious nature, and merciful inclinations, and the many promises and declarations, of thyself which thou hast made to returning sinners in Jesus Christ! Thou hast sent thine only Son to be our only Saviour; and he that did no sin was manifested to take away our sins. O for his sake be thou pleased to pity us, and spare us, and forgive us. Turn away thy wrath from us; receive us to thy blessed favour; and comfort us with the sure persuasion, that our great and many sins are remitted.

And because such is the infirmity of our nature, that without thy grace we have not the least power to keep ourselves even from the greatest sins; O grant us the increase of thy grace, and such help of thy good Spirit, as may fortify us against all temptation, and make us willing and faithful, and diligent in thy service. And be pleased, O Lord, yet further to discover and manifest thyself to our souls, that we may know aright thee, the only true God, and Jesus Christ whom thou hast sent. And give us power from on high, to enable us so to live and practise, according to that light and knowledge of our duty which thou art pleased to impart unto us, that we may not hold the truth in unrighteousness, knowing the better, and doing the worse, but may walk in the light, as children of light, while we have it; that we may never in judgment be deprived of it. O let us not only be almost, but altogether Christians; sincere converts, true penitents, and sound believers. And wilt thou, O God, that workest all in all, do that work of thy grace thoroughly upon all our hearts; for which we may have cause to give thee praise and glory to all eternity.

Which things we beg not only for ourselves, but for all the partakers of our nature, whom thou hast made to share in our hopes and capacities of eternal happiness; especially for thy whole church, wheresoever or howsoever disposed of over all the earth; for all in authority, from the highest even to the lowest; for our ministers and teachers; for our relations and neighbours; our friends and benefactors; and for all thy afflicted, whatsoever be their trials and troubles. O supply all their wants, and fulfil all their desires, so as thy wisdom sees best, for thy own mercy's sake in Jesus Christ.

Thou, Lord, art the great preserver of men, who hast kept and blessed us to-day, and all our days. Praised be thy name for all thy goodness, which we so long and largely have experienced. O make us sensible and thankful, as we are obliged to be. Take care of us, O Lord, and be good to us this night. Give us bodily rest in our beds, and rest for our souls in thyself. And be thou our God and guide, our hope and help, our joy and comfort, and all in all to us this night, and for evermore. *Amen.*

FRIDAY MORNING. *Jenks.*

O Lord our God! thy name is most excellent in all the earth: thou hast set thy glory above the heavens, and thou art worthy to be celebrated with everlasting praises of men and angels; for thou hast created all things, and for thy pleasure they are and were created. Thy hands, O Lord, have made us and fashioned us, and thou hast breathed into our nostrils the breath of life; yea, still thou holdest our souls in life, and givest us every good thing that makes our lives a blessing and a comfort to us. Thou hast formed us for thyself, that we should show forth thy praise, and live to thy glory, as we do continually live upon thy bounty.

But, O Lord our God! we have not brought thee the glory thou hast made us capable of, and so many ways obliged us to; instead of that, O how greatly have we dishonoured thee, our God, in the whole course and conduct of our lives! time after time, forgetting the gracious Giver of all our good things, who art never unmindful of us. And O how soon have we been weary to do thee service, who art never weary to do us good! Yea, we have not only neglected thy work, but have been disobedient against thy word, and have gone after our own foolish and hurtful lusts, in such ways of living as thy laws and our own hearts disallow and condemn us for.

And for these things we desire to pour out our hearts, and to humble ourselves here before thee; entreating thy gracious favour, for the sake of thy mercy in Christ Jesus, that thou wilt be pleased to give us repentance and pardon for all that is past, wherein we have offended thee; whether in omitting of our duty, or failing in it, or doing contrary to it. However we have transgressed, O humble us duly under the sense of it; and for thy dear Son's sake, absolve us thoroughly from the guilt of it.

And strengthen us, good Lord, with might, by thy Spirit in the inner man, to make us more watchful against, and more victorious over, the corruption of our nature, the temptations of the devil, and the distractions and allurements of this sinful world, wherein we live. O destroy in us every vicious inclination, every evil habit, and rebellious notion, that exalts itself against the knowledge of God, and against the obedience of our Lord Jesus Christ. And increase and confirm in us still more and more, thy true knowledge, and faith, and fear, and love; and every grace of thy Holy Spirit, which thou knowest to be most wanting in us, and necessary for us; such as may make our lives still more comfortable to ourselves, more profitable to others, and more to the glory of thy name. And however it goes with us, as to the concerns of this present time, O that we may still be found in the way of our duty, fearing God, and working righteousness; that we may secure our interest in the great Saviour of the world, so that when all here shall fail us, thou mayest take us up, and be the strength of our hearts, and our portion for evermore.

Day by day we magnify thee, O Lord, who makest every day of our lives still a further addition to thy mercies. We bless thee for our last night's preservation and protection, and for the rest and refreshment which thou hast given us therein. O cause us to hear thy loving-kindness in the morning, for in thee do we trust; cause us to know the way wherein we should go, for we lift up our souls to thee. Cast us not away from thy presence; take not thy Holy Spirit from us; but direct all our ways to please thee, our God, that thou mayest crown us with blessing and good success. Help us to see thy power, to own thy presence, to admire thy wisdom, and to love thy goodness in all thy creatures. And by all the comforts of creatures, O draw our hearts still nearer to thyself the blessed Creator of every comfort; and let our meditations of God be sweet as well as frequent, that delighting ourselves in the Lord, thou mayest give unto us the desires of our hearts. Such thy mercy and grace we beg for ourselves, and all ours, and thine every where, in our great Mediator's form of prayer. Our Father, &c.

FRIDAY EVENING. *Jenks*

Our ever blessed and most gracious God! thou art the Lord and Giver of our lives and hopes, and of all our enjoyments and comforts. To thee we do owe ourselves, and all that ever we are capable of rendering and ascribing. For by thee, O Lord, we were created and have our being; and through thy good providence it is, that we still have been spared and preserved, and cared and provided for, throughout our whole lives unto this present time. From thee, our God, comes all our help, and in thee is reposed all our hope. Thou art the bountiful

Giver of all the good that our souls desire, and the merciful withholder of all the evils that our sins deserve. We acknowledge thy great and daily goodness to us, and our own exceeding unworthiness of the least of all thy mercies. We take shame and confusion to ourselves, that we have so little improved, and so greatly abused, all thy patience with us, and all the various instances of thy bounty to us. For even thy mercies help to inflame the heavy reckoning of our offences, because we have done so much against thee, after all the great things thou hast done for us. We desire, O Lord, to be penitent, and humbled for our sins; and to entreat thy gracious favour in Jesus Christ, for the pardon of them. Forgive us, we pray thee, for his sake, all the sins that ever we have committed against thee, and absolve us from all the evils whereof we now stand guilty before thee. And being justified by faith, grant us peace with God, through our Lord Jesus Christ.

And we pray that thou wilt be to us a Father of mercies and a God of consolation; so that thou wilt make us followers of God, as dear children; ever jealous over our hearts, and watchful over our ways; continually fearing to offend, and endeavouring to please thee: and keeping our hearts with all diligence, that they may not be hardened through the deceitfulness of sin. Thou knowest, O Lord, our weakness and danger of temptation; our danger from the cruel, subtle enemy of our souls; and from this present world that is so full of snares; and from our own vile flesh and deceitful hearts, so apt to betray us into the enemies' hands; we pray, therefore, good Lord, that thou wilt arm us with the whole armour of God, and uphold us with thy free Spirit, and watch over us for good evermore. Especially in the times of our sorest trials, let us experience the strongest aids of thy heavenly grace, that we may never fall a prey to those deadly enemies that seek to devour us.

And teach us, our God, to know the day of our grace, and the time of our visitation, and to see the things of our peace, and duly to mind and settle the great eternal affairs of our souls, in this our day, before they be hid from our eyes. And while we have time, O enable us to use and improve it, to those great ends for which thou art pleased to put that precious talent into our hands, that we may make the short and uncertain stay which we have here, an opportunity of securing to ourselves a sure and everlasting well-being, when we shall depart from hence.

And seeing thou art pleased yet to hold our souls in life, and to make us find and feel, by every day's experience, how abundantly gracious and merciful thou art, with much patience and long suffering, enduring us, and with loving-kindness and manifold blessings, still preventing and following us; O give us hearts more sensible of thy love, more affected with thy mercy, and more thankful for those continued favours which thou art pleased to multiply upon us. And help us to show forth thy praise and the truth of our thanks, not only in speaking good of the name of God, but so ordering our conversation as becomes the gospel of our Lord Jesus Christ.

And to thy mercy in him, most merciful Father, we do now humbly commend ourselves, and all that we are, and have, this present night; beseeching thee to preserve and defend, and bless and keep us, both in soul and body, from all evils and dangers, to which the weakness of our frame, and the greatness of our sins, do expose us. And grant us such comfortable repose, whereby our frail nature may be refreshed, and our decayed strength recovered, that we may rise again better fitted and enabled to serve thee according to thy will in all the duties of the following day, if thou shalt be pleased to make addition of another day to our lives. And as thou addest days and mercies, be pleased also to add repentance and amendments to our lives; that, as we come nearer to our end, we may be made still fitter for the enjoyment of thy heavenly kingdom; that every day may bring us still so much nearer to those everlasting joys and glories which thou hast prepared for them that love thee. And for all the good things that ever we have had, and do at present enjoy, and yet hope for from thy bountiful hands, thine, O blessed glorious Lord our God, be the praise, and honour, and glory, offered up with all grateful hearts, by us, and the whole church, now and for evermore, through the merits and intercession of Jesus Christ our Redeemer, to whom be praise and glory for ever. *Amen.*

SATURDAY MORNING. *Jenks.*

WE do here present ourselves this morning before thy heavenly glorious Majesty, most blessed Lord our God, with the desire of our souls, to pay unto thee that tribute of homage and service, and prayer and praise, which thou hast made us capable of, and every way obliged us to. We desire to perform the same in such a manner, that thou mayest mercifully accept us and our services, at the hands of Christ Jesus. In his great name we come to thee, at thy command, and worship here at thy footstool, to beg thy pardon and peace, the increase of thy grace, and the tokens of thy love. For we are not worthy that thou shouldst in any way of mercy take notice of us, or be entreated by us: but worthy is the Lamb of God, slain to take away the sins of the world, for whose sake do thou, O Lord, mercifully look upon us; for he has fulfilled those holy laws, which we have broken, and perfectly satisfied the justice of heaven for all our breaches of them. And in him thou art a God gracious and merciful, to poor sinners, who deserve nothing from thee, but to be forsaken and abhorred by thee. Unto us belong shame and confusion of face for our sins, and fearful expectation of all the judgments and miseries which thy laws denounce against sinners; if thou, Lord, shouldst be extreme to mark what we have done amiss; if thou shouldst deal with us and proceed against us as in justice thou mightest.

But, O gracious Father, regard not what we have done against thee, but what our blessed Saviour has done for us; not what we have made ourselves, but what he is made of thee, our God, unto us. And O that Christ may be to every one of our souls, what he is to all thy faithful people, wisdom, and righteousness, and sanctification, and redemption; that his precious blood may cleanse us from all our sins; and that the grace of thy Holy Spirit may further renew and sanctify our souls, and subdue our iniquities, and mortify our lusts; and quicken us to, and enable us for, the performance of all the duties of thy holy service. O let not sin reign in our mortal bodies, that we should obey it in the lust thereof. Let there be no sin in us but what is felt and hated, bewailed and resisted by us; and let us approve our very hearts to thee, the Searcher of them; and all our ways be still pleasing in thy sight.

O teach us to know thee, our God, and enable us to do thy will as we ought to do. Give us hearts to fear thee, and love thee; to trust and delight in thee, and to adhere and cleave in faithfulness unto thee. That no temptations may draw us, nor any tribulations drive us from thee; but that all thy dispensations to us, and all thy dealings with us, may be the messengers of thy love to our souls, to bring us still nearer to thy blessed self, and to make us still fitter for thy heavenly kingdom. Quicken us, O Lord, in our dulness; that we may not serve thee in a lifeless and listless manner; but may abound in thy work, and be fervent in spirit, serving the Lord. And make us also faithful in all the offices of intercourse with our neighbours; that we may be ready to do good, and bear evil, and forbear revenge; and be just and kind, merciful and meek, peaceable and patient, sober and temperate, humble and self-denying, inoffensive and useful in the world. That so glorifying thee here upon earth, we may, at our departure hence, enter into the joy of our Lord, and be forever glorified in thy heavenly kingdom.

O Thou that hast kept us alive to this day, and hast been still good and kind to us all our days, renew thy mercy to us, we beseech thee, together with this morning light; and as thou makest the outgoings of the morning and evening to rejoice, so lift up the light of thy countenance upon us, and make us glad with the tokens of thy love; and thou that art ever present with us, O make us ever well aware of thy presence, that we duly remember thee in all our ways, and wisely and piously demean ourselves in all our affairs. Be with us, good Lord, at our going out, and our coming in; and let thy grace follow us this day, and all the days of our life. Be thou our guide unto death, in death our comfort, and after death our portion and happiness everlasting. O hear us from heaven, thy dwelling-place; and, when thou hearest, have mercy; forgive the sins of our persons, and the sins of our prayers; and do more for us than we are worthy to expect at thy hands, for his sake, who alone is worthy; in whose comprehensive words we sum up all our desires. Our Father, &c.

SATURDAY EVENING. *Jenks.*

O LORD, we desire to seek thy face, and to wait upon thee in the duties of thy worship; entreating thy gracious favour with our whole hearts, that we may do all as we ought, with good acceptance to our God. And to whom should we make our applications, but unto thee, the Father of mercies and the fountain of all goodness, who art able to do exceeding abundantly for us, even above all that we can ask or think; and who hast declared thy willingness to be solicited by us; and thy readiness to hear, and help, and answer us, in those things which we beg at thy gracious and bountiful hands, in the name and mediation of our great Lord and Saviour: O let our prayer be set before thee as incense, and the lifting up of our hands be as the evening sacrifice. It is in his blessed name alone, that we have the encouragement and boldness to beg of thy infinite goodness all that thou knowest to be needful and expedient for us; seeing there is in ourselves no good thing to recommend us to thy favour and acceptance; but a proneness and inclination to what is displeasing in thy eyes, and destructive to our souls. For besides that we were by nature the children of wrath, a seed of evil doers, the sinful offspring of rebellious parents; we have been daily trespassing upon thee, and still adding to the heavy score of our offences against thee. There is nothing in us, O Lord, but what may provoke thee to reject us: but there is enough in thy beloved Son, of all grace and goodness, to move thee mercifully to accept us. He was made sin for us, who knew no sin, that we might be made the righteousness of God in him; and that we might be saved through faith in his merits, where we could not be saved by any desert of our own works. As the chastisement of our peace was upon him, so let the merits of his righteousness be upon us; and by his stripes let our souls be healed.

Nor do we only beg for pardon of our sins, but also for power against them, and grace sufficient for us to break them off, and to walk more pleasingly before thee, in all the ways and duties of righteousness and holiness, which thy word prescribes to us. O never suffer us to be tempted above what we are able; but make our temptations less, or thy grace in us, and our spiritual strength, still greater than all our temptations; that no iniquities may prevail against us, nor any presumptuous sin have dominion over us. O make us more conformable to the pattern and the precepts of our Saviour, and more transformed into his holy image and likeness. So that our light may shine before men, to the glory of thee our heavenly Father, and to the edification of those with whom we have our conversation.

And together with our own, we commend to thy mercy, O God of the spirits of all flesh, the necessities and distresses of all our brethren throughout the world. O enlighten the ignorant, quicken the careless, awake the secure, convince the erroneous, reclaim the vicious, establish the unsettled, and comfort the dejected. Bring all to the knowledge and love of thy truth, and to the participation of thy grace, and the obedience of Christ and so to the blessed hope of thy heavenly glory, and to the eternal salvation of our souls. We pray more particularly for all our magistrates and ministers of the gospel; and all our friends and relations; and all thy servants; and all the afflicted every where; especially those for whose happiness and salvation thou knowest us to be chiefly concerned. O do thou for us, and for them, as thou knowest best, and most needful and expedient, for thy own mercy's sake in Jesus Christ.

To thee we now render humble and hearty thanks for thy mercy to our family during another week. We thank thee that during its days and nights thou hast watched around our dwelling — hast met our returning wants — hast given us food convenient for us, and the protection of raiment, and a home. We praise thee that so many of our friends have been continued to us; and that thou dost still preserve to us the enjoyments of a Christian land. Thou hast in mercy brought us again near to the day of sacred rest. If it be thy good pleasure to keep us through this night — which we humbly implore — we pray that thou wilt prepare us for the duties of another holy day. Awake us in the morning with a lively sense of thy mercies; with a spirit of prayer; with hearts fitted to be impressed by religious truth; and with a deep conviction of thy goodness in the resurrection of our Lord Jesus from the grave. Go with us, if we may go, to the house of worship; and meet us in the sanctuary and bless us. Aid all thy ministering servants, that they may declare thy truth with simplicity and power. May thy Spirit descend on the churches; on all Sunday schools; and on all who are engaged in designs of benevolence; and may the morrow be a day long to be remembered in Zion, and the time soon come when thy Sabbath shall be observed by all the family of mankind.

And now that the night is upon us, and we are ready to betake ourselves to our rest, we commit ourselves to thy gracious protection, who never sleepest nor slumberest, but hast still a watchful eye upon thy people. O watch over us, our God, we pray thee, for good; that none of the evils or harms which our sins have deserved may befall us. Preserve us from the works, and from the powers of darkness, and from all the terrors and dangers of the night. Let all our sins, to-day or any time heretofore committed, be removed out of thy sight, and show us the light of thy countenance, O Lord, to refresh us with the sense of thy blessed love and favour, in our dear Redeemer; for whom, and to whom, with thy eternal self, and Holy Spirit, be all thanks, and praise, and honour, and glory, ascribed of us and all thy church, from this time forth, world without end. *Amen.*

THIRD WEEK.

SABBATH MORNING. *Smith*

O Thou who art the Author and Preserver of our lives, unto thee we would now lift up our voice and our hearts. Teach us to approach unto thee with that reverence which becometh all thy creatures; and vouchsafe to draw near unto us, as a God of pity, of mercy, and of grace.

We adore thee, O God, who hast made us for thy service; that thou hast given us thy word to direct us in thy worship; and that one day in every seven of our lives is appointed for this purpose. As the unworthy, but professing disciples of Jesus Christ, who hope for acceptance only through his merits and mediation, we would now offer up our morning sacrifice to the God, and Father, and fountain of all. This is the day which thou hast made; the day upon which thy Son rose from the dead, finishing the work of our redemption; that happy day when the love of God, the grace of Jesus Christ, and the fellowship of the Holy Ghost, may be humbly expected wherever two or three are met together in the name of the adorable Trinity. Wilt thou then, O most high and incomprehensible Jehovah! accept of the dedication which we now make thee of our bodies and souls?

We are sensible that we have rendered ourselves unworthy of thy notice, having lost thy image, and broken thy commandments. But, God of all grace, thou art in Christ again reconciling a guilty world unto thyself, not imputing unto men their trespasses; and, therefore, we would now believingly, although humbly, draw near, asking and hoping every thing for his sake. Let those sins which we have formerly committed against much goodness, much love, and much light, be all blotted out of the book of thy remembrance. Let these worthless souls of ours be clothed with the wedding garment of a Redeemer's righteousness, that we may thus be interested in the privileges of his kingdom. O thou Giver of every good and perfect gift, create in us all clean hearts, and renew right spirits within us, that we may love thee —that we may fear thee—that it may be as our meat and our drink at all times to do thy holy will. We thank thee, O God, for that providential care and goodness which thou hast exercised towards us during the past week, and the past night. Prepare us for all the duties in which we are this day to be engaged. When we are allowed to enter into thine earthly temple, let all worldly wishes, worldly cares, and worldly thoughts of every sort, be banished from our minds. Enable us to sing thy praises with gratitude in our hearts. Grant that we may read thy holy Scriptures for our instruction and comfort. May the prayers which we shall this day offer up for ourselves and others, so far as is consistent with thy glory, be accepted; and let thy word preached enlighten our understandings, spiritualize our hopes, confirm our faith, rekindle our love, and inspire us with new resolutions to live more becoming the professions we make, and the privileges we enjoy.

And when we return from thy house, forbid, O God, that we should spend any part of thy day in thinking our own thoughts, speaking our own words, or minding our own pleasures; but let it be an entire Sabbath of rest unto our souls, reflecting upon what we have heard, laying up thy doctrines and precepts in our memories, examining by thy word and Spirit, into our state; and renewing, by thine all-sufficient grace, our broken vows, and unfulfilled engagements.

And thus, O Father, into whose hands we have committed our immortal spirits, by thus wisely and profitably spending our Sabbaths on earth, may we all be trained up and prepared for that eternal Sabbath in heaven, where we shall see thee as thou art, feel all thy perfections conspiring to make us happy, join in endless worship with an innumerable company of angels and dignified spirits, be introduced into thy presence, where there is fulness of joy, and be admitted to sit down at thy right hand, where there are pleasures for evermore.

O Lord, might we still intercede in behalf of our brethren of mankind! Thou hast promised by the blood of thy covenant, to speak peace unto the heathen. Soon, O God, give them to thy Son as his inheritance, with the utmost parts of the earth for his possession. Where the gospel is preached and professed, may multitudes be converted, and made a willing people in the day of thy power. Pour out, O God, a double portion of thy Holy Spirit, upon all the ministers of the everlasting gospel; and may they be enabled to discharge the important trust committed to them with fidelity and diligence, with thy approbation, and with abundant success. Let the churches with which we are more immediately connected have rest; and walking together in the fear of the Lord, and comforts of the Holy Ghost, may they be edified and multiplied.

Our relatives and friends, wherever they are, may their bodies be the objects of thy providential care, and all their souls the subjects of thy saving grace. If it be thy will, let us have many comfortable and useful meetings in this world, and may none of us be found wanting in that day when thou countest thy jewels. Such as may now be more immediately under thy afflicting hand, O God, console, support, and in thy due time deliver; and may we all have an interest in that sure promise, that all things at last shall work together for good.

Now, unto the King eternal, immortal, and invisible, the only wise God, be honour and glory, for ever and ever. *Amen.*

SABBATH EVENING. *Smith.*

Our Father that art in heaven, hallowed be thy sacred name. For we, that are in ourselves but as dust and ashes, have, nevertheless, been permitted again and again this day to draw near and supplicate at the throne of thy grace. We confess, that even the iniquities of our holy things testify against us; and hadst thou been strict to mark our vain, polluted, and sinful thoughts, even in thy worship, thou mightest have cast us off. But, O Lord, we admire, and adore; and would even rejoice in these gracious declarations, which thou hast given us in thy word, that thou takest no pleasure in the destruction of sinners: and knowing our frame, remembering we are but dust, and therefore exacting of us less than our iniquities deserve, thou art long-suffering, slow to anger, full of compassion, and plenteous in mercy.

Blessed God, may every returning consideration of thy glorious attributes, but especially these astonishing expressions of thy loving-kindness and tender mercy to the human race, so conquer and soften our hard and stony hearts, as that they may now melt down, and flow out, in ardent love, and humble gratitude; thus ending thy day, as we sweetly began it, with thine easy yoke, in thy delightful service.

O God, keep us in patient waiting until that glorious hour, when we may hope to join that blessed company around thy throne, and sing the song of Moses and the Lamb. Make us thankful for those communications of thy love and grace, which, but tasted here below, give more true peace, and solid pleasure, than the men of the world enjoy, when their corn, and wine, and creature comforts, do most abound.

O God, give us a greater relish for these pure and spiritual joys. We long to have more of the temper and disposition of the holy Psalmist, when he said, "As the hart panteth after the water brooks, so panteth my soul after thee, O God!" We wish to say, "How amiable are thy tabernacles, O Lord of Hosts! a day spent in thy courts, is better than a thousand otherwise employed."

Lord, grant that the worship and services in which we have lately been engaged, may be followed not only by thy gracious pardon, but with thy efficacious benediction. May neither the cares nor the pleasures of this world destroy the seed of the word which may have been this day sown in our hearts; but may it spring up, and bear fruit, some thirty, sixty, or an hundred fold.

We have desired the sincere milk of the word, that we may grow thereby. We are one Sabbath day's journey nearer the end of life. God grant that we be nearer to heaven in our tempers, in our conduct, in our desires and affections.

From this night we would desire to lead a life more conformable to the holy gospel we profess, and to the glorious hopes we are permitted to entertain.

Will the Lord be pleased to follow with his blessing the preaching of the gospel every where! Wherever the name of Christ hath this day been named, may multitudes see their need of his salvation, and be constrained to fly to him as their city of refuge. And, let the glorious period spoken of in an ancient prophecy, soon come, when the whole earth shall be full of the knowledge of the Lord, as the waters cover the channel of the sea.

Will God be pleased to hear the intercessions which have this day been put up through all his churches; more especially for our native country, the government under which we live, thy church as established among us, and all sects and denominations of real Christians. Be pleased, O

Lord, to pardon what may have been asked amiss; and where thy servants may have neglected to ask for needful blessings to themselves and others, do thou, of thine infinite goodness, supply the deficiency. And now, O God, permit us to commend our bodies and souls to thy paternal care this night. Thou art the keeper of Israel, who never slumbereth nor sleepeth. Give us composed and refreshing sleep. Be at our right hand, and we will not fear what evil men or evil spirits can do to us; and having found that thou hast been our refuge and defence all the night long, may we awake in the morning disposed to meditate upon thy goodness and mercy. O may we live in thy love and fear all our days, and improve by every dispensation of thy providence and grace, and at last be admitted, with all ours, into thy heavenly kingdom. We ask and hope for every blessing, in the name, and for the sake, of our dear Redeemer. *Amen.*

MONDAY MORNING. *Smith.*

INCOMPREHENSIBLE, but infinitely great and glorious Jehovah! we are again this morning permitted to lift up our hearts and voice unto thee. Thou didst at the first make man after thine own image, a little lower than the angels, and crowned him with honour and with glory; but our first parents broke thy covenant, and we have fallen from this holy and happy condition, into a state of guilt, pollution, and misery.

We are but of yesterday, and know nothing. We are a seed of evil-doers, who have gone astray from every right path; and thy pure and perfect law hath justly concluded us all under sin, that every mouth may be stopped, and the whole world become guilty before God.

But thou hast not left us altogether, nor in any age in this dark and forlorn situation. For, when the world by wisdom knew not God, and the way of man was not in himself, God, at sundry times, and in divers manners, spake in times past to our fathers by the prophets, and in these last days hath spoken still more clearly and fully by his own Son.

O God, our Father, through the operation of the Holy Spirit, engage us all to make a saving application of this Son of thine, as the Lamb slain from the foundation of the world; and to whom all the prophets gave witness, and now once in the end of the world hath appeared to put away sin by the sacrifice of himself.

Receive, we beseech thee, O God, this morning, our sincere and united thanks for that protection which thou hast afforded us, and the refreshing sleep we have enjoyed during the past night. Be with us, O our heavenly Father, through the whole of this day, and of this week, whose secular employments we are now about to enter upon. In all our transactions with the world, may we be conscientiously just, knowing that all who do unrighteously are an abomination unto the Lord.

Let us guide our affairs with discretion, so as that we may have it in our power to show favour, and assist our neighbour, in whatsoever business he hath need of us, as becometh saints.

Enable us, O God, upon all occasions, and in all situations, to show mercy, that we may never have judgment without mercy from thee. If thou shouldst see meet to crown our lawful endeavours, so as that we increase and abound in the good things of this life, Lord, let our rising in the world go hand in hand with the preservation and comfortable subsistence of all around us.

But, O, let us take heed from morning to night, lest at any time our hearts be overcharged with the cares of this life; for thou hast expressly said, "He that maketh haste to be rich, shall not be innocent."

Lord, deliver us from the inordinate love of money, which is the root of all evil; which, while some coveted after, they have erred from the faith, and pierced themselves through with many sorrows.

O Lord, we would not be over-anxious to lay up for ourselves treasures on earth, where moth and rust doth corrupt, and where thieves may break through and steal;

but would be laying up for ourselves treasures in heaven, that where our treasure is, there our hearts may be also forever.

Lord, we would keep alive upon our minds, both the shortness and the uncertainty of time. May this engage us to redeem it, and so to number all our days, as to be applying them toward an habitual preparation for death. Lord, give us this day our daily bread. Forgive us our numberless failings, and short-comings in duty. Forbid that we indulge either envy or malice in our hearts toward any fellow-creature. If it be thy holy will, may we fall into no temptation, but which thou wilt enable us to resist and overcome. And in the evening may we return to a throne of grace, with a conscience void of offence, and a heart replenished with gratitude to God, for the privileges and blessings of another day. Now unto the Three that bear record in heaven, the Father, the Word, and the Holy Spirit, be ascribed, as is most due, all praise, and power, dominion, and glory, world without end. *Amen.*

MONDAY EVENING. *Smith.*

Our Father, in heaven—evening, as well as morning, would we approach thy more immediate presence, with our humble tribute of adoration and praise. Thou art the greatest and the best of beings. There is none like unto thee in all the earth. Among the gods there is none like unto thee, O Lord! none like unto thee in heaven above, or on the earth beneath. Thou art the eternal God, with whom a thousand years are as one day, and one day as a thousand years.

Of old hast thou laid the foundation of the earth, and the heavens are the work of thy hands: they shall perish, but thou shalt endure; yea, all of them shall wax old like a garment; as a vesture shalt thou change them, and they shall be changed: but thou art the same, and thy years shall have no end.

The eyes of the Lord are in every place, beholding the evil and the good.

How then "shall we go from thy Spirit, or whither shall we flee from thy presence? If we ascend up into heaven, thou art there; if we make our bed in hell, behold, thou art there: if we say, Surely the darkness shall cover us, even the night shall be light about us: for the darkness hideth not from thee, but the night shineth as the day; the darkness and the light are both alike to thee."

How then ought our hearts to tremble, O Lord, when we consider also that thou art infinitely pure and just! Thou art the Holy One of Israel, whose name is holy, and who dwellest in the high and holy place.

And surely God will not do wickedly, neither will the Almighty pervert judgment: for the work of a man will he render unto him, and cause every man to find according to his ways. Yet, notwithstanding all this, we lift up our heads and hearts in hope. Blessed be God's name for that reviving declaration: "O Israel, thou hast destroyed thyself, but in me is thine help." To bring about our salvation, thou didst not spare thy Son; but in due time sent him into the world. We rejoice that Christ came not to do away the law, but to fulfil it; that by fulfilling all righteousness, he became the Mediator of a better covenant; that by his death upon the cross, the hand-writing of ordinances, that was against us, is blotted out; for he took it out of the way, nailing it to his cross. By him we have now received the atonement; and to him alone we look, and in him alone would we confide as our Mediator and Advocate with the Father. Yea, doubtless, and we would count all things but loss for the excellency of the knowledge of Jesus Christ our Lord, that we may win Christ, and be found in him; not having our own righteousness, which is of the law, but that which is through the faith of Christ, even the righteousness which is of God by faith.

Lord, enable us to walk worthy of this holy vocation wherewith we are called, and to put our trust in thee, that we may never be ashamed, and that thou mayest deliver us in thy righteousness. O that we could at all times say, Whom have we in heaven but God? and there is none upon earth that we desire in comparison with him: our flesh and our heart faileth, but he is the strength of our heart, and, we would hope, our portion for ever.

Lord, help us to consider that the end of all things, as to us, may be near at hand, and therefore we should be sober, and watch unto prayer; looking diligently unto ourselves, lest any of us fail of the grace of God; and so numbering all our days, as that we may apply our hearts unto true wisdom.

God grant that we may never be like the men of the world, which have all their portion in this life, and who say of it, "This is my rest, *here* will I dwell, for I have desired it;" but, on the contrary, finding that for true happiness we here have laboured in vain, and spent our strength for nought, and that all our days are vanity, may we cry out, I loathe it, I would not live always! O, that I had wings like a dove! for then would I fly away, and be at rest. Lord, keep us ever in a waiting posture, and enable us to see thy hand, and to acknowledge thy will, in every thing that befalls us.

For the health of body and composure of mind which we have this day enjoyed, we would express our thankfulness to a gracious God. Be with us, heavenly Father, during the silent watches of the ensuing night. Preserve us still from disease of body, and from distress of mind: or, if it should be thy will that we receive such chastisements from thy hand, Lord, give us patience to endure them, and a happy issue out of them in due time. Let the putting off of our clothes this night remind us of the putting off of these mortal bodies, which must, ere long, return to the dust: and O grant that we may be both habitually and actually prepared for the important event. May the like blessings, both temporal and spiritual, be bestowed upon all who are near and dear to us. In thy fear and love, and in mutual good offices, may we live whilst in this world, and ere long meet together in that kingdom, and in those mansions, which our dear Redeemer hath been preparing from the beginning of time.

In his name we ask every blessing; and to him, with thee, O Father, and the Eternal Spirit, be all praise, and honour, and glory. *Amen.*

TUESDAY MORNING. *Smith.*

O Thou Creator and Preserver of all things, behold us again, this morning, at the footstool of thy throne. We draw near, permitted and encouraged by thy word, to adore thy perfections, and to give thee thanks for the many favours conferred upon us. We come also to confess our demerit and sinfulness, and to plead for thy pardoning mercy and recovering grace. And who is like unto thee, O thou great, eternal, invisible, and incomprehensible Object of our spiritual worship! Before all things thou didst exist; from everlasting to everlasting thou art the only living and true God, infinite in wisdom, power, goodness and mercy. Of thy good-will and pleasure thou didst at first bring us out of nothing into existence. But that rank of being which we hold in the scale of creation, demands our further and most grateful acknowledgment. We are wiser than the fowls of heaven and have more understanding than the beasts that perish. We bless God that we are endued with rational and immortal souls, and made capable of knowing, worshipping, and enjoying him. We would express our thankfulness this morning for all that care, protection, and kindness, which we have experienced from our birth to the present hour; for sparing us in childhood, guiding us in youth, and preserving us amidst the numberless diseases and dangers of riper years. We thank thee for our daily food, for our warm and decent clothing, for all the necessaries of life, and those many conveniencies and comforts which we enjoy beyond thousands of our fellow creatures around us. But, above all, we would ever adore and praise God for his inestimable love and grace in Jesus Christ.

We had destroyed ourselves, but in God there was help found. When there was no eye to pity, nor hand to help, he sent his Son to be the Saviour of the world. We believe that Jesus of Nazareth is the only true Messiah, and that he died for our offences, and rose again for our justification.

We fly to thee in him, as the alone foundation for pardon, reconciliation, adoption into the family of heaven, and every spiritual blessing. O let the Holy Spirit be given unto us, to seal our souls unto the day of redemption. Let him be as a Spirit of wisdom to guide us at all times; as a Spirit of holiness, to regenerate and cleanse our souls from every impure desire; and as a Spirit of might and power, to strengthen us, that we may neither be ashamed nor afraid, when we have respect unto all thy commandments. Lord, we are poor, short-sighted creatures, and know not what temporal blessings to ask at thy hands; for we know not what shall eventually be best for us. If consistent with thy will, may we hope that goodness and mercy shall still follow us.

What are we, and what is our father's house, that thou hast brought us up hitherto? When we think of what we have received, O God, and compare it with what we deserve, we are lost in wonder and astonishment at thy goodness. Let it not be altogether lost: may it lead us to gratitude and humility, to repentance, and to a mindfulness of our latter end: for we know not what is between us and the grave. Thou mayest yet see meet to teach us in the school of adversity. Help us then to say, "It is the Lord's will, let him do what seemeth him good. Shall we receive good at the hand of the Lord, and shall we not also receive evil?" Lay not upon us more than thou wilt enable us to bear, that the issue of all shall be to thy glory, and for our greater good.

Lord, accept of our sincere thanks for that freedom from pain, both of body and mind, which we have enjoyed during the past night. There are many no doubt, whose cry, during the lingering hours, hath been, Would God it were morning! and who even now (the distress remaining) may be saying, Would God it were evening! Lord God, take pity upon such, and in thy good time relieve them: and elevate all our hearts towards that time and place, when God shall wipe away all tears from our eyes, and there shall be no more death; neither sorrow nor crying; neither shall there be any more pain; the former things being for ever passed away. Until this period come, until death, which leadeth unto it, may we all be kept in a waiting posture. May we watch as well as pray, that we be *actually* as well as *habitually*, prepared for death: for blessed are those servants whom the Lord, when he cometh, shall find watching. Now, unto Him that supplieth all our need, according to his riches in glory, by Jesus Christ; to the Three that bear record in heaven, the Father, the Word, and the Holy Ghost, be honour and glory, thanksgiving and praise, for ever and ever. *Amen.*

TUESDAY EVENING. *Smith.*

God of all goodness and grace, hear our prayer this evening, and give ear to the words of our mouth. We would call upon thee, who alone art worthy to be praised, and who hast given us reason to hope that thou wilt send out thy light and thy truth, to lead and bring us to thy holy hill, even unto a throne of grace, where we may obtain mercy to pardon, and grace to help in time of need. We know, and would have ever deeply impressed on our minds, that the Lord, he is great, and that our Lord is above all gods. Thou remainest for ever the same, and thy throne is from generation to generation. One day is with thee as a thousand years, and a thousand years as one day. The Most High, whom we would now worship, dwelleth not in temples made with hands. Heaven is his throne, and the earth is his footstool; yet his eyes run to and fro through the world: from the place of thy habitation thou lookest down upon all the inhabitants of the earth, and considerest all their works. There is no iniquity with the Lord our God: thou art the Lord who lovest righteousness, and exercisest judgment in the earth; and thou hast appointed a day when thou wilt judge the world in righteousness. What then must become of us, O Lord, who have always been ungrateful, and so often broken thy most just and easy commandments? To us, indeed, O God, belongeth shame and confusion of face; and more especially when we think of thy holiness, and our impurity and sinfulness.

Thou didst create us after thy image, but we have let it be defaced. Thou hast favoured us with the light of revelation; but we have loved the ways and works of darkness. Thy law, O God, which is exceeding broad, hath been often read to us, and its precepts impressed on our minds, but in how many instances have we transgressed against it!

O deal not with us according to our folly, but see our shield, and look upon the face of thine Anointed; that he, like unto Aaron of old, may bear our iniquity, and we be accepted at a throne of grace through him.

We look to Christ alone for acceptance with the Father, who blotted out the hand-writing of ordinances that was against us, and took it out of the way, nailing it to his cross; even thy Son, O God, who thus (as it became him) fulfilled all righteousness; and being the Mediator of a better covenant, brought in a better hope, by the which hope we draw nigh unto God. And thus looking, O God, and thus hoping, we would not only humbly expect the pardon of all our sins, but even a comfortable persuasion thereof in our own minds, with all those advantages which accompany or flow from it.

Lord, give us that best of evidences which ariseth from a conformity of mind and will to thee, and to our blessed Master. Let us have grace, whereby we may serve God acceptably. None of us would henceforward live unto ourselves. We are not our own, for we are bought with a price. May we therefore glorify God in our body, and in our spirit, which are God's.

We would, we hope and trust, form sincere resolutions this evening, to live more and more soberly, honestly and godly, in this present evil world. And to this purpose, O God, teach us to reflect seriously upon the shortness of life; the rapidity with which our days, and weeks, and months, and years, pass away. Help us to consider that our career may terminate every moment, when death shall summon us to judgment, and the consequences be eternal. Lord, teach us therefore so to number and estimate every day as if it were our last. Like the foolish virgins, may we not sleep, or even slumber, in a cold outward profession; but having our loins girded, and our lamps burning, may we imitate the wise virgins, be ever watching, and making ready for the coming of our Lord; and thus we may hope to appear before him with confidence and holy joy.

Keep us this night, O God, under the shadow of thy wings, and defend our bodies and souls from all evil. Refresh us with sleep; and if thou art pleased to grant us the privilege of another day in this state of probation, may our renewed strength be employed to advance thy glory and promote the best interests of all around us. O Lord, continue still to be kind and favourable to all our relations and friends. May we all be united in the same covenant of redemption here, and be permitted to enjoy its more glorious privileges together hereafter. Let the country where we live, and while we live, O God, if consistent with the great designs of thy providence, never be the seat of war, but the residence of liberty and peace. We long for the time when wars shall cease to the ends of the earth, and there shall be nothing to hurt or destroy in all thy holy mountain. Hasten that happy time, O God, and prepare the world for it. And now the God of Israel cause us to go from his throne in peace, and with the hope of pardon and acceptance: and to the Father, Son, and blessed Spirit, be eternal praises. *Amen.*

WEDNESDAY MORNING. *Smith.*

O Thou most holy, blessed, and glorious Lord God, whom we are bound by every tie to worship and obey; behold us again, this morning, before the throne of thy grace. We laid ourselves down in peace—we have during the past night taken our rest in safety; and by thy kind providence we are entering upon the duties and enjoyments of another day.

A wearisome night might have been appointed us; thou mightest have alarmed us with dreams, and terrified us through visions; and we might have been full of tossings to and fro, until the dawning; but thou hast bestowed on us sleep, such as thou givest to thy beloved, and our beds have comforted and refreshed us. Blessed be the God and Father of our Lord Jesus Christ, for this renewed instance of his sustaining power and preserving goodness.

This morning again would we say, Come and hear, all ye that fear God, and we will declare what he hath done for our bodies and souls. Thine hand, O God, created us at the first. And we thank thee, O Lord, that thou hast not only granted us life, and thy visitation to preserve our spirit in the helpless state of infancy and childhood; but that thou hast cast our lot in a part of the world where light and liberty, peace and plenty, have so long existed and flourished.

Incomprehensible Being, who searchest the heart, and to whom every secret motion within us is known, behold our souls prostrate before the throne of thy grace this morning, ready again to take hold of thy covenant and strength, that we may make peace with thee, and that thou mayest make peace with us. Look down, O God of mercy, upon us; and for thine own sake, and according to thy express word and promise, blot out our transgressions, and remember our sins no more.

Behold, O God, our shield, and look upon the face of thine anointed, thy beloved Son, in whom thou art ever well pleased; who appeared in our world to put away sin by the sacrifice of himself; and by this one offering hath perfected for ever them that are sanctified. O! for his sake, forgive us our sins, and cleanse us from all unrighteousness. And now may the peace of God, which passeth all understanding, keep our hearts and minds, through Christ Jesus. We would not be over-anxious for that peace and prosperity which the world giveth. But we pray for that peace, which Jesus Christ hath promised, and left for all his disciples; a peace which the world can neither give nor take away; and through which our hearts may not be troubled, or in any degree afraid.

We must confess, O God, that if thou shouldest be strict to mark iniquities, we have often had cause to be both ashamed and afraid.

Thou hast also said in thy word, that the just shall live by faith; but if any man draw back, my soul shall have no pleasure in him. Wilt thou heal our backslidings, and pardon our numberless failings in duty. Thou hast said, Return, thou backsliding Israel, and I will not cause mine anger to fall upon you. Turn thou us unto thee, O Lord, and we shall be turned; and from this day enlighten and renew, more and more, every faculty and power of our mind and soul, that we may give all diligence to add to our faith, virtue, knowledge, temperance, patience, godliness, brotherly kindness, and charity; that these things being in us, and abounding, we may neither be barren, nor unfruitful in the saving knowledge of our Lord Jesus Christ.

For that protection which thou hast afforded us during the past night, and that refreshing sleep which our bodies have enjoyed, we desire, O God, to be more and more thankful. To thy care and keeping we again commit ourselves this day. Compass us about with thy favour as with a shield.

If consistent with thy will, prosper us in all our lawful employments, and give us comfort in all our worldly enjoyments. The same blessings we would ask in be half of our relations, our friends, our benefactors, and well-wishers. Our enemies, Father, forgive them, and enable us to do the same.

Lord, plead thine own cause in the world. Let ignorance, idolatry, superstition, and wickedness, come to an end. Erect the throne of thy Son's dominion upon the ruins of Satan's kingdom. Let the happy time be approaching when there shall be universal peace on earth and good-will amongst all mankind. Lord, continue kind to our native country. Provide for us, O God, rulers and magistrates, such as are able men, who fear thee, and hate covetousness. Prosper, O God, the means of instruction provided for our youth, and let the hoary heads be found in the way of righteousness; that they may look backward with satisfaction, and forward with hope. Pity the sick and afflicted; spare young and useful lives; and prepare us all for death and judgment. Now, blessed be God for all his gifts, both of nature and of grace! And to the Three that bear record in heaven, the Father, the Word, and Holy Spirit, be ascribed all honour and glory. *Amen.*

WEDNESDAY EVENING. *Smith.*

GLORIOUS JEHOVAH! by which name thou didst desire to be known by thy people of old, O take us (like them) into covenant with thee, and draw near in mercy to hear and help us. We would ever consider it as our highest honour, and greatest privilege, to call upon God by prayer and supplication, with thanksgiving.

We adore thee as the alone true object of all spiritual worship. Though there be that are called gods, whether in heaven or on earth, (as there be gods many, and lords many,) to us there is but one God the Father, of whom are all things, and we in him; and one Lord Jesus Christ, by whom are all things, and we by him, and one Spirit, the Eternal Spirit, who searcheth all things, yea, the deep things of God, by whom, through Jesus Christ alone, we have access unto the Father. In this new and living way may we be permitted to approach, at this time, to offer up our evening sacrifices.

And we would say, Blessed be the name of the Lord, from this time forth, and for evermore: from the rising of the sun unto the going down of the same, the Lord's name be praised; for the Lord is high above all nations, and his glory above the heavens. There is none like unto thee: rich in mercy, glorious in holiness, fearful in praises, ever doing wonders. But we would more especially praise thee this night for the unmerited, yet still continued, communications of thy goodness and grace to us.

We would more particularly thank and praise thy name for what we have experienced of it during the past day. Thou hast protected our going out and our coming in. The Lord is our keeper; he hath been as a shade upon our right hand, and preserved us from all evil.

We would be thankful, O God, unto thee for these temporal blessings; and pray earnestly that they may produce in our souls humility, gratitude, and love. But let us not be over-anxious about any worldly enjoyments or advantages. We would be convinced that all things here are unsatisfactory, or fleeting in their nature.

Blessed Saviour, impress thine own injunction upon our minds—Labour not for the meat which perisheth, but for that meat which endureth unto everlasting life, and which the Son of man shall give to all that come unto him.

Help us each to say with the apostle: "We are crucified with Christ, nevertheless we live; yet not we, but Christ liveth in us: and the life that we now live in the flesh, we live by the faith of the Son of God, who loved us, and gave himself for us, that we should no longer live the rest of our time in the flesh to the lusts of men, but to the will of God."

Thus living and walking no longer according to our old natural state, but according to the new one which we receive by faith, and the principles and means of practice, properly belonging thereunto, may we now strive to continue and increase in all Christian duties and graces. May we continue to love God in Christ as our supreme good. We pray for that fear of the Lord which is the beginning of wisdom, and by which every wise man departeth from evil. We would submit ourselves to him, saying, upon all proper occasions, the will of the Lord be done. May God, of his infinite mercy, grant that we may continue in the faith, grounded and settled, and that we be not moved away from the hope of the gospel. Let our love to mankind be without dissimulation, and may we be kindly affectioned one to another, with brotherly love. Instead of stirring up strife, by giving way to anger at any time, and using grievous words, help us, O Lord, by a soft answer to turn away wrath.

Lord, enable us daily to do good, that we may be rich in good works, ready to distribute, willing to communicate; laying up in store for ourselves a good foundation against the time to come. But, at the same time, keep us humble, O God, and let us never be desirous of vain glory.

May we be temperate in all things; and as we would ascend at last into the hill of the Lord, and stand accepted in his holy place—to this end, bless us, O God, with a pure heart, and with clean hands, and may we every day be growing wiser and better. We would thank the Lord, who hath preserved us this day from all evil.

Help us to know the measure of our days, and to keep in constant remembrance how frail we are; our wasting frames requiring a fresh supply of spirits and strength, by means of rest and repose through the night.

May we be secure during the night, and take our rest in safety; and let the same privileges be conferred upon all our brethren and kindred, according to the flesh; that we may all have the blessedness of those who make the Lord their trust.

Now unto Him that is able to do exceeding abundantly above all that we ask, or think, according to the power that worketh in us, unto him be glory in the church, by Christ Jesus, throughout all ages, world without end **Amen.**

THURSDAY MORNING. *Smith*

Thou hast sworn by thyself, O Lord! the word is gone out of thy mouth in righteousness, and shall not return, that unto thee "every knee shall bow, and every tongue confess." We would, therefore, seek unto God betimes, and make our supplications unto the Almighty; pressing ever at the same time upon our spirits that important consideration,—though the Lord's throne be in heaven, and he dwell by his special presence in his holy temple there, yet his eyes for ever behold, and his eyelids try the children of men. Neither is there any creature that is not manifest in his sight, but all things are naked and open unto the eyes of him with whom we have to do.

Well may we, indeed, say, "O Lord, thou hast searched us and known us. Thou knowest our down-sitting and our up-rising: thou understandest our thoughts afar off. Thou compassest our path, and our lying down, and art acquainted with all our ways; for there is not a word in our tongue, but lo! O Lord, thou knowest it altogether. Such knowledge is too wonderful for us; it is high, we cannot attain unto it. Oh the depth of the riches both of the wisdom and knowledge of God!"

When we consider all this, "What is man, that thou art mindful of him; and the sons and daughters of men, that thou thus visitest them?" In us, that is, in our flesh, dwelleth no good thing: we are all as an unclean thing, and all our righteousnesses are as filthy rags. If thou, Lord, shouldst mark iniquities, O Lord, who shall stand. In thy sight shall no man living be justified. And in this guilty and sinful state to which we have reduced ourselves, what can we do but fall down in humble adoration at the throne of thy grace, that according to the multitude of thy tender compassions, thy merited wrath and indignation may be turned away from us?

When we consider what we have merited, we tremble, and are afraid; but when we consider what thy Son has done and suffered for sinners, our broken hearts and contrite spirits revive. Remember in mercy, O God, that *he* hath satisfied thy justice for us; and notwithstanding we may have been the very chief of sinners, we would through him look for pardon, acceptance, and every spiritual blessing.

O thou that bindest up the broken in heart, and healest the wounded in conscience, say unto our souls, "Go in peace, thy faith hath made thee whole." Set us as a seal upon thine arm, and may we be as one who hath found favour in thine eyes. And knowing, O God, that every one who hath this hope in him purifieth himself, even as thou art pure, may we be anxious to follow after righteousness and godliness, and to be walking in all the commandments and ordinances of the Lord blameless. We will serve the Lord with fear, and let our hearts stand in awe of his word. We will love the Lord our God with all our heart, and with all our mind; and our neighbour as ourselves, for his sake. We bless God, who hath kept and preserved us during the past night, and safely and happily conducted us to the commencement of a new day. If consistent with thy sovereign will, continue thy guardianship and paternal goodness throughout its fleeting course.

Lord, we would renew this morning the consecration of our bodies, our souls, our life, our labour, all that is in us, and all that belongs to us. We desire to be more and more engaged in studying thy will, in promoting thy glory, doing good to our fellow-creatures, and working out with fear and trembling our own salvation. O God! all good! accept of this sincere and renewed sacrifice; let it ascend, through thy forbearance, to a throne of grace, and may it be accompanied with the merits of that sacrifice which thy dear Son offered up for our pardon and reconciliation.

Grant, O God, that we may henceforth detach our affections more and more from the things of time, and whilst we are daily labouring for the meat which perisheth, may we be truly mindful of that which endureth unto everlasting life.

May we never forget that we have precious and immortal souls, which demand our first and chief attention; and that the gain of the whole world will profit us nothing, if, in too anxiously caring about this, we should lose our souls.

And, O Lord, whilst we are anxious about the salvation of our own souls, we would not be unmindful of the eternal interests of all our fellow-creatures. We earnestly pray for the fulfilment of thine ancient promise, which saith, "As the earth bringeth forth her bud, and as the garden causeth the things that are sown in it to spring forth, so the Lord God will cause righteousness and praise to spring forth before all nations." Let the number of thy spiritual children be as the sand of the sea, which cannot be measured, or numbered; and let it come to pass, that in the place where it was said unto them, "Ye are not my people," there it shall be said, "Ye are the sons and daughters of the living God."

O let thy sun still rise upon the just and the unjust among us, and fulfil thy gracious promise, giving us rain in due season, that our land may yield her increase, and the trees of the field their fruit. O God, for the sake of thy chosen people, overlook the infidelity and profligacy of thousands around us. Hear the prayers of thy servants for a general reformation. O that we might be a holy, and then we shall be a happy people. Continue, O God, to be the guide, the protector, and the portion of all in this family; and, if consistent with the great designs of thy providence, let goodness and mercy follow us all the days of our lives. Hear us, O God, from thy dwelling-place, and send us an answer of peace, for his sake who alone is worthy, with the Father, and blessed Spirit, to receive endless praises. *Amen.*

THURSDAY EVENING. *Smith.*

We would, this evening, lift up our voice unto God most high, unto God who doeth all things for us.

Having obtained help of God, we have continued until this day, monuments of his sparing mercy. Thou art God, and not man, and therefore it is that we have not long ere now been cut off from the land of the living.

We would have these words deeply impressed on our minds: "It is the will of God, in Christ Jesus, concerning us, that in every thing we give thanks; for the Lord hath done great things for us, whereof we are glad; and every creature of God is good, if it be received with thanksgiving." Let us, therefore, whether we eat or drink, or whatsoever we do, give thanks unto God always, and for all things, through Jesus Christ our Lord. In God we live and move. We are the monuments of his wisdom, power, and goodness.

From our youth upward, we have had food to eat and raiment given us to put on, with a quiet and peaceable habitation to dwell in; a lodging-place where we have taken our rest in safety: yea, both lain down, and risen up, from month to month, and from year to year, without any daring to make us afraid. But what is all this, O God, to thy spiritual blessings? It is our privilege, and happiness, that we can now say, "God hath visited and redeemed his people, as he spake by the mouth of all his holy prophets which have been since the world began; and hath performed the mercy promised to our fathers, and remembered his holy covenant, even that covenant which thou wast pleased to make with thy servants, Abraham and Isaac, that in their seed should all the nations of the earth be blessed."

Forbid, O God, that any of us should be among that unhappy number, who despise or abuse the riches of thy goodness, and forbearance, and long suffering patience, not knowing that this should lead us to immediate repentance. For we know not what another night may bring forth; and "what shall it profit us if we gain the world, and lose our own souls?" Merciful and gracious God, deliver us from a hard and impenitent heart, lest we should treasure up unto ourselves wrath against the day of wrath, and revelation of thy righteous judgment.

O that we may say, with an inspired apostle, "We know whom we have believed, and we are persuaded that he will keep that which we have committed unto him (our precious and immortal souls) safe and secure until that day." O that we could say, "We love God, because he first loved us," and that we have known and believed the love which God hath for us; and therefore the desire of our soul is to his name, and towards the remembrance of his holiness.

O that we may delight ourselves more in God, and that our hearts might become the dwelling-place of the Holy Spirit. We would be washed and sanctified, as well as justified, in the name of the Lord Jesus, and by the Spirit of our God.

If thou wilt, O God, that we live to-morrow, may it be to begin a new life; a life more conformable to our professions and privileges: a life which shall turn out more to the advancement of God's glory, the edification of our fellow-creatures, and the eternal safety and happiness of our own souls.

But if it should please thee to terminate our course during the night, may our souls find pardon and acceptance with thee; and, disengaged from this prison of clay, take their flight to the regions of glory, where they shall behold thy face in righteousness, and be forever satisfied with thy glorious resemblance.

We would remember with affection, and in a way of prayer, all who are near and dear to us. The Lord be their shepherd, that they may never want: not want what may be requisite for the support and safety of their bodies; but more especially we pray, that our God may supply all their spiritual needs, according to his riches in glory, by Christ Jesus. Again we commit this house, with every inhabitant therein, young, and old, and of middle age, to the Keeper of Israel, who never slumbereth nor sleepeth, that he may watch over our lying down and rising up, and preserve us from all evil. In this hope, we ascribe to the Father, to the Son, and to the blessed Spirit, honour and glory, world without end. *Amen.*

FRIDAY MORNING. *Smith.*

BEHOLD us, O good and gracious God, at the footstool of thy throne this morning. We come to present our humble, and sincere adorations to the Author of our life, and lengthener out of our days: for it is to thee that we are indebted for our preservation during the past night; and thou alone hast caused us to see the beginning of this day. Let thy gracious presence be with us during the course of it, and all the succeeding days and nights of our earthly pilgrimage. And to the end that thou mayst hear us, notwithstanding our unworthiness and sinfulness, look upon us, O God, in the face of thine Anointed; and cause us to be partakers of all the blessed fruits of his death and resurrection. We look to the unsearchable riches of Christ, that we may see what is the fellowship of the mystery which from the beginning of the world hath been hid in God; who not only created all things by Christ, but was in him reconciling the world unto himself; and hath now exalted him to be a Prince and a Saviour, to give repentance unto his people, as well as the remission of all their sins. O that our bodies may henceforth be the temples of God, through the Holy Spirit dwelling in us, and uniting us to Jesus Christ by a true and living faith. We would count all things but loss, that we may win Christ, and be found in him, not having our own righteousness, which is of the law, but that which is through the faith of Christ, the righteousness which is of God by faith; and that we may know him, and the power of his resurrection, and the fellowship of his sufferings, and be made conformable unto his death: not as though we had already attained, either were already perfect; but this one thing we desire to do— "forgetting those things which are behind, and reaching forth unto those things which are before, we would press toward the mark for the prize of the high calling of God, in Christ Jesus our Lord." Thou knowest, O God, and we would at the same time acknowledge and confess, the weakness and corruption of our nature, and to how many dangers and temptations we are continually exposed. Lord, give us thy strength, and thy grace, to preserve and keep us at all times. Let neither the world nor the flesh this day seduce us from the paths of duty; but, ever thinking and acting as under God's more immediate inspection, may we keep in the love and fear of all God's holy commandments. Teach us in every circumstance, O God, to know thy will, and give us inclination and ability to do it. Continue of thy bounty to provide for all our necessities; and support and comfort us under every disappointment and trial which thou mayest see proper to bring upon us.

May we live in thy fear, that we may die in thy favour, and so be made both happy and glorious through eternity.

For thy distinguishing, although unmerited goodness and mercy towards us, and all who are near and dear to us, we once more offer up our united thanksgivings; saying at the same time, Let every creature that is in heaven, and on the earth, give glory to God for ever and ever. And now, Lord, what wait we for? our hope is in thee. Let the words of our mouths, and the meditations of our hearts, be acceptable in thy sight, O Lord, our strength and our Redeemer. *Amen.*

FRIDAY EVENING. *Smith.*

O LORD, our God, with humble gratitude we would appear in thy presence this evening, to bless thy name for our preservation hitherto; and more especially for the renewed tokens of thy kindness and love during the past day.

We pray that our humble and sincere thanks to God for all his mercies may ascend now as incense, and the lifting up of our hands be as acceptable as the evening sacrifices of old. When we recollect the mercies of the past day, O God, and thy goodness towards us ever since we had a being, our souls should be overwhelmed with wonder, love, and gratitude; but ah, how cold and insensible! and what poor returns of love do we make! O Lord, forgive the past, and make us more grateful to thee in future. We have not rendered unto the Lord according to the benefits done unto us; and if thou, Lord, shouldst be strict to mark our deficiencies, alas! where would be our hope? What, indeed, would our situation be, wert thou not a God of infinite mercy, and were not severity and judgment thy strange work.

Yet thy mercy, O Lord, is everlasting, and thy compassions fail not. Thou hast said, "As I live, I have no pleasure in the death of the wicked; but that the wicked turn from his way and live." And again: "Come now, and let us reason together: though your sins be as scarlet, they shall be as white as snow; though they be red like crimson, they shall be as wool." Who then is a God like unto thee, that pardoneth iniquity, and passeth by the transgressions of thy people; who retainest not thine anger because thou delightest in mercy? For the display of this attribute, and that a solid foundation might be laid for our hope, thou didst not spare thine only begotten Son, but sent him in due time, to suffer and die in the room of sinners. It is a faithful saying, and not only worthy of all acceptation, but of our highest and daily praise, that "God was in Christ, reconciling the world unto himself, not imputing their trespasses unto them;" and hath committed to his servants, in every age, the word of reconciliation. Forbid it, then, O heavenly Father! that any of us here present, should be amongst that unhappy number to whom thy

Son shall at last say, "Ye would not come unto me, that ye might have life." But deeply sensible of our present sinful and miserable state, convinced that there is no other name under heaven by which we can be saved, and divinely persuaded of the willingness, as well as all-sufficiency of the Son of God, for this purpose, may we each, in due time, believe to the saving of the soul.

Through him alone we look for pardon, for justification, for adoption into the family of heaven, and for a renovation of all the powers and faculties of our mind and soul, to enlighten and fit us for a holy practice.

We know from past experience that we are not sufficient of ourselves, either to will or to do; but thy grace is sufficient for us, and thy strength can be perfected in our weakness. We pray that the law of the Spirit of life which is in Christ, may make us free from the law of sin and death. We shall then, O God, enjoy comfort through life, peace at death, and glory in heaven.

This night would we again commend ourselves, and all that is near and dear to us, unto thy fatherly care and special protection. Preserve us from every danger, and let us never be separated from thy love in Christ Jesus. Grant, O God, the pardon of all the sins which we have committed during the past day; as well those that lie heavy upon our consciences, as those which through infirmity we have forgotten.

Give thine angels charge, O God, in a particular manner, with respect to this family, that heads, and domestics, and children belonging to it, may all be preserved from the malice and power of the prince of darkness. Should our souls be required at our hands this night, may we be ready to resign them into the arms of a covenant God in Christ: but should our life be spared, may we more cheerfully and entirely dedicate it to Him unto whom it best belongs, and who alone can make us happy here and hereafter. Now unto the King eternal, immortal, and invisible, the only wise God, be honour, and glory: for of him, and through him, and to him, are all things. *Amen.*

SATURDAY MORNING *Smith.*

Lord God Almighty! which was, and is, and art to come: with thee is the fountain of life, and thou art the Author of every good and perfect gift. We would, therefore, give unto the Lord the glory and thanksgiving which is due unto his name, and worship him this morning in the beauty of holiness. But how shall we, whose thoughts are vanity, and whose hands and hearts are so impure, presume to address the sacred Majesty of heaven and earth? We take encouragement only, O God, from thy perfections, and from the gracious declarations of thy revealed will. "Thou art infinitely wise, and holy, and just, and good; but thou hast magnified thy mercy above thy great name." Blessed, for ever blessed, be the God and Father of our Lord Jesus Christ, who sent not his Son into the world to condemn the world, but that the world through him might be saved. O God, for Christ's sake, forgive us all our sins; and according to the good pleasure of thy will, and to the praise of the glory of thy grace, may we be accepted in the Beloved. We would be justified by faith alone, and thus have peace with God through our Lord Jesus Christ; for we believe that he is the end of the law for righteousness to every one that believeth. And may this faith, O God, not be of a dead and barren nature, but may it work by love, and purify our hearts.

O God, thy word is truth; sanctify us through belief of the truth. According to thine own promise, give unto each of us a new spirit, and take away the stony heart out of our flesh, that we may walk in thy statutes, and keep thine ordinances, and do them. Thus may we hope that we shall be thy people, and that thou wilt continue to be our God, and portion, in time and through eternity.

Accept of our thanks, O God, for all that mercy and goodness which hath followed us through every period of our past life; for sparing us under the weakness and diseases of childhood; conducting our steps through the slippery paths of youth; and preserving us still amidst the no less surrounding dangers of riper years.

We thank thee for the food we have to eat, the raiment wherewith we are clothed, for the comfortable habitations we have to dwell in, and the many conveniences and privileges that we enjoy above numbers around us, and in other parts of this habitable world.

We thank thee, O God, for another night's comfortable rest. We have laid us down and slept in peaceful security. Thou hast caused the out-goings of another morning to rejoice over us. We are brought in safety and health to the light and enjoyments of another day. Defend and keep us in the same, O God, from all harm, whether of a temporal or spiritual nature. Prosper us in all our lawful undertakings this day; and give us humble and thankful hearts to enjoy the good things which thou hast provided for us.

Provide, O God, in thy mercy and goodness, for the wants of the poor and needy. Thou hast promised to regard the prayer of the destitute. Help them to wait upon thee in the use of every lawful mean, and then to see that their expectation shall not perish. O thou who art in thy holy habitation a Father to the fatherless, and the Judge of the widow, according to thy word, help and relieve all those who commit themselves unto thee.

Lord, be merciful to the sick and afflicted part of mankind. Spare young and useful lives; and prepare the dying for their last change. It is said in thy word, "The Lord is nigh unto them that are of a broken heart, and saveth such as be of a contrite spirit." Lord, fulfil this promise in respect unto all such as may be distressed in mind. May it please thee to have compassion according to the multitude of thy tender mercies. And wilt thou be pleased to sanctify bereaving dispensations to all concerned. May neither we, nor ours, sorrow as those who have no hope: but ever remembering that as Jesus Christ himself died and rose again from the dead, so them that sleep in Jesus will God bring with him: may we comfort ourselves and one another with these words. As those who are near and dear to us are daily dropping off the stage of life, may we love heaven better, and strive to have clearer views of our interest in gospel privileges and hopes. To us to live, and while we live, may it indeed be Christ, and then to die will be everlasting gain. And now, O our God, hear the prayer of thy servants, and their supplications. O Lord, hear; O Lord, forgive; O Lord, hearken, and do, and defer not, for thine own name's sake and for thy Son's sake; who, with the Holy Spirit, are worthy to receive all honour and glory, world without end. *Amen.*

SATURDAY EVENING. *Smith.*

Lord God of Israel, according to thy promise in these latter days, pour out thy Spirit upon all thy servants here present; even the spirit of wisdom and of truth. Let him teach us all things, and bring all things to our remembrance whatsoever we should say unto thee, and then give ear to our prayer, O God, and hide not thyself from our supplications; but hearken thou, and hear in heaven thy dwelling-place, and when thou hearest, forgive, and accept of our persons, and this our evening sacrifice. We would review, and acknowledge all thy merciful dealings towards us this week. Six days more thou hast added to our lives, and every morning we have experienced thy loving-kindness; and every evening we have had reason to celebrate thy faithfulness. Whilst many have been exposed to hunger and cold, we have been fed and clothed by thy bounty. Multitudes in the world have this week been suddenly called from time to eternity; but God is still holding our soul in life. Night after night we have laid ourselves down to sleep, and we have awakened in the morning, for the Lord sustained us; yea, we have lain down in peace, and our sleep hath been sweet. For all this we would be thankful to thee,

7 *

O Lord, who makest us to dwell in safety, and whose visitation alone preserveth our spirit. But we would be chiefly thankful for the continuance of our spiritual privileges and comforts.

Blessed be God, that our land is still the land of gospel light and liberty; and that we can worship thee both in private and public, without any one daring to disturb us. God grant that we may never undervalue or abuse these privileges; as knowing that our guilt and condemnation will then be severer in the day of judgment.

We would be more and more thankful for the means of grace, and all the ordinances of divine appointment. May the daily reading of thy word increase our spiritual knowledge, confirm our faith, and animate our hopes. Let our morning and evening sacrifices keep us in a holy and watchful frame through the day, and dispose us to resign ourselves to thy gracious keeping during the night.

And O may the return of every Sabbath be looked forward to with increasing delight! Lord, make us thankful for the near approach of another Lord's day Sabbath.

Shouldst thou see meet in thy goodness, and by thine all-protecting providence, to spare us to see the light of another morning, may we all be in the Spirit upon the Lord's day, and worship God, who is a Spirit, in spirit and in truth. We would not forsake the assembling of ourselves together, as the manner of some is. May we love the habitation of thy house, and the place where thine honour dwelleth; thither would our willing feet repair, that we may publish, with the voice of thanksgiving, God's manifold mercies, and tell of all his wondrous works. Lord, bless the studies and preparation of thy ministering servants; may they be as scribes who are well instructed unto the kingdom of Heaven, and bring forth, out of their treasures, things new and old! May they convince and convert sinners, and build up and comfort the saints.

Permit us once more to commit, to thy care and keeping, our absent relatives and friends. Although at a distance from us, may they be nigh unto the Lord our God day and night, that he may maintain their cause at all times, as the matter shall require.

Lord, be merciful to the sick and afflicted part of mankind. Whatever be the cause, or the event of their present visitation, may they have reason to say with thy servant of old, "It is good for us that we have been afflicted; for thereby have we learned thy statutes."

Merciful and gracious God, lay not upon such more than thou wilt enable them to bear; and soon, if it be thy holy will, let the language of the Psalmist be theirs— "Return unto thy rest, O my soul, for the Lord hath dealt bountifully with thee."

For the world in general we would once more entreat at a throne of grace. Look down from heaven, O God, and behold from the habitation of thy holiness and glory, a world lying in ignorance and wickedness. God be merciful to us, and bless us, and cause thy face to shine upon us, that thy way may be known upon earth, and thy saving health among all nations. Blessed Jesus, thou hast expressly declared that thy gospel shall be preached in all the world, for a witness unto all nations. We long for that happy time when the Jews shall be brought in with the fulness of the Gentiles. Then should we behold mercy and truth meet together, righteousness and peace mutually embrace. Nation shall not then lift up sword against nation, neither shall they learn war any more. Lord, although not permitted to see these happy times, may we now rejoice in the prospect, and at last die in the comfortable hope of their arrival. This night we would again commit ourselves, and all our concerns, to God's paternal care and keeping, in the hope of being raised up in the morning to see and enjoy another day of the Son of man. For his sake, we ask every blessing.—And to him, with thee, O Father, and the Holy Spirit, be all glory, and praise, and humble worship, for ever. *Amen.*

FOURTH WEEK.

SABBATH MORNING. *Bickersteth.*

O ALMIGHTY GOD, Creator, Governor, and Upholder of all things, who, after making the heaven and earth, didst rest on the seventh day, and bless and sanctify it, teach us now, resting from our worldly labours, to devote the day to thy service. O thou, whose Son did, as on this day, rise again from the dead, grant us grace to rise from the death of sin to the life of righteousness. Help us now, in his name, to seek thy blessing on those holy duties to which the Sabbath is set apart.

We bless and praise thee for the appointment of this day, and for all the means of grace which we enjoy in this highly favoured land. We bless thee that thy house is open, that thy ministers have liberty to preach, and we have opportunity and inclination to assemble with thy people and hear thy holy word.

Above all, we thank thee for the knowledge of Jesus Christ; for free justification and salvation through his life, death, and resurrection. We praise thee for the gift of thy Holy Spirit. Blessed, for ever blessed, be thou, the God and Father of our Lord Jesus Christ, for all these thy benefits.

Great have been thy mercies to us; but with shame we confess that we have slighted thy goodness, and carelessly regarded thy great salvation. How many Sabbaths have we broken; how many invitations of mercy have we neglected; how many warnings and threatenings have we trifled with! How cold have been our prayers; how great our irreverence; how inexcusable our unbelief!

Forgive us, O forgive us, all our negligences, and infirmities, and all our sins and iniquities. To the Lord our God belong mercies and forgivenesses, though we have rebelled against him. Return again and bless us.

Graciously be present with us, through all the solemn services of this day. Enable us to go to thy house in the spirit of prayer. Pour out upon us, and all that shall meet in thy name, the spirit of grace and supplication. Let none of us draw near to thee with our lips only, while our hearts are far from thee; but enable us to worship thee in spirit and in truth. Cause thy face to shine upon us. Grant that we may find that the Lord is in his holy temple, and be able to say, It was good for us to have been there! Prepare our hearts to receive thy holy word, that it may be sown in good ground, and bring much fruit to perfection.

Bless especially all such as hope this day again to receive the memorials of our Saviour's sufferings and death. May contrition, penitence, faith, humility, and love, be in lively exercise, and be greatly increased.

Help all of us, not only to abstain from engaging in our usual business and occupation, but also keep us from worldly conversation, and from vain thoughts. Raise our affections to things above, and let our conversation be in heaven. Enable us to give this day to reading and hearing thy word, to meditation, self-examination, and prayer; and be thou with us to bless us in our retired devotions.

And, Father of mercies, we beseech thee to bless all that minister in holy things. Multiply unto them thy grace, that they may be faithful, diligent, and laborious. Grant them humility, disinterestedness, watchfulness, and zeal; may all have grace to take heed to themselves, and to the flock over which the Holy Ghost has made them overseers, feeding the church of God which he has purchased with his own blood. Stand by and strengthen them this day. Open thou their mouths, and enable them to testify boldly the gospel of the grace of God. We especially pray for him who ministers among us. May he this day be enabled to speak a word in season to us, and to all that hear him.

And, we beseech thee, grant that this thy Sabbath may be distinguished by great and singular mercies to thy church. Be thou with all Christian congregations meeting to worship thee. By the ministry of thy word this day, convert many sinners; heal those that have backslidden, strengthen those that are weak, and confirm those that are strong. Give thy holy word free course, and let it be glorified in every land, and among every people. Hear us, and answer us, for our Lord Jesus Christ's sake. *Amen.*

Our Father, &c.

SABBATH EVENING. *Bickersteth.*

Holy, holy, holy, Lord God Almighty, which was, and is, and art to come! Thou art of purer eyes than to behold iniquity; thou chargest thine angels with folly, and in thy sight the heavens are not clean; we approach thee, then, only in the name of Jesus Christ.

We confess, O Lord, how defective and defiled all our services are. We acknowledge that our prayers are full of distractions. Our very petitions need thy pardon, our cold intercessions for others increase our own guilt, and our unworthy thanksgivings fall utterly short of thy great goodness to us. We carelessly and unbelievingly hear thy word. All we do is polluted and sinful. O forgive us. Forgive the sins of solemn duties; and let that great High Priest, who is passed into the heavens, bearing the iniquities of our holy things, plead for us in thy sight.

And grant, most merciful Lord, that it may not be in vain that we enjoy such distinguished privileges as thou hast given to us, lest it be more tolerable for Sodom and Gomorrah in the day of judgment than for us. Let not the seed of the word of God which has this day been sown in our hearts, be plucked away by Satan, lost through temptation, or choked with the cares of this life; but having heard it and received it, incline us to keep it, and do thou cause it to bring forth fruit, an hundred fold.

Grant that our lives may exhibit whose we are, and whom we serve: remembering that if we know our

Lord's will, and do it not, we shall justly have the severer punishment. We humbly beseech thee, strengthen our resolutions to live more decidedly to thee. We feel that we now have again to enter into the contest with our spiritual enemies; make us more than conquerors through him that loved us. We have again to exert ourselves to run the race set before us; teach us ever to look unto Jesus as the author and finisher of our faith. O let us take the more earnest heed never to let slip the things which we have heard.

And we pray for all those who have this day assembled before thee, and heard the word of salvation. Grant unto them the same mercies which we ask for ourselves. Let thy ministers, that water others, be themselves abundantly watered in their own soul. Strengthen them for thy work, both in body and soul.

Remember, in mercy, those who by thy providence have been kept from thy house, and let them receive a special supply of thy grace. Grant that those who have wilfully or ignorantly deprived themselves of public worship, may have their eyes opened to see, and their hearts awakened to feel their guilt and their danger, and learn to flee from the wrath to come. O hasten the time when thy house shall be a house of prayer for all nations, and the whole world shall worship in thy courts.

Thanks be unto God for all the privileges of the past Sabbath. Blessed be thy name that we were permitted to hear thy word, to join thy people in prayer and praise, and to enjoy so plentifully the means of grace. Blessed be our God for any thing of communion with him, or desire after him. Blessed be God, if the grace of our Lord Jesus Christ, or his holy word, be more understood or valued by us. Our cup runneth over with mercies.

O Lord, if, amid our infirmities, thy Sabbaths here below rejoice the heart; if to rest from earthly labours, and enjoy the privileges of thy house in this world be delightful; how should we thank thee for the prospect of an eternal Sabbath, where thy servants shall serve thee without one wandering thought, without weariness, and without distraction! O grant, in mercy grant, that none of those who have this day met together in thy house, may be wanting in the number of those who shall dwell in that house not made with hands, eternal in the heavens, for Jesus Christ's sake. *Amen.*

Our Father, &c.

MONDAY MORNING. *Bickersteth.*

ALMIGHTY GOD, the Father of our Lord Jesus Christ, of whom the whole family in heaven and earth is named, who hast said that thou wilt be the God of all the families of Israel, and they shall be thy people; dispose our hearts by the gracious influence of thy Holy Spirit, to worship thee through one Mediator, Jesus Christ our Lord.

Thou art God, and there is none beside thee: the Creator of heaven and earth, the Lord of glory, the Lord God, merciful and gracious, long suffering, abundant in goodness and truth, keeping mercy for thousands, forgiving iniquity, and transgressions, and sin, and that will by no means clear the guilty. We bow and worship at thy footstool; we acknowledge thee to be the Lord.

Accept, through thy Son Jesus Christ, our Lord, our unfeigned thanksgivings for the mercies of another day. Thou gavest us our being, and thou preservest us from day to day. Through the defenceless hours of the night thou hast kept us in safety. Thou hast given us a soul capable of knowing and rejoicing in thee, and a body by which we may serve thee.

We bless thee for the seeing eye, and the hearing ear, for the free use of our limbs and our senses, for the power of the mind, and the affections of the heart.

But, O Lord, we thank thee most of all for thy spiritual blessings. We bless thee that we were not born in heathen lands, but in this favoured country, where the light of thy truth clearly shines. We thank thee for the comfort of the Holy Scriptures, for the labours of faithful ministers, and for all the means of grace. O how great has been thy love to us! Thou sparedst not thine own Son, but deliveredst him up for us all, and with him thou hast freely given us all things.

What reward shall we render unto the Lord for all his benefits? We desire now afresh to devote ourselves to thy service. We give up ourselves, our whole selves unto thee. God of peace, sanctify us wholly: God of our life, grant that our whole spirit, and soul, and body, may be preserved blameless unto the coming of our Lord Jesus Christ.

But with shame and confusion of face, we would confess that we have been rebellious and disobedient. Thou art holy, but we are unholy. Thou art merciful, but we have often been selfish and unkind. Thou art pure, but we are impure. Thou art patient, but we are impatient. We have abused all thy gifts, and made them occasions of sin. Lord, we acknowledge our impenitence, we confess our unbelief, we bewail our self-righteousness.

Forgive us all our offences, remember not against us our transgressions, but remember thy great and tender mercies which have been ever of old. Grant unto every one of us a saving interest in the death of Christ, full and free forgiveness of all our sins, and grace and strength to go and sin no more. Lord, help us to love thee, teach us to serve thee. Give us thy strength that we may overcome our corrupt nature. Grant that this day we may have power from on high to resist every temptation, to confess Christ before men, to labour steadfastly with a single eye to thy glory, to live in the spirit of prayer, in faith, humility, self-denial, and love, and to walk before thee in that narrow way which leads to eternal life. Fill us with love to others. Teach us to do good to all men, [and to seek according to our means to visit and relieve the fatherless and the widows in their affliction,] and do thou keep us unspotted from the world.

Lord, for thy name's sake, hear us. We beseech thee, according to thy infinite mercy, give us grace to serve thee, constantly and unfeignedly. Herein art thou glorified, that we bear much fruit. For thine own glory, grant us thy Spirit, that we may bring forth all the fruits of righteousness.

And hear us farther in behalf of our relations and friends, our neighbourhood, our minister, and all for whom we ought to pray. Help those that are weak. Comfort those that are cast down. Heal those that are sick. Relieve those that are in distress. Be merciful unto thy church. O bless us, and cause thy face to shine upon us, that thy way may be known upon earth, thy saving health among all nations. Bring the Gentiles to Christ. Gather thy people Israel into thy fold. Give wisdom and power to every effort of Christian love for spreading thy gospel. Bless all societies formed for this end, and let those who support and conduct them, have thy direction and guidance. Lord, grant that the power of the cross of Christ, may at length fully triumph over all error and superstition, all idolatry, and delusion, and sin.

Gracious Lord, not for our worthiness, but for the only name's sake of Jesus Christ, hear these our prayers, which we sum up in his own words.

Our Father, &c.

MONDAY EVENING. *Bickersteth.*

O ETERNAL GOD, whose name is love, and who so loved the world that thou gavest thine only-begotten Son, that whosoever believeth in him should not perish but have everlasting life, help us, by the Holy Spirit, to believe in Christ Jesus; and trusting in him to have access unto thee.

We feel our need of a Saviour for sinners; for we all have sinned, and come short of the glory of God. When we look back even on the past day, thy law accuses us of many sins, and our own consciences justly condemn us. We have been forgetful of thy presence; our conversation has been light and trifling; and we have not with a single eye sought thy glory, or copied the holy life of our Saviour Christ. He left us a perfect example, but how seldom we tread in his steps: how little we have of his meekness and lowliness of heart, of his zeal and love! We have sinned, notwithstanding the light of thy word, and the checks of our own consciences.

Grant us thy grace that we may not be hardened through the deceitfulness of sin. Give us true repentance, and such a sense of our sinfulness as may lead us to despair of salvation by any works of our own; and bring us humbled and penitent to the foot of the cross. Help us by faith to behold the Lamb of God which taketh away the sin of the world. Teach us to renounce our own righteousness, and to depend wholly on Jesus Christ: may we be able to say and feel, "In the Lord have I righteousness and strength."

Teach us to come to Jesus Christ, and now to look to him, not only for pardon and peace, but also for grace and strength. We are weak, but Jesus is strong: grant that we may be made strong in and through him. Draw us to Christ, that we may receive out of his fulness all that we need, repentance, remission of sins, and the gift of thy Holy Spirit; that he may dwell in our hearts by faith, and we be rooted and grounded in love.

We commend ourselves to thy care during the night. Let no evil come nigh us. May our last thoughts be with thee; and when we awake, may we be still with thee. Refresh our bodies with the quiet repose of the night, and renew our spiritual strength. Teach us ever to watch and pray, and to be always ready, seeing we know neither the day nor the hour when the Son of Man shall come.

Extend thy merciful care to all that are near and dear to us. We pray for all our relatives. May those that are endeared to us by the ties of nature, be yet more dear by the stronger bonds of grace. Grant that we may be all one in Christ Jesus our Lord. We pray for our Christian friends, for our neighbours, and all with whom we have intercourse.

Bless those that minister before the Lord. May they be

faithful, wise, humble, and devoted servants of the Lord Jesus Christ. Every where raise up pastors according to thine heart, which shall feed thy people with knowledge and understanding. Grant thy blessing to every missionary now preaching Christ to the Gentiles. Cause Jew and Gentile to turn to the Lord, that they may be saved. Bring on the happy day, when there shall be one fold and one Shepherd; and they shall not hurt, nor destroy, in all thy holy mountain.

O thou Giver of every good and perfect gift, we praise and bless thee for thy great and continued mercies to us. All things thou givest to us richly for enjoyment. We receive from thee full provision for all our temporal wants, and thou forgivest our iniquities.

Like as a father pitieth his children, so thou our Lord and Father pitiest them that fear thee. Thou knowest our frame; thou rememberest that we are dust. Thou hast had compassion on us in our low and lost estate, and thou gavest thy Son to die for us; and now thou offerest and givest us thy Holy Spirit, to soften our hard hearts and to help our infirmities. Thou justifiest us freely by thy grace, adoptest us into thy family, and givest us a hope full of glory.

Behold what manner of love thou our Father hast bestowed upon us that we should be called the sons of God! God of mercy, grant, only grant, that we may be followers of thee as dear children, and show forth thy praise, not only with our lips, but in our lives, through Jesus Christ.

And now blessing, and honour, and glory, and power, be unto Him that sitteth upon the throne, and unto the Lamb, for ever and ever. *Amen.*

Our Father, &c.

The Lord bless us, and keep us.

The Lord make his face to shine upon us, and be gracious unto us.

The Lord lift up his countenance upon us, and give us peace.

TUESDAY MORNING. *Bickersteth.*

ALMIGHTY GOD, source of every good, and fountain of every blessing, the God and Father of our Lord Jesus Christ, and in him our God and Father, give us the Spirit of adoption, and enable us to cry, Abba, Father. Help us to come and pour out our hearts before thee with the same confidence and affection with which children go to an earthly parent. Enable us to repose on thy love, to tell thee all our desires, and all our sorrows; and from the heart, to thank thee for all thy goodness to us.

Great and abundant cause we have to bless our God for all that he is in himself, and for all that he is to us. Thy mercies are new every morning. We thank thee that we meet together in peace and safety. Thou hast been our defence and our refuge. Let then the outgoings of the morning and of the evening praise thee.

We thank thee more especially for all the mercies of redemption. In the gospel of Christ, mercy and truth meet together, and righteousness and peace kiss each other. Thus can even we rejoice in thy power and justice, thy holiness, mercy, and love; and bless thee that the light of the knowledge of this thy glory shines, in the hearts of thy people, in the face of Jesus Christ. Blessed be thou, the just God and the Saviour.

O how unworthy we are of the least of thy mercies! We are all sinful and guilty. We have turned every one to his own way. We would give thee glory by an ingenuous and free confession that in many things we have all offended thee. From our youth up, even till now, we have been great sinners.

We dare not justify ourselves in thy sight, for if we should attempt it, even our own mouths would condemn us. We have omitted to perform many plain duties. We have done many things for which our consciences justly accuse us. All our righteousnesses are defiled. All our prayers and services are polluted.

Yet spare us, good Lord, spare us, according to thy great compassion and thy tender mercy. Lord God of our salvation, it is thy gracious promise on which our souls rely, that if we confess our sins thou art faithful and just to forgive us our sins, and to cleanse us from all unrighteousness. We now confess our sins, and we ask that they may be forgiven, and that our souls may be purified from sin. We plead for thy mercy, for Jesus bore our sins in his own body on the tree. We plead thy faithfulness according to thy many precious promises.

Cleanse, we beseech thee, the thoughts of our hearts, by the influence of thy Holy Spirit, that we may perfectly love thee, and worthily magnify thy holy name. Strengthen us for the duties of this day. Suffer us not to be tempted above what we are able to bear; but with every temptation, make a way to escape. Incline and enable us to walk in that way.

Hold thou up our goings in thy paths, that our footsteps slip not. Set a watch before our mouths, and keep the door of our lips, that we offend not with our tongue. May we always speak that which is good to the use of edifying, that it may minister grace to the hearers. Enable us also to keep our heart with all diligence, seeing that out of it are the issues of life. Increase our faith, enliven our hope, and enlarge our charity, that we may faithfully serve thee, and in all things glorify thy holy name.

We pray for all our relatives and friends. Give them prosperity both of body and soul.* Grant that grace and

---

* When any member of the family is sick, add—

We particularly commend unto thee that member of our family now in affliction, may faith, patience, submission, and resignation, be granted in this hour of trial, and in thy own good time remove the affliction. And, Lord, grant that all our tribulations here below may lead us to look at the things which are above, and work out for us a far more exceeding and eternal weight of glory. Ever give us a spirit of sympathy, and tender feeling, and love for each other, and may we always be ready to weep with those that weep, and rejoice with those that rejoice.

peace may be multiplied to all those that call on the name of the Lord Jesus Christ, their Lord and ours. Seek and save the lost sheep of the house of Israel. Let the light of life shine into every benighted heart. Increase especially among the people of this nation, the number of those who know, and love, and serve thee. Bless our rulers, and guide our statesmen; teach thy ministers and prosper thy people, that there may be no complaining in our streets; and that it may be said of us, "Happy is the people that is in such a case; yea, happy is that people whose God is the Lord."

These prayers we offer up in the name and through the mediation of thy Son, Jesus Christ, our Lord.

Our Father, &c.

TUESDAY EVENING. *Bickersteth.*

O Thou, who art the God of all the families of the earth, who didst favourably notice Abraham's commanding his children and his household after him to keep the way of the Lord; be thou present with us now, and enable us by thy Holy Spirit, and through thy Son's intercession, to worship thee in spirit and in truth.

We come before thee, acknowledging that we were all born in sin, the children of wrath, and have in common a corrupt nature and a continual propensity to depart from thee. And O how often have we offended thee, the God of all the earth, by actual transgressions!

Even in the day that is past, by vain thoughts, by idle words, by sinful indulgences, we have grieved thy Spirit, and we have incurred thy displeasure. Our only refuge is in thy promised mercy in Christ Jesus. We

---

When any member of the family is on a journey, add—

O Lord, we beseech thee, regard with thy favour, protect and defend *him* who is now absent from us. Take *him* under thy special care. Preserve *him* from every temptation. Prosper *him* in *his* undertakings. May *he* be a blessing every where *he* goes; and bring *him* in health and peace among us again, that we may together have fresh cause to praise and bless thy holy name.

cast ourselves wholly on that mercy. Fixing all our hopes on our Saviour Jesus, we confess our guilt, and earnestly pray that his blood may cleanse us from all sin.

And give us, we beseech thee, the comfortable assurance that our sins are forgiven. Let thy Holy Spirit bear witness with our spirits that we are children of God. Plentifully impart to us the gift of thy Spirit, that we may bring forth love, joy, peace, gentleness, goodness, meekness, long-suffering, forbearance, and temperance. Grant that we may so copy the example of our Saviour, as to be the epistles of Christ, known and read of all men; and have clear evidence of our own salvation. Teach us so to live, that we may glorify thee who hast bought us with a price of such amazing value as the blood of thine own Son.

O that all now kneeling together may indeed obtain mercy in Christ Jesus, may pass from death unto life, and love and serve thee unfeignedly. But, O Lord, how cold is our love to thee! how dead, how dull are our hearts! Help us to love thee; to love God with all our heart, with all our mind, with all our soul, and with all our strength. Shed abroad the love of God in our hearts, by giving us the Holy Ghost; and may we be taught of God to love one another. Be thou present with us in our more retired devotions; praying to our Father which is in secret in our closet, may we find his presence and blessing there.

Bless, O Lord, all that are near and dear to us. Many beloved relatives and friends are now absent from us; but thou art with them, and all their wants are known to thee. Give them thy grace; ever guide them here by thy counsel, and may none of them be wanting in thy heavenly kingdom.

We pray for all in authority; Lord, may their counsels be ordered by thee as may be most for the good of our country.

Give, we beseech thee, to all ministers of Jesus Christ every where, true knowledge and understanding of thy word; and may they set it forth in their lives accordingly. Make them wise to win souls. Lord, call forth and send out many faithful labourers to the work of the ministry. May the distant isles wait on thee, and the Gentiles come to thy light. Bless every society established for benefiting the bodies or the souls of men, and especially those in which we are more immediately engaged and interested.

Thanks be unto thee, Holy Lord God, for all thy goodness towards us. How multiplied are thy mercies every day! How excellent is thy loving-kindness! We bless thee for all thy long suffering and forbearance towards us. We bless thee for the infinite mercies of redeeming love. We bless thee for the knowledge of thy salvation, and for the light of thy truth; for protection from every danger during the night, and provision for all our wants by day. Thou hast spread our table with food, and thou givest us every needful good. Accept these our prayers and our praises, which we offer up in and through Jesus Christ, our only Mediator and Advocate. *Amen.*

Our Father, &c.

WEDNESDAY MORNING. *Bickersteth.*

O LORD GOD Almighty, the Creator of heaven and earth, the Lord of glory, who art greatly to be feared in the assembly of thy saints, and to be had in reverence of all them that are round about thee; who dwellest in heaven, surrounded with angels and archangels, with cherubim and seraphim, who veil their faces while they praise and worship; we bow down before thee in the name of Jesus Christ. None other name, but the name of Jesus; none other merits, but the merits of Jesus, would we plead in thy sight: but by him, through one Spirit, may we now have access with confidence to the throne of grace.

O Thou whose name is holy, who hast required that

we confess our faults one to another; we would now confess our many and our great sins. We have often sinned against thee, and against each other, in thought, word, and deed. O forgive our hardness of heart, and our earthly-mindedness; all our want of charity, all our hastiness of spirit, all our bad tempers, and every sinful action.

For thine own name's sake blot out our transgressions, and remember not our sins.

Lord of all grace, help us ever hereafter to walk worthy of the vocation wherewith we are called. May we, with all lowliness, and meekness, with long-suffering, forbearing one another in love, endeavour to keep the unity of the Spirit in the bond of peace. Give us grace so to live, that we may find more and more how good and how pleasant it is for brethren to dwell together in unity.

Give unto each of us grace to fulfil our duties toward each other. As *parents*, may we bring up our children in the nurture and admonition of the Lord; and as *children*, obey our parents in all things.

We ask for blessings on our native land. Lord, we would sigh before thee for all the abominations of our country. O how the swearer, the Sabbath-breaker, the covetous, the licentious, and the blasphemer, abound on every side! Because of these things the wrath of God comes on the children of disobedience. Spare us, good Lord, spare us, for thy name's sake. Grant, we beseech thee, that as we have been peculiarly distinguished by thy mercies, so it may have to be said of us, "Surely this great nation is a wise and understanding people, for what nation is there so great, who hath God so nigh unto them, as the Lord our God is in all things that we call upon him for."

Pour out of thy Spirit on all who have the direction of public affairs; on all who minister in holy things; on the magistrates; and on the people; that a general revival of religion may appear among us. Cause thy church every where to flourish and increase. We pray especially for an increase of the zeal, purity and love, humility and devotion of thy people. Let Zion break forth on the right hand and on the left. Add daily to thy church, in our own country, and in heathen lands, such as shall be saved. Bless every missionary gone forth to preach to the Gentiles the unsearchable riches of Christ, and may more and more grace be given unto them all, that they may labour zealously, wisely, and abundantly in thy cause.

And now, Lord, accept our unfeigned thanksgivings, for all those blessings which we daily so richly enjoy, and especially for the kind protection of another night. We thank thee more especially for those many dear ties of relationship, affection, and Christian principles, which bind us together. We bless thee for all that sympathy of feeling and union of heart which thou hast given us; and we pray that we may be more and more knit together in Christian love.

But, beyond all other mercies, we bless thee for the common salvation of Jesus Christ; for his birth, his life, his death, and his resurrection; for all that he was, and is, and will be. Blessed be God for the gift of his Son Jesus Christ, our only Saviour, our only hope, and our sure refuge.

We trust that we may say we are one in Christ, members of that body of which he is the head; and we bless and praise thee for this thy unspeakable mercy. We thank thee for this opportunity of assembling ourselves together, to pay our morning sacrifice; and we pray that however we may be separated here below, or however scattered in different stations; as we have now met together here on earth, we may hereafter all meet in heaven, for Jesus Christ's sake. *Amen.*

WEDNESDAY EVENING. *Bickersteth.*

GRACIOUS and merciful God, slow to anger, great in power, and rich in mercy to all them that call upon thee, help us now so, in the name of Christ, to ask, that we may have; and so to seek, that we may find.

Enter not into judgment with us, O Lord, for in thy sight we cannot be justified. However unblameable we may appear before men, before Him who knows the heart we confess and would mourn over innumerable sins in the past day, and in every day of our life.

We acknowledge with shame and sorrow our hypocrisy and pride, our vanity and selfishness, our unbelief and impatience, our self-indulgence and self-righteousness, our obstinacy and self-will, our disregard of thy law and thy glory, our living to ourselves and not to thee. And, O how hard is our heart, that feels so little the guilt and the evil of so many and such great sins!

Lord of all power and might, soften and break these hard hearts. Give us a contrite spirit. There is mercy with thee. There is forgiveness with thee. O may thy great mercy be displayed towards us, in pardoning all our sins, and in renewing our souls. Give us penitence, faith, and self-denial. Bestow on us the graces of sincerity, humility, and love.

May the love of Christ be more known and felt by us, and let it constrain us to live not to ourselves, but to him that died for us. Grant us thy Holy Spirit, teaching those things of which we are ignorant, taking of the things of Christ to show them unto us, and daily sanctifying our hearts.

We ask for heavenly wisdom, holy simplicity, ardent zeal, and purity of heart. Incline us to study to be quiet, and to do our own business, and to work with our own hands. Prepare us, day by day, more and more, for the coming of our Lord Jesus Christ. Make us meet to be partakers of the inheritance of the saints in light.

We commend ourselves to thy care during the night. May we lie down at peace with thee, through Christ, and in peace with all the world.

O Lord, though we be unworthy, through our manifold transgressions, to approach thee at all, yet thou hast commanded that intercessions be made for all men; hear us, therefore, unworthy though we be, in behalf of all that need our prayers. May the Lord comfort his people, and have mercy upon his afflicted. Let all nations whom thou hast made come and worship before thee, and glorify thy name. Let every obstacle which may hinder the progress of thy truth, be removed in mercy. Bless all the members of the church of Christ, and all his ministers, and especially those with whom we are more intimately connected.

Give to our parents, our brothers, our sisters, and our relatives, all those temporal and spiritual blessings of which they stand in need. Bless our superiors, our companions, and all about us. Continue the blessing of peace to our country. Pardon any who may have injured us; and if we have injured any, may we be ready to confess our fault, and to make restitution for any wrong done, and may they be disposed to forgive us.

We would not, O thou gracious Giver of every good, close our evening prayer, without offering up, through Christ Jesus, our sincerest thanksgiving for all the mercies of the past day. For any help vouchsafed in our duties; for any stand which we may have been enabled to make against sin, Satan, and the world; for any measure of light, knowledge, or grace, given unto us, all praise, all glory be to thee. If we are still kept in thy way, and yet spared from that ruin which we have deserved, while we live, let us praise and bless thee.

How great is the sum of thy mercies! When we look back on thy past blessings, when we read thy promises relating to that which is to come, and when we look around us on every side, and especially when we regard that cross on which thy Son died for sinners, we would say from the heart, Our mouths shall speak the praise of the Lord, and let all flesh bless his holy name for ever.

Hear us, for the only sake of Jesus Christ.

Our Father, &c.

THURSDAY MORNING. *Bickersteth.*

Merciful God, give ear unto us, when we cry to thee, in the name of Jesus Christ. Our voices shalt thou hear in the morning, O Lord; in the morning will we direct our prayer unto thee, and will look up. Lord, help us to pray.

Great is the need that we have to seek the Lord while he may be found, and to call upon him while he is near. We know that in us, that is, in our flesh, there dwelleth no good thing. The things of the world, the lust of the eye, and the lust of the flesh, and the pride of life, are continually tempting us, and leading us astray from thee. Our affections towards thee, O God, are cold and dull. Our tempers are often unsanctified. We are prone to depart from thee, and lukewarm and indifferent when we ought to have a holy zeal. We too much neglect and trifle with our own salvation, and the salvation of our relatives and friends. We have little of that spiritual mind which is life and peace. Our temptations are many, we often yield to them; we have no strength of our own to resist them.

We beseech thee, therefore, O our God, to be very merciful to us, sinners. Incline and enable us to come to Jesus Christ, weary and heavy laden as we are, and may we find rest in him. Teach us our own guilt and ruin; and help us to rely on his blood, and build all our hopes on his righteousness. God grant that, being grafted in Christ, we may live to him. Suffer us not to deceive ourselves by a mere form and profession of religion; but give us true faith, that we may really abide in Christ and bear much fruit. Quicken thou our souls. Make our hearts pure, humble, and devout; and our conversation holy and heavenly. Thou art our Rock, and in thee do we trust. Thou art our Strength, O establish us. Help us to live near to thee all the day long; and do thou preserve us from that sin which does so easily beset us.

Give us grace this day to overcome temptation, and to

mortify all our corrupt affections. Grant unto us the abundance of thy Holy Spirit. Lord, we deserve not the blessing; we have forfeited the mercy: but, O Thou, with whom is the residue of the Spirit, for the glory of thy name, and according to thy faithful promise, give us thy Spirit, that we may never dishonour thee by inconsistency and unfruitfulness, but abound in every good work, and walk worthy of the gospel of Christ. Enable us to begin anew this day, in seriousness and entire dedication of heart, to give ourselves to thee.

Lord, help us this day to live in prayer, to watch against the peculiar temptations of our station, to embrace every opportunity of doing good, to redeem the time, and to make steady advances in that narrow way which leadeth to eternal life.

And while we pray to thee for those mercies which we need, we would from the heart thank thee for all those great blessings which we have received, and do from day to day enjoy. The benefit of quiet repose, the renewal of our strength, the light which we enjoy, and the better light of life; these, and all the mercies which surround us on awaking, call for our unfeigned thanksgiving, and we do praise and bless thee for them. Blessed be thou, for redeeming mercy. Blessed be thou, that Jesus died for sinners, even for us. Thanks be unto thee, that grace, pardon, peace, strength, the Holy Spirit, and eternal life, are given to sinners, through faith in Christ. Unto Him that loved us, and washed us from our sins in his own blood, and hath made us to be kings and priests unto God, and his Father, to him be glory and dominion for ever and ever.

O Lord God, let the bright glory and happy dominion of our Lord Jesus Christ be spread through the world. Increase both the number and the zeal of those seeking the good of Zion, and the enlargement of thy Son's kingdom. Grant thy blessing to every effort to make the unsearchable riches of Christ known to the Gentiles. Give unto thy people Israel the new heart and the new spirit. Bless our favoured country, so that it may be a highly honoured instrument in diffusing the light of truth abroad; and grant that every exertion for that end may be a means of reviving true religion in all our hearts at home. Bless all in authority. Let thy priests be clothed with righteousness, and thy people sing for joy. May peace and mercy be granted to all our relatives, and rest on our own souls, and in our own family. May we, and all thy people, be united in one heart and mind in thy service and love, praying for each other, bearing one another's burdens, and so fulfilling the law of Christ. Hear us for his name's sake.

Our Father, &c.

THURSDAY EVENING. *Bickersteth*.

ALMIGHTY GOD, Father of mercies, and God of all comfort, according to thy gracious promise, give us thy Holy Spirit to help our infirmities, and enable us, in the name, and through the mediation of thy Son Jesus Christ, our Lord, to call upon thee.

Great is thy goodness to us sinners, in that we, who have grievously offended thee, have such a Mediator, who ever liveth to make intercession for us. Without a Saviour we can have no hope; for we have sinned against thee, and done evil in thy sight day by day.

We confess and mourn before thee the manifold sins of the past day. We daily offend thee by pride, impenitence, hardness of heart, unbelief, and forgetfulness of thee, and in many other ways: leaving undone the things which we ought to have done, and doing those things which we ought not.

Lord, let thy Holy Spirit convince us of our sinfulness. We pray that we may see more of the extent of our iniquities, and feel more of their guilt. Thus may we be led to hate sin, and to feel the need and value of that Saviour who came to seek and to save that which was lost. Grant that we may be partakers of his great salvation. Whatever else we lose, may we win Christ and be found in him.

Lord, we are unclean; if thou wilt, thou canst make us clean. We believe that thou art able, we believe that thou art willing. Lord, help our unbelief; Lord, make us clean.

Give us, we beseech thee, such a sense of thy mercy in free forgiveness, through the blood of Christ, that we may be constrained to present our bodies a living sacrifice unto thee. Enable us daily to crucify the lusts of the flesh. Give us such a measure of thy grace, that all the powers of our minds, all the affections of our hearts, and all the talents entrusted to us, may be unreservedly engaged for thee. Lord, incline us to spend ourselves and be spent for thee; strengthen our desire to do so, and enable us ever hereafter to bring this desire to good effect.

Let the number of thy willing and devoted servants be every where increased. Be thou exalted, O God, above the heavens, and thy glory above all the earth. Pour out thy Spirit upon all flesh, that all the ends of the earth may remember and turn unto the Lord, and all the kindreds of the nations may worship before thee. Let thy great name, now so little known, and so much profaned, be magnified and sanctified in every country and by every tongue.

Bless the land in which we dwell; its government, the ministers of Jesus Christ, and all its people. May we be a people fearing God and working righteousness. Look with thine especial favour on our relatives and friends, our family connexions and acquaintance. May they all be partakers of the grace of Christ here, and of his glory hereafter.

We will bless the Lord at all times, his praise shall continually be in our mouths. Bless the Lord, O our souls, and forget not all his benefits. How great and how numerous they are!

Blessed be the Lord, who daily loadeth us with benefits. All the temporal mercies granted so abundantly to us, our food, our clothing, our home, our friends, the daily provisions for our various necessities, these are from thee, who openest thy hand and fillest all things living with plenteousness. But, above all, blessed be the God and Father of our Lord Jesus Christ, who hath blessed us with all spiritual blessings in heavenly things in Christ Jesus. Thanks be unto God for his unspeakable gift.

Now unto the King eternal, immortal, invisible, the only wise God, be honour and glory for ever and ever.

These prayers and praises we offer up in the name of the Lord Jesus Christ, the Saviour of perishing sinners: trusting only in his mediation and merits.

Our Father, &c.

FRIDAY MORNING. *Bickersteth.*

ALMIGHTY and heavenly Father, who art about our path, and about our bed, and spiest out all our ways; we come to thee in the name of thy beloved Son, to supplicate thy mercy as we enter upon the duties of another day.

Thou, O Lord, art a shield for us, our glory, and the lifter up of our heads. We laid us down, and slept; we awaked, for thou, Lord, hast sustained us. For restored light, for life, and health, and strength, we praise and bless thee. Thou, Lord, only, keepest us in safety, and free from evil. Thou providest for all our wants. May our souls, and all that is within us, magnify God for all his goodness, and especially for his wonderful mercy in redeeming sinners by Jesus Christ; for the light of that Sun of Righteousness, which arises with healing in his wings on benighted souls; for all the blessings of free salvation through him, all the means of grace, and the hope of future glory.

Sad are the returns which we have made for so many mercies. How ungrateful have we been! We acknowledge and bewail our manifold sins and rebellions. We were born in sin, and we find continually the flesh lusting against the spirit, and the spirit against the flesh, so that we cannot do the things that we would. We are guilty, sinful, and weak. Lord, save us, or we perish. We entirely depend on thy mercy, in Christ Jesus, for the gift and continuance of every good, and for deliverance from all those evils which we have justly deserved.

For that mercy we now earnestly look to thee, O Father of mercies. Remember us, O Lord, with the favour that thou bearest unto thy people. O visit us with thy salvation; that we may see the good of thy chosen, that we may rejoice in the gladness of thy people, that we may glory with thine inheritance. May the grace of God which bringeth salvation, teach us, and all men, to deny ungodliness and worldly lusts, and to live soberly, righteously, and godly, in this present world. Enable us now, and ever hereafter, to seek the glory of thy holy name, by fulfilling every duty of our station conscientiously and diligently.

Give us grace to be continually looking to thee, through this day, for direction, assistance, and strength. Be thou in all our thoughts, and let us acknowledge thee in all our ways.

Give us the same mind that was in Christ Jesus, that we may be humble, patient, gentle, and full of love, even as he was. Teach us to be poor in spirit, and meek; to mourn for sin, and to hunger and thirst after righteousness; and thus shall we obtain the blessings of the kingdom of Christ. Grant that we may love that Saviour whom we have not seen, and believing in him may we rejoice with joy unspeakable and full of glory.

And here, constrained by thy mercies, we would afresh present our bodies a living sacrifice, holy and acceptable unto thee, which is our reasonable service. We renew in thy presence all our solemn vows, renouncing the world, the flesh, and the devil; and steadfastly purposing, by thy help, to keep thy holy will and commandments, and walk in the same this and every day of our lives. We take thee, O God, for our portion, and thy laws as our rule, and thy service as our duty, entreating thee to give us grace that we may be wholly thine.

And O that all mankind knew and served thee. Grant that the kingdom which is righteousness, and peace, and joy in the Holy Ghost, may be established in every land, in every heart. Fulfil thy gracious promises. Send thy gospel to the Gentiles, and let them be turned from darkness to light. Let the kingdoms of this world speedily become the kingdoms of our God and his Christ, that he may reign for ever.

Grant the abundance of thy Holy Spirit to the ministers of Christ every where, and especially to him who watches over our souls. Bless the place and the neighbourhood in which we live, and prosper every effort to do good.

Lord, we beseech thee also to bless our more immediate relations. Regard with thy favour our parents, our brothers and sisters, our benefactors and friends, our connexions and acquaintance. Look upon them in mercy, and visit them with thy salvation. Hear these prayers, for the only sake of the Lord Jesus Christ.

Our Father, &c.

FRIDAY EVENING. *Bickersteth*

ALMIGHTY GOD, the Father of our Lord Jesus Christ, and the God of the spirits of all flesh, the earth is thine, and the fulness thereof, the round world, and they that dwell therein.

We come, as sinners, but trusting in thy beloved Son, our Advocate, and the propitiation for our sins, and looking for the promised spirit of grace and supplication.

Lord, we confess before thee our own sins, and those of our country. Like thy people of old, while we have been greatly distinguished by privileges, we have also been a sinful nation, a people laden with iniquity, a seed of evil-doers, children that are corrupters. We have forsaken the Lord, and have provoked the Holy One of Israel. And chiefly, now, we would confess our coldness and indifference in extending the blessings of that glorious Gospel which thou hast entrusted to us. How slothful and unconcerned have we been to communicate to others the privileges which we enjoy, and to use all the means which thou hast given unto us of imparting the knowledge of Christ to distant lands! To us belong shame and confusion of face, because we have sinned against thee. But to the Lord our God belong mercies and forgiveness, though we have rebelled against him.

We beseech thee give us a zeal for thy glory. Fountain of light, and life, and grace, pour upon us thy quickening Spirit, to animate and excite us to devote ourselves to thee. Raise up, we pray thee, those who shall unceasingly pray, and give, and think, and labour, for the spread of thy truth. Revive the days of the primitive church, when thy people, walking in the fear of the Lord, and in the comfort of the Holy Ghost, were multiplied.

May the true light come more and more to thy church, and the glory of the Lord rise upon her; and may the Gentiles come to this light, and kings to the brightness of thy rising.

Lord, we plead the glory of thy great name, the faithfulness of thy promises, and the happiness of thine own creation; and with these pleas, we ask, that the heathen may be given to Christ for his inheritance, and the uttermost parts of the earth for his possession.

O Lord, hast thou not said, "It shall come to pass in the last days that I will pour out of my spirit upon all flesh?" Behold! in these last days! give now to us that ask. With thee is the residue of the Spirit; and the Lord's hand is not shortened that it cannot save, nor his ear heavy that it cannot hear.

Have respect unto the Covenant, for the dark places of the earth are full of the habitations of cruelty. May the Sun of righteousness arise with healing in his wings, on those people now sitting in darkness and the shadow of death.

We pray thee to hasten the coming of that time, when it shall not be asked, Who hath believed our report? and to whom is the arm of the Lord revealed? but it shall be said, The Lord hath made bare his holy arm in the sight of all nations, and all the ends of the earth have seen the salvation of our God.

And grant, gracious Lord, that while the fulness of the Gentiles is come in, all Israel may also be saved. May the veil which remains upon their hearts when Moses is read, be taken away by their turning to the Lord. May this branch, which has so long been broken off, at length be grafted into its own Olive-tree.

O let the Deliverer come out of Zion, and turn away ungodliness from Jacob.

And while we thus pray, we thank thee, good and gracious Lord, for all the blessed signs of the times in which we live. We bless thee for the beginning of a general desire to spread thy truth through the world, and that societies have been raised in these latter days, among all denominations of thy servants, for evangelizing the heathen, and for their conversion from dumb idols to the living God. We thank thee for any success given to these efforts, and would thereby be encouraged to persevere in more zealous labours, and more fervent prayers.

*In this great work, O Lord, may we, as a family, partake. Thou hast cast our lot in a Christian land, and surrounded us with Christian enjoyments. In all our comforts, may we regard thy hand, and while we enjoy so richly the light of thy gospel, may we remember that there are millions who are destitute. Thou hast brought us in safety, and amid many blessings, through another day. Thou hast caused the light of truth, like the light of the sun, to shine around us, and our dwelling. Thou hast encompassed our path; and hast given to us mercies bestowed on few of the human family. While we taste these blessings, and while we render thee praise for them, we would also pray, that they may be soon enjoyed by all nations. In the midst of a Christian land, and surrounded with the mercies of religion, liberty, education, and peace, we now commit ourselves to thy fatherly protection through the dangers of this night. Preserve us,

O God, we pray thee, from all harm, and bless those who have no home, no pillow, no quiet abode—those that wander, without any one to guide them; those that are confined in prison, with no one to comfort them; those that are oppressed and in bondage, with no one to relieve; those that are in danger by land or by sea, and no one to protect them; those that are sick, with none to minister to them; and those that are dying, with no one to break to them the bread of life.—These blessings, for ourselves and our fellow-creatures, we humbly beg, in the name of that merciful Redeemer, who, by the grace of God, tasted death for every man; and to whom, with thee and the Holy Ghost, be honour and glory, both now and forever. *Amen.**

SATURDAY MORNING. *Bickersteth.*

*We appear before thee, O Lord, our most merciful Father, to give thee thanks for preserving mercy through another night. To thy goodness we owe it, that we have laid us down and slept, for thou hast sustained us. Our voice shalt thou hear in the morning. To thee would we come, and to thee would we look, O thou preserver of men.

Spared by thy mercy, we enter upon the duties and dangers of another day. Our bodies and souls—our life, our property, our health, our talents, are all thine. Thou hast formed us, and not we ourselves. These bodies, fearfully and wonderfully made, are the proofs of thy wisdom and power. Thou art the Father of our spirits, and the God of our lives. Thou hast redeemed us by the blood of Christ, thine only Son. Thou hast sent down thy Holy Spirit to renew and sanctify our hearts. And to thee, and thy holy service, O Lord our God, we desire now unfeignedly and entirely to devote our lives. Make us useful to our fellow-creatures. Open before us paths of benevolence, and dispose us to walk therein. May our time, and influence, and property, and all that we have and are, be consecrated to thy holy service. May we not live in vain. When we die, whether it be this day, or at a future period, may we have the satisfaction of reflecting that we have been enabled by thy grace, to do something for that blessed cause, in behalf of which thy Son, though he was rich, yet became poor, and who gave himself unto death, that he might save a lost world.*

Holy, holy, holy Lord, we acknowledge it to be owing to thy infinite mercy, that we are not left in the darkness of heathen lands. Thou didst incline thy servants of old to send faithful missionaries to preach thy glorious gospel; thou didst support them in all their trials and difficulties, and at length this favoured country became a Christian land. And, Lord, how hast thou since blessed us above other nations, in the enjoyment of the light of thy truth, and the power and means to communicate it! We feel that our privileges imply duties. Give us grace, then, to labour, that the word of the Lord may from us sound out in every place. We thank thee that thou hast given many the disposition to aid in this work, and that numbers of thy servants are united in societies, to send abroad the tidings of salvation. Lord, bless them all. Greatly increase the number of such as have at heart the good of Zion.

We thank thee, O Lord, that thy holy word is translating into numerous different languages, and that now so many nations may hear in their own tongues the wonderful works of God. Give yet greater success to these efforts. Facilitate this work by imparting, more and more, peculiar talents to those engaged therein.

Lord, do thou prepare and call forth labourers. Qualify fit instruments to conduct missionary efforts, and give them faith, wisdom, and judgment, uprightness, patience, and self-denial, a single eye, and a single heart, in all their proceedings. So incline their minds, that they may send none to labour among the heathen but those that are first chosen of thee: men anointed with the Holy Ghost. Do thou raise up meek, humble, patient, believing, laborious, and persevering men, counting their word their wages, and looking for the recompense of reward hereafter: men suited to the exigencies of the heathen, in their various degrees of civilization and knowledge, and adapted to meet their wants in each particular situation; men willing to spend themselves, and be spent for Christ. Lord, send forth, we beseech thee, send forth such labourers.

Regard, we beseech thee, O Lord, with thy infinite love, those who have gone forth in thy name to heathen lands, to labour in making Christ known to the Gentiles. Help them to be followers of thy Apostles. Grant that they may never lose that first love and ardour of mind which induced them, for Christ's sake, to leave country, home, friends, and relatives. Preserve them sound in doctrine, and pure in their life and conversation. In the faith of Christ may they vanquish the world, the flesh, and the devil, and overcome apparently insurmountable difficulties. Give unto them utterance, that they may open their mouth boldly, to make known the mystery of the gospel. Give them grace to hope even against hope; and in thy own good time remove every opposing obstacle to the universal diffusion of thy truth. Let the course of thy providence prepare the way for thy servants. Let every fresh advance, either in commerce, science, or arts, aid the coming on of the Redeemer's kingdom; all things work together for good, till all shall know thee, the only true God, from the least to the greatest.

And for this we entreat the full out-pouring of thy Holy Spirit upon all flesh; upon kings of the earth and all people; upon all Christian ministers; upon princes, senators, and magistrates; young men and maidens, old men and children. Let them praise the name of the Lord, for his name alone is excellent, his glory is above the earth and heaven.

O Lord, it is not our glory we seek, but thine. We long, we ask, we pray, that thy will may be done on earth as it is in heaven; that all nations whom thou hast made may come and worship before thee, and glorify thy name. Lord, thou knowest our desires: we know not how to express them as we should. Do for us and thy church exceeding abundantly above all that we ask or think, for thy great name's sake.

These prayers we offer up in the name of our Lord Jesus Christ.

Our Father, &c.

SATURDAY EVENING. *Bickersteth.*

O GOD, thou art the God of all the families of the earth; for they are formed by thy will, and supported by thy providence. But thou art, in a peculiar manner, the God of those families, in which thy name is known, and loved, and honoured. Thou blessest the habitation of the just. Whatever be the disposition of others, we desire to say, As for us, and our house, we will serve the Lord. Thy yoke is easy, thy burden is light; thy work is honourable and glorious; and in keeping thy commandments, there is great reward. Thou art the best of all masters; thou hast promised to bear with our infirmities, and to suffer us to want no good thing.

Already thou hast laid us under infinite obligations, as the God of providence and of grace; thou hast dealt well with thy servants, O Lord. Bless the Lord, O our souls, and all that is within us, bless his holy name. Bless the Lord, O our souls, and forget not all his benefits.

By thy good hand upon us, we have been conducted through the perils, not only of another day, but another week; a period, during which many have been carried down to their graves, and we have been brought so much nearer to our own. Impress us with the lapse of our time, and so teach us to number our days, that we may apply our hearts unto wisdom. Many have been involved in perplexities, and exposed to want; many have been confined to the house of mourning, or the bed of sickness; but we have been indulged with liberty, and ease, and health, and strength; we have seen thy loving-kindness every morning, and thy faithfulness every night; and have had all things richly to enjoy.

But, O how little have we been affected by the instances of thy undeserved goodness; how imperfectly have we improved our religious privileges; how negligent have we been in seizing opportunities of doing good to the bodies and souls of our fellow-creatures—and how well does it become each of us to exclaim, Behold, I am vile; what shall I answer thee? wherefore I abhor myself, repenting in dust and ashes.

We appear before thee, this evening, in our trespass; enter not into judgment with thy servants, O Lord. Our only hope is, that to the Lord our God belong mercies and forgiveness, though we have rebelled against him. Have mercy upon us, O God, according to thy loving-kindness, according to the multitude of thy tender mercies, blot out our transgressions.

And may a confidence in thy goodness, instead of encouraging us to sin, that grace may abound, inspire us with that godly sorrow which worketh repentance unto life. May we hate and forsake every false way. May we be attentive to our condition, and study our character; may we bridle our tongue, and keep our heart with all diligence.

May we often look back and see, how at any time we have been ensnared or overcome; and watch and pray in future, lest we enter into temptation. And do thou keep us by thy power; uphold us by thy free Spirit; and not only restrain us from sin, but mortify us to it.

May sleep refresh our bodies, and fit them for thy service on the ensuing day; and may thy grace prepare our minds. May we leave all the cares of the world for awhile, behind; that we may attend on the Lord without distraction. May we repair to the hallowed exercises of devotion, as the hart panteth after the water brooks. May we call the Sabbath a delight, and be glad when they say to us, Let us go into the house of the Lord.

And, O thou God of all grace, do as thou hast said;

fulfil thy word unto thy servants, upon which thou hast caused them to hope. Bless abundantly the provisions of thy house, and satisfy thy poor with bread. Clothe thy priests with salvation, and let thy saints shout aloud for joy.

And to the God of all grace, the Father, the Word, and the Holy Ghost, be all honour and glory, both now and for ever. *Amen.*

FIFTH WEEK

SABBATH MORNING. *Cotterill.*

O Thou, Lord of the Sabbath, who hast set apart this day for thyself, and hast commanded us to keep it holy to thy name, look down upon a family of sinful creatures who are assembled together to acknowledge thy goodness in bringing us to see it.

We adore thee for thy patience and forbearance in not dealing with us according to our deserts, nor rewarding us according to our iniquities. And we beseech thee to pour down upon us the abundance of thy grace, that we may rest this day according to thy commandment. Let not thy sabbath be a weariness to us, but our delight. Let us honour thee, by not doing our own ways, nor finding our own pleasure, nor speaking our own words.

Bless us, O Lord, with all spiritual blessings in Christ Jesus: bless us, we pray thee, in turning away every one of us from our iniquities. Wash us in the fountain of that blood which cleanseth from all sin. Clothe us with the robe of that righteousness, which is, by faith of Jesus Christ, unto all and upon all them that believe.

Prepare us for the various duties which are now before us.

Sanctify unto us thy appointed means of grace. Send

out thy light and thy truth; let them lead us; let them bring us to thy holy hill, and to thy tabernacle. May we go with the multitude to thy house of prayer, with the voice of joy and praise, with the multitude that keep holy-day. There may we give thee the glory which is due unto thy name, and worship thee in the beauty of holiness. May we see thy power and thy glory, so as thy servants see them in the sanctuary; and be satisfied with the goodness of thy house, even of thy holy temple.

Grant, O Lord, that the Scriptures, which thou hast caused to be written for our learning, may be applied to our hearts in the demonstration of the Spirit, and of power. May we in such wise hear them, read, mark, learn, and inwardly digest them, that we may embrace, and ever hold fast the blessed hope of everlasting life, through a crucified Redeemer.

Hear our prayers, O God, for all Christian ministers; [especially for *him* whom thou hast appointed over us;] and endue them with the grace of thy Holy Spirit. Give unto them the spirit of love, and of power, and of a sound mind. Make them able ministers of the New Testament, faithful stewards of thy mysteries. Help them to take heed to themselves and to the doctrine; that so, according to thy promise, they may both save themselves and those who hear them.

We beseech thee to inspire continually the Universal Church with the spirit of truth, unity, and concord; and grant that all they who do confess thy name, may agree in the truth of thy holy word, and live in unity and godly love. May numbers be added to it, every Sabbath day, of such as shall be saved.

Look in mercy upon such as have hitherto neglected thy Sabbaths. Teach them to improve those that remain; and so to redeem the time which they have lost, that they may be numbered among thy true people.

Remember for good as many as, through sickness, or any other impediment, may be prevented from attending the ordinances of thy house, and the habitation which their soul loveth. Let thy presence be with them in their private meditations, even as with those who shall assemble together in the place where thy honour dwelleth.

We pray thee, also, to have compassion upon those who as yet belong not to thy visible Church.

O Thou who art a light to lighten the Gentiles, and the glory of thy people Israel, shine upon the nations which are sitting in darkness, and in the shadow of death.

Give, O Lord, the word, that great may be the company of the preachers, who shall go forth into all the world, and preach the gospel to every creature. Let nation after nation be converted to the Christian faith, till the kingdoms of this world become the kingdoms of our Lord and of his Christ, and the earth be filled with the knowledge of thy glory, as the waters cover the sea.

Hear, we beseech thee, O heavenly Father, these our imperfect petitions; and answer them in the multitude of thy tender mercies, for the sake of Jesus Christ, our only Lord and Saviour; to whom, with thee and the Holy Ghost, be all honour and glory, world without end.

Our Father, &c.

SABBATH EVENING. *Cotterill.*

O GOD, whose nature and property is ever to have mercy, and to forgive, receive our humble petitions; and though we be tied and bound with the chain of our sins, yet let the pitifulness of thy great mercy loose us, for the honour of Jesus Christ, our Mediator and Advocate.

O Lord, the only begotten Son, Jesus Christ; O Lord God, Lamb of God, Son of the Father, that takest away the sins of the world, have mercy upon us. Thou that takest away the sins of the world, have mercy upon us. Thou that takest away the sins of the world, receive our prayer. Thou that sittest at the right hand of God the Father, have mercy upon us. For thou only art holy: thou only art the Lord: thou only, O Christ, with the

Holy Ghost, art most high in the glory of God the Father.

And as we beseech thee, O Lord, to forgive us all our sins, negligences, and ignorances, (particularly those of the past day,) so may it please thee to give us true repentance; and to endue us with the grace of thy Holy Spirit, to amend our lives according to thy holy word.

O Thou, from whom all good things do come, grant to us, thy humble servants, that, by thy holy inspiration, we may think those things that be good, and by thy merciful guiding, may perform the same.

Accept, we beseech thee, O Lord, our hearty thanks for the means of grace which have been vouchsafed us this day; and for every blessing which thou hast bestowed upon us.

To thee be ascribed all the good which we have received ourselves, and all which has been wrought in others.

We bless thee in behalf of those who may have been turned from their evil ways, or who have been comforted, instructed, and in any way edified, in thy house of prayer.

For these, and all thy other mercies, our souls do magnify thy glorious name, which is exalted above all blessing and praise.

We further beseech thee, O Father Almighty, to open the ears of thy compassion to our supplications for others.

Mercifully look upon the Universal Church which thou hast purchased to thyself with the precious blood of thy dear Son.

And to those that shall be ordained to any holy function, give thy grace and heavenly benediction; that, both by their life and doctrine, they may set forth thy glory, and set forward the salvation of all men.

Bless the words which have been spoken in thy name this day; and let them not prove to any the savour of death unto death, but of life unto life, to all who have heard them.

Be gracious unto thy servants who have met together with us in thy courts: and grant that as many as are planted into this house of the Lord, may flourish in the courts of the house of our God.

Have mercy on those by whom the day of rest has been disregarded. Father, forgive them, for they know not what they do.

Be favourable, also, unto those who have been kept by sickness, or any other necessity, from joining the public assemblies of thy Church. Do thou, Almighty Lord, who art a most strong tower unto them that put their trust in thee, to whom all things in heaven, and in earth, and under the earth, do bow and obey; be now and evermore their defence, and make them to know and to feel that there is none other name under heaven given to man, in whom and through whom, they may receive health and salvation, but only the name of our Lord Jesus Christ.

We give thee hearty thanks, likewise, for such of them as it may have pleased thee this day to deliver out of the miseries of this sinful world; beseeching thee, that it may also please thee, of thy gracious goodness, shortly to accomplish the number of thy elect, and to hasten thy kingdom; that we, with all those that are departed in the true faith of thy holy name, may have our perfect consummation and bliss, both in body and soul, in thy eternal and everlasting glory, through Jesus Christ, our Lord; in whose name we offer up these our prayers; and conclude them in the words which he himself has taught us to use.

Our Father, &c.

MONDAY MORNING. *II. More.*

ALMIGHTY and most merciful Father! thou art a God that hearest prayer; and we are encouraged to draw nigh unto thy throne of grace, most humbly beseeching thee to look upon us, according to thy tender mercy in Jesus Christ. We confess our daily offences against thee in thought, word, and deed. If thou shouldst be extreme to mark what is done amiss, O Lord, who might abide it! Deal not with us after our sins, neither reward us after our iniquities. We bless thee for that all-prevailing Advocate, Jesus Christ, the righteous: by his cross and intercession, good Lord, deliver us.

We are now about to enter upon the worldly employments of another week: strengthen us with thy grace, that these may not withdraw our hearts from thee, nor make us negligent of our souls, and our salvation. May the influences of the Sabbath rest upon us through the week, and may the solemn and blessed truths which we heard yesterday, in the house of prayer, abide in our memories, and direct our conduct!

With many thanks for thy mercies during the past night, we now cast ourselves upon thy protection, not knowing what this day may bring forth; but trusting in that wisdom which cannot err, and in that love which cannot fail; do thou appoint our lot as seemeth good to both. Father, not our will, but thine be done! Preserve us from temptation; preserve us from sin; preserve us from our own evil hearts; and if we are permitted to see the close of this day, let us look back upon it as one in which we have walked with God.

Preserve us from the power of evil; from the sin that doth so easily beset us; from the lusts of the flesh, and the vanities of a wicked world.

Send thy good Spirit to direct and guide us in the ways and works of godliness; purify our affections; enliven our devotion; teach us how to pray, and how to hear, and read, and profit by thy holy word. Make us Christians, not only in name, but also in heart and in hope. Teach us the value of our souls, and the salvation which has been wrought for them by Christ Jesus. May we never be ashamed of confessing him before men, but, amidst all discouragements and difficulties, give us boldness to show ourselves his true disciples.

Let our conversation be such as becometh his gospel; and whatsoever we do in word or in deed, let us do all in his name, giving thanks to God and the Father through him. And let the words of our mouths, and the meditations of our hearts be acceptable in thy sight, O Lord, our strength, and our Redeemer.

Our Father, &c.

MONDAY EVENING.   *II. More.*

O Lord God Almighty, we bless thee for all the mercies of the past day, and we pray thee now to take us under thy care, and to deliver us from all the perils and dangers of this night. Preserve us, O Lord, both in body and soul, from every evil, and keep us from all sinful thoughts when we are about to close our eyes in sleep.

And pardon, we beseech thee, all our offences, for the sake of Jesus Christ. We confess, O Lord, that we have this day left undone many things which we ought to have done, and done many things which we ought not to have done. Pardon all our pride and vanity, our idleness and self-indulgence, our impatience, fretfulness, and discontent. Pardon, O Lord, all the rash and angry words which we have this day spoken, and all the sinful thoughts which have arisen up in our minds, and which we have not been careful to resist. And especially, we pray thee, to pardon our forgetfulness of thee, our God, and our want of gratitude and love to Jesus Christ. For these, and all our other sins, which, from time to time, we have committed, we here implore thy pardon and forgiveness, in the name of our most merciful Saviour.

And since we know that our life is so short and uncertain, help us, day by day, to think of our latter end. O Lord, grant us grace so to live that we be not afraid to die; and do thou receive our souls at last into thine eternal kingdom.

Enable us this night to shake off all worldly cares and desires, and to meditate upon thee; let thy Holy Spirit be present with us, to purify our hearts, and to bring before us the things which concern our peace, and to inspire us with godly resolutions.

Above all things, make us rightly to understand thine infinite mercy in the redemption of mankind by Jesus Christ, and diligently to avail ourselves of all our privileges, as his disciples, and thy children by adoption and grace.

O heavenly Father, we commit ourselves to thy holy keeping this night, and desire to rest securely under the shadow of thy protection. Defend us from all perils and dangers, and especially from those which may assault and hurt the soul. Prepare us, by comfortable repose, for the duties of the morrow; and grant that we may rise disposed and strengthened for thy service, as faithful and diligent disciples of thy blessed Son; in whose words we further pray:

Our Father, &c.

TUESDAY MORNING. *Com. Prayer.*

OUR FATHER, who art in heaven, hallowed be thy name; thy kingdom come; thy will be done on earth, as it is in heaven; give us this day our daily bread; and forgive us our trespasses, as we forgive those who trespass against us; and lead us not into temptation, but deliver us from evil; for thine is the kingdom, and the power, and the glory, for ever and ever.

Almighty and everlasting God, in whom we live, and move, and have our being; we, thy needy creatures, render thee our humble praises for thy preservation of us from the beginning of our lives to this day, and especially for having delivered us from the dangers of the past night. To thy watchful providence we owe it, that no disturbance hath come nigh us or our dwelling, but that we are brought in safety to the beginning of this day. For these thy mercies, we bless and magnify thy glorious name; humbly beseeching thee to accept this our morning sacrifice of praise and thanksgiving, for his sake who lay down in the grave, and rose again for us, thy Son, our Saviour, Jesus Christ.

And since it is of thy mercy, O gracious Father, that another day is added to our lives, we here dedicate both our souls and our bodies to thee and thy service, in a sober, righteous, and godly life; in which resolution, do thou, O merciful God, confirm and strengthen us; that, as we grow in age, we may grow in grace, and in the knowledge of our Lord and Saviour, Jesus Christ.

But O God, who knowest the weakness and corruption of our nature, and the manifold temptations which we daily meet with; we humbly beseech thee to have compassion on our infirmities, and to give us the constant assistance of thy Holy Spirit; that we may be effectually restrained from sin, and excited to our duty. Imprint upon our hearts such a dread of thy judgments, and such a grateful sense of thy goodness to us, as may make us both afraid and ashamed to offend thee. And, above all, keep in our minds a lively remembrance of that great day, in which we must give a strict account of our thoughts, words, and actions; and, according to the works done in the body, be eternally rewarded or punished, by him whom thou hast appointed the judge of quick and dead, thy, Son, Jesus Christ our Lord.

In particular, we implore thy grace and protection for the ensuing day. Keep us temperate in our meats and drinks, and diligent in our several callings. Grant us patience under any afflictions thou shalt see fit to lay on us, and minds always contented with our present condition. Give us grace to be just and upright in all our dealings; quiet and peaceable; full of compassion; and ready to do good to all men according to our abilities and opportunities. Direct us in all our ways, and prosper the works of our hands in the business of our several stations. Defend us from all dangers and adversities; and be graciously pleased to take us, and all things belonging to us, under thy fatherly care and protection. These things, and whatever else thou shalt see necessary and convenient to us, we humbly beg, through the merits and mediation of thy Son, Jesus Christ, our Lord and Saviour.

The grace of our Lord Jesus Christ, and the love of God, and the fellowship of the Holy Ghost, be with us all evermore. *Amen.*

TUESDAY EVENING. *Com. Prayer*

OUR FATHER, who art in heaven, hallowed be thy name; thy kingdom come; thy will be done on earth, as it is in heaven; give us this day our daily bread; and forgive us our trespasses, as we forgive those who trespass against us; and lead us not into temptation, but deliver us from evil; for thine is the kingdom, and the power, and the glory, for ever and ever.

Most merciful God, who art of purer eyes than to behold iniquity, and hast promised forgiveness to all those who confess and forsake their sins; we come before thee in an humble sense of our own unworthiness, acknowledging our manifold transgressions of thy righteous laws. But, O gracious Father, who desirest not the death of a sinner, look upon us, we beseech thee, in mercy, and forgive us all our transgressions. Make us deeply sensible of the great evil of them; and work in us an hearty contrition; that we may obtain forgiveness at thy hands, who art ever ready to receive humble and penitent sinners; for the sake of thy Son Jesus Christ, our only Saviour and Redeemer.

And lest, through our own frailty, or the temptations which encompass us, we be drawn again into sin, vouchsafe us, we beseech thee, the direction and assistance of thy Holy Spirit. Reform whatever is amiss in the temper and disposition of our souls; that no unclean thoughts, unlawful designs, or inordinate desires, may rest there. Purge our hearts from envy, hatred, and malice; that we may never suffer the sun to go down upon our wrath; but may always go to our rest in peace, charity, and good-will, with a conscience void of offence towards thee and towards men; that so we may be preserved, pure and blameless, until the coming of our Lord and Saviour Jesus Christ.

And accept, O Lord, our intercessions for all mankind. Let the light of thy gospel shine upon all nations; and may as many as have received it, live as becomes it. Be gracious unto thy church; and grant that every member of the same, in his vocation and ministry, may serve thee faithfully. Bless all in authority over us; and so rule their hearts, and strengthen their hands, that they may punish wickedness and vice, and maintain thy true religion and virtue. Send down thy blessings, temporal and spiritual, upon all our relations, friends, and neighbours. Reward all who have done us good, and pardon all those who have done or wish us evil, and give them repentance and better minds. Be merciful to all who are in any trouble; and do thou, the God of pity, administer to them according to their several necessities, for his sake who went about doing good, thy Son, our Saviour, Jesus Christ.

To our prayers, O Lord, we join our unfeigned thanks for all thy mercies; for our being, our reason, and all other endowments and faculties of soul and body; for our health, friends, food and raiment, and all the other comforts and conveniences of life. Above all, we adore thy mercy in sending thy only Son into the world to redeem us from sin and eternal death, and in giving us the knowledge and sense of our duty towards thee. We bless thee for thy patience with us, notwithstanding our many and great provocations; for all the directions, assistances, and comforts of thy Holy Spirit; for thy continual care and watchful providence over us through the whole course of our lives; and particularly for the mercies and benefits of the past day; beseeching thee to continue these thy blessings to us; and give to us grace to show our thankfulness in a sincere obedience to his laws, through whose merits and intercession we received them all, thy Son, our Saviour, Jesus Christ.

In particular, we beseech thee to continue thy gracious

protection to us this night. Defend us from all dangers and mischiefs, and from the fear of them; that we may enjoy such refreshing sleep as may fit us for the duties of the following day. Make us ever mindful of the time when we shall lie down in the dust; and grant us grace always to live in such a state, that we may never be afraid to die: so that living and dying we may be thine, through the merits and satisfaction of thy Son, Christ Jesus, in whose name we offer up these our imperfect prayers.

The grace of our Lord Jesus Christ, and the love of God, and the fellowship of the Holy Ghost, be with us all evermore. *Amen.*

WEDNESDAY MORNING. *Cotterill.*

ALMIGHTY and most merciful Father, we have erred and strayed from thy ways like lost sheep. We have followed too much the devices and desires of our own hearts. We have offended against thy holy laws. We have left undone those things which we ought to have done; and we have done those things which we ought not to have done; and there is no health in us. But thou, O Lord, have mercy upon us, miserable offenders. Spare thou them, O God, which confess their faults. Restore thou them that are penitent; according to thy promises declared unto mankind, in Christ Jesus our Lord.

And grant, O most merciful Father, for his sake, that we may hereafter live a godly, righteous, and sober life, to the glory of thy holy name.

Help us, especially, so to live through the day upon which we have entered.

Bless us in all our ways; and, whatever we do, may we do it heartily as unto thee, with a single eye to thy glory, and a humble dependence on thy fatherly protection.

Enlighten our understanding; control our wills; and sanctify our affections. Preserve us, that neither the pleasures, nor the cares, nor the honours of this life, turn away our thoughts from the life which is to come. May we learn and labour daily to live above the world; and to follow all our occupations in it with a heavenly mind.

Enable us faithfully to discharge our several duties to thee and to our fellow-creatures; that we may be useful in our generation among men, and steadfast in our covenant with thee. Having had much forgiven of thee, may we love thee much, and strive to please thee in all our ways.

And grant that nothing may ever separate between us and thee, by causing us to grow weary of thy service. But may we keep thy covenant for ever; and think upon thy commandments to do them, finding thy yoke easy, and thy burden light; yea, accounting thy service perfect freedom, and the very joy of our heart.

Lord, we pray thee that thy grace may always attend us, and make us continually to be given to all good works.

We desire to offer up our unfeigned thanksgivings for the good which thou mayest already have wrought in us, and for every mercy which thou hast vouchsafed to our bodies and our souls. Day by day we give thanks unto thee, and praise thy name.

Glory be to God on high, and on earth peace, good will towards men. We praise thee, we bless thee, we worship thee, we glorify thee, we give thanks unto thee, for thy great glory, O Lord God, heavenly king, God the Father Almighty.

We beseech thee, O Lord, to embrace with the arms of thy mercy, not only ourselves, but all who partake of our fallen nature. Pity and convert the wicked. May they no longer make a mock at sin, but learn to tremble at that wrath which thou hast revealed against all ungodliness and unrighteousness of men, fearing thee who art able to destroy both body and soul in hell. Give them grace to stand in awe of thy judgments, and to sin no more.

Bless thy faithful people with knowledge and good understanding in the ways of godliness: and let not the children of this world be wiser in their generation than the children of light.

And since many are the afflictions of the righteous,

Lord, remember them, and all their troubles: yea, may they be had before thee in everlasting remembrance. Though troubled on every side, let them not be distressed; though perplexed, let them not be in despair; though persecuted, let them not be forsaken; though cast down, let them not be destroyed. In all their afflictions be thou afflicted; and let the angel of thy presence save them. In thy love, and in thy pity, do thou redeem them; and bear them, and carry them, as in the days of old.

Grant that every affliction, though not for the present joyous, but grievous, may yield the peaceable fruits of righteousness to such as are exercised thereby.

And do thou bring them, at the last, to that place of rest and peace, where thou wilt wipe away all tears from their faces; where there shall be no more sorrow, nor crying; neither shall there be any more pain; and the former things shall pass away.

Assist us mercifully, O Lord, in these our supplications and prayers; and dispose the way of thy servants towards the attainment of everlasting salvation; that, among all the changes and chances of this mortal life, we may ever be defended by thy most gracious and ready help, through Jesus Christ our Lord.

Our Father, &c.

WEDNESDAY EVENING. *Cotterill.*

O Lord, thou hast been our refuge from one generation to another. Before the mountains were brought forth, or ever the earth and the worlds were made, thou art God from everlasting, and world without end.

Upon thy mercy-seat in the heavens thou waitest to be gracious; and we, thy sinful creatures, draw nigh unto thee, as unto a God in Christ, reconciling the world unto thyself, not imputing their trespasses unto them.

We trust, O Lord, to the word of thy promise, that though we have sinned, we have an Advocate with thee,

Jesus Christ the righteous, who is the propitiation for our sins; and not for ours only, but for the sins of the whole world.

If we say that we have no sin, we deceive ourselves, and the truth is not in us; but if we confess our sins, thou art faithful and just to forgive us our sins, and to cleanse us from all unrighteousness.

We pray thee, therefore, to create and make in us new and contrite hearts; that we, worthily lamenting our sins, and acknowledging our wretchedness, may obtain of thee, the God of all mercy, perfect remission and forgiveness. Regard us no longer as children of wrath, but as dear children; heirs of the kingdom of heaven, and joint-heirs with Christ. Satisfy us with thy mercy, and that soon, that we may rejoice and be glad in thee all our days.

Grant us, according to the riches of thy glory, to be strengthened with might, by thy Spirit, in the inner man. Let Christ dwell in our hearts by faith, that being rooted and grounded in love we may be able to comprehend, with all saints, what is the breadth, and length, and depth, and height, and to know the love of Christ, which passeth knowledge, that we may be filled with all the fullness of thee our God.

Thou hast brought and defended us, O heavenly Father, through the dangers of another day; and hast blessed us with every needful blessing, in our going out and coming in.

But, we beseech thee, O God of the spirits of all flesh, in whom alone we live, and move, and have our being, to touch our hearts with the solemn and affecting truth, that we know not what shall be on the morrow. Keep us constantly mindful, that in the midst of life we are in death. Of whom may we seek for succour but of thee, O Lord, who, for our sins, art justly displeased? Yet, O Lord God, most holy, O Lord, most mighty, O holy and merciful Saviour, thou most worthy judge eternal, suffer us not, at our last hour, for any pains of death to fall from thee.

Give ear, O Lord, to our prayers for our fellow-creatures.

Put the ungodly in fear, that they may know themselves to be but men. Incline them seriously to think on their ways, and turn their feet unto thy testimonies.

Let all those who trust in thee rejoice; because their redemption draweth nigh; and their salvation is nearer than when they first believed.

Be gracious unto such as, in this transitory world, are suffering, either for their sins or for righteousness sake; and sanctify their sufferings to the good of their souls.

Lastly, we pray thee, Almighty God, with whom do live the spirits of just men made perfect, after they are delivered from their earthly prisons, to look with compassion on all whom the sorrows of death are encompassing about. We commend their souls into thy hands, as into the hands of a faithful Creator and most merciful Saviour; humbly beseeching thee, that they may be precious in thy sight. Wash them in the blood of that spotless Lamb that was slain to take away the sins of the world, that they may be presented pure, and without spot before thee.

And teach us who survive, in every daily spectacle of mortality to remember how frail and uncertain our own condition is; and so to number our days that we may apply our hearts unto wisdom. Grant that neither the splendour of any thing that is great, nor the conceit of any thing that is good in us, may withdraw our eyes from looking upon ourselves as sinful dust and ashes: but that we may press forward to the prize of the high calling that is before us, in faith and patience, humility and meekness, mortification and self-denial, charity and constant perseverance unto the end; and all this for thy Son, our Lord Jesus Christ's sake: to whom, with thee and the Holy Ghost, be all honour and glory, world without end.

Our Father, &c.

THURSDAY MORNING. *Cotterill.*

Almighty God, whose eyes run to and fro throughout all the earth, we adore and magnify thee, as the author of all our blessings, and the source of all our happiness.

Every good gift, and every perfect gift, is from above, and cometh down from thee, the Father of lights, with whom is no variableness, neither shadow of turning.

Thou preservest to us our life and health, our food and raiment, our friends and benefactors, our private and public blessings, the means of grace, and the hope of glory. Thou art worthy of our highest adoration, our liveliest gratitude, and our most unfeigned praise.

But wherewithal shall we come before thee? And how shall we give unto thee the honour due unto thy name? All that we have is unworthy of thy regard; and our best returns serve only to remind us, how gracious thou art in receiving them. Not for our sakes, O Lord, not for our sakes, dost thou continue to bless us from day to day, and permit us to come into thy presence; but because thou delightest in mercy; because thy goodness is from everlasting to everlasting; and because, above all, thou hast respect unto the sacrifice of thy beloved Son, who gave himself a ransom for our souls.

For his sake, O Lord, continue to us all our blessings; and be gracious unto us, even as thou art wont. Grant that the number of thy mercies, in Christ Jesus, may ever triumph over the multitude of our sins; and that our supplications and praises, stained as they are with imperfection and defilement, may, through his most precious blood-shedding, daily enter with acceptance into thy ears, O Lord of hosts.

In his all-prevailing name we beseech thee to look down upon us in compassion this morning. Let thy thoughts towards us be thoughts of peace, and not of evil.

As thou hast kept us from the terror by night, and from the pestilence that walketh in darkness, so may it please thee to save us from the arrow that flieth by day, and from the destruction that wasteth at noon.

O merciful Father, that despisest not the sighing of a contrite heart, nor the desire of such as be sorrowful, mercifully assist our prayers that we make before thee, in all our troubles and adversities, whensoever they oppress us; and graciously hear us, that those evils which the craft and subtlety of the devil or man worketh against us, be brought to nought, and by the providence of thy goodness they may be dispersed, that we, thy servants, being hurt by no persecutions, may evermore give thanks unto thee, and praise thy holy name.

Enable us to pass this day, and all our days, in thy faith and fear.

Preserve us, that our minds be not overcharged with the cares of this life.

Make us humble in prosperity, and patient and thankful in the time of adversity.

Suffer us not to be occupied in ungodly works with the men that work wickedness. Let us not do the things that please them, and so become partakers of their sins. But give us grace to set our face as a rock against sin, and vanity, and every appearance of evil; and let not our hearts be inclined to any evil thing, but only to that which pleaseth thee.

Thou hast showed us, O Lord, what is good, and what thou requirest of us. Help us to obey thy commandment, to do justly, to love mercy, and to walk humbly with thee, our God. And, having received how we ought to walk and please thee, may we abound more and more. Vouchsafe, we beseech thee, continually to direct, sanctify, and govern, both our hearts and bodies in the ways of thy laws, and in the works of thy commandments; that through thy most mighty protection, both here and ever, we may be preserved in body and soul.

O thou God of kingdoms, and Lord of heaven and earth, give thy blessing to all nations; especially to that in which thou hast cast our lot.

We are, indeed, a sinful people, laden with iniquity, and it is entirely of thy mercies that we have not been consumed. But continue, we pray thee, to spare and bless us; and grant that all thy goodness towards us may lead us to repentance. Be thou our God, and may we be thy people; that all the world may know that thou art our Defender and Almighty Deliverer.

Bless the neighbourhood in which we dwell, and the families with whom we are more immediately connected. May they be taught of thee to be kindly affectioned one toward another; and to dwell together in peace and love, and do thou, the God of peace and love, be with them now and evermore.

We further pray thee to shed thy favour and blessing upon this family. Increase our love to thee, and to each other; and make it our delight thus to meet before thy throne, to offer up our prayers and praises, through Jesus Christ, our only Mediator and Advocate.

Our Father, &c.

THURSDAY EVENING. *Cotterill.*

ALMIGHTY and everlasting Lord God, the Creator of the ends of the earth, that faintest not, neither art weary, whose mercy endureth forever, who is a God like unto thee, that pardonest iniquity, that passest by the transgression of thy heritage; and retainest not thy anger forever, because thou delightest in mercy?

When we call to remembrance the days that are gone, from our youth up even until now, and consider how many of them have been spent in forgetfulness of thee, innumerable sorrows might well encompass us; and our sins take such hold upon us, that we should not be able to look up. Seeing they are more in number than the hairs of our head, our hearts might well fail because of them, did we not know that thy compassions fail not.

We have abundant cause, O Lord, to remember and to be confounded, and never to open our mouth any more because of our shame, even though thou shouldst be pacified towards us for all that we have done.

We therefore bless thee for Jesus, the Mediator of the new covenant; through whom we hope to be justified from all things, from which we could not be justified by any righteousness of our own.

We adore and magnify thy name, O Father of mercies, and God of all consolation, for having called us with a holy calling, not according to our works, but according to thy own purpose and grace, given us in Christ Jesus before the world began; whom having not seen, we love, and in whom, though we see him not, yet believing, we may rejoice with joy unspeakable and full of glory.

O for a song of praise! for a psalm of everlasting thanksgiving unto thee, the God of our salvation! O Lamb of God, worthy art thou that wast slain; for thou hast redeemed us unto God by thy blood! Worthy art thou that wast slain, to receive power, and riches, and wisdom, and strength, and honour, and glory, and blessing!

Teach us, O Lord, to live, day by day, in humble dependence on thy promises, in cheerful obedience to thy laws, and in a sure and certain hope of a blessed immortality.

Keep us, we beseech thee, with thy perpetual mercy; and because the frailty of man, without thee, cannot but fall, keep us ever by thy help from all things hurtful, and lead us to all things profitable to our salvation.

From all our enemies, temporal and spiritual, defend us, O Christ.

In all time of our tribulation, in all time of our prosperity, in the hour of death, and in the day of judgment, good Lord deliver us.

Grant that, being received for thy own children by adoption, and being incorporated into thy holy church we may receive the fulness of thy grace, and ever remain in the number of thy faithful children; and finally, with the residue of thy people, may be made partakers of thy heavenly kingdom.

Preserve us, especially, from all the evils to which we may be exposed this night. Graciously give thy angels charge concerning us, to pitch their tents around our beds: and grant that our friends, our neighbours, and all who are dear to us, may be brought in safety to the beginning of another day.

As often as we are about to lie down on the bed of sleep, help us to look forward to that sleep in the dust of the earth, from which all shall awake at the last, some to everlasting life, and some to shame and everlasting contempt.

And may we be found meet, in that day, to join in that glorious song which thou hast prepared for those who wait for thy appearing: "Lo! this is our God: we have waited for him, and he will save us. This is the Lord; we will rejoice and be glad in his salvation."

Almighty and everlasting God, who dost govern all things in heaven and earth, mercifully hear these our supplications; and grant us thy peace all the days of our life, through Jesus Christ, our Lord.

Our Father, &c.

FRIDAY MORNING.   *Cotterill.*

ALMIGHTY GOD, whose ears are always open to the petitions of thy humble servants, unto thee do we lift up our souls. We would seek thee whilst thou mayest be found; and call upon thee whilst thou art near.

Dispose us ever to direct our prayer unto thee, and to look up; and, daily, at thy footstool, to wait for thy blessing, more than they who watch for the morning, yea, more than they who watch for the morning.

Let every day begin with thee. For thou, O Lord, art a God full of compassion, and gracious, long-suffering, and plenteous in goodness and truth. How precious are thy thoughts which are to us-ward!

Thou hast protected us during the hours of darkness; for the darkness is no darkness with thee; but the night shineth as the day: the darkness and the light to thee are both alike. We have slept and awoke, and are still with thee. Thou art a God at hand, and not afar off; and none can hide themselves in secret places, where thou canst not see them.

Whither shall we go from thy Spirit? And whither shall we flee from thy presence? If we ascend up into heaven, thou art there; if we go down to hell, thou art there also. If we should take the wings of the morning, and remain in the uttermost parts of the sea, even there would thy hand lead us, and thy right hand hold us.

We humble ourselves before thee, for the sins which thy all-seeing eyes have beheld in the course of our lives. Very grievous are they, O Lord, and more than we are able to express; and not one of them is forgotten before thee. If thou shouldst be extreme to mark what is done amiss, O Lord, who may abide it? We confess that our hearts cannot endure, nor our hands be strong, in that day when thou shalt deal with us, if thou deal with us according to our sins, and reward us according to our iniquities.

But, we beseech thee, O Lord, deal not thus with thy servants. Blot out the hand-writing that is against us; and take it out of the way, nailing it to the cross of thy beloved Son. Grant unto us redemption through his blood, even the forgiveness of sins, according to the riches of thy grace. May we be washed; may we be sanctified; may we be justified, in the name of the Lord Jesus, and by thy Spirit, O Lord God.

Let a sense of thy presence abide with us this day. May we set thee always before us, remembering that thou, O God, seest us. And since unto thee all hearts are open, all desires known, and from thee no secrets are hid; cleanse, we beseech thee, the thoughts of our hearts, by the inspiration of thy Holy Spirit, that we may perfectly love thee, and worthily magnify thy holy name.

And while we acknowledge thee in all our ways, do thou in mercy direct our paths. As thou didst vouchsafe to lead thy people Israel in safety through the wilderness, going before them by day in a pillar of cloud, and in a pillar of fire by night; so be thou mercifully pleased to lead and protect us in the way in which we should go. Stand continually at our right hand, that we may not be moved. Strengthen us with the Holy Ghost, the Comforter; and daily increase in us thy manifold gifts of grace; the spirit of wisdom and understanding, the spirit of counsel and strength, the spirit of knowledge and true piety; and fill us, O Lord, with thy holy fear, now and evermore.

We beseech thee, also, O Lord, to give unto our fellow-creatures a due reverence of thy holy presence.

May the ungodly remember that thou knowest their manifold transgressions; and that there is no darkness, or shadow of death, where the workers of iniquity may hide their heads.

May those who have hitherto been deceiving themselves or others, with vain professions of religion, be brought to see that they cannot deceive thee; and so may be led to seek thee in truth and sincerity.

O Lord, we beseech thee, let thy continual pity cleanse and defend thy church; and because it cannot continue in safety without thy succour, preserve it evermore by thy help and goodness.

Let thy presence comfort and support thy afflicted people,: and be a refuge to them in all their troubles.

Furthermore, we pray thee to dwell in the hearts of all who are near and dear to us; and to make them a holy temple in the Lord, the habitation of thy blessed Spirit, through Jesus Christ our Saviour and Redeemer.

Our Father, &c.

FRIDAY EVENING. *Cotterill.*

ALMIGHTY and immortal God, the aid of all that need, the helper of all that flee to thee for succour, the life of them that believe, and the resurrection of the dead, receive us, as thou hast promised by thy well-beloved Son, saying, Ask, and ye shall have; seek, and ye shall find; knock, and it shall be opened unto you. So give now unto us that ask; let us that seek find; open the gate unto us that knock, that we may enjoy the everlasting benediction of thy heavenly grace, and may come to the eternal kingdom which thou hast promised by Christ our Lord.

We draw nigh unto thee in his great name, trusting to thy word, that whosoever believeth in thy beloved Son shall be saved. And we beseech thee to grant, that we may come unto him this night, weary and heavy laden with the burden of our sins, and may thus find rest to our souls.

As the heavens are higher than the earth, so great let thy mercy be towards us. Far as the east is from the west, so far do thou remove our transgressions from us. Yea, like as an earthly father pitieth his children, so do thou, our heavenly Father, pity and have mercy upon us. Adopt us into thy family; take away our guilt; accept our persons; and reconcile us unto thyself, through the blood of thy beloved Son.

We pray thee, also, O Lord, to show unto us more of the evil of sin, that we may know more of thy wonderful grace and mercy in pardoning it; and more of the loving-kindness of God our Saviour, in dying to redeem us from it.

O the depths of the riches of thy wisdom, thy knowledge, and thy love! Thou, O God, the merciful and gracious Lord, hast so done thy marvellous works, that they ought to be had in remembrance. Thou hast sent redemption unto thy people; thou hast commanded thy covenant for ever; holy and reverend is thy name. It is a good thing to give thanks unto thee, O Lord; and to sing praises unto thy name, O thou, Most Highest; to show forth thy loving-kindness in the morning, and thy faithfulness every night. We, thy unworthy servants, therefore, do give thee most humble and hearty thanks for all thy goodness and loving-kindness to us and to all men. We bless thee for our creation, preservation, and all the blessings of this life; but, above all, for thine inestimable love in the redemption of the world, by our Lord Jesus Christ; for the means of grace, and for the hope of glory. And, we beseech thee, give us that due sense of all thy mercies, that our hearts may be unfeignedly thankful, and that we may show forth thy praise, not only with our lips but in our lives, by giving up ourselves to thy service, and by walking before thee in holiness and righteousness all our days, through Jesus Christ our Lord; to whom with thee and the Holy Ghost, be all honour and glory, world without end.

Vouchsafe, O Lord, to hear our prayers for those whom it is our duty and our desire to remember at the throne of grace.

May it please thee to bring into the way of truth all such as have erred, and are deceived.

May it please thee to defend and bless all who are in authority; to rule their hearts in thy faith, fear, and love, that they may ever seek thy honour and glory.

May it please thee to guide and protect our magistrates, that they may be a terror to evil-doers, and for the praise of them that do well.

May it please thee to illuminate all the ministers of thy blessed gospel with true knowledge and understanding of thy word; and that both by their preaching and living, they may set it forth and show it accordingly.

May it please thee to bless the faithful in Christ Jesus, and to give them grace to continue faithful unto death.

May it please thee to bless the rising generation, especially the generation of those that seek thee, and of all our kindred, friends, and neighbours. Grant that our children, as they grow in stature, may grow in wisdom and in grace, and in favour with thee and man: and thus may become thy sons and daughters, O Lord Almighty.

Finally, may it please thee to stand at the right hand

of the poor and destitute, and to be unto them a tower of strength against all their enemies.

Grant, O Lord, these our petitions, through the merits of Jesus Christ our Saviour; who liveth and reigneth with thee, in the unity of the Holy Ghost, one God, world without end.

Our Father, &c.

SATURDAY MORNING. *Bp. Bloomfield.*

Almighty and most merciful Father, who, for our many sins committed against thee, mightest most justly have cut us off in the midst of our days, we humbly thank thee, that in the multitude of thy mercies thou hast hitherto spared us.

Accept, we beseech thee, our unfeigned sorrow for our past transgressions; and grant that we may never so presume upon thy mercy, as to despise the riches of thy goodness; but let a sense of thy forbearance and long-suffering work in us repentance and amendment of life, to thy honour and glory, and to our final acceptance in the last day, through the merits of our Saviour Jesus Christ.

Keep alive in us, O Lord, a true spirit of devotion: and preserve us from the great sin of praying to thee with our lips only, and not with our heart and mind.

Convince us of our entire dependence upon thee; quicken us in the pursuit of things eternal; that we may continually press forward to obtain the prize of our high calling in Christ Jesus.

Dispose us, we beseech thee, rightly to discharge the duties of this day. Watch over our path; compass us about with thy favour; preserve us in our going out and coming in; and direct all our steps in the way of thy commandments.

Make us truly honest and conscientious in all our dealings; diligent in the performance of our duty; innocent in our conversation; meek, charitable, and forgiving towards others; watchful over ourselves, and ever mindful of thy presence.

Sanctify unto us our crosses and afflictions, if it be thy good pleasure to afflict us; and give us such a measure of patience and godly resolution, that we may be willing to take up our cross daily, and to follow the Lamb, whithersoever he goeth.

O Lord, if we have now asked any thing amiss, we pray thee pardon our ignorance and infirmity; and whatsoever is good for us, even if we ask it not, be pleased to grant to us, in the name and for the sake of thy dear Son Jesus Christ, our only Mediator and Advocate.

Our Father, &c.

SATURDAY EVENING. *H. More.*

IN an humble acknowledgement of our manifold sins and iniquities, which we from time to time, and more especially this day, have committed against thee, both in thought, word, and deed, we now prostrate ourselves before thee, O Lord of heaven and earth, beseeching thee, for the sake of Jesus Christ, our only Lord and Saviour, to be merciful unto us. Forgive us, O Lord, that we have not rendered unto thee according to thy mercy and loving-kindness; that we have been forgetful and disobedient, and have sinned against heaven, and in thy sight. Let thy Holy Spirit sanctify us throughout, and give us more and more grace and strength, whereby we may be enabled to subdue all our sinful and corrupt affections; grant that we may improve the remainder of our days with all possible care, and give all diligence to make our calling and election sure, that we may so persevere therein unto death, that at last we may attain everlasting life.

Accept our praises and thanksgivings for all thy mercies vouchsafed us in this life, and for the hopes of a better. And now that we are going to take our rest and sleep, let us consider that thou, Lord, only makest us to dwell in safety; whether we sleep or wake, live or die, let us be found thine own, to thy eternal glory, and our everlasting salvation, through Jesus Christ.

O our God, another week has just passed away, and we are still in the land of the living, while so many of our fellow-creatures have passed from time into eternity. Blessed be God for the continuance of life and health, and for prolonged opportunities of preparing for death and judgment.

O gracious God, let not this continuance of mercy increase our condemnation, by encouraging us to commit sin, because hitherto thine anger has been withheld from falling upon us. Let us not treasure up wrath unto ourselves against the day of wrath; but teach us to number our days, that we may apply our hearts unto wisdom.

Prepare us, most blessed God, by sleep and rest, to take our part in the duties of the Sabbath to-morrow. Give us that sense of sin which leads to a full confession of its guilt, and to faith in the atonement of Christ for its pardon. Give us that adoring gratitude for all thy mercies, more especially for the great mercy of a Saviour, which may incline us to praise thee with joyful lips. Give us that sense of the value of our souls, and of the greatness of thy salvation, which may lead us to seek life and mercy with all our hearts. O let not the coming Sabbath be defectively used, like those which are passed; but let it be so improved, by public and private means of grace, as to advance our meetness for the service of that eternal Sabbath that remaineth for the people of God; through the merit and mediation of Jesus Christ.

Our Father, &c.

PRAYERS AND THANKSGIVINGS

FOR

PARTICULAR OCCASIONS.

LAST EVENING OF THE OLD YEAR. *Jay*

O God, thou hast been our refuge and dwelling-place in all generations; before the mountains were brought forth, or ever thou hadst formed the earth and the world, even from everlasting to everlasting, thou art God. A thousand years in thy sight are but as yesterday when it is past, and as a watch in the night. But as for man, his days are as grass, as a flower of the field, so he flourisheth; for the wind passeth over it, and it is gone, and the place thereof knoweth it no more.

We appear before thee, to close in thy presence, another of the revolutions of our fleeting existence, earnestly praying that the season may not pass away, without suitable and serious reflections. We know that our life is a vapour, that appeareth for a little time, and then vanisheth away; we know the frailty of our frame, and the numberless diseases and disasters to which we are exposed—so teach us to number our days that we may apply our hearts unto wisdom.

What numbers of our fellow-creatures have, during the past year, been carried down to their long home— but we have been preserved; and are living to praise thee this day. Blessed be the God of salvation, to whom belong the issues from death, that we are yet in the regions of hope, that we have yet an accepted time, and a day of salvation; and that our opportunities of doing good, as well as of gaining good, are still prolonged.

Thou hast commanded us to remember all the way, which thou hast led us in the wilderness. The scene of our journeying has indeed been a wilderness; but the hand that has conducted us is divine; and a thousand privileges have been experienced in it.

Thou hast corrected us, but it is of the Lord's mercies we are not consumed.

We have had our afflictions, but how few have they been in number; how short in continuance; how alleviated in degree; how merciful in design; how instructive and useful in their results.

Thou hast not dealt with us after our sins, neither hast thou rewarded us according to our iniquities.

But O what a series of bounties and blessings present themselves to our minds, when we look back upon the year through which we have passed: and to what, but to thine unmerited goodness in the Son of thy love, are we indebted for all. Health, strength, food, raiment, residence, friends, relations, comfort, pleasure, hope, usefulness,—all our benefits have dropped from thy gracious hand; and there has not been a day, or an hour, or a moment, but has published thy kindness and thy care.

Especially would we acknowledge thy goodness, in continuing to us the means of grace. Whatever has been denied us, we have had the provisions of thy house. The toils and trials of the week have been refreshed and relieved by the delights of the Sabbath. Our eyes have seen our teachers. Our ears have heard the joyful sound of the gospel; and our hearts have often said, Lord, it is good for us to be here.

And we especially praise thy name, O thou God of grace, for all the success which has attended the means of grace. We thank thee that thy Holy Spirit has been sent down upon thy churches. We praise thee that thy grace has been imparted to any to comfort the disconsolate; to strengthen the feeble; to support the dying. We bless thee that the preached gospel has been attended with success; and that the reviving influences of thy Holy Spirit have been felt in our land. We thank thee for all the mild and benignant influences of our holy religion upon the nation amid whom we live; and that the inestimable blessings of liberty, peace, prosperity, and education, are still continued with us. And we give praise to thy name that thou hast remembered thy promises to thy church — that thou hast extended its cords, and strengthened its stakes — that thou hast excited thy people to the great work of spreading thy gospel among the nations — and hast crowned their efforts with so cheering success.

And O, that every moment of the past year could, if called upon — and it will be called upon, bear witness to our gratitude, love and obedience. O, that it was not in its power to convict us of the most unworthy requitals of thy goodness. To thee, O Lord, belong glory and honour, but to us shame and confusion of face. O, who can understand his errors? O how many duties have we neglected or improperly performed! How little have we redeemed our time, or improved our talents! How little have we been alive to thy glory, or sought, or even seized, when presented, opportunities of serving our generation! How unprofited have we been under the richest means of religious prosperity — and, when for the time we ought to be able to teach others, we need to be again taught ourselves, what are the first principles of the oracles of God.

God be merciful to us sinners. Pardon our iniquity, for it is great. Cleanse us from all unrighteousness; and work in us to will and to do of thy good pleasure. Let us not carry one of our old sins with us into the new year — unforgiven — unrepented of — unbewailed — unabhorred. With a new portion of time, may we have new hearts; and become new creatures.

If this coming year we should die — and in the midst of life we are in death — may death prove our eternal gain: and if our days are prolonged, may we walk before the Lord in the land of the living, and show forth all thy praise. The number of our months is with thee. In thy hand our breath is, and thine are all our ways. Prepare us for all: and be with us in all: and bring us safely through all, into the rest that remains for thy people; for the sake of our Lord and Saviour; in whose words we call thee, Our Father, &c. *Amen.*

FIRST MORNING OF THE NEW YEAR. *Jay.*

O Lord, of old hast thou laid the foundation of the earth, and the heavens are the work of thy hands. They shall perish, but thou shalt endure; yea, all of them shall wax old like a garment; as a vesture shalt thou change them, and they shall be changed; but thou art the same, and thy years shall have no end. We desire, O God, with the profoundest reverence to contemplate the eternity of thy nature. May our minds be filled with elevation and grandeur, at the thought of a Being with whom one day is as a thousand years, and a thousand years as one day; a Being who, amidst all the revolutions of empire, and the lapse of ages, feels no variableness nor shadow of turning. How glorious, with immortality attached to them, are all thy attributes; and how secure are the hopes and happiness of all those who know thy name and put their trust in thee.

May we rejoice, that while men die, the Lord liveth; that while all creatures are found broken reeds and broken cisterns, he is the Rock of Ages, and the fountain of living waters. O that we may turn away our hearts from vanity; and among all the uncertainties of the present state, look after an interest in that everlasting covenant, which is ordered in all things and sure. May we seek after an union with thyself, as the strength of our heart, and our portion forever, for thou hast assured us that while the world passeth away, and the lusts thereof, he that doeth the will of God abideth forever.

We thank thee that thou hast revealed to us the way in which a fallen and perishing sinner can be eternally united to thyself; and that Jesus is the way, the truth and the life. In his name we come; O, receive us graciously; justify us freely; renew us in the spirit of our minds; and bless us with all spiritual blessings in heavenly places in Christ.

By the lapse of our days, and weeks, and years, which we are called upon so often to remark, may we be reminded how short our life is, and how soon we shall close our eyes on every prospect below the sun; and, O, suffer us not to neglect the claims of eternity, in the pursuit of the trifles of time; but knowing how frail we are, may we be wise enough to choose that good part which shall not be taken away from us; and before we leave the present evil world, may we secure an inheritance in another and a better. May thoughts of death and eternity so impress our minds, as to put seriousness into our prayers, and vigour into our resolutions; may they loosen us from an undue attachment to things seen and temporal; so that we may weep as though we wept not, and rejoice as if we rejoiced not.

And remembering that the present life, so short, so uncertain—and so much of which is already vanished, is the only opportunity we shall ever have for usefulness, may we be concerned to redeem the time. May we be alive and awake at every call of charity and piety. May we feed the hungry, and clothe the naked; may we instruct the ignorant; reclaim the vicious; forgive the offending; diffuse the gospel; and consider one another to provoke one another unto love and good works, not forsaking the assembling ourselves together as the manner of some is, but exhorting one another, and so much the more as we see the day approaching.

As we have entered on a new period of life, may we faithfully examine ourselves, to see what has been amiss in our former temper or conduct; and in thy strength may we resolve to correct it. And may we inquire for the future — with a full determination to reduce our knowledge to practice — Lord, what wilt thou have me to do?

Prepare us for all the duties of the ensuing year. All the wisdom and strength necessary for the performance of them must come from thyself; may we, therefore, live a life of self-distrust, of divine dependence, and of prayer; may we ask and receive, that our joy may be full; may we live in the Spirit, and walk in the Spirit.

If we are indulged with prosperity, O let not our prosperity destroy us, or injure us. If we are exercised with adversity, suffer us not to sink in the hour of trouble, or sin against God. May we know how to be abased, without despondence; and to abound, without pride. If our relative comforts are continued to us, may we love them without idolatry, and hold them at thy disposal; and if they are recalled from us, may we be enabled to say, the Lord gave, and the Lord hath taken away; and blessed be the name of the Lord.

Fit us for all events. We know not what a day may bring forth; but we encourage ourselves in the Lord our God, and go forward. Thou hast been thus far our helper; thou hast promised to be with us in every condition; thou hast engaged to make all things work together for good; all thy ways are mercy and truth. May we, therefore, be careful for nothing; but in every thing, by prayer and supplication with thanksgiving, may we make known our requests unto God; and may the peace of God, that passeth all understanding, keep our hearts and minds through Christ Jesus.

Bless, O bless the young; may each of them, this day, hear thee saying, My son give me thy heart; and, from this time, may they cry unto thee, as the guide of their youth. Regard those who have reached the years, wherein they say, we have no pleasure in them. If old in sin, may they be urged to embrace, before it be forever too late, the things that belong to their peace; and if old in grace, uphold them with thy free Spirit, and help them to remember, that now is their salvation nearer than when they believed.

Bless all the dear connexions attached to us by nature,

friendship, or religion. Grace be to them, and peace be multiplied.

Let our country share thy protection and smiles. Bless all our rulers and magistrates.

We commend to thee, most merciful Father, the interests of thy church in the advancing year. Not knowng that it will be thy good pleasure to keep us in the land of the living, yet we pray that thou wilt regard with special favour thy holy church; and smile continually upon Zion. Give grace to thy ministers that they may preach thy gospel with simplicity, power, and success. Bless all Sunday schools. And may thy Spirit be given to enlighten all Sunday school teachers, and to sanctify all Sunday school scholars. May thy Holy Spirit descend upon the churches. Let pure and undefiled religion prevail in all the congregations of thy people. May sinners be converted in great numbers to thyself; and may this year be distinguished by great and successful efforts to spread the gospel through this land, and through all the world. Smile, O gracious God, on all missionaries of the cross; amid all their labours and sufferings, and privations, do thou sustain them. Let not thy people faint, and grow weary in this work; and during the advancing year, grant, we beseech thee, that the power of thy gospel may be felt in all lands, and soon may the whole family of man be brought under the saving power of divine truth.

Our Father, which art in heaven, hallowed be thy name; thy kingdom come; thy will be done on earth as it is in heaven; give us this day our daily bread, and forgive us our trespasses, as we forgive those that trespass against us; and lead us not into temptation; but deliver us from evil: for thine is the kingdom, and the power, and the glory, for ever. *Amen.*

FOR CHRISTMAS DAY. *Cotterill,*

MORNING.

Almighty God, the Father of our Lord Jesus Christ, we humbly beseech thee to accept our hearty thanks for the manifold mercies which thou hast poured upon us.

We bless thee, especially, for sending thy well beloved Son, to take our nature upon him, and to be made in the likeness of sinful flesh.

We rejoice that unto us a Child is born; that unto us a Son is given. And we would join the multitude of the heavenly host, in ascribing glory to thee in the highest; peace on earth; good will toward men.

We praise thee for revealing to us the way in which mercy and truth have met together; in which righteousness and peace have kissed each other. And we account it a faithful saying, and worthy of all acceptation, that Christ Jesus came into the world to save sinners.

Help us, O Lord, to employ this day in meditating on this great mystery of godliness, God manifest in the flesh, which thy holy angels desire to look into.

And as, when thou didst bring thy first-begotten into the world, thou didst command all the heavenly host to worship him, so may we also give unto him the glory which is due unto his name.

O thou great and glorious Redeemer, who art Wonderful, Counsellor, the Mighty God, the Everlasting Father, the Prince of Peace, we praise thee; we bless thee; we worship thee; we glorify thee; we give thanks to thee for thy great glory, O Lord God, Lamb of God, the only begotten Son, Jesus Christ, King of kings, and Lord of lords, Emmanuel, God with us. For thou only art holy; thou only art the Lord; thou only, O Christ, with the Holy Ghost, art most high in the glory of God the Father.

But chiefly, at this time, we adore thee for leaving the glory which thou hadst with the Father before the world began. We know thy grace, O Lord Jesus Christ, that though thou wast rich, yet for our sakes thou didst become poor, that we, through thy poverty, might be made rich. We beseech thee, by the mystery of thy holy incarnation and nativity, good Lord, deliver us. O Son of David, have mercy upon us. Thou, who didst come that we might have life, and might have it more abundantly, be gracious unto us.

Thou who wast called Jesus, that thou mightest save thy people from their sins, save us, and help us, we humbly beseech thee, O Lord.

And give unto us grace, Almighty God, that we may cast away the works of darkness, and put upon us the armour of light, now in the time of this mortal life, in which thy Son, Jesus Christ, came to visit us in great humility.

As he came not to be ministered unto, but to minister, and hath left us an example to do unto others as he hath done unto us, so may we learn to take his yoke upon us, and to learn of him, who was meek and lowly in heart, that we may find rest unto our souls. Grant, that we, being regenerate and made thy children by adoption and grace, may daily be renewed by thy Holy Spirit, and follow the blessed steps of his most holy life; ever remembering that he gave himself for us, to redeem us from all iniquity, and to purify us unto himself a peculiar people, zealous of good works.

Vouchsafe, O Lord, thy special blessing to us this day.

Have compassion, also, on those who have never heard of the coming of our blessed Lord in the flesh. In him who hath arisen to rule over the Gentiles, let the Gentiles trust, and find his rest to be glorious.

Mercifully with thy favour look upon the whole Christian world. May all that name the name of Christ depart from iniquity. Especially preserve them from turning this season into an occasion of revellings and unholy mirth. Let them rejoice, as Christians, in Christ their Saviour; and let thy grace teach them to deny all ungodliness and worldly lusts, and to live soberly, righteously, and godly, in this present world.

And, as at thy first coming, O Lord Jesus Christ, thou didst send thy messenger to prepare thy way before thee, we beseech thee, finally, to grant that the ministers and stewards of thy mysteries, may likewise so prepare and make ready thy way, by turning the hearts of the disobedient to the wisdom the just; that, at thy second coming to judge the world, we may be found an acceptable people in thy sight, through Jesus Christ, our Lord, in whose name we further pray:—

Our Father, &c.

FOR CHRISTMAS DAY.

EVENING.

O Holy and merciful God, who art of purer eyes than to behold iniquity, and yet long-suffering towards sinners, we approach thy throne, acknowledging our unworthiness, and putting our whole trust and confidence in the promises which thou hast made unto us in Christ Jesus our Lord.

We have greatly provoked thee to anger by our manifold offences; and, were not judgment thy strange work, we should long since have received at thy hands the just reward of our evil-doings.

But thou declarest thy almighty power most chiefly in showing mercy and pity. Thou hast not stretched forth the right hand of thy majesty to avenge thee of thine enemies; but with thine own arm thou hast wrought out redemption for us. Thou hast not sent thy Son into the world to condemn the world, but that the world through him might be saved.

We bless thee for revealing to us this great mystery, which was hid from ages and generations, but is now made manifest unto the sons of men. We rejoice that unto us was born a Saviour, which is Christ the Lord. Our souls do magnify the Lord, and our spirits do rejoice in God our Saviour. Hosanna to the Son of David!

Blessed be he that cometh in the name of the Lord: Hosanna in the highest!

Blessed be thou, the God of Israel, for visiting and redeeming thy people, and raising up a horn of salvation for them; for performing the promise made unto their fathers, and for remembering thy holy covenant.

Praised be thy name, for sending forth, in the fulness of time, thy only begotten Son, made of a woman, made under the law, that we might receive the adoption of sons.

Glory be unto thee, for causing thy loving-kindness toward us to appear. Not by works of righteousness which we have done, but according to thy mercy, thou hast saved us.

O Thou, who wast in Christ reconciling the world unto thyself, not imputing their trespasses unto them, forgive us all our trespasses. Through him who was made in the likeness of sinful flesh, and came to seek and to save that which was lost, have mercy upon us. By the mystery of his holy incarnation and nativity, good Lord, deliver us.

And, since thy blessed Son was manifested that he might destroy the works of the devil, to make us the children of God and heirs of eternal life, grant, we beseech thee, that having this hope, we may purify ourselves, even as he is pure; and that, when he shall come again, in power and great glory, we may be made like unto him, in his eternal and glorious kingdom.

But who may abide the day of his coming? And who may stand when he appeareth? O thou compassionate and faithful High Priest, partaker of our flesh and blood, who wast in all points tempted like as we are, yet without sin, and art not ashamed to call us brethren, have pity upon our infirmities; and grant unto us, that we, being delivered out of the hands of our enemies, may serve thee, without fear, in holiness and righteousness before thee, all the days of our life.

Fill our hearts with love to thee for the unspeakable gift which thou didst vouchsafe to bestow upon a sinful world; and dispose us always most thankfully to receive the same.

Let the same mind, also, be in us, which was in Christ Jesus; who being in the form of God, and thinking it not robbery to be equal with God, yet made himself of no reputation, and took upon him the form of a servant, and was found in fashion as a man, a man of sorrows and acquainted with grief.

Help us continually to follow the example of his great humility. In lowliness of mind may we esteem others better than ourselves. And give us grace so to walk in all holiness of living, that we may not be ashamed before him at his coming.

We pray likewise, O heavenly Father, that, through thy tender mercies, the Day-Spring from on high, which hath visited us, may arise, and shine upon the nations that are sitting in darkness and in the shadow of death, to guide their feet into the way of peace.

Grant that it may both be a light to lighten the Gentiles, and be the glory of thy people Israel.

And may none of those who behold it, love darkness rather than light, because their deeds are evil.

Raise up faithful and able ministers of the New Testament, to go before the face of the Lord, to prepare his ways, to give knowledge of salvation to his people, by the remission of their sins.

Pour down thy grace and heavenly benediction upon all who are called Christians. May the children of Zion be joyful in their King! And may they so truly follow the blessed steps of their Lord and Master, that they may be saved by him in the great day of his appearing and glory. Grant this for Jesus Christ's sake, our only Lord and Saviour.

Our Father, &c.

FOR A SACRAMENT SABBATH. *Cotterill*

MORNING.

O HOLY and gracious Lord God, who wilt by no means clear the guilty, yet sparest those who confess their sins unto thee, look down with compassion upon us, thy servants, who are now humbled before thee, imploring thy fatherly forgiveness. Spare us, good Lord, spare us, for we are miserable sinners! We cannot set all our transgressions in order before thee, nor confess them so truly as we ought to do; yet we desire not to cloak and dissemble them before thy face, O heavenly Father, trusting to thy word, that if we confess our sins, thou art faithful and just to forgive us our sins, and to cleanse us from all unrighteousness. Be merciful unto us, we most humbly beseech thee; for we put our whole trust and confidence in thy mercy, and not in anything that we do. We have destroyed ourselves, but in thee is our help. Save, Lord, or we perish; for there is salvation in no other. To whom else should we go? Thou only hast the words of eternal life. Grant unto us, O Lord, we beseech thee, pardon and peace; that we may be cleansed from all our sins, and may serve thee with a quiet mind.

We praise thee, O God, for the multitude of thy blessings vouchsafed unto us, particularly for the many opportunities which thou affordest us of becoming wise unto salvation.

What shall we render unto thee this day, for all the benefits which thou hast done unto us? We will receive the cup of salvation, and call upon the name of the Lord. We will pay our vows in the courts of thy house and in the presence of all thy people.

We give thee most humble and hearty thanks, O Almighty God, our heavenly Father, for that thou hast given thy Son, our Saviour Jesus Christ, not only to die for us, but to be our spiritual food and sustenance in the holy sacrament of his body and blood. Dispose us religiously and devoutly to receive the same, in remembrance of his meritorious cross and passion; whereby alone we obtain the remission of our sins, and are made partakers of the kingdom of heaven. Teach us to consider the dignity of that holy mystery, and so to search and examine our own consciences, that we may come holy and clean to such a heavenly feast, in the marriage garment required by thee in holy Scripture, and may be received as worthy partakers of that holy table.

May we spiritually eat the flesh of Christ, and drink his blood! May we dwell in Christ, and Christ in us! May we be one with Christ, and Christ with us! And may his body, which was given for us, and his precious blood, which was shed upon the cross, preserve our bodies and souls unto everlasting life!

Mercifully vouchsafe, O Lord, to extend unto all our fellow-creatures the inestimable benefits of Christ's suffering and death.

Give grace, O heavenly Father, to all thy ministering servants, that they may, both by their life and doctrine, set forth thy true and lively word, and rightly and duly administer thy holy sacraments. And to all thy people give thy heavenly grace; especially to such as shall assemble with us in thy holy temple, and shall come to the holy communion of the body and blood of our Saviour Christ. May they diligently examine themselves before they eat of that bread, and drink of that cup, and so judge themselves, that they be not judged of thee. May they examine themselves, whether they repent truly of their former sins, steadfastly purpose to lead a new life, have a lively faith in thy mercies through Christ, with a thankful remembrance of his death, and be in charity with all men. And may numbers be added to thy church continually, of those who are willing to join themselves unto thee in an everlasting covenant, not to be forgotten.

Pitifully behold the sorrows of those who are filled with groundless fears, lest they should eat and drink unworthily. May they hear and receive the comfortable things which Christ our Saviour saith unto all who truly turn unto him. May they come unto him labouring and heavy laden with the burden of their sins, and so find rest unto their souls.

Finally, we beseech thee to have compassion upon those who shall most unthankfully refuse to come to thy table, though so graciously called and bidden. May they take heed, lest, by withdrawing themselves from this holy supper of their Lord, they provoke his just indignation against them. May they earnestly consider how little their excuses will avail before thee, and by thy grace be brought to a better mind; seriously remembering, that if they eat not the flesh of the Son of man, and drink not his blood, they have no life in them, and neither part nor lot in his salvation.

Grant this, O God of mercy, for the sake of Jesus Christ, our only Lord and Saviour.

Our Father, &c.

FOR A SACRAMENT SABBATH. *Cotterill.*

EVENING.

Almighty God and Father, who, according to the multitude of thy mercies, dost so put away the sins of those who truly repent, that thou rememberest them no more, open thine eye of mercy upon us, thy servants, who earnestly desire thy pardon and forgiveness. Renew in us, O heavenly Father, whatever hath been decayed by the fraud and malice of the devil, and by our own carnal will and frailty. And forasmuch as we put our full trust and confidence in thee, impute not unto us our manifold transgressions, but wash them away in the blood of thy beloved Son. Graciously vouchsafe to receive us to thy favour. Sanctify us and strengthen us by thy Holy Spirit; and at length bring us unto the kingdom of heaven, and to everlasting life.

We praise thee for thy promises of forgiveness to those who truly turn unto thee.

We bless thee for another day of sacred rest, which thou hast vouchsafed unto us, and for all the blessings of the same.

Above all things, we give thee most humble and hearty thanks for the redemption of the world by the death of our Lord and Saviour, Jesus Christ. May we always remember the exceeding great love of our Master and only Saviour, Jesus Christ, thus dying for us, and the innumerable benefits which, by his precious blood-shedding, he hath obtained unto us, and also his goodness and loving-kindness in instituting and ordaining holy ordinances as pledges of his love, to our great and endless comfort.

Grant that we, who have eaten and drunk in thy presence, may receive the strengthening and refreshing of our souls by the body and blood of Christ. Help us to remember the solemn vows which we have this day renewed in thy presence, and in the presence of all thy people; and enable us truly to perform them. May we go forth into the world bearing about us the marks of a crucified Saviour. Having enlisted ourselves again under the banners of the Captain of our salvation, may we manfully fight the good fight of faith, and continue his faithful soldiers and servants unto our lives' end. Grant that we may have power and strength to have victory, and to triumph against the devil, and the world, and the flesh. May we be encouraged in our holy warfare by the ensamples of the glorious company of the apostles, the goodly fellowship of the prophets, the noble army of martyrs, and of all the holy church triumphant, who have been made more than conquerors through him who loved them, and bought them with his blood.

As thou hast knit together thine elect in one communion and fellowship, in the mystical body of thy Son Jesus Christ our Lord; grant us grace so to follow thy blessed saints in all virtuous and holy living, that we may enter into those unspeakable joys, which thou hast prepared for them that unfeignedly love thee. And when he shall come to be glorified in his saints, and to be admired in all them that believe, may we sit down with Abraham, Isaac, and Jacob, and all thy redeemed people, at the marriage supper of the Lamb.

Grant, also, O Lord, we beseech thee, that those who have waited on thee this day in thy holy temple, and around thy table, may renew their spiritual strength.

May all men see that they are thy disciples, by the love which they have one to another. O God, who hast taught us that all our doings without charity are nothing worth, send thy Holy Ghost, and pour into our hearts that most excellent gift of love, the very bond of peace and of all virtues, without which whosoever liveth is counted dead before thee. Let there be no schism in the body of Christ; but let the members have the same care one of another, knowing, that if any sin against their brother, and wound his weak conscience, they sin against Christ.

And since the offence of the cross is not ceased, comfort and succour all those who may any ways suffer from love to thee and thy cause. Hide them under thy wing. Enable them to witness a good confession, and to give no just occasion to their enemies to blaspheme. By well-doing, let them put to silence the ignorance of foolish men, in meekness instructing those that oppose themselves, if peradventure thou mayest give them repentance to the acknowledging of the truth.

Convert the hearts of all those who are thrusting away from them thy great mercies: especially of such as have this day neglected thy ordinances, and turned aside from thy holy table.

And, if any have there appeared before thee with unclean hands and unsanctified hearts, without the marriage-garment required by thee in holy scripture, not discerning the Lord's body, may they search and examine their conscience, and repent; lest, after the taking of this holy sacrament, Satan enter into them as he entered into Judas, and fill them full of all iniquity, and bring them to destruction both of body and soul.

We ask these blessings in the name of Jesus Christ, our only Lord and Saviour.

Our Father, &c.

FAST DAY.—MORNING. *Jenks.*

O Lord God, glorious in holiness, and of purer eyes than to behold any iniquity without abhorrence of it, and indignation against it! How shall man, sinful man, that drinks in iniquity like water, appear before thee? And how shall we, vile and frail, polluted and depraved as we are, show ourselves in the presence of such a great and wise, just and holy God, as thou art? When we look upon thy perfect law, and see what we should be, what manner of persons, in all holy conversation and godliness; and when we reflect on our own hearts and lives, and find what we are; how wanting in our duty, and how contrary to that holy rule which thou dost prescribe to us, by which to keep our hearts and to order our conversation; we cannot come into thy presence, O Lord, without confusion of face, and anguish of soul, and remorse of conscience, to think how foolishly and wickedly we have done; and how abject and wretched we have made ourselves.

We have not glorified thee, O Lord, in bearing fruits of holiness answerable to thy revealed will, and to thy love; but we desire to give glory to God, in confessing our sins, and humbling our souls, and acknowledging our desert of all thy judgments; and admiring and magnifying the riches of that grace and mercy, which has spared us so long a time, and showed us such marvellous kindness still, notwithstanding all the high provocations of our sins. With thee, our God, there is mercy, that thou mayest be feared; that our sins, though great and manifold, may be pardoned; and that our souls may be recovered and healed, and eternally saved: O help us so to judge ourselves, that we may not be judged of the Lord, to be condemned with the world; and so to lay our sins to heart, that thou mayest never lay them to our charge, but upon the account of thy Son our Saviour; whom thou hast given to be the propitiation for our sins; and in whom thou art a God gracious and merciful to poor sinners; that deserve nothing at all from thee, but to be forsaken and abhorred by thee. For his sake, O God! give us repentance and pardon for all that is past, wherein we have offended thee; whether they be our sins of omission or commission; sins of weakness or wilfulness; failings or presumptions; the sins of ignorance, or such as we have committed against light and knowledge; O gracious Lord, humble us duly under the sense of them, and absolve us thoroughly from the guilt of them. O set our sins in order before us, and make us to know our transgressions, and the evil of our own hearts; and every one of us so to search and try our ways, that we may turn to the Lord, and bring forth fruits meet for repentance; and not only loathe ourselves in our own sight, for the evils whereof we have been guilty; but also loathe, as much as ever we have loved, the things which displease thy holy will, and dishonour thy blessed name. O that we may forsake our sins, not only in the outward commission, but in the inward affection; not reserving to ourselves any sin or lust to be spared, nor any way of wickedness, wherein we would be allowed; but keeping at that distance which thy holy word teaches to keep, from every evil and accursed thing, that is abomination in thy sight, and destructive to our souls; and cleansing ourselves from all filthiness of flesh and spirit, endeavouring to perfect holiness in the fear of God.

O pour out a spirit of serious repentance and reformation upon the whole nation: to heal the distempers of our souls, to curb the disorders of our lives, and to recover the decayed power of godliness in the land; and so prepare and dispose us not only for thy temporal mercies, but for the mercy of our Lord Jesus Christ to eternal life. Help us so to turn from the evil of our ways, that thou mayest turn from the fierceness of thy wrath, and cause thy anger towards us to cease. O that we may fear the rod, and who has appointed it! And so prepare to meet thee, our God, in the way of thy judgments, that the God of peace may think thoughts of peace to us, and not of evil; and to give us an unexpected end, and the desired issue, of all our fears and dangers.

Thou canst show us great and mighty things, which we know not, and exceed all our expectations, as well as our deservings, by thy bountiful favours: and though thou mightest make us know the worth of slighted mercies by their want, and deprive us of all the good which we have so little improved, and so greatly abused: yet, O how many promises of thy word, and what frequent experience, which we have had of thy mercy, in time of our need, do encourage us still with hope to look unto thee, our God, and to wait for the salvation of the Lord! O how long, in all our provocations, hast thou spared us! And how often, in our distresses, sent wonderful redemption to us! And to thee, who hast helped and delivered, in time past, do we look still for help and deliverance. O, our God, be thou pleased to help and deliver us, for the glory of that mercy which first made us thy people, and still has owned us for thy peculiar care. O do not abhor us, nor forsake us, for thy name's sake; but be jealous for thy land, and pity thy people. Turn us again, O Lord God of hosts, and cause thy face to shine, and we shall be saved.

Either in mercy turn away the evils from us; or prepare us for them, and support us under them, and bring us happily out of them; that we may not sink and perish in them, but find spiritual good, by temporal evils; and find the light momentary afflictions to work for us a far more exceeding and eternal weight of glory; and all things concurring to promote our grace and our peace with God, through Jesus Christ. And though thou shouldst feed us with bread of adversity, and water of affliction, yet let not our teachers be removed; nor bring us under a famine of the word of the Lord: nor give us over to the formality of a lifeless profession; under all the means of grace, to send leanness into our soul. Though thou permit the floods and storms to arise and increase, yet fortify us so by thy grace, that we may not be moved by any of those afflictions, so as to turn the blessed advantage of suffering for thee into an occasion of falling from thee.

O help us, Lord, to rid our hands and our hearts of all the accursed things that provoke thy wrath and indignation against us. And let us wisely consider of thy doings, and know the time of our visitation, and hearken to the calls, and take the warnings, and improve the means and mercies vouchsafed to us, while we have them; and follow the conduct of thy good providence, and comply with all thy gracious methods used to reclaim us from our sins, and to reform our lives, and save our souls; that all may not be in vain to us, but at least effect the purpose of thy saving mercy upon us; to deliver us from the evils to come, and to set us safe into the hands of Jesus Christ, our blessed Lord and Saviour. *Amen.*

FAST DAY.—EVENING. *Jay*

O God, thou hast established thy throne in the heavens, and thy kingdom ruleth over all. We prostrate ourselves before thee, deeply impressed with a sense of the vastness of thy agency and dominion. Thou changest the times and the seasons; thou removest kings, and settest up kings. Empires rise and fall, and fade and flourish, at thy bidding; and all nations are in thy hand, but as clay in the hand of the potter.

But none of thy dispensations are arbitrary. Whatever thou doest, is done because, O Father, it seemeth good in thy sight; and thy judgment is always according to truth. Thou art holy in all thy ways, and rightcous in all thy works—and thou art good; even in wrath thou rememberest mercy, and dost not afflict willingly, nor grieve the children of men.

Therefore it is, that we have been this day humbling ourselves in thy presence.

For we acknowledge that we have been deeply guilty. Thou hast nourished and brought up children, but we have rebelled against thee. The ox knoweth his owner, and the ass his master's crib; but we have not known, we have not considered. Thou hast given us our corn, and wine, and oil, and multiplied our silver and gold; and we have prepared them for Baal. Because of swearing, the land has mourned. Pride has compassed us about as a chain. Discontent has rebelled against thine appointments. How has the love of money, which is the root of all evil, abounded among us. How have thy Sabbaths been profaned, and thy ordinances disregarded. How has the gospel been undervalued, neglected, despised.

And all our transgressions have been more aggravated than those of any other people, because thou hast favoured us unspeakably more than all the families of the earth.

Therefore thou couldest easily and justly have destroyed us; but thou hast not stirred up all thy wrath. In all that has come upon us, for our evil deeds, thou hast punished us less than our iniquities deserve. Yet thou hast testified thy displeasure, and visited us with thy judgments; so that when we looked for light and peace, we have seen darkness and trouble.

O, let us not be inattentive to the design of thy dealings, or insensible under thy rebukes. O, let it not be said of us as it was of the Jews, the harp, and the viol, and the tabret, and pipe, and wine are in their feasts, but they regard not the word of the Lord, neither consider the operation of his hand. Thou hast stricken them, but they have not grieved; thou hast consumed them, but they have refused to receive correction; they have made their faces harder than the rock; they have refused to return.

In the way of thy judgments, O Lord, may we wait for thee. Thou hast said, Is any afflicted? let him pray. Call upon me in the day of trouble, and I will deliver thee, and thou shalt glorify me. Fulfil the word unto thy servants, upon which thou hast caused us to hope. And O, let not the calamity be removed only, but above all, sanctified; let it appear that we have heard the rod, and him that appointeth it: and be able to say, It is good for us that we have been afflicted.

For which purpose, bless, we beseech thee, the word of thy grace, which has been spoken; and grant that the professed humiliation of the day may be real — for thou lookest to the heart. And let it also be universal; may it extend from the highest to the lowest; may it pervade every part of our country; may it enter every church, and every family — let none of us lose sight of ourselves in the public calamity. May each individual retire and ask, What have I done, and what wilt thou have me to do? And though other lords have had dominion over us, henceforth, by thee only, may we make mention of thy name.

Regard the government under which we live, and the magistracy of the land — may all be wise in counsel, exemplary in conduct, and faithful to their trust.

And thus may we be reformed, and not destroyed. Thus may we be a holy, that we may be a happy people, whose God is the Lord. Return, O Lord, how long? and let it repent thee concerning thy servants. O, satisfy us early with thy mercy, that we may rejoice and be glad all our days. Make us glad according to the days wherein thou hast afflicted us, and the years wherein we have seen evil. Let thy work appear unto thy servants; and thy glory unto their children. And let the beauty of the Lord our God be upon us; and establish thou the work of our hands upon us; yea, the work of our hands, establish thou it.

And to the Father, the Son, and the Holy Spirit, be rendered the kingdom, power, and glory, for ever and ever. *Amen.*

IN TIME OF PESTILENCE. *Jenks.*

O Lord God, the giver of our health, it is only of thy mercy that we have so much health continued, after the manner in which we have lived. And O how just were it with thee, utterly to take away that health from us which we have so greatly abused to a forgetfulness of thee, and wantonness against thee! How justly mightest thou smite us with the most sharp and noisome diseases, which our nature most abhorreth: to hurry us out of the land of the living, and put a sorrowful end to our wretched days! Our flesh trembles for fear of thee, and we are afraid of thy judgments, lest thou shouldst strike into us the arrows of the Almighty, for the poison thereof to drink up our spirits: lest thou shouldst give unto death a command to come in at our doors, and sweep us away with the besom of destruction. But, O thou Hope of Israel, the Saviour thereof in time of trouble! regard not our ill deserts; but remember thy own tender mercies, and gracious promises; and take pity on us, and turn away this plague from us. Put a stop to the raging pestilence, and say to the destroying angel, It is enough. That so we may not be afraid of the terror by night, nor for the arrow that flies by day; nor for the pestilence that walketh in darkness; nor for the destruction that wasteth at noon day: but with calmness in our minds, and gladness in our hearts, may serve thee faithfully and cheerfully all our days: and devote our spared lives, which we have begged at thy hands, and our health and every mercy, to thy honour and glory; through the strength and the righteousness of thy dear Son, our most compassionate and prevailing Mediator, Jesus Christ. *Amen.*

FOR RAIN. *Jenks.*

We confess, O Lord, that we have so greatly abused the comforts of thy good creatures, that thou mightest justly withdraw them from us, and make the heavens over us as brass, and the rain of our land dust, and the land itself to mourn, and all that grows upon it to wither. But O thou Father of mercies, who in judgment rememberest mercy, consult not now our merits, but thy own mercies, how to use us. Thou that hast the bottles and treasures of heaven at thy command, be pleased now to open the windows of heaven, and cause the rain to come down in its season; making grass to grow for the cattle, and herbs and fruits of the earth for the service of men. And however thou art pleased to deal with us, O suppress all our repinings at any of thy dealings: and let them all amend and better us: and make us a people prepared to receive the mercies which we want, and wait and beg for, at thy gracious hands, upon the account of Jesus Christ. *Amen.*

FOR FAIR WEATHER. *Jenks*

LORD, if thou shouldst turn a fruitful land into barrenness, for the wickedness of them that dwell therein; yet righteous wert thou, and just would be thy judgments; and we must not open our mouths to reply against God; but bear the indignation of the Lord which our sins have so much deserved; when our iniquities have turned away the blessings, and withholden the good things from us. But, O Father of mercies, spare us, and forgive us, for thy own mercy's sake; and put a stop to the calamity that threatens destruction to the works of thy hands; that the rain which is thy blessing may not be turned into a curse; nor descend from heaven to corrupt and spoil the fruits of the earth. O cause the overflowing showers to cease, which damp the joy of the harvest, and endanger the blasting of our blessings. And as thou hast given us plenty, and caused our land to yield its increase, so give us, we pray thee, a seasonable time to gather in the fruits which thy bounty has provided for us; that in the use of them we may joyfully and cheerfully serve thee; and not consume them upon our lusts, but live to thy glory, as we do upon thy bounty. And when thy judgments are in the land, O that we, who inhabit it, may learn righteousness! nor let our anxieties be so great for our bodies as for our souls; that however we fare here, it may go well with us forever. O let us not labour for the meat that perisheth, but for that which endures to everlasting life; which everlasting provision for our unchangeable condition, above all we beg at thy hands, O Lord God our heavenly Father, for the sake of Jesus Christ our only Saviour. *Amen.*

UNDER FAMILY AFFLICTION. *Cotterill.*

MORNING OR EVENING.

ALMIGHTY GOD, the Father of mercies and the God of all consolation, our only help in time of need, we flee unto thee for succour in this season of tribulation and distress. Out of the deeps we call unto thee, O Lord. Lord, hear our voice. O let thine ears consider well the voice of our complaint.

We acknowledge, O God, that for our iniquities we are visited, and for our sins are we troubled. We are born to trouble as the sparks fly upward, because we have been transgressors from the womb. And if thou shouldst be extreme to mark what we have done amiss, our present sorrows would only be the beginning of sorrows which should know no end. Wherefore should a living man complain? a man for the punishment of his sins?

But thou art gracious and merciful; full of compassion and of great goodness. Thou hast not dealt with us according to our sins: nor rewarded us according to our iniquities. Blessed be thy name, that thou not only hast opened unto us a way of escape from the wrath to come, but hast mercifully ordained the sufferings of the present life to work together for good to them that love thee.

Thy wise providence ordereth all things both in heaven and earth. Not a sparrow falleth to the ground without thy knowledge and appointment; and the very hairs of our head are all numbered. Thou assurest us, that thou dost not willingly afflict or grieve the children of men, but for their profit, that they may be partakers of thy holiness. Whom thou lovest, thou chastenest; and scourgest every son whom thou receivest.

Thou afflictest us to humble us, and to prove us, and to know what is in our hearts; and whether we will love thee, and keep thy commandments, or no.

Give us grace therefore to consider, in this day of our adversity, wherefore thou contendest with us, and art wroth. Let us not despise thy chastening, nor faint when we are rebuked of thee; nor be weary of thy correction. But let us be still, and know that thou art God. In patience enable us to possess our souls. Grant that our tribulation may work patience; and patience experience; and experience hope; and our hope, let it not make ashamed; but let thy love be shed abroad in our hearts, through the Holy Ghost given unto us. Let us not cast away our confidence, which hath great recompense of reward. Though troubled on every side, let us not be distressed; though perplexed, let us not be in despair; though cast down, let us not be destroyed. And be pleased to cause our light afflictions, which are but for a moment, to work out for us a far more exceeding and eternal weight of glory; while we look not at the things that are seen, but at the things which are not seen: for the things which are seen, are temporal; but the things which are not seen, are eternal. Though no chastening for the present seemeth to be joyous, but grievous; yet afterwards let it yield the peaceable fruit of righteousness unto us who are now exercised thereby. Grant that we may find it good to be afflicted, and see that thou, of very faithfulness, hast caused us to be in trouble.

And whenever it may please thee to deliver us out of the miseries of this sinful world, of thy gracious goodness receive us into that blessed kingdom, where thou shalt wipe away all tears from our eyes; where there shall be no more death, neither sorrow nor crying, neither shall there be any more pain; for the former things are passed away.

We beseech thee, also, O Lord, to have compassion on our brethren and companions in tribulation.

Have mercy upon all sick persons; and make all their bed in their sickness. Eternal God, be thou their refuge, and place underneath them thy everlasting arms. Look graciously upon them, O Lord; and the more the outward man decayeth, strengthen them, we beseech thee, so much the more continually, by thy grace and Holy Spirit, in the inward man. Give them unfeigned repentance for all the sins of their past lives, and steadfast faith in thy Son Jesus; that their sins may be done away by thy mercy, and their pardon sealed in heaven, before they go hence, and are no more seen.

We commend into thy hands, as into the hands of a faithful Creator and most merciful Saviour, the souls of those who are departing this life; most humbly beseeching thee, that they may be precious in thy sight. Wash them, we pray thee, in the blood of that spotless Lamb which was slain to take away the sins of the world; that whatsoever defilements they may have contracted in the midst of this miserable and wicked world, through the lusts of the flesh or the wiles of Satan, being purged and done away, they may be presented pure and without spot before thee.

Be gracious also unto thy people who are weeping, and refuse to be comforted for the loss of beloved friends and relations, departed this life in thy faith and fear. Let them not be sorry, as men without hope, for those that sleep in thee: but comfort them with the joyful expectation, that they shall see each other again at the resurrection in the last day.

May it please thee, likewise, to defend and provide

for the fatherless children and widows, and all that are desolate and oppressed.

And, since many are the afflictions of the righteous, Lord, remember them and all their troubles. Regard those who are in heaviness through manifold temptations. Graciously hear us, that those evils which the craft and subtilty of the devil or man worketh against them be brought to nought, and by the providence of thy goodness they may be dispersed; that they, thy servants, being hurt by no persecutions, may evermore give thanks unto thee, and glorify thy name.

Finally, we commend to thy fatherly goodness all those who are any ways afflicted or distressed in mind, body, or estate. That it may please thee to comfort and relieve them, according to their several necessities; giving them patience under their sufferings, and a happy issue out of all their afflictions.

[Hear us, especially, in behalf of thy servant, for whom we desire especially to pray. We look up unto thee, O thou compassionate Saviour, who wast thyself a man of sorrows, and acquainted with grief. O thou, who didst weep at the tomb of Lazarus, and art still touched with the feeling of our infirmities, pitifully behold the sorrows of our hearts, and graciously look upon our afflictions. O thou, who, of old, didst cure all manner of sickness, and all manner of disease among the people, be gracious unto us. Let not this sickness be unto death; but for the glory of thy name. Speak the word only, and thy servant shall be healed. Have mercy upon *him*, O Lord, have mercy upon *him;* and not on *him* only, but on us also, lest we should have sorrow upon sorrow. If it be possible, let this cup pass away from us, without our drinking all its bitterness; but, if not, thy will be done. Only be pleased to sanctify this thy fatherly correction to *him*, that the sense of *his* weakness may add strength to *his* faith, and efficacy to *his* repentance; that, if it should be thy good pleasure to restore *him* to *his* former health, *he* may lead the residue of *his* life in thy fear and to thy glory; or else give *him* grace so to take thy visitation, that after this painful life is ended, *he* may dwell with thee in life everlasting.]

And this we beg for Jesus Christ's sake.

Our Father, &c.

FOR A SICK CHILD. *Jenks*

O God of the spirits of all flesh, the only giver and preserver of life in every living soul; the smallest, as well as the greatest, are thy work and thy care; and neither without the compass of thy providence, nor below the notice and regard of our heavenly Father, who, though so great above all, yet despiseth not any! O Lord, let thy thoughts be full of pity and tender mercy to this poor sick child, for whose afflictions we are now concerned; and send *him* that relief and comfort from above, which none of us are able to give. Either lighten the load, or increase the strength to bear it; and deal gently and graciously with *him*, O Lord, beyond what we are worthy to ask at thy hands, even for thy own goodness and mercy's sake. Spare *him*, O Father of mercies, and grant *him* ease and release from his trouble; yea, make haste to deliver *him*, we beseech thee; and in submission to thy will we beg the recovery of *his* health, and the continuance of *his* life, to be spent in thy fear, and to thy praise, that *he* may continue to do thee service, and bring thee glory in *his* days upon earth. But, forasmuch as children themselves, who are shapen in iniquity, and conceived in sin, are therefore subject to death, if thou art pleased, Lord, to take *him* away so early, O let it be in mercy, and prepare *him* then so for thyself, that it may be to *him* the greatest gain to die; that *he* may not only be delivered from the miseries and dangers of this world, and that to come, but may be made ripe and ready for heaven and eternal glory, through the infinite satisfaction and merits of thy beloved Son, our compassionate Saviour, who so kindly embraced blessed young children, and ever lives at thy right hand to intercede for young and old; the only prevailing advocate for us all. And to thy mercy in him, O most gracious God, we commend this afflicted child, beseeching thee to deal well by *him*, and be good and kind to *him;* and out of the riches of thy grace, provide and do abundantly, as thou knowest best for *him*, in life and death, and for evermore. *Amen.*

UNDER DANGEROUS SICKNESS. *Jenks.*

O Lord God Almighty, in whom we all ever live, and move and are; we acknowledge it to be of thy mercy we are not consumed, because thy compassions fail not. If thou hadst, long before this time, cut us off in our sins, and shut us up under final despair of thy mercies, yet righteous hadst thou been, O Lord; and justly mightest thou now refuse to hear us calling upon thee in our prayers, as we so often have refused to hear thee calling upon us by the motions of thy Holy Spirit. But thou art God, and not man; and thy thoughts are not as our thoughts, nor thy ways as our ways; but as the heavens are higher than the earth, so are thy thoughts and thy ways above ours. Thou art our refuge and strength, a present help in time of trouble.

And now we come to thee, O Lord our God, in behalf of this thy servant, that lies here in a low and distressed state, under thy chastening hand. Look down, we beseech thee, mercifully upon *him;* and be thou gracious and favourable to *him*, according to the multitude of thy tender mercies in Christ Jesus. If thou but speak the word, *he* will be healed.—And in submission to thy most wise and good disposal of all things, we would beg this mercy at thy hands, that thou wouldst be pleased to rebuke *his* distemper, to remove thy stroke, and cause the bitter cup which thou hast given *him* to pass away from *him*, and make *him* a way to escape out of the affliction that is upon *him;* and to this end, that thou wouldst direct to the means proper for *his* help, and command a blessing upon them to promote *his* recovery. Spare him, good Lord, and restore *him*, if it be thy will, that *he* may have a long time to work out *his* salvation, and be more useful in *his* place, and do more good in *his* generation; or however thou shalt be pleased to deal with *him* as to the concerns of *his* body, which we pray may be in a way of gentleness and tender mercy; yet Lord, let *his* soul be ever precious in thy sight; and may this sickness be for the health of that immortal better part, to promote *his* salvation everlasting.

O give *him* a right discerning of the things belonging to *his* peace, before they be hid from *his* eyes; show *him* what *he* is to do; enable *him* for the doing of it, that *he* may have the sound peace with God, through Jesus Christ; give *him* the true repentance towards God, and the right faith in the only Saviour of the world; wash and cleanse *his* soul with the blood of thy Son, and the graces of thy Spirit, that it may be delivered from all defilements it has contracted in this present evil world, and be found safe and happy in the hour of death, and in the great day of our Lord Jesus Christ. Fit *him*, O Lord, for living or dying, whatever in thy wise and righteous providence thou hast designed for *him*, that it may be unto *him* Christ to live, and gain to die, that in all *he* may find cause to glorify thy name, still experiencing thy gracious goodness to him in the Son of thy love: if thou shalt please yet to release *him* from *his* bed of languishing, to live longer upon earth, O that *he* may live to thee in thy fear, and to thy praise, and do thee better service, and bring thee greater glory; or, if thou hast determined that this sickness shall be a sickness unto death, and this visitation *his* last visitation, prepare *him*, O merciful God, by thy grace, for thy blessed self; and grant *him* a safe and comfortable passage out of this wretched life, to an infinitely better, through the merits and mediation of thy beloved Son, our only Saviour, Jesus Christ. *Amen.*

FOR ONE DYING. *Jenks*

O THE hope of Israel, and the Saviour thereof in time of trouble! when all other hope and help fail, it is not in vain to seek unto thee for succour, who canst bring back from the mouth of the grave, and where thou art not pleased any further to prolong the temporal life, yet canst deliver from eternal death, and bring safe to the blessed life everlasting. We beg the recovery of thy servant, O Lord, now that *he* seems to us going the way of all flesh, and launching forth into his everlasting condition.

O Lord our God, leave *him* not, nor forsake *him*, but support and assist *him* now in *his* sorest extremities, in *his* last agonies, when *he* is to conflict with the king of terrors; let *him* find the most sweet and seasonable aids from the Almighty God of *his* salvation, and take *him* not out of this life till thou hast fitted *him* for a better. O thou ever living God, stand by *him* in the dying hour, and secure *him* in thy hands from the enemies of *his* soul, and finish all that is wanting of the work of thy grace upon *his* heart. Freely and fully pardon and deliver *him* from all *his* sins, and fit *him* to appear with comfort and rejoicing in thy blessed presence. O make *his* departure easy, and full of peace and hope; carry *him* safe through the dark passage, upon which *he* is entering, and let *him* find it the gate of glory, and a door opened into the everlasting kingdom and joy of *his* Lord. Into thy hands we commend *his* spirit. O thou Father of mercies, be merciful to *him*, and receive *his* departing soul; and when *he* is numbered among the dead, let *him* also be numbered among the redeemed and blessed of the Lord, for his sake who himself died for sinners, and rose again, and lives, and is alive for ever more, and has the keys of death and hell. To thy mercy, in that blest Saviour of the world, O most merciful Father, we now humbly commend *him*; beseeching thee to be all in all to *him*, and infinitely better than we are worthy or able to ask for *him;* and let *him* be thine in life and death, and for ever more, through the all-sufficient mediation of thy dear Son, our prevailing Advocate and Redeemer, Jesus Christ. *Amen.*

THE EVENING AFTER A FUNERAL. *Jay*

O THOU Father of mercies, and God of all comfort. Thou hast often invited us to thyself, by kindness; and it manifests our depravity, that we think of thee so little in the hour of ease and prosperity. But we are now before thee in affliction and distress. Yet we rejoice to know, that thou art a very present, and an all-sufficient help in trouble.

Thou takest away, and who can hinder thee, or say unto thee, What doest thou? Thou hast a right to do what thou wilt with thine own. Thou art a Sovereign, and the reasons of thy conduct are often far above, out of our sight; but thy work is perfect, thy ways are judgment. All thy dispensations are wise, and righteous, and kind—kind, even when they seem to be severe.

May we hear thy voice in thy rod, as well as in thy word: and gathering, from the corrections with which we are exercised, the peaceable fruit of righteousness, be able to acknowledge, with all our suffering brethren before us, It is good for me that I have been afflicted.

It is not the Scripture only that reminds us of our living in a dying world, but all observation and experience. Man is continually going to his long home, and the mourners daily go about the streets. And we are all accomplishing, as an hireling, our day; and in a little time our neighbours, friends, and relations, will seek us —and we shall not be. Our days are swifter than a weaver's shuttle, and are spent without hope. Thou hast made our days as an hand's breadth, and our age is as nothing before thee: verily, every man at his best state is altogether vanity. For our days are not only few, but full of evil. Anxieties perplex us; dangers alarm us; infirmities oppress us; disappointments afflict us; losses impoverish us — we are consumed by thine anger, and by thy wrath are we troubled. O, shut not thy merciful ear to our prayers; but spare us, O Lord, most holy; O God, most mighty; O holy and most merciful Saviour; thou most worthy Judge eternal, suffer us not, at our last hour, for any bitter pains of death, to fall from thee.

We acknowledge, O God, with shame and sorrow, that the state of degradation and mortality in which we groan, was not our original condition. Thou madest man upright; but he sought out many inventions. By one man, sin entered into the world, and death by sin; and so death hath passed upon all men, for that all have sinned.

And we bless thee that this is not our final state. By the discoveries of faith, we see new heavens, and a new earth, wherein dwelleth righteousness. We see the spirits of just men made perfect. We see our vile bodies changed, and fashioned like the Saviour's own glorious body; and man, the sinner, raised above the angels, who never sinned.

We bless thee for this purpose of grace, formed before the world began, and accomplished in the fulness of time, by the Son of thy love, who hath abolished death, and brought life and immortality to light by the gospel; and who among the ravages of the grave, says, I am the resurrection, and the life; he that believeth in me, though he were dead, yet shall he live; and whosoever liveth and believeth in me shall never die.

So teach us to number our days that we may apply our hearts unto wisdom — that wisdom which will lead us to prefer the soul to the body, and eternity to time; that wisdom which will lead us to secure an interest in a better world, before we are removed from this.

O let not the trifles of time induce us to neglect the one thing needful. While each of us is compelled to say, I know thou wilt bring me to death, and to the house appointed for all living, may we be enabled also to say, I know whom I have believed, and am persuaded that he is able to keep that which I have committed to him against that day.

And, O, let not the solemnities we have this day witnessed, be ever forgotten; for often, our most serious impressions have worn off, and our goodness has been as the morning cloud and early dew that soon passeth away.

Thou hast permitted death to invade our circle, and hast turned our dwelling into a house of mourning. May we find that it is better to be in the house of mourning than in the house of mirth. By the sadness of the countenance may the heart be made better, more serious to reflect, and more softened to take impression.

With the feelings of the creature, may we blend the views and the hopes of the Christian. May we remember that thou hast bereaved us, resuming what was lent us for a season, but never ceased to be thine own. May we, therefore, be dumb, and open not our mouth, because thou hast done it; or if we speak, may it be to acknowledge and pray—I know, O Lord, that thy judgments are right, and that thou in faithfulness hast afflicted me; let thy loving-kindness be for my comfort, according to thy word unto thy servant.

Now, unto Him that is able to keep us from falling, and to present us faultless before the presence of his glory, with exceeding joy, to the only wise God our Saviour, be glory and majesty, dominion and power, both now and ever. *Amen.*

MOURNING FOR THE LOSS OF RELATIVES AND FRIENDS. *Smith.*

O THOU who art our great Creator, and, by thy good hand upon us, still our merciful Preserver, may we at this time approach the footstool of thy throne, with thy divine forgiveness and gracious acceptance. To whom can we go but unto thee, who art the Father of lights, and fountain of every blessing; and who hast said in thy Holy Scriptures, "Call upon me in the day of trouble, I will deliver thee, and thou shalt glorify me." In this word, O God, we find it written, "It is better to go to the house of mourning than to go to the house of feasting; for that is the end of all men, and the living will lay it to his heart."

By thy wise and special appointment, our deceased [brother] [sister] is cut off from the land of the living; [his] [her] body returns to the earth out of which it was taken, and [his] [her] spirit hath returned to thee, who gave it. We would desire upon this, as upon every occasion, to submit ourselves to God; saying, "The will of the Lord be done." Be pleased to grant, O thou Author of every good and perfect gift! grant, that we may be enabled to say, with the same resignation as thy servant of old: "The Lord gave, and the Lord hath taken away; blessed be the name of the Lord."

Blessed Jesus, thou hast said, "I am the resurrection and the life. He that believeth in me, though he were dead, yet shall he live." And, O heavenly Father, help us all to extend our views forward to that day when thou shalt redeem *our* souls from the power of the grave; and when these bodies, which are sown in corruption, dishonour, and weakness, shall be raised in incorruption, glory, and power; and that saying be brought to pass — "Death is swallowed up in victory." In this important and interesting day, when the world shall be judged in righteousness by that Immanuel whom God the Father hath appointed, may we, and all our deceased friends, appear clothed with his righteousness, and hear him pronounce, "Come, ye blessed of my Father, inherit the kingdom prepared for you from the foundation of the world."

Knowing these things, may we be enabled, O God, to comfort ourselves together, and edify one another, ever reckoning that "the sufferings of this present time are not worthy to be compared to the glory that shall be revealed in us;" nay, assured "that our light affliction, which is but for a moment, worketh for us a far more exceeding and eternal weight of glory."

Now, unto Him that is able to keep us from falling, and to present us faultless before the presence of his glory with exceeding joy, to the only wise God, our Saviour, be glory and majesty, dominion and power, both now and ever. *Amen.*

SPRING. *Jay.*

Thou art the fountain of life; in thee we live, move, and have our being—and the prerogative of that being is, that we are able to contemplate thy perfections, and rise from thy works—to thyself.

Thou sendest forth thy Spirit, and renewest the face of the earth; and, from apparent death, all nature starts into reanimated vigour and joy. In what myriads of productions art thou displaying afresh, the wonders of thy wisdom, power, and goodness—the whole earth is full of thy riches.

While we partake of the general sympathy and delight, may we join with all thy works to praise thee. And, O thou God of all grace, bless us with the renewing of the Holy Ghost, in all the powers of our souls. May old things pass away, and all become new in Christ; may the beauty of the Lord be upon us; and the joy of the Lord be our strength.

May the young remember, that they are now in the spring of life; and that *this* spring, once gone, returns no more. May they, therefore, eagerly seize, and zealously improve, the short, but all-important season, for the cultivation of their minds, the formation of their habits, the correction of their tempers, their preparation for future usefulness, and their gaining that good part which shall not be taken away from them.

W

SUMMER. *Jay.*

We hail Thee in the varying aspects of the year, and bless Thee for all their appropriate influences and advantages. O, let us not view them and enjoy them as men only, but as Christians also; and ever connect with them, the better blessings of thy grace.

How wise, and useful, and necessary, are these intermingled rains and sunbeams—may Jesus, as the Sun of Righteousness, arise upon us, with healing under his wings; and may he come down as rain upon the mown grass, and as showers that water the earth.

When we walk by the cooling brook—may we think of that river, the streams whereof make glad the city of God.

When we retire from the scorching warmth of the day, into the inviting shade—may we be thankful for a rest at noon, a shelter from the heat, the shadow of a great rock in a weary land.

May thy servants behold the moral fields, that are already white unto harvest, and be all anxiety to save the multitudes that are perishing for lack of knowledge.

The harvest truly is great, but the labourers are few; we therefore pray, that Thou wilt send forth labourers into thy harvest.

He that gathereth in summer, is a wise son; he that sleepeth in harvest, is a son that causeth shame. Now is our accepted time, now is our day of salvation. O, let us not waste our precious privileges, and in a dying hour exclaim—The harvest is past, the summer is ended, and we are not saved.

AUTUMN. *Jay.*

How fleeting as well as varying are the seasons of the year! How insensibly have the months of spring and summer vanished! and nature has no sooner attained its maturities, than we behold its declension and decay

The fields are now shorn of their produce; the beauties of the garden are withered; the woods are changing their verdure, and the trees shedding their foliage—we also never continue in one state. Many of our connexions and comforts have already dropped away from us; and the remaining are holden by a slender tenure; while we ourselves do all fade as a leaf, and in a little time, our places will know us no more.

Blessed be the God and Father of our Lord Jesus Christ, for the announcement of an inheritance that fadeth not away. O for a hope full of immortality! for a possession of that good part, which shall not be taken away from us!

WINTER. *Jay.*

O Thou God of nature and providence; manifold are thy works; in wisdom thou hast made them all; and all are full of thy goodness. The welfare of thy creatures requires the severity of winter as well as the pleasures of spring. We adore thy hand in all. Thou givest snow like wool: thou scatterest the hoar frost like ashes. Thou sendest abroad thine ice like morsels: who can stand before thy cold?

But we bless thee, for a house to shelter us; for raiment to cover us; for fuel to warm us; and all the accommodations, that render life, even at this inclement season, not only tolerable, but full of comfort.

May we be grateful; and may we be pitiful. May we reflect on the condition of those who are the victims of every kind of privation and distress—and waste nothing; hoard nothing; but hasten to be ministers of mercy, and the disciples of Him, who went abroad, doing good.

O, let the rich, *now*, deservedly prize their wealth, and use it as the instrument of usefulness. May they be willing to communicate, and ready to distribute; and enjoy the blessing of him that is ready to perish; and make the widow's heart to sing for joy.

FOR A DAY OF THANKSGIVING. *Jay*

MORNING.

God, thou art very great—thou art clothed with honour and majesty; thou coverest thyself with light as with a garment; thou walkest upon the wings of the wind. When we reflect on the glory of thy majesty, we are filled with wonder at the vastness of thy condescension. For thou condescendest even to behold things that are in heaven. What, then, is man, that thou art mindful of him, or the son of man, that thou visitest him?

We rejoice, that we are under the governance of a Being, who is not only Almighty, but perfectly righteous, and wise, and good; that all things, in our world, are appointed and arranged by thy paternal agency; that thy providence numbers the very hairs of our head, and that a sparrow falleth not to the ground, without our heavenly Father.

Hitherto hath the Lord helped us. We bless thee for personal mercies. If we are called, it is by thy word. If we are renewed, it is by thy Spirit. If we are justified, it is freely by thy grace through the redemption that is in Christ Jesus. It is in thee we live, and move, and have our being. Thy goodness has been always near us, to hear our complaints, to soothe our sorrow, and to command deliverance for us. And numberless are the instances of loving-kindness, that now, from ignorance, or inattention, elude our notice; the discovery of which will awaken our songs, when we mingle with those who dwell in thy house above, and are still praising thee.

We thank thee for relative benefits; for blessings on our families, blessings on our churches, and blessings on our country. We confess that we are not worthy of the least of all thy mercies, and of all the truth which thou hast showed unto thy servants. Sins of every kind and of every degree, have reigned among us; have spread through all ranks and orders; and continued, notwithstanding all warnings and corrections; and if thou hadst dealt with us after our sins, or rewarded us according to our iniquities, we should long ago have had no name or place among the nations of the globe.

But to the Lord, our God, belong mercies and forgivenesses, though we have rebelled against him. All thy dispensations towards us have said, with a tenderness that ought to penetrate our hearts—How shall I give thee up! Our privileges, never properly improved, and forfeited times without number, have been continued. We still behold our Sabbaths, and our ears still hear the joyful sound. Our constitution, liberties, and laws, have not been subverted, or impaired. Thou hast given us rains, and fruitful seasons; thou hast filled us with the finest of the wheat; our garners have been affording all manner of store. Thou hast spread thy wing, and sheltered us from the pestilence that walketh in darkness, and the destruction that wasteth at noonday. Civil discord has not raged in our land; our shores have not been invaded; we have not heard the confused noise of warriors, nor seen garments rolled in blood — it has not come nigh us. Our enemies have often threatened to swallow us up, but the Lord has been on our side, and they have not prevailed against us. We are this day called upon to acknowledge thy goodness in (———). [Here let the particular causes for thankfulness be expressed.]

May we never convert our blessings into instruments of provocation, by making them the means of nourishing pride and presumption, wantonness and intemperance; and compel thee to complain—Do ye thus requite the Lord, O foolish people, and unwise? Is not he thy Father, that hath bought thee? Hath he not made thee, and established thee?

For this purpose meet with us in thy house; and may the goings of our God and our King be seen in the sanctuary. Be with the preacher, and with the hearers; and let the words of his mouth, and the meditation of their hearts be acceptable in thy sight, O Lord, our strength, and our Redeemer. May public instruction awaken the ardour of our feelings: May our gratitude not only be lively, but practical and permanent. And by all thy mercies, may we present our bodies a living sacrifice, holy and acceptable unto thee, which is our reasonable service.

Bless the Lord, ye his angels, that excel in strength, that do his commandments, hearkening unto the voice of his word. Bless ye the Lord, all ye his hosts; ye ministers of his, that do his pleasure. Bless the Lord, all his works, in all places of his dominion; bless the Lord, O my soul. *Amen.*

FOR A DAY OF THANKSGIVING. *Jay.*

EVENING.

O God, thou art good, and doest good. Thou art good to all, and thy tender mercies are over all thy works.

We have thought of thy loving-kindness this day, in the midst of thy temple; and are again surrounding this domestic altar, to exclaim, O that men would praise the Lord for his goodness, and for his wonderful works to the children of men.

We lament to think, that a world so filled with thy bounty, should be so alienated from thy service and glory. We mourn over the vileness of our ingratitude, and abhor ourselves, repenting in dust and ashes.

O thou God of all grace, make us more thankful. In order that we may be more thankful, may we be more humble; impress us with a deep sense of our unworthiness, arising from the depravity of our nature, and countless instances of unimproved advantages, omitted duties, and violated commands. May we compare our condition with our desert, and with the far less indulged circumstances of others. May we never be inattentive to any of thy interpositions on our behalf: but be wise, and observe these things, that we may understand the loving-kindness of the Lord.

How many blessings, temporal and spiritual, public and private, hast thou conferred upon us! Thy mercies have been new every morning, and every moment.

Our afflictions have been few and alleviated, often short in their continuance, and always founded in a regard to our profit. Thy secret has been upon our tabernacle; and we have known thee in thy palaces for a refuge. The lines have indeed fallen to us in pleasant places, yea, we have a goodly heritage. Thou hast not dealt so with any people. It is a good land, which the Lord our God has given us — a land distinguished by knowledge; dignified as the abode of civil and religious freedom; endeared by the patriot's zeal, and the ashes of our forefathers; a land the Lord careth for, and upon which his eye has been from the beginning even to the end of the year.

Thou hast been a wall of fire round about us, by thy providential protection, and the glory in the midst of us, by the gospel of our salvation, the ordinances of religion, and the presence of thy Holy Spirit.

What shall we render unto the Lord for all his benefits towards us? Because thou hast been our help, therefore under the shadow of thy wing may we rejoice. Because thou hast heard our voice and our supplication, therefore may we call upon thee as long as we live; and in every future difficulty and distress, make thee our refuge and our portion.

Enable us to bless thee at all times; may thy praise continually be in our mouth; and may we show forth thy praise, not only with our lips, but in our lives.

Being delivered from the peril and calamity of (———) with which we have been exercised, may we serve thee without fear, in holiness and righteousness all the days of our lives.

We dare not trust our own hearts. We have often resembled thy people of old, who, in the hour of deliverance and indulgence, sang thy praise, and said — All that the Lord commandeth us, will we do; but soon forgot his works and the wonders which he had showed them. Keep these things for ever in the imagination of our hearts; and not only draw us, but bind us to thyself, with the cords of love, and the bonds of a man.

And with all our calls to gratitude and joy, may we remember that we have also reason for sorrow and humiliation. O give us that repentance which is unto life. Reform, as well as indulge us; and pardon, as well as spare. Let not our prosperity destroy us, nor our table become a snare. Let us not, by our perverse returns, provoke thee to visit us with heavier afflictions; and turn the rod into a scorpion. May our ways please the Lord, that we may hope for continuance of thy favour, and know that all things shall work together for our good.

Do good in thy good pleasure unto Zion. Build thou the walls of Jerusalem. And as the churches have rest, may they walk in the fear of the Lord, and in the comforts of the Holy Ghost, and be multiplied.

Preside over our national councils; impart wisdom to those who conduct our public affairs; and may all the various classes in the community pursue that righteousness which exalteth a nation, and forsake that sin which is a reproach to any people.

Regard the services in which we have been engaged with the thousands of our Israel; accept of the poor and imperfect thanksgivings we have offered; and let thy word which has been dispensed, in aid of the devotion of the day, accomplish all the good pleasure of thy goodness — through Jesus the Lord, our righteousness and strength; and in whose words we address thee, as

Our Father, which art in heaven, hallowed be thy name; thy kingdom come; thy will be done on earth as it is in heaven; give us this day our daily bread, and forgive us our trespasses as we forgive those that trespass against us; and lead us not into temptation; but deliver us from evil; for thine is the kingdom, the power, and the glory, for ever. *Amen.*

FOR RAIN AFTER A DROUGHT. *Jay*

THOU hast never left thyself without witness, but hast been continually doing good, even for the unthankful and unworthy, in giving them rain from heaven, and fruitful seasons, and filling their hearts with joy and gladness. We acknowledge that the heavens over us might have been brass, and the earth under us iron. We have justly deserved the calamity; and thy power, without a miracle, could have inflicted it; but though thou hast tried our patience and awakened our fears, thou hast not forgotten to be gracious. We praise thee for sending us the seasonable and plentiful rain, by which thou hast refreshed and revived the drooping fields, so that the earth promises to yield her increase.

FOR FAIR WEATHER AFTER RAIN. *Jay*

O GOD, thou art good and doest good. Thou hast again surpassed our deserts, and been better to us than our fears. Thou hast caused the clear shining after rain; so that in the meadows the hay appeareth; and in the fields, thou art preparing of thy goodness for the poor. Thou preservest man and beast. May we feel our entire dependence upon thee; and by prayer and praise, give thee the glory that is due unto thy holy name.

FOR A GOOD HARVEST. *Jay.*

AGAIN thou hast crowned the year with thy goodness. The grain might have perished in the earth, or have failed of maturity, for want of the showers, and of the sunshine; but thou hast pleased to bless the springing thereof; and we saw first the blade, then the ear, and after that the full corn in the ear. We hailed the valleys standing thick with corn, and heard the little hills rejoicing on every side. In due time the mower filled his hands, and the binder of sheaves his bosom; and the appointed weeks of harvest have been afforded us to gather in the precious produce. O that men would praise the Lord for his goodness, and for his wonderful works to the children of men! For he satisfieth the longing soul, and filleth the hungry soul with goodness.

We have again witnessed thy faithfulness and truth in the promise—while the earth remaineth, seed time and harvest, and cold and heat, and summer and winter, and day and night, shall not cease—may we learn to trust thee in all thy engagements.

And make us thankful, that, as we have no famine of bread, so we have no famine of hearing the word of the Lord. With regard to the soul, as well as to the body, Thou fillest us with the finest of the wheat.

FOR THE RESTORATION OF PLENTY. *Jenks.*

O GOD, the Fountain of all goodness! thou didst threaten with famine to destroy the blessings of the earth, which we have so wickedly abused; but remembering thy own tender mercies, and not our ill deserts, hast raised a new and plentiful supply for us. And now thou crownest the year with thy goodness, and thy paths drop fatness. Thou hast loaded the earth with the fruits of thy bounty, and sent abundance of all good things for the service and comfort of man. O make us more sensible of the obligation which thy love has laid upon us. And as thou fillest us with thy good things, so fill our hearts with thy love and grace, to use every gift aright to thy glory; that in the use and strength of what we are continually receiving from thee, we may devote ourselves to live unto thee, and to serve thee with gladness and rejoicing for all thy rich mercy to us in Jesus Christ.

FOR A SAFE RETURN FROM A JOURNEY.   *Jay.*

As the Keeper of Israel, Thou hast been with us, not only in the house, but by the way. We might have been injured by wicked and unreasonable men. We might have been left groaning under the pain of bruised or fractured limbs. Our lives might have been spilt, like water on the ground, which cannot be gathered up again; and the first tidings that reached our friends, might have plunged them into anguish.

Thy mercy, too, in our absence, has been upon our tabernacle, and secured it from all evil—O that it may be a tabernacle of the righteous; and be ever filled, not only with the voice of rejoicing, but of praise.

And be with us in all the future journey of life; guide us by thy counsel, uphold us by thy power; and supply all our wants, till we come to our Father's house in peace.

FOR RECOVERY FROM SICKNESS.   *Jay.*

ALL our times are in thy hand. All diseases come at thy call, and go at thy bidding. Thou redeemest our life from destruction, and crownest us with loving-kindness and tender mercies. We bless thee, that thou hast heard our prayer, and commanded deliverance for our friend and thy servant, who has been under thine afflicting hand. He (*or she*) was brought low, but thou hast helped *him:* thou hast chastened *him* sore, but not delivered *him* over unto death. May *he* not only live, but declare the works of the Lord.

As thou hast delivered *his* eyes from tears, *his* feet from falling, and *his* soul from death, may *he* daily inquire, What shall I render unto the Lord for all his benefits towards me? and resolve to offer unto thee, the sacrifices of thanksgiving, and to call upon the name of the Lord.

And may we ever remember, that a recovery is only

a reprieve; that the sentence which dooms us to the dust is only suspended; and, that at most, when a few years are come, we shall go the way whence we shall not return. May we therefore secure the one thing needful, and live with eternity in view.

PRAYERS AT TABLE.

BEFORE MEAT. *Jay.*

ALMIGHTY GOD! the eyes of all wait upon thee, and thou givest them their meat in due season. Bless, we beseech thee, the provisions of thine earthly bounty, which are now before us; and let them nourish and strengthen our frail bodies, that we may the better serve thee, through Jesus Christ. *Amen.*

OR THUS:

Bountiful Giver of every good and perfect gift! thou art never weary of supplying our returning wants—grant, we pray thee, that the food of which we are about to partake, may contribute to the comfort and support of our bodies,—and enable us to engage with more zeal in thy service; which we ask for Jesus Christ's sake. *Amen.*

OR THUS:

Let thy blessing, Almighty God, descend on this portion of thy bounty, and on us, thy unworthy servants, through Jesus Christ our Lord.

OR THUS:

Almighty God, we beseech thee to pardon our sins: to bless the refreshment now before us, to our use, and us to thy service, through Jesus Christ.

OR THUS:

Father of lights, from whom cometh down every good and perfect gift, enable us to receive these fruits of thy bounty with humility and gratitude, and give us grace, that, whether we eat or drink, or whatever we do, we may do all to thy glory, and be accepted through the great Redeemer.

OR THUS:

Bounteous God, we acknowledge our dependence on thee, and our unworthiness of thy benefits. We pray thee to forgive our sins: to bless us in the reception of this food, and enable us to improve the strength we may derive from it to thy glory, for Christ's sake.

OR THUS:

Sanctify, O Lord, we beseech thee, these thy productions to our use, and us to thy service, through Jesus Christ, our Lord. *Amen.*

AFTER MEAT. *Jay.*

WE thank thee, O God, our heavenly Father! for the innumerable good gifts of thy providence. Especially do we thank thee for the rich provision thou hast made for our souls—accept our grateful acknowledgments for the food we have now received; and enable us to prove our sincerity by the holiness and obedience of our lives, for the sake of our Lord and Saviour, Jesus Christ. *Amen.*

OR THUS:

What shall we render to thee, O God, for all thy benefits? Every day of our lives we are receiving fresh tokens of thy favour. O, let thy goodness lead us to repentance. And if we can do no more than express our gratitude, help us to do that in the sincerity of our souls, and thine shall be the glory, for ever, through Jesus Christ. *Amen.*

OR THUS:

Accept, heavenly Father, our humble thanks for this, and for all thy blessings through Jesus Christ.

OR THUS:

We thank thee, our heavenly Father, for the rich provision thou hast made for our temporal and eternal welfare; especially for the food we have now received. May thy goodness lead us to repentance, and thy grace prepare us for heavenly entertainments, through Jesus Christ our Lord.

OR THUS:

We praise thee, O Lord, for the provisions of thy providence and grace, and in particular for this renewed token of thy favour. May we feel our increased obligations to be thine, and be fitted at length, to eat bread in thy heavenly kingdom, through our Lord Jesus Christ.

OR THUS:

We bless thee, O Lord, for this kind refreshment. Be pleased to continue thy favours, and feed us with the bread of life. Supply the wants of the needy, and enable us, while we live on thy bounty, to live to thy glory, for Christ's sake. *Amen.*

OR THUS:

Blessed and praised be thy holy name, O Lord, for this and all thy other blessings, bestowed upon us through Jesus Christ our Lord. *Amen.*

HYMNS

(CHIEFLY ADAPTED TO)

FAMILY WORSHIP.

HYMNS

CHIEFLY ADAPTED TO FAMILY WORSHIP.

MORNING HYMNS.

1 HYMN. C. M.

1 ONCE more, my soul, the rising day
   Salutes thy waking eyes;
 Once more, my voice, thy tribute pay
   To Him who rules the skies.

2 Night unto night his name repeats;
   The day renews the sound,
 Wide as the heavens on which he sits
   To turn the seasons round.

3 'Tis he supports my mortal frame;
   My tongue shall speak his praise;
 My sins would rouse his wrath to flame,
   And yet his wrath delays.

4 How many wretched souls have fled
   Since the last setting sun!
 And yet thou lengthenest out my thread,
   And yet my moments run.

5 Great God, let all my hours be thine,
   While I enjoy the light;
 Then shall my sun in smiles decline,
   And bring a peaceful night.

2   HYMN. L. M.

1 AWAKE, my soul, and with the sun
Thy daily stage of duty run;
Shake off dull sloth—and joyful rise
To pay thy morning sacrifice.

2 Glory to Thee, who safe hast kept,
And hast refreshed me while I slept:
Grant, Lord, when I from death shall wake,
I may of endless life partake.

3 Direct, control, suggest, this day,
All I design, or do, or say;
That all my powers, with all their might,
In thy sole glory may unite.

3   HYMN. L. M.

1 GOD of the morning, at thy voice
    The cheerful sun makes haste to rise,
And like a giant doth rejoice
    To run his journey through the skies.

2 O! like the sun, may I fulfil
    Th' appointed duties of the day;
With ready mind, and active will,
    March on, and keep my heav'nly way.

3 Lord, thy commands are clean and pure,
    Enlightening our beclouded eyes;
Thy threatenings just—thy promise sure
    Thy gospel makes the simple wise.

4 Give me thy counsels for my guide,
    And then receive me to thy bliss;
All my desires and hopes beside
    Are faint and cold compared with this.

4   HYMN. C. M.

1 GOD of my life, my morning song
    To thee I cheerful raise:
Thy acts of love 'tis good to sing,
    And pleasant 'tis to praise.

2 Preserv'd by thy almighty arm,
   I pass'd the shades of night,
Serene, and safe from every harm,
   To see the morning light.

3 While numbers spent the night in sighs,
   And restless pains and woes,
In gentle sleep I closed my eyes,
   And rose from sweet repose.

4 Oh, let the same almighty care
   Through all this day attend:
From every danger—every snare,
   My heedless steps defend.

5 Smile on my minutes as they roll,
   And guide my future days;
And let thy goodness fill my soul
   With gratitude and praise.

5   HYMN. 7's.

1 THOU that dost my life prolong,
Kindly aid my morning song;
Thankful from my couch I rise,
To the God that rules the skies.

2 Thou didst hear my ev'ning cry;
Thy preserving hand was nigh;
Peaceful slumbers thou hast shed,
Grateful to my weary head.

3 Thou hast kept me through the night
'Twas thy hand restor'd the light:
Lord, thy mercies still are new,
Plenteous as the morning dew.

4 Still my feet are prone to stray;
Oh! preserve me through the day
Dangers every where abound;
Sins and snares beset me round.

5 Gently, with the dawning ray,
On my soul thy beams display;
Sweeter than the smiling morn,
Let thy cheering light return.

6   HYMN. L. M.

God our Defence.

1 O LORD, how many are my foes,
    In this weak state of flesh and blood
My peace they daily discompose,
    But my defence and hope is God.

2 Tired with the burdens of the day,
    To thee I raised an ev'ning cry;
Thou heardst, when I began to pray,
    And thine almighty help was nigh.

3 Supported by thine heav'nly aid,
    I laid me down and slept secure;
Not death should make my heart afraid,
    Though I should wake and rise no more

4 But God sustain'd me all the night;
    Salvation doth to God belong:
He raised my head to see the light,
    And makes his praise my morning song

7   HYMN. C. M.

1 THOU, gracious Lord, art my defence:
    On thee my hopes rely;
Thou art my glory, and shalt yet
    Lift up my head on high.

2 Guarded by him, I laid me down,
    My sweet repose to take;
For I through him securely sleep,
    Through him in safety wake.

Salvation to the Lord belongs;
    He only can defend;
His blessing he extends to all
    That on his power depend.

8   HYMN. S. M.

Prayer for spiritual light.

1 WE lift our hearts to Thee,
    Thou Day-Star from on high;
The sun itself is but thy shade,
    Yet cheers both earth and sky

2 O, let thy rising beams
    Dispel the shades of night;
And let the glories of thy love
    Come like the morning light.

3 How beauteous nature now!
    How dark and sad before!
With joy we view the pleasing change
    And nature's God adore.

4 May we this life improve
    To mourn for errors past;
And live this short revolving day
    As if it were our last.

9   HYMN. S. M.

Morning Meditation.

1 AWAKE, my drowsy soul,
    These airy visions chase;
Awake, my active pow'rs renew'd,
    To run the heav'nly race.

2 See how the rising sun
    Pursues his shining way;
And wide proclaims his Maker's praise,
    With ev'ry bright'ning ray!

3 Thus would my rising soul
    Her heav'nly Parent sing;
And to her great Original
    Her humble tribute bring.

4 Serene, I laid me down
    Beneath his guardian care;
I slept, and I awoke, and found
    My kind preserver near.

12*

5 Dear Saviour, to thy cross,
  I bring my sacrifice;
Ting'd with thy blood, it shall ascend
  With fragrance to the skies.

10   HYMN. C. M.

God's goodness renewed every Morning and Evening.

1 GREAT GOD! my early vows to thee
  With gratitude I'll bring,
And at the rosy dawn of day
  Thy lofty praises sing.

2 Thou, round the heav'nly arch dost draw
  A dark and sable veil,
And all the beauties of the world,
  From mortal eyes conceal.

3 Again the sky with golden beams
  Thy skilful hands adorn,
And paint, with cheerful splendour gay
  The fair ascending morn.

4 And as the gloomy night returns,
  Or smiling day renews,
Thy constant goodness still my soul
  With benefits pursues.

5 For this will I my vows to thee
  With ev'ning incense bring;
And at the rosy dawn of day
  Thy lofty praises sing.

11   HYMN. 8. 8. 6.

1 ONCE more my eyes behold the day,
And to my God, my soul would pay
  Its tributary lays:
O may the life preserv'd by thee
With all its powers and blessings be
  Devoted to thy praise.

2 Beneath the shadow of thy wings,
  (Israel's great Keeper, King of kings)
    My weary head found rest:
  No dire alarms, or racking pains,
  Devouring flames or galling chains,
    Disturb my peaceful breast.

3 How many, since I laid me down,
  Have launch'd into a world unknown,
    To meet a dreadful doom;
  While some on watery billows toss'd,
  Or wand'ring on an unknown coast,
    Have sigh'd in vain for home.

4 But, I am spar'd to see thy face,
  A monument of saving grace,
    And live to praise thy name
  Still be thou near, my gracious Lord,
  To keep and guide;—and by thy word
    Peace to my soul proclaim.

5 Let me enjoy thy presence here,
  In every storm my heart to cheer,
    Till thou shalt bid me rise,
  Where sin and sorrow never come,
  Till at my blest eternal home,
    I wake in sweet surprise.

12   HYMN. C. M.

The fear of God.   Prov. xxiii. 17.

1 THRICE happy souls, who, born of heav'n
    While yet they sojourn here,
  Humbly begin their days with God,
    And spend them in his fear.

2 So may our eyes with holy zeal
    Prevent the dawning day;
  And turn the sacred pages o'er,
    And praise thy name and pray.

3 Midst hourly cares may love present
    Its incense to thy throne;
  And, while the world our hands employs,
    Our hearts be thine alone.

4 At night we lean our weary heads
    On thy paternal breast;
  And, safely folded in thine arms,
    Resign our powers to rest.

5 In solid, pure delights, like these,
    Let all my days be past;
  Nor shall I then impatient wish,
    Nor shall I fear the last.

13   HYMN. 7's.

1 NOW the shades of night are gone;
  Now the morning light is come;
  Lord, may I be thine to-day—
  Drive the shades of sin away.

2 Fill my soul with heav'nly light,
  Banish doubt, and cleanse my sight;
  In thy service, Lord, to-day,
  Help me labour, help me pray

3 Keep my haughty passions bound—
  Save me from my foes around;
  Going out and coming in,
  Keep me safe from ev'ry sin.

4 When my work of life is past
  Oh! receive me then at last!
  Night of sin will be no more,
  When I reach the heav'nly shore.

EVENING HYMNS.

14   L. M.

1 THUS far the Lord has led me on;
   Thus far his power prolongs my days,
And ev'ry ev'ning shall make known
   Some fresh memorial of his grace.

2 Much of my time has run to waste,
   And I, perhaps, am near my home;
But he forgives my follies past;
   He give me strength for days to come.

3 I lay my body down to sleep;
   Peace is the pillow for my head;
While well appointed angels keep
   Their watchful stations round my bed.

4 Thus, when the night of death shall come
   My flesh shall rest beneath the ground
And wait thy voice to break my tomb,
   With sweet salvation in the sound.

15   HYMN. C. M.

1 DREAD Sov'reign, let my ev'ning song
   Like holy incense rise;
Assist the offering of my tongue
   To reach the lofty skies.

2 Through all the dangers of the day
   Thy hand was still my guard;
And still to drive my wants away,
   Thy mercy stood prepar'd.

3 Perpetual blessings from above
   Encompass me around,
But oh! how few returns of love
   Hath my Redeemer found!

4 What have I done for him who died
   To save my guilty soul?
Alas! my sins are multiplied,
   Fast as my minutes roll!

Y

5 Yet, with this guilty heart of mine,
   Lord, to thy cross I flee,
And to thy grace my soul resign,
   To be renew'd by thee.

16   HYMN. S. M.

1 GREAT God, to thee my ev'ning song
   With humble gratitude I raise;
Oh let thy mercy tune my tongue,
   And fill my heart with lively praise.

2 My days unclouded as they pass,
   And ev'ry gently rolling hour,
Are monuments of wond'rous grace,
   And witness to thy love and pow'r.

3 Thy love and pow'r, celestial guard,
   Preserve me from surrounding harm:
Can danger reach me while the Lord
   Extends his kind, protecting arm?

4 Let this blest hope my eyelids close
   With sleep refresh my feeble frame:
Safe in thy care may I repose,
   And wake with praises to thy name.

17   HYMN. L. M.

1 GLORY to thee, my God, this night,
For all the blessings of the light;
Keep me, O keep me, King of kings,
Beneath thine own almighty wings.

2 Forgive me, Lord, for thy dear Son,
The ill that I this day have done;
That with the world, myself, and thee,
I, ere I sleep, at peace may be.

3 Let my blest guardian, while I sleep,
His watchful station near me keep,
My heart with love celestial fill,
And guard me from th' approach of ill.

4 Teach me to live, that I may dread
   The grave as little as my bed;
   Teach me to die, that so I may
   Rise glorious at the awful day.

18   HYMN. C. M.

1 INDULGENT God, whose bounteous care
    O'er all thy works is shown,
  Oh let my grateful praise and prayer
    Arise before thy throne.

2 What mercies has this day bestow'd!
    How largely hast thou blest!
  My cup with plenty overflow'd,
    With cheerfulness my breast.

3 Now may soft slumber close my eyes,
    From pain and sickness free;
  And let my waking thoughts arise,
    To meditate on thee.

4 Thus bless each future day and night,
    Till life's vain scene is o'er;
  And then to realms of endless light,
    Oh let my spirit soar.

19   HYMN. S. M.

1 ANOTHER day is past,
    The hours forever fled;
  And time is bearing me away,
    To mingle with the dead.

2 My mind in perfect peace
    My Father's care shall keep
  I yield to gentle slumber now
    For thou canst never sleep.

3 How blessed, Lord, are they
    On thee securely stayed!
  Nor shall they be in life alarmed
    Nor be in death dismayed.

20   HYMN. S. M.

1 THE day is past and gone,
   The ev'ning shades appear;
Oh, may I ever keep in mind,
   The night of death draws near.

2 Lord, keep me safe this night,
   Secure from all my fears;
May angels guard me while I sleep,
   Till morning light appears.

3 And when I early rise,
   To view th' unwearied sun,
May I set out to win the prize,
   And after glory run.

4 Lord, when my days are past,
   And I from time remove,
O may I in thy bosom rest,
   The bosom of thy love.

21   HYMN. 7's.

1 SOFTLY now the light of day
Fades upon my sight away;
Free from care—from labour free,
Lord, I would commune with thee.

2 Soon, for me, the light of day
Shall for ever pass away:
Then from sin and sorrow free,
Take me, Lord, to dwell with thee!

22   HYMN. C. M.

Evening Prayer and Praise.

1 INDULGENT Father, by whose care,
   I've pass'd another day,
Let me this night thy mercy share;
   O, teach me how to pray.

2 Show me my sins, that I may mourn
  My guilt before thy face;
Direct me, Lord, to Christ alone,
  And save me by thy grace.

3 Let each returning night declare
  The tokens of thy love;
And ev'ry hour thy grace prepare
  My soul for joys above.

4 And when on earth I close mine eyes,
  To sleep in death's embrace,
Let me to heav'n and glory rise,
  To see thy smiling face.

23 HYMN. 7's.
Evening Communion with God.

1 NOW, from labour and from care,
Twilight shades have set me free;
In the work of praise and pray'r
Lord, I would converse with thee.
O, behold me from above,
Fill me with a Saviour's love.

2 Sin and sorrow, guilt and wo,
Wither all my earthly joys;
Nought can charm me here below,
But my Saviour's melting voice,
Lord, forgive; thy grace restore;
Make me thine for evermore.

3 For the blessings of this day,
For the mercies of this hour,
For the gospel's cheering ray,
For the Spirit's quick'ning pow'r,
Grateful notes to thee I raise;
O, accept my song of praise.

24 HYMN. C. M.

1 IN mercy, Lord, remember me,
  Through all the hours of night,
And grant to me most graciously
  The safeguard of thy might.

2 With cheerful heart I close my eyes
  Since thou wilt not remove;
 Oh, in the morning let me rise,
  Rejoicing in thy love!

3 Or, if this night should prove the last,
  And end my transient days;
 Lord, take me to thy promis'd rest,
  Where I may sing thy praise.

25   HYMN. C. M.

1 FATHER, by saints on earth ador'd,
  By saints beyond the skies,
 Accept, through Jesus Christ, our Lord,
  Our ev'ning sacrifice.

2 If kept to-day from wilful sin,
  We magnify thy grace;
 Thou hast our kind preserver been,
  And thine be all the praise.

3 We live to testify the grace,
  Which sure salvation brings;
 And sink to night in thine embrace,
  And rest beneath thy wings.

4 But whether, Lord, we wake or sleep,
  The charge of love divine,
 We trust thy providence to keep
  Our souls for ever thine.

26   HYMN. 8's & 7's.

1 SAVIOUR, breathe an ev'ning blessing,
  Ere repose our spirits seal:
 Sin and want we come confessing,
  Thou canst save, and thou canst heal.
 Though destruction walk around us,
  Though the arrow past us fly,
 Angel-guards from thee surround us,
  We are safe, if thou art nigh

2 Though the night be dark and dreary,
    Darkness cannot hide from thee;
Thou art He, who, never weary,
    Watchest where thy people be;
Should swift death this night o'ertake us,
    And our couch become our tomb;
May the morn in heav'n awake us,
    Clad in light and deathless bloom!

27   HYMN. C. M.

1 O LORD, another day is flown,
    And we, a lonely band,
Are met once more before thy throne,
    To bless thy fost'ring hand.

2 And wilt thou bend a list'ning ear
    To praises low as ours?
Thou wilt! for thou dost love to hear
    The song which meekness pours.

3 And, Jesus, thou thy smiles wilt deign,
    As we before thee pray;
For thou didst bless the infant train,
    And we are less than they.

4 Oh, let thy grace perform its part,
    And let contentions cease;
And shed abroad in ev'ry heart
    Thine everlasting peace.

28   HYMN. L. M.

1 THE night shall hear me raise my song,
And in her silent courts my tongue
Shall pour the solitary lay,
For all the mercies of the day.

2 Nor will my God disdain to hear
The sigh I breathe—the fervent pray'r:
When, sinking to oblivious rest,
I seek the pillow of his breast.

3 And when the blushing morn shall **rise,**
  To tinge with gold the eastern skies;
  With strength renew'd, my thankful lay
  Shall hail the new-born beams of day.

29   HYMN. 8's.

1 INSPIRER and Hearer of pray'r,
    Before whom a sinner may bend;
  My all to thy covenant care,
    I sleeping or waking commend.

2 If thou art my shield and my sun,
    The night is no darkness to me;
  And fast as my moments roll on,
    They bring me but nearer to thee.

3 From evil secure, and its dread,
    I rest, if my Saviour be nigh;
  And songs his kind presence indeed,
    Shall in the night season supply.

4 He smiles, and my comforts abound;
    His grace as the dew shall descend·
  And walls of salvation surround
    The soul he delights to defend.

30   HYMN. C. M.

1 IN all my vast concerns with thee,
    In vain my soul would try
  To shun thy presence, Lord, or flee
    The notice of thine eye.

2 Thy all-surrounding sight surveys
    My rising and my rest,
  My public walks, my private ways,
    And secrets of my breast.

3 My thoughts lie open to the Lord,
    Before they're form'd within;
  And ere my lips pronounce the word,
    He knows the sense I mean.

Oh wondrous knowledge, deep and high,
  Where can a creature hide?
Within thy circling arms I lie,
  Enclos'd on ev'ry side.

5 So let thy grace surround me still,
  And like a bulwark prove,
To guard my soul from ev'ry ill,
  Secur'd by sov'reign love.

31 HYMN. C. M.

1 LORD, thou wilt hear me when I pray
  I am for ever thine:
I fear before thee all the day,
  Nor would I dare to sin.

2 And while I rest my weary head,
  From cares and business free,
'Tis sweet conversing on my bed
  With my own heart and thee.

3 I pay this evening sacrifice;
  And when my work is done,
Great God, my faith and hope relies
  Upon thy grace alone.

4 Thus with my thoughts compos'd to peace,
  I'll give mine eyes to sleep;
Thy hand in safety keeps my days,
  And will my slumbers keep.

32 HYMN. C. M.

Saturday Night.

1 BEGONE, my worldly cares, away,
  Nor dare to tempt my sight;
Let me begin th' ensuing day,
  Before I end this night.

2 Yes, let the work of pray'r and praise
  Employ my heart and tongue;
Begin, my soul;—thy Sabbath days
  Can never be too long.

3 Let the past mercies of the week
  Excite a grateful frame;
Nor let my tongue refuse to speak
  Some good of Jesus' name.

4 On wings of expectation borne,
  My hopes to heav'n ascend;
I long to welcome in the morn.,
  With thee the day to spend.

33   HYMN. 7's.

Sabbath-Eve.   Heb. iv. 9.

1 SAFELY through another week,
God has brought us on our way;
Let us now a blessing seek,
On th' approaching Sabbath day.
Day of all the week the best,
Emblem of eternal rest.

2 When the morn shall bid us rise,
May we feel thy presence near!
May thy glory meet our eyes
When we in thy house appear
There afford us, Lord, a taste
Of our everlasting feast.

MORNING OR EVENING HYMNS.

34   HYMN. L. M.

A Hymn for Morning or Evening.

1 MY God, how endless is thy love!
  Thy gifts are ev'ry evening new;
And morning mercies from above
  Gently distil like early dew.

2 Thou spread'st the curtains of the night,
  Great Guardian of my sleeping hours;
Thy sov'reign word restores the light,
  And quickens all my drowsy pow'rs

3 I yield my pow'rs to thy command,
  To thee I consecrate my days;
Perpetual blessings from thine hand
  Demand perpetual songs of praise.

35   HYMN. C. M.

1 HOSANNA, with a cheerful sound,
  To God's upholding hand;
Ten thousand snares attend us round,
  And yet secure we stand.

2 That was a most amazing pow'r
  That rais'd us with a word;
And ev'ry day, and ev'ry hour,
  We lean upon the Lord.

3 The rising morn cannot assure
  That we shall end the day;
For death stands ready at the door
  To hurry us away.

4 Our life is forfeited by sin
  To God's avenging law;
We own thy grace, immortal King,
  In ev'ry breath we draw.

5 God is our sun—whose daily light
  Our joy and safety brings;
Our feeble frame lies safe at night,
  Beneath his shady wings.

36   HYMN. C. M.

1 ON thee, each morning, O my God,
  My waking thoughts attend;
In thee are founded all my hopes,
  In thee my wishes end.

2 My soul, in pleasing wonder lost,
  Thy boundless love surveys;
And, fir'd with grateful zeal, prepares
  A sacrifice of praise.

3 When ev'ning slumbers press my eyes,
    With his protection blest,
  In peace and safety I commit
    My weary limbs to rest.

4 My spirit, in his hand secure,
    Fears no approaching ill;
  For, whether waking or asleep,
    Thou, Lord, art with me still.

37   HYMN. L. M.
Daily Devotion.

1 MY God, accept my early vows,
  Like morning incense in thine house;
  And let my nightly worship rise,
  Sweet as the ev'ning sacrifice.

2 Watch o'er my lips, and guard them, Lord,
  From every rash and heedless word;
  Nor let my feet incline to tread
  The guilty path where sinners lead.

3 Oh, may the righteous, when I stray,
  Smite, and reprove my wandering way;
  Their gentle words, like ointment shed,
  Shall never bruise, but cheer my head.

4 When I behold them press'd with grief,
  I'll cry to heaven for their relief;
  And by my warm petitions, prove
  How much I prize their faithful love.

FAMILY RELIGION.

38   HYMN. L. M.

1 FATHER of all, thy care we bless,
  Which crowns our families with peace;
  From thee they spring, and by thy hand
  They have been, and are still sustain'd.

2 To God, most worthy to be prais'd,
   Be our domestic altars rais'd;
   Who, Lord of heav'n, scorns not to dwell
   With saints in their obscurest cell.

3 To thee may each united house,
   Morning and night present its vows;
   Our servants there, and rising race,
   Be taught thy precepts, and thy grace.

4 Oh, may each future age proclaim
   The honours of thy glorious name;
   While, pleas'd and thankful, we remove
   To join the family above.

39   HYMN. S. M.

Love to the Brethren.

1 Blest be the tie that binds
     Our hearts in Christian love;
   The fellowship of kindred minds
     Is like to that above.

2 Before our Father's throne
     We pour our ardent prayers;
   Our fears, our hopes, our aims, are one,
     Our comforts and our cares.

3 We share our mutual woes;
     Our mutual burdens bear;
   And often for each other flows
     The sympathizing tear.

4 When we asunder part,
     It gives us inward pain;
   But we shall still be join'd in heart,
     And hope to meet again.

5 This glorious hope revives
     Our courage by the way;
   While each in expectation lives,
     And longs to see the day.

6 From sorrow, toil, and pain,
   And sin, we shall be free;
And perfect love and friendship reign
   Through all eternity.

40   HYMN. C. M.

1 LO! what an entertaining sight,
   Those friendly brethren prove,
Whose cheerful hearts in bands unite,
   Of harmony and love!

2 Where streams of bliss, from Christ the spring,
   Descend to every soul;
And heav'nly peace, with balmy wing,
   Shades and bedews the whole.

3 'Tis pleasant as the morning dews,
   That fall on Zion's hill;
Where God his mildest glory shows,
   And makes his grace distil.

41   HYMN. S. M.

1 BLEST are the sons of peace,
   Whose hearts and hopes are one;
Whose kind designs to serve and please
   Through all their actions run.

2 Blest is the pious house,
   Where zeal and friendship meet;
Their songs of praise—their mingled vows,
   Make their communion sweet.

3 From those celestial springs
   Such streams of pleasure flow,
As no increase of riches brings,
   Nor honours can bestow.

4 Thus on the heavenly hills
   The saints are blest above;
Where joy, like morning dew, distils,
   And all the air is love.

42 HYMN. S. P. M.

1 HOW pleasant 'tis to see
  Kindred and friends agree,
Each in his proper station move;
  And each fulfil his part,
  With sympathizing heart,
In all the cares of life and love!

2 Like fruitful showers of rain,
  That water all the plain,
Descending from the neighbouring hills,
  Such streams of pleasure roll
  Through every friendly soul,
Where love, like heav'nly dew, distils.

43 HYMN. C. M.

1 AUTHOR of good—to thee we turn:
    Thine ever wakeful eye
  Alone can all our wants discern—
    Thy hand alone supply.

2 O let thy love within us dwell,
    Thy fear our footsteps guide;
  That love shall vainer loves expel,
    That fear all fears beside.

3 And O, by error's force subdued,
    Since oft, by stubborn will,
  We blindly shun the latent good,
    And grasp the specious ill;—

4 Not what we wish—but what we **want**,
    Let mercy still supply:
  The good we ask not, Father, grant—
    The ill we ask—deny.

44 HYMN. C. M.

1 GOD of our fathers! by whose hand
    Thy people still are blest,
  Be with us through our pilgrimage,
    Conduct us to our rest.

2 Through each perplexing path of life
   Our wandering footsteps guide;
Give us each day our daily bread,
   And raiment fit provide

3 O spread thy sheltering wings around,
   Till all our wanderings cease,
And at our Father's lov'd abode
   Our souls arrive in peace.

4 Such blessings from thy gracious hand
   Our humble prayers implore;
And thou, the Lord, shalt be our God
   And portion evermore.

45   HYMN. L. M.

1 THOU, Lord, through every changing scene
Hast to the saints a refuge been;
Through every age, eternal God!
Their pleasing home—their safe abode.

2 In thee our fathers sought their rest,
And were with thy protection blest;
Behold their sons, a feeble race!
We come to fill our fathers' place.

3 Through all the thorny paths we tread,
Ere we are number'd with the dead,
When friends desert—and foes invade,
Be thou our all-sufficient aid!

4 And when this pilgrimage is o'er,
And we must dwell on earth no more,
To thee, great God! may we ascend,
And find an everlasting friend.

5 To thee our infant race we'll leave;
Them may their fathers' God receive;
That voices, yet unform'd, may raise
Succeeding hymns of humble praise.

SABBATH MORNING.

46   HYMN. C. M.

1 LORD, in the morning thou shalt hear
    My voice ascending high;
  To thee will I direct my prayer,
    To thee lift up mine eye;—

2 Up to the hills, where Christ is gone
    To plead for all his saints,
  Presenting at his Father's throne
    Our songs and our complaints.

3 Thou art a God, before whose sight
    The wicked shall not stand;
  Sinners shall ne'er be thy delight,
    Nor dwell at thy right hand.

4 But to thy house will I resort,
    To taste thy mercies there;
  I will frequent thine holy court,
    And worship in thy fear.

5 Oh may thy Spirit guide my feet
    In ways of righteousness,
  Make every path of duty straight,
    And plain before my face.

47   HYMN. C. M.

1 SOON as the morning rays appear,
    I'll lift my eyes above;
  My voice shall reach thy listening ear,
    And supplicate thy love.

2 Within thy house my voice shall rise
    Before thy mercy-seat;
  There will I fix my steadfast eyes,
    And worship at thy feet.

3 In righteousness thy strength display,
    And my protection be;
  Teach me to know that only way,
    Which leads to heav'n and thee.

48   HYMN. S. M.
The Sabbath welcomed.

1 WELCOME, sweet day of rest,
   That saw the Lord arise;
Welcome to this reviving breast,
   And these rejoicing eyes!

2 Jesus himself comes near,
   And feasts his saints to-day;
Here we may sit, and see him here,
   And love, and praise, and pray.

3 One day, amid the place
   Where God my Saviour's been,
Is sweeter than ten thousand days
   Of pleasure and of sin.

4 My willing soul would stay
   In such a frame as this,
Till call'd to rise, and soar away,
   To everlasting bliss.

49   HYMN. P. M.

1 WELCOME, delightful morn!
   Thou day of sacred rest;
I hail thy kind return;
   Lord make these moments blest.
From low delights, and mortal toys,
I soar to reach immortal joys.

2 Now may the King descend,
   And fill his throne of grace;
Thy sceptre, Lord, extend,
   While saints address thy face;
Let sinners feel thy quick'ning word,
And learn to know and fear the Lord.

3 Descend, celestial Dove,
   With all thy quick'ning powers;
Disclose a Saviour's love,
   And bless these sacred hours:
Then shall my soul new life obtain,
Nor Sabbaths be indulg'd in vain.

50   HYMN. 10's.

1 HAIL, happy day! thou day of holy rest!
What heav'nly peace and transport fill our breast,
When Christ, the God of grace, in love descends,
And kindly holds communion with his friends.

2 Let earth and all its vanities be gone,
Move from my sight, and leave my soul alone;
Its flattering, fading glories I despise,
And to immortal beauties turn my eyes.

3 Fain would I mount and penetrate the skies,
And on my Saviour's glories fix my eyes:
Oh! meet my rising soul, thou God of love,
And waft it to the blissful realms above!

51   HYMN. L. M.

The Rest of the Sabbath.

1 ANOTHER six days' work is done;
Another Sabbath is begun:
Return, my soul—enjoy thy rest;
Improve the day thy God has blest.

2 Oh that our thoughts and thanks may rise,
As grateful incense, to the skies;
And draw from heav'n that sweet repose,
Which none but he that feels it knows.

3 This heav'nly calm within the breast!
The dearest pledge of glorious rest,
Which for the church of God remains—
The end of cares—the end of pains.

4 With joy, great God, thy works we view
In varied scenes, both old and new;
With praise, we think on mercies past
With hope, we future pleasures taste.

5 In holy duties let the day—
In holy pleasures, pass away;
How sweet, a Sabbath thus to spend
In hope of one that ne'er shall end.

52 HYMN. C. M.

1 COME, let us join with sweet accord
   In hymns around the throne;
This is the day our rising Lord
   Hath made, and call'd his own.

2 This is the day which God hath blest,
   The brightest of the seven;
Type of that everlasting rest,
   The saints enjoy in heav'n.

53 HYMN. L. M.

Preparation for the Duties of the Sabbath implored

1 COME, dearest Lord, and bless this day;
Come, bear our thoughts from earth away;
Now, let our noblest passions rise
With ardour to their native skies.

2 Come, Holy Spirit, all divine,
With rays of light upon us shine;
And let our waiting souls be blest
On this sweet day of sacred rest.

3 Then, when our Sabbaths here are o'er,
And we arrive on Canaan's shore,
With all the ransom'd, we shall spend
A Sabbath which shall never end.

54 HYMN. L. M.

1 GREAT God! this sacred day of thine
   Demands the soul's collected pow'rs;
With joy we now to thee resign
   These solemn, consecrated hours:
Oh may our souls adoring own
The grace that calls us to thy throne.

2 All-seeing God! thy piercing eye
   Can every secret thought explore;
May worldly cares our bosoms fly,
   And where thou art intrude no more
Oh may thy grace our spirits move,
And fix our minds on things above!

3 Thy Spirit's powerful aid impart,
And bid thy word, with life divine,
Engage the ear—and warm the heart;
Then shall the day indeed be thine:
Our souls shall then adoring own
The grace that calls us to thy throne.

55   HYMN. P. M.

Resurrection of Christ celebrated.

1 AWAKE, our drowsy souls,
And burst the slothful band;
The wonders of this day
Our noblest songs demand:
Auspicious morn! thy blissful rays
Bright seraphs hail, in songs of praise.

2 At thy approaching dawn,
Reluctant death resign'd
The glorious Prince of life,
In dark domains confin'd
Th' angelic host around him bends,
And midst their shouts the God ascends.

3 All hail, triumphant Lord!
Heav'n with hosannas rings;
While earth, in humbler strains,
Thy praise responsive sings!
"Worthy art thou, who once wast slain
Through endless years to live and reign."

4 Gird on, great God, thy sword,
Ascend thy conqu'ring car,
While justice, truth, and love,
Maintain the glorious war:
Victorious, thou thy foes shalt tread,
And sin and hell in triumph lead.

56   HYMN. C. M.

1 AGAIN the Lord of life and light
Awakes the kindling ray;
Dispels the darkness of the night,
And pours increasi   y.

13*

2 Oh! what a night was that, which wrapt
    A sinful world in gloom!
Oh! what a Sun, which broke, this day,
    Triumphant from the tomb!

3 This day be grateful homage paid,
    And loud hosannas sung;
Let gladness dwell in ev'ry heart,
    And praise on ev'ry tongue.

4 Ten thousand thousand lips shall join
    To hail this welcome morn,
Which scatters blessings from its wings
    To nations yet unborn.

57   HYMN. 7's.

1 SAFELY through another week,
    God has brought us on our way;
Let us now a blessing seek,
    Waiting in his courts to-day:
Day of all the week the best,
Emblem of eternal rest.

2 While we seek supplies of grace,
    Through the dear Redeemer's name;
Show thy reconciling face—
    Take away our sin and shame;
From our worldly cares set free,
May we rest this day in thee.

3 May the gospel's joyful sound
    Conquer sinners—comfort saints;
Make the fruits of grace abound,
    Bring relief from all complaints:
Thus let all our Sabbaths prove,
Till we join the church above.

58   HYMN. 7's.
The Sabbath Morning.

1 IN this calm impressive hour,
  Let my pray'r ascend on high;
  God of mercy, God of pow'r,
  Hear me when to thee I cry:
  Hear me from thy lofty throne,
  For the sake of Christ thy Son.

2 With this morning's early ray,
  While the shades of night depart,
  Let thy beams of light convey
  Joy and gladness to my heart:
  Now o'er all my steps preside,
  And for all my wants provide.

3 O what joy that word affords,
  "Thou shalt reign o'er all the earth;"
  King of kings, and Lord of lords,
  Send thy gospel heralds forth:
  Now begin thy boundless sway,
  Usher in the glorious day.

59   HYMN. C. M.
The Resurrection Sabbath.

1 BLEST morning, whose first dawning rays
  Beheld our rising God;
  That saw him triumph o'er the dust,
  And leave his dark abode!

2 In the cold prison of the tomb
  Our dear Redeemer lay,
  Till the revolving skies had brought
  The third, th' appointed day.

3 Hell and the grave unite their force
  To hold our God in vain;
  The sleeping conqueror arose,
  And burst their feeble chain.

4 To thy great name, Almighty Lord,
 These sacred hours we pay,
And loud hosannas shall proclaim
 The triumph of the day.

60   HYMN. C. M.

1 WHEN, on the third auspicious day,
 While yet the blushing dawn
Shed forth its earliest smiling ray
 To gild the rising morn;

2 The "holy women" sought the place
 Where their belov'd was laid,
And shining angels preach'd the grace
 That rais'd him from the dead;

3 They hasted from the hallow'd ground,
 Where his dear flesh had lain,
To tell his mourning friends around,
 That Jesus lives again.

4 This day, as days of older time,
 Is one of heav'nly joy;
Good tidings reach to ev'ry clime,
 And ev'ry tongue employ.

SABBATH EVENING.

61   HYMN. C. M.

1 FREQUENT the day of God returns
 To shed its quick'ning beams;
And yet how slow devotion burns,
 How languid are its flames!

2 Accept our faint attempts to love;
 Our frailties, Lord, forgive:
We would be like thy saints above,
 And praise thee while we live.

3 Increase, O Lord, our faith and hope,
 And fit us to ascend,
Where the assembly ne'er breaks up
 The Sabbath ne'er shall end;

4 Where we shall breathe in heav'nly air,
   With heav'nly lustre shine;
Before the throne of God appear,
   And feast on love divine;

5 Where we, in high seraphic strains,
   Shall all our pow'rs employ;
Delighted range th' ethereal plains,
   And take our fill of joy.

62   HYMN. L. M.
   The Eternal Sabbath.   Heb. iv. 9.

1 THINE earthly Sabbaths, Lord, we love,
But there's a nobler rest above;
To that our longing souls aspire,
With ardent pangs of strong desire.

2 No more fatigue, no more distress,
Nor sin, nor hell, shall reach the place;
No groans to mingle with the songs,
Which warble from immortal tongues.

3 No rude alarms of raging foes;
No cares to break the long repose;
No midnight shade, no clouded sun,
Obscures the lustre of thy throne.

4 Around thy throne, grant we may meet,
And give us but the lowest seat;
We'll shout thy praise, and join the song
Of the triumphant, holy throng.

63   HYMN. L. M.

1 IS there a time when moments flow,
   More peacefully than all beside?
It is, of all the times below,
   A Sabbath eve in summer tide.

2 O then the setting sun smiles fair,
   And all below, and all above,
The diff'rent forms of nature wear
   One universal garb of love.

3 And then the peace that Jesus beams,
   The life of grace, the death of sin;

With nature's placid woods and streams,
   Is peace without, and peace within.

4 Delightful scene! a world at rest,
   A God all love, no grief nor fear;
 A heav'nly hope, a peaceful breast,
   A smile unsullied by a tear.

5 If heav'n be ever felt below,
   A scene so heav'nly, sure, as this,
 May cause a heart on earth to know
   Some foretaste of celestial bliss

6 Delightful hour, how soon will night
   Spread her dark mantle o'er thy reign;
 And morrow's quick returning light
   Must call us to the world again.

7 Yet will there dawn at last a day,
   A Sun that never sets shall rise;
 Night will not veil his ceaseless ray,
   The heav'nly Sabbath never dies!

64   HYMN. C. M.
Evening Twilight.

1 I LOVE to steal awhile away
   From every cumb'ring care,
 And spend the hours of setting day
   In humble, grateful prayer.

2 I love in solitude to shed
   The penitential tear,
 And all his promises to plead,
   Where none but God can hear.

3 I love to think on mercies past,
   And future good implore,
 And all my cares and sorrows cast
   On him whom I adore

4 I love by faith to take a view
   Of brighter scenes in heav'n;
 The prospect doth my strength renew
   While here by tempests driv'n.

5 Thus, when life's toilsome day is o'er,
   May its departing ray
 Be calm as this impressive hour,
   And lead to endless day.

FOR THE BEGINNING OF THE YEAR.

65 HYMN. L. M.

1 GREAT God! we sing thy mighty hand;
By that supported still we stand:
The op'ning year thy mercy shows,
Let mercy crown it till it close.

2 By day, by night—at home, abroad,
Still we are guarded by our God;
By his incessant bounty fed—
By his unerring counsels led.

3 With grateful hearts the past we own,
The future—all to us unknown—
We to thy guardian care commit,
And peaceful leave before thy feet.

4 In scenes exalted or depress'd,
Be thou our joy—and thou our rest;
Thy goodness all our hopes shall raise,
Ador'd through all our changing days.

5 When death shall close our earthly songs,
And seal in silence mortal tongues,
Our helper, God, in whom we trust,
In brighter worlds our souls shall boast.

66 HYMN. L. M.

1 ETERNAL God! I bless thy name,
The same thy power—thy grace the same;
The tokens of thy friendly care
Begin, and close, and crown the year.

2 Supported by thy guardian hand,
Amid ten thousand deaths I stand,
And see, when I survey thy ways,
Ten thousand monuments of praise.

3 Thus far thine arm has led me on—
Thus far I make thy mercy known;
And while I tread this desert land,
New mercies shall new songs demand.

4 My grateful voice on Jordan's shore,
  Shall raise one sacred pillar more;
  Then bear in thy bright courts above,
  Inscriptions of immortal love.

67   HYMN. 7's.

1 WHILE with ceaseless course the sun
    Hasted through the former year,
  Many souls their race have run,
    Never more to meet us here:
  Fixed in an eternal state,
    They have done with all below
  We a little longer wait,
    But how little—none can know.

2 Spared to see another year,
    Let thy blessing meet us here;
  Come, thy dying work revive,
    Bid thy drooping garden thrive;
  Sun of Righteousness, arise!
    Warm our hearts and bless our eyes;
  Let our prayer thy pity move;
    Make this year a time of love.

3 Thanks for mercies past received,
    Pardon of our sins renew;
  Teach us henceforth how to live
    With eternity in view;
  Bless thy word to old and young,
    Fill us with a Saviour's love;
  When our life's short race is run,
    May we dwell with thee above.

68   HYMN. 5's & 11's.

A New Year.

1   COME, let us anew
    Our journey pursue,
    Roll round with the year,
  And never stand still, till the Master appear

FOR THE CLOSE OF THE YEAR.

2   Our life is a dream,
      Our time as a stream
      Glides swiftly away;
And the fugitive moment refuses to stay.

3   The arrow is flown,
      The moment is gone;
      The millennial year
Rushes on to our view, and eternity's here.

4   O that each in the day
      Of his coming may say,
      "I've fought my way through,
I've finish'd the work thou did'st give me to do!'

5   O that each from his Lord
      May receive the good word,
      "Well and faithfully done!
Enter into my joy, and sit down on my throne!"

FOR THE CLOSE OF THE YEAR.

69   HYMN. C. M.

Reflections at the End of the Year.

1 AND now, my soul, another year
    Of thy short life is past;
I cannot long continue here,
    And this may be my last.

2 Much of my dubious life is gone,
    Nor will return again;
And swift my passing moments run,
    The few that yet remain.

3 Awake, my soul—with utmost care
    Thy true condition learn:
What are thy hopes?—how sure? how fair?
    What is thy great concern?

4 Behold, another year begins!
    Set out afresh for heaven;
Seek pardon for thy former sins,
    In Christ so freely given.

5 Devoutly yield thyself to God,
   And on his grace depend;
With zeal pursue the heav'nly road,
   Nor doubt a happy end.

70   HYMN. S. M.

Rapid flight of Time.

1 MY few revolving years,
   How swift they glide away!
How short the term of life appears,
   When past—'tis but a day!—

2 A dark and cloudy day,
   Made up of grief and sin;
A host of dang'rous foes without,
   And guilt and fear within.

3 Lord, through another year,
   If thou permit my stay,
With watchful care may I pursue
   The true and living way!

71   HYMN. C. M.

Praise for Providential Goodness.

1 GOD of our lives, thy various praise
   Our voices shall resound:
Thy hand directs our fleeting days,
   And brings the seasons round.

2 To thee shall grateful songs arise,
   Our Father and our Friend:
Whose constant mercies from the skies,
   In genial streams descend.

3 In ev'ry scene of life, thy care,
   In ev'ry age, we see;
And, constant as thy favours are,
   So let our praises be.

4 Still may thy love, in every scene,
   To ev'ry age, appear;
And let the same compassion deign
   To bless the op'ning year.

72 HYMN. C. M.

The House appointed for all living.

1 HOW still and peaceful is the grave,
  Where, life's vain tumults past,
Th' appointed house by heav'n's decree,
  Receives us all at last!

2 The wicked there from troubling cease—
  Their passions rage no more;
And there the weary pilgrim rests
  From all the toils he bore.

3 All, levell'd by the hand of death,
  Lie sleeping in the tomb,
Till God in judgment calls them forth,
  To meet their final doom.

THE SEASONS.

73 HYMN. P. M.

1 HOW pleasing is the voice
  Of God, our heav'nly King,
Who bids the frosts retire,
  And wakes the lovely spring!
    Bright suns arise,
  The mild wind blows,
  And beauty glows,
    Thro' earth and skies.

2 The morn, with glory crown'd
  His hand arrays in smiles:
He bids the eve decline,
  Rejoicing o'er the hills:
    The ev'ning breeze
  His breath perfumes;
  His beauty blooms
    In flow'rs and trees.

3 With life he clothes the spring,
   The earth with summer warms:
  He spreads th' autumnal feast,
   And rides on wintry storms;
    His gifts divine
   Thro' all appear;
   And round the year
    His glories shine.

74 HYMN. L. M.

1 THE flow'ry spring, at God's command,
  Perfumes the air, and paints the land:
  The summer rays with vigour shine,
  To raise the corn and cheer the vine.

2 His hand in autumn richly pours,
  Through all her coasts, redundant stores;
  And winters, soften'd by his care,
  No more the face of horror wear.

3 The changing seasons, months and days,
  Demand successive songs of praise;
  And be the cheerful homage paid,
  With morning light and ev'ning shade.

4 And oh, may each harmonious tongue
  In worlds unknown the praise prolong,
  And in those brighter courts adore,
  Where days and years revolve no more.

75 HYMN. C. M.

Spring.

1 WHEN verdure clothes the fertile vale,
   And blossoms deck the spray,
  And fragrance breathes in ev'ry gale,
   How sweet the vernal day!

2 Hark! how the feather'd warblers sing!
   'Tis nature's cheerful voice;
  Soft music hails the lovely spring,
   And woods and fields rejoice.

3 O God of nature, and of grace,
   Thy heav'nly gifts impart;
  Then shall my meditation trace
   Spring blooming in my heart.

4 Inspir'd to praise, I then shall join
    Glad nature's cheerful song;
  And love, and gratitude divine
    Attune my joyful tongue.

76   HYMN. S. M.
The Spring.

1 SWEET is the time of spring,
    When nature's charms appear;
  The birds with ceaseless pleasure sing,
    And hail the op'ning year:
  But sweeter far the spring
    Of wisdom and of grace,
  When children bless and praise their King
    Who loves the youthful race.

2 Sweet is the dawn of day,
    When light just streaks the sky;
  When shades and darkness pass away,
    And morning's beams are nigh:
  But sweeter far the dawn
    Of piety in youth;
  When doubt and darkness are withdrawn
    Before the light of truth.

3 Sweet is the early dew,
    Which gilds the mountain's tops,
  And decks each plant and flow'r we view,
    With pearly glitt'ring drops:
  But sweeter far the scene
    On Zion's holy hill;
  When there the dew of youth is seen
    Its freshness to distil.

77   HYMN. S. M.

1 GREAT God, at thy command
    Seasons in order rise:
  Thy pow'r and love in concert reign
    Through earth, and seas, and skies.

2 How balmy is the air!
    How warm the sun's bright beams!
  While, to refresh the grounds, the rains
    Descend in gentle streams.

3 With grateful praise we own
   Thy providential hand,
 While grass, and herbs, and waving corn,
   Adorn and bless the land.

4 But greater still the gift
   Of thine incarnate Son;
 By him forgiveness, peace, and joy,
   Through endless ages run.

78   HYMN. 8's.

1 THE winter is over and gone,
   The thrush whistles sweet on the spray,
 The turtle breathes forth her soft moan,
   The lark mounts and warbles away.

2 Shall every creature around
   Their voices in concert unite,
 And I, the most favour'd, be found,
   In praising to take less delight?

3 Awake, then, my harp, and my lute!
   Sweet organs, your notes softly swell!
 No longer my lips shall be mute,
   The Saviour's high praises to tell!

4 His love in my heart shed abroad,
   My graces shall bloom as the spring
 This temple, his Spirit's abode,
   My joy, as my duty, to sing.

79   HYMN. 7's.

1 PLEASING spring again is here!
 Trees and fields in bloom appear!
 Hark! the birds, with artless lays,
 Warble their Creator's praise!

2 Lord, afford a spring to me!
 Let me feel like what I see;
 Ah! my winter has been long,
 Chill'd my hopes, suppress'd my song.

3 How the soul in winter mourns,
 Till the Lord, the Sun, returns!
 Till the Spirit's gentle rain
 Bids the heart revive again!

4 O beloved Saviour, haste,
   Tell me all the storms are past:
  Speak, and by thy gracious voice
   Make my drooping soul rejoice.

80   HYMN. C. M.

Summer—A Harvest Hymn.

1 TO praise the ever bounteous Lord,
   My soul, wake all thy pow'rs;
  He calls, and at his voice come forth
   The smiling harvest hours.

2 His cov'nant with the earth he keeps;
   My tongue, his goodness sing;
  Summer and winter know their time,
   His harvest crowns the spring.

3 Well pleas'd the toiling swains behold
   The waving yellow crop;
  With joy they bear the sheaves away,
   And sow again in hope.

4 Thus teach me, gracious God, to sow
   The seeds of righteousness;
  Smile on my soul, and with thy beams
   The rip'ning harvest bless.

5 Then, in the last great harvest, I
   Shall reap a glorious crop;
  The harvest shall by far exceed
   What I have sow'd in hope.

81   HYMN. C. M.

Winter.

1 STERN winter throws his icy chains,
   Encircling nature round;
  How bleak, how comfortless the plains,
   Late with gay verdure crown'd!

2 The sun withdraws his vital beams,
   And light and warmth depart;
  And drooping lifeless, nature seems
   An emblem of my heart.

3 My heart, where mental winter reigns,
   In night's dark mantle clad,
Confin'd in cold, inactive chains,
   How desolate and sad!

4 Return, O blissful Sun, and bring
   Thy soul-reviving ray;
This mental winter shall be spring,
   This darkness cheerful day.

5 O happy state, divine abode,
   Where spring eternal reigns;
And perfect day, the smile of God,
   Fills all the heav'nly plains!

6 Great Source of light, thy beams display,
   My drooping joys restore,
And guide me to the seats of day,
   Where winter frowns no more.

82   HYMN. L. M.

Goodness of God in the Seasons.

1 ON God the race of man depends,
Far as the earth's remotest ends;
At his command the morning ray
Smiles in the east, and leads the day.

2 Seasons and times obey his voice;
The morn and ev'ning both rejoice
To see the earth made soft with showers,
Laden with fruit, and dress'd in flowers.

3 The desert grows a fruitful field;
Abundant food the valleys yield;
The plains shall shout with cheerful voice,
And neighbouring hills repeat their joys.

4 Thy works pronounce thy power divine;
O'er every field thy glories shine;
Through ev'ry month thy gifts appear:
Great God, thy goodness crowns the year

83   HYMN. C. M.

1 THE Lord is good, the heav'nly King,
   He makes the earth his care;
Visits the pastures ev'ry spring,
   And bids the grass appear.

2 The times and seasons—days and hours,
  Heav'n, earth, and air, are thine;
When clouds distil in fruitful show'rs,
  The Author is divine.

3 The soften'd ridges of the field
  Permit the corn to spring;
The valleys rich provision yield,
  And all the lab'rers sing.

4 The various months thy goodness crowns;
  How bounteous are thy ways!
The bleating flocks spread o'er the downs,
  And shepherds shout thy praise.

84   HYMN. L. M.

1 SING to the Lord, exalt him high,
Who spreads his clouds around the sky;
There he prepares the fruitful rain,
Nor lets the drops descend in vain.

2 He makes the grass the hills adorn,
And clothes the smiling fields with corn;
The beasts with food his hands supply,
And feed the ravens when they cry.

3 What is the creature's skill or force,
The vig'rous man, the warlike horse,
The sprightly wit, the active limb!
All are too mean delights for him.

4 His saints are lovely in his sight;
He views his children with delight;
He sees their hopes, he knows their fear,
And finds and loves his image there.

85   HYMN L. M.

1 LET Zion praise the mighty God,
And make his honours known abroad;
For sweet the joy our songs to raise,
And glorious is the work of praise.

2 Our children live secure and blest;
Our shores have peace, our cities rest;
He feeds our sons with finest wheat,
And adds his blessings to their meat.

3 The changing seasons he ordains,
　The early and the latter rains;
　His flakes of snow like wool he sends,
　And thus the springing corn defends.

4 With hoary frost he strews the ground;
　His hail descends with dreadful sound;
　His icy bands the rivers hold,
　And terror arms his wintry cold.

5 He bids the warmer breezes blow,
　The ice dissolves, the waters flow;
　But he hath nobler works and ways
　To call his people to his praise.

6 Through all our land his laws are shown:
　His gospel through our borders known;
　He hath not thus reveal'd his word
　To every land—Praise ye the Lord!

86　　　　HYMN. C. M.

1 WITH songs and honours sounding loud,
　　Address the Lord on high;
　Over the heavens he spreads his cloud,
　　And waters veil the sky.

2 He sends his showers of blessings down
　　To cheer the plains below;
　He makes the grass the mountains crown,
　　And corn in valleys grow.

3 He gives the grazing ox his meat,
　　He hears the ravens cry;
　But man, who tastes his finest wheat,
　　Should raise his honours high.

4 His steady counsels change the face
　　Of the declining year;
　He bids the sun cut short his race,
　　And wintry days appear.

5 His hoary frost, his fleecy snow,
　　Descend and clothe the ground;
　The liquid streams forbear to flow,
　　In icy fetters bound.

6 When from his dreadful stores on high
　　He pours the sounding hail,
　The wretch that dares his God defy
　　Shall find his courage fail.

7 He sends his word, and melts the snow,
   The fields no longer mourn;
  He calls the warmer gales to blow,
   And bids the spring return.

8 The changing wind, the flying cloud,
   Obey his mighty word;
  With songs and honours sounding loud,
   Praise ye the sov'reign Lord.

THE SPREAD OF THE GOSPEL.

87 HYMN. 8's, 7's, 4's.

Prayer for a Revival. Ps. lxxxv. 7.

1 SAVIOUR, visit thy plantation:
   Grant us, Lord, a gracious rain!
  All will come to desolation,
   Unless thou return again.
     Lord, revive us;
   All our help must come from thee.

2 Keep no longer at a distance;
   Shine upon us from on high,
  Lest, for want of thine assistance,
   Ev'ry plant should droop and die.

3 Let our mutual love be fervent,
   Make us prevalent in pray'rs;
  Let each one esteem'd thy servant,
   Shun the world's bewitching snares.

4 Break the tempter's fatal power:
   Turn the stony heart to flesh;
  And begin from this good hour
   To revive thy work afresh.

88 HYMN. P. M.

1 SOV'REIGN of worlds above,
   And Lord of all below,
  Thy faithfulness and love,
   Thy pow'r and mercy show;
     Fulfil thy word;
     Thy Spirit give;
     Let heathens live
     And praise the Lord.

2 On lands that lie beneath
   Foul superstition's sway,
Whose horrid shades of death
   Admit no heav'nly ray,
     Blest Spirit! shine,
     Their hearts illume;
     Dispel the gloom
     With light divine.

3 Father, who to thy Son
   Thy steadfast word has given,
That thro' the earth shall run
   The news of peace with heav'n,
     Extend his fame;
     Thy grace diffuse;
     And let the news
     The world reclaim.

4 Few be the years that roll,
   Ere all shall worship thee;
The travail of his soul,
   Soon let the Saviour see;
     O God of grace!
     Thy pow'r employ,
     Fill earth with joy,
     And heav'n with praise.

89   HYMN. C. M.

1 OH, when shall Afric's sable sons
   Enjoy the heav'nly word;
And vassals, long enslaved, become
   The freemen of the Lord?

2 When shall the untutor'd heathen tribes,
   A dark, bewilder'd race,
Sit down at our Immanuel's feet,
   And learn and sing his grace!

3 Haste, sovereign mercy, and transform
   Their cruelty to love;
Soften the tiger to a lamb,
   The vulture to a dove.

90   HYMN. 8, 7, 4.

1 O'ER the gloomy hills of darkness,
   Cheer'd by no celestial ray,
Sun of Righteousness, arising,
   Bring the bright, the glorious day;
     Send the gospel
To the earth's remotest bound.

2 Kingdoms wide that sit in darkness!
   Grant them, Lord, the glorious light;
And from eastern coast to western,
   May the morning chase the night;
     And redemption,
Freely purchased, win the day.

3 Fly abroad, thou mighty gospel—
   Win and conquer, never cease;
May thy lasting, wide dominions
   Multiply and still increase;
     Sway thy sceptre,
Saviour, all the world around.

91   HYMN. L. M.

1 SOV'REIGN of worlds! display thy pow'r
Be this thy Zion's favour'd hour;
Bid the bright Morning Star arise,
And point the nations to the skies.

2 Set up thy throne where Satan reigns,
On Afric's shore, on India's plains,
On wilds and continents unknown;
And be the universe thine own.

3 Speak! and the world shall hear thy **voice**;
Speak! and the desert shall rejoice;
Scatter the gloom of heathen night,
And bid all nations hail the light.

92   HYMN. 8, 7, 4.
For the Influence of the Spirit.

1 WHO, but thou, Almighty Spirit,
   Can the heathen world reclaim?
Men may preach, but till thou favour,
   Heathens will be still the same:
     Mighty Spirit!
Witness to the Saviour's name.

2 Thou hast promised by the prophets,
   Glorious light in latter days:
Come, and bless bewilder'd nations,
   Change our pray'rs and tears to praise;
    Promis'd Spirit!
Round the world diffuse thy rays.

3 All our hopes, and prayers, and labours,
   Must be vain without thine aid:
But thou wilt not disappoint us—
   All is true that thou hast said
    Faithful Spirit!
O'er the world thine influence shed.

93   HYMN. 7, 6.

1 FROM Greenland's icy mountains,
   From India's coral strand:
Where Afric's sunny fountains
   Roll down their golden sand;
From many an ancient river,
   From many a palmy plain,
They call us to deliver
   Their land from error's chain.

2 What tho' the spicy breezes
   Blow soft o'er Ceylon's Isle,
Tho' ev'ry prospect pleases,
   And only man is vile;
In vain with lavish kindness
   The gifts of God are strown;
The heathen in his blindness
   Bows down to wood and stone.

3 Shall we, whose souls are lighted
   With wisdom from on high,
Shall we to men benighted
   The lamp of life deny!
Salvation! O Salvation!
   The joyful sound proclaim,
Till earth's remotest nation
   Has learn'd Messiah's name.

4 Waft, waft, ye winds, his story,
   And you, ye waters, roll,
Till, like a sea of glory,
   It spreads from pole to pole;

Till o'er our ransom'd nature,
  The Lamb for sinners slain,
Redeemer, King, Creator,
  In bliss returns to reign.

94 HYMN. C. M.

1 GREAT Saviour, let thy pow'r divine
  O'er all the earth be known;
Let all, to thee, their will resign,
  And make thy will their own.

2 Perversion marks the guilty way,
  Which heathens madly tread;
From all thy laws they go astray,
  And hasten to the dead.

3 Thou, Saviour-God, hast pow'r alone
  To turn their wand'ring feet;
To bend their souls before thy throne,
  Low at thy mercy-seat:

4 For all the pow'r, beneath, above,
  Thy wounded hands sustain;
Then sway the sceptre of thy love,
  And let thy mercy reign.

95 HYMN. L. M.

The Glory of God in his Works and in his Word.

1 GREAT Sun of Righteousness, arise!
  O bless the world with heav'nly light!
Thy gospel makes the simple wise:
  Thy laws are pure—thy judgments right.

2 Thy noblest wonders here we view,
  In souls renew'd and sins forgiv'n:—
Lord, cleanse my sins—my soul renew,
  And make thy word my guide to heav'n.

96 HYMN. L. M.

Universal Reign of Christ.

1 GREAT God! whose universal sway
The known and unknown worlds obey,
Now give the kingdom to thy Son,
Extend his pow'r—exalt his throne.

2 As rain on meadows newly mown,
  So shall he send his influence down;
  His grace, on fainting souls, distils,
  Like heav'nly dew, on thirsty hills.

3 The heathen lands, that lie beneath
  The shades of overspreading death,
  Revive at his first dawning light,
  And deserts blossom at the sight.

4 The saints shall flourish in his days,
  Dress'd in the robes of joy and praise;
  Peace, like a river, from his throne,
  Shall flow to nations yet unknown.

97   HYMN. L. M.

1 JESUS shall reign where'er the sun
  Doth his successive journeys run;
  His kingdom stretch from shore to shore,
  Till moons shall wax and wane no more.

2 For him shall endless pray'r be made,
  And endless praises crown his head;
  His name, like sweet perfume, shall rise
  With ev'ry morning sacrifice.

3 People and realms of ev'ry tongue
  Dwell on his love with sweetest song;
  And infant voices shall proclaim
  Their early blessings on his name.

4 Blessings abound where'er he reigns,
  The joyful pris'ner bursts his chains;
  The weary find eternal rest,
  And all the sons of want are blest.

5 Let every creature rise and bring
  Peculiar honours to our king;
  Angels descend with songs again,
  And earth repeat the loud amen.

98   HYMN. L. P. M.

Rejoicing in View of God's Universal Reign.

1 LET all the earth their voices raise,
  To sing a psalm of lofty praise,
    To sing and bless Jehovah's name;
  His glory let the heathen know,
  His wonders to the nations show,
    And all his saving works proclaim.

2 Oh! haste the day—the glorious hour,
When earth shall feel his saving pow'r,
And barb'rous nations fear his name:
Then shall the race of man confess
The beauty of his holiness,
And in his courts his grace proclaim.

99   HYMN. S. M.

1 I LOVE thy kingdom, Lord,
The house of thine abode,
The church, our blest Redeemer sav'd
With his own precious blood.

2 I love thy church, O God!
Her walls before thee stand,
Dear as the apple of thine eye,
And graven on thy hand.

3 For her my tears shall fall;
For her my prayers ascend;
To her my cares and toils be given,
Till toils and cares shall end.

4 Beyond my highest joy
I prize her heav'nly ways,
Her sweet communion—solemn vows
Her hymns of love and praise.

5 Jesus, thou friend divine,
Our Saviour, and our King,
Thy hand from every snare and foe,
Shall great deliv'rance bring.

6 Sure as thy truth shall last,
To Zion shall be giv'n
The brightest glories earth can yield,
And brighter bliss of heaven.

100   HYMN. C. M.

Christ crowned as Lord of all.

1 ALL hail, the great Immanuel's name!
Let angels prostrate fall:
Bring forth the royal diadem,
And crown him Lord of all.
14*

2 Crown him, ye martyrs of our God,
   Who from his altar call;
Praise him who shed for you his blood,
   And crown him Lord of all.

3 Ye chosen seed of Israel's race,
   A remnant weak and small,
Hail him who saves you by his grace,
   And crown him Lord of all.

4 Ye Gentile sinners, ne'er forget
   The wormwood and the gall;
Go spread your trophies at his feet,
   And crown him Lord of all.

5 Let ev'ry kindred—ev'ry tribe,
   On this terrestrial ball,
To him all majesty ascribe,
   And crown him Lord of all.

6 Oh! that with yonder sacred throng,
   We at his feet may fall;
And join the everlasting song,
   And crown him Lord of all.

101   HYMN P. M.

1 SOV'REIGN of worlds above,
   And Lord of all below,
Thy faithfulness and love,
   Thy power and mercy show.
   Fulfil thy word,
     Thy Spirit give;
   Let heathens live,
     And praise the Lord.

2 Few be the years that roll,
   Ere all shall worship thee;
The travail of his soul
   Soon let the Saviour see:
   O God of grace!
     Thy power employ;
   Fill earth with joy,
     And heav'n with praise.

102   HYMN. 7's.

1 WAKE the song of jubilee,
   Let it echo o'er the sea!
Now is come the promis'd hour;
   Jesus reigns with sov'reign pow'r!

2 All ye nations, join and sing,
  "Christ, of lords and kings is King!"
  Let it sound from shore to shore,
  Jesus reigns for evermore!

3 Now the desert lands rejoice,
  And the islands join their voice;
  Yea, the whole creation sings,
  "Jesus is the King of kings."

103   HYMN. L. M.

Exhortation to Universal Praise.

1 FROM all that dwell below the skies,
  Let the Creator's praise arise:
  Let the Redeemer's name be sung,
  Through ev'ry land—by ev'ry tongue.

2 Eternal are thy mercies, Lord;
  Eternal truth attends thy word;
  Thy praise shall sound from shore to shore,
  Till suns shall rise and set no more.

EARLY PIETY.

104   HYMN. L. M.

1 NOW in the heat of youthful blood,
  Remember your Creator, God:
  Behold the months come hast'ning on,
  When you shall say—"My joys are gone.'

2 Behold, the aged sinner goes,
  Oppress'd with guilt and heavy woes,
  Down to the regions of the dead,
  With endless curses on his head.

3 The dust returns to dust again;
  The soul, in agony of pain,
  Ascends to God—not there to dwell,
  But hears her doom—and sinks to hell.

4 Eternal King! I fear thy name;
  Teach me to know how frail I am:
  And when my soul must hence remove,
  Give me a mansion in thy love.

105   HYMN. C. M.

*Youth admonished to remember their **Creator**.*

1 CHILDREN, to your Creator, God
   Your early honours pay;
While vanity and youthful blood
   Would tempt your thoughts astray.

2 Be wise—and make his favour sure,
   Before the mournful day,
When youth and mirth are known no more,
   And life and strength decay.

3 The mem'ry of his mighty name
   Demands your first regard;
Nor dare indulge a meaner flame,
   Till you have lov'd the Lord.

106   HYMN. C. M.

1 WHILE in the tender years of youth,
   In nature's smiling bloom,
Ere age arrive, and trembling wait
   Its summons to the tomb;—

2 Remember thy Creator, God;
   For him thy pow'rs employ;
Make him thy fear, thy love, thy hope,
   Thy portion, and thy joy.

3 He shall defend and guide thy course
   Through life's uncertain sea,
Till thou art landed on the shore
   Of blest eternity.

107   HYMN. S. M.

The Young asking for Divine Guidance.

1 FROM earliest dawn of life,
   Thy goodness we have shared;
And still we live to sing thy praise,
   By sov'reign mercy spared.

2 To learn and do thy will,
   O Lord, our hearts incline;
And o'er the paths of future life
   Command thy light to shine.

EARLY PIETY.

3 While taught thy word of truth,
  May we that word receive;
And when we hear of Jesus' name,
  In that blest name believe!

4 O, let us never tread
  The broad, destructive road,
But trace those holy paths which lead
  To glory, and to God.

108   HYMN. S. M.

1 MY son, know thou the Lord,
  Thy father's God obey:
Seek his protecting care by night,
  His guardian hand by day.

2 Call, while he may be found,
  And seek him while he's near;
Serve him with all thy heart and mind,
  And worship him with fear.

3 If thou wilt seek his face,
  His ear will hear thy cry;
Then shalt thou find his mercy sure,
  His grace forever nigh.

4 But if thou leave thy God,
  Nor choose the path to heav'n;
Then shalt thou perish in thy sins,
  And never be forgiv'n.

109   HYMN. C. M.

Youth.

1 COME, let us now forget our mirth,
  And think that we must die;
What are our best delights on earth,
  Compar'd with those on high!

2 Our pleasures here will soon be past—
  Our brightest joys decay;
But pleasures there for ever last,
  And cannot fade away.

3 Here sins and sorrows we deplore,
  With many cares distrest;
But there the mourners weep no more,
  And there the weary rest.

4 Our dearest friends, when death shall call,
    At once must hence depart;
But there we hope to meet them all,
    And never, never part.

5 Then let us love and serve the Lord,
    With all our youthful pow'rs;
And we shall gain this great reward,
    This glory shall be ours.

110   HYMN. C. M.

1 RELIGION is the chief concern
    Of mortals here below;
May I its great importance learn,
    Its sov'reign virtue know!

2 Religion should our thoughts engage,
    Amidst our youthful bloom;
'Twill fit us for declining age,
    And for the awful tomb.

111   HYMN. L. M.

1 YE lovely bands of blooming youth,
Warn'd by the voice of heav'nly truth,
Now yield to Christ your youthful prime,
With all your talents and your time.

2 Think on your end, nor thoughtless say,
"I'll put far off the evil day;"
Ah! not a moment's in your pow'r,
And death stands ready at the door.

3 Eternity!—how near it rolls!
Count the vast value of your souls!
Beware! and count the awful cost,
What they have gain'd whose souls are lost.

4 Pride, sinful pleasures, lusts and snares,
Beset your hearts, your eyes, your ears—
Take the alarm—the danger fly!
"Lord! save me," be your earnest cry

112 HYMN. S. M.
Prayer of a Youth. Ps. cxix. 9.

1 WITH humble heart and tongue,
   My God, to thee I pray;
 Oh, make me learn, while I am young,
   How I may cleanse my way.

2 Make an unguarded youth
   The object of thy care;
 Help me to choose the way of truth,
   And fly from every snare.

3 My heart, to folly prone,
   Renew by power divine;
 Unite it to thyself alone,
   And make me wholly thine.

4 Oh, let thy word of grace
   My warmest thoughts employ;
 Be this, through all my foll'wing days,
   My treasure and my joy.

5 To what thy laws impart,
   Be my whole soul inclin'd;
 Oh, let them dwell within my heart,
   And sanctify my mind.

6 May thy young servant learn,
   By these to cleanse his way;
 And may I here the path discern
   That leads to endless day.

113 HYMN. L. M.

1 HOW soft the words my Saviour speaks!
   How kind the promises he makes!
 A bruised reed he never breaks,
   Nor will he quench the smoking flax.

2 The humble poor he won't despise,
   Nor on the contrite sinner frown;
 His ear is open to their cries,
   He quickly sends salvation down.

3 When piety, in early minds,
   Like tender buds, begins to shoot,
 He guards the plants from threat'ning winds,
   And ripens blossoms into fruit.

4 With humble souls he bears a part
   In all the sorrows they endure;
 Tender and gracious is his heart,
   His promise is for ever sure.

5 He sees the struggles that prevail
   Between the powers of grace and sin
 He kindly listens while they tell
   The bitter pangs they feel within.

6 Though press'd with fears on every side,
   They know not how the strife may end
 Yet he will soon the cause decide,
   And judgment unto vict'ry send.

MISCELLANEOUS.

114   HYMN. C. M.

1 WHILST thee I seek, protecting Power!
   Be my vain wishes still'd;
 And may this consecrated hour
   With better hopes be fill'd.

2 Thy love the pow'r of thought bestow'd,
   To thee my thoughts would soar:
 Thy mercy o'er my life has flow'd,
   That mercy I adore.

3 In each event of life, how clear
   Thy ruling hand I see!
 Each blessing to my soul most dear,
   Because conferr'd by thee.

4 In ev'ry joy that crowns my days,
   In ev'ry pain I bear,
 My heart shall find delight in praise,
   Or seek relief in pray'r.

5 When gladness wings my favour'd hour,
   Thy love my thoughts shall fill;
 Resign'd, when storms of sorrow low'r,
   My soul shall meet thy will.

 My lifted eye, without a tear,
   The gath'ring storm shall see;
 My steadfast heart shall know no fear;
   That heart will rest on thee.

115   HYMN. 8 s, 7's, and 4's.

God, the Pilgrim's Guide.

1 GUIDE me, O thou great Jehovah,
   Pilgrim through this barren land;
I am weak, but thou art mighty;
   Hold me with thy pow'rful hand:
     Bread of heaven,
   Feed me till I want no more.

2 Open, Lord, the crystal fountain,
   Whence the healing waters flow,
Let the fiery, cloudy pillar,
   Lead me all my journey through.
     Strong Deliv'rer,
   Be thou still my strength and shield.

3 When I tread the verge of Jordan,
   Bid my anxious fears subside;
Death of death, and hell's destruction,
   Land me safe on Canaan's side:
     Songs of praises
   I will ever give to thee.

116   HYMN. L. M.

Crucifixion to the World.

1 WHEN I survey the wond'rous cross,
On which the Prince of glory died,
My richest gain I count but loss,
And pour contempt on all my pride.

2 Forbid it, Lord, that I should boast,
Save in the death of Christ, my God,
All the vain things that charm me most,
I sacrifice them to his blood.

3 See, from his head, his hands, his feet,
Sorrow and love flow mingled down!
Did e'er such love and sorrow meet,
Or thorns compose so rich a crown?

4 Were the wide realm of nature mine,
That were a present far too small;
Love so amazing, so divine,
Demands my soul, my life, my all.

117   HYMN. C. M.

Holy Fortitude.

1 AM I a soldier of the cross?
    A follower of the Lamb!
  And shall I fear to own his cause,
    Or blush to speak his name!

2 Shall I be carried to the skies,
    On flow'ry beds of ease,
  While others fought to win the prize,
    And sail'd through bloody seas!

3 Are there no foes for me to face?
    Must I not stem the flood!
  Is this vain world a friend to grace,
    To help me on to God!

4 Sure I must fight, if I would reign;
    Increase my courage, Lord,
  To bear the cross, endure the shame,
    Supported by thy word.

5 The saints, in all this glorious war,
    Shall conquer, tho' they die;
  They see the triumph from afar,
    With faith's discerning eye.

118   HYMN. C. M.

Salvation welcomed.

1 SALVATION! O, the joyful sound!
    'Tis pleasure to our ears:
  A sov'reign balm for every wound,
    A cordial for our fears.

2 Buried in sorrow and in sin,
    At hell's dark door we lay;
  But we arise by grace divine
    To see a heav'nly day.

3 Salvation! let the echo fly
    The spacious earth around,
  While all the armies of the sky
    Conspire to raise the sound.

119 HYMN. L. M.

A Broken and a Contrite Heart.

1 SHOW pity, Lord; O Lord, forgive;
Let a repenting rebel live;
Are not thy mercies large and free?
May not a sinner trust in thee?

2 O wash my soul from every sin,
And make my guilty conscience clean;
Here on my heart the burden lies,
And past offences pain mine eyes.

3 My lips with shame my sins confess,
Against thy law, against thy grace;
Lord, should thy judgments grow severe,
I am condemn'd, but thou art clear.

4 Yet save a trembling sinner, Lord,
Whose hope, still hov'ring round thy word,
Would light on some sweet promise there
Some sure support against despair.

120 HYMN. C. M.

Repentance at the Cross.

1 'TWAS for my sins, my dearest Lord
Hung on the cursed tree,
And groan'd away a dying life
For thee, my soul, for thee.

2 O, how I hate those sins of mine
That shed the Saviour's blood;
That pierc'd and nail'd his sacred flesh
Fast to the fatal wood!

3 Whilst with a melting broken heart
My murder'd Lord I view,
I here renounce my darling sins,
And slay the murd'rers too.

121 HYMN. L. M.

Sufferings and Death.

1 STRETCH'D on the cross, the Saviour dies;
Hark! his expiring groans arise:
See from his hands, his feet, his side,
Runs down the sacred crimson tide.

2 But life attends the deathful sound,
  And flows from ev'ry bleeding wound·
  The vital stream, how free it flows,
  To save and cleanse his rebel foes!

3 Can I survey this scene of wo,
  Where mingling grief and wonder flow,
  And yet my heart unmov'd remain,
  Insensible to love, or pain?

4 Come, dearest Lord, thy grace impart,
  To warm this cold, this stupid heart!
  'Till all its pow'rs and passions move
  In melting grief, and ardent love.

122   HYMN.   8's, 7's, 4's.

It is finished.   John xix. 30.

1 HARK! the voice of love and mercy!
  Sounds aloud from Calvary!
  See, it rends the rocks asunder—
  Shakes the earth and veils the sky!
    "It is finished!"—
  Hear the Saviour—dying—cry.

2 It is finish'd!—Oh, what pleasure
  Do these precious words afford!
  Heav'nly blessings without measure,
  Flow to us from Christ the Lord:
    It is finish'd!—
  Saints the dying words record.

3 Finish'd—all the types and shadows
  Of the ceremonial law!
  Finish'd—all that God had promised;
  Death and hell no more shall awe;
    It is finish'd!—
  Saints, from hence your comforts draw.

4 Tune your harps anew, ye seraphs,—
  Join to sing the pleasing theme!
  All on earth, and all in heav'n,
  Join to praise Immanuel's name:
    Hallelujah!
  Glory to the bleeding Lamb!

123 HYMN. C. M.

Breathing after the Holy Spirit.

1 COME, Holy Spirit, heav'nly Dove,
   With all thy quick'ning pow'rs,—
Kindle a flame of sacred love
   In these cold hearts of ours.

2 In vain we tune our formal songs;
   In vain we strive to rise;
Hosannas languish on our tongues,
   And our devotion dies.

3 Dear Lord! and shall we ever live
   At this poor dying rate?
Our love so faint, so cold to thee,
   And thine to us so great!

4 Come, Holy Spirit, heav'nly Dove,
   With all thy quick'ning pow'rs,—
Come, shed abroad a Saviour's love,
   And that shall kindle ours.

124 HYMN. L. M.

Parting with carnal joys.

1 I SEND the joys of earth away;
Away, ye tempters of the mind,
False as the smooth deceitful sea,
And empty as the whistling wind.

2 Your streams were floating me along,
Down to the gulf of black despair
And whilst I listen'd to your song,
Your streams had e'en conveyed me there

3 Lord, I adore thy matchless grace,
That warn'd me of that dark abyss;
That drew me from those treach'rous seas,
And bade me seek superior bliss.

4 Now to the shining realms above,
I stretch my hands, and glance my eyes;
Oh, for the pinions of a dove,
To bear me to the upper skies.

125   HYMN. 7's.

1 JESUS, lover of my soul,
    Let me to thy bosom fly,
  While the billows near me roll,
    While the tempest still is high;
  Hide me, O my Saviour, hide,
    Till the storm of life be past;
  Safe into the haven guide,
    Oh, receive my soul at last!

2 Other refuge have I none;
    Lo! I, helpless, hang on thee;
  Leave, Oh, leave me not alone,
    Lest I basely shrink and flee:
  Thou art all my trust and aid,
    All my help from thee I bring;
  Cover my defenceless head
    With the shadow of thy wing.

3 Thou, O Christ, art all I want;
    Boundless love in thee I find:
  Raise the fallen, cheer the faint,
    Heal the sick, and lead the blind.
  Just and holy is thy name:
    I am all unrighteousness;
  Vile and full of sin I am,
    Thou art full of truth and grace.

4 Plenteous grace with thee is found,
    Grace to pardon all my sin;
  Let the healing streams abound,
    Make and keep me pure within.
  Thou of life the fountain art,
    Freely let me take of thee:
  Reign, O Lord, within my heart,
    Reign to all eternity

126   HYMN. 7, 6.
          Pilgrim's Song.

1 RISE, my soul, and stretch thy wings,
    Thy better portion trace;
  Rise from transitory things,
    Tow'rds heav'n thy native place.
  Sun, and moon, and stars decay—
    Time shall soon this earth remove;
  Rise, my soul, and haste away
    To seats prepared above.

2 Rivers to the ocean run,
 Nor stay in all their course:
Fires ascending seek the sun
 Both speed them to their source;
So a soul that's born of God,
 Pants to view his glorious face;
Upward tends to his abode,
 To rest in his embrace.

3 Fly me riches, fly me cares,
 While I that coast explore;
Flatt'ring world, with all thy snares,
 Solicit me no more.
Pilgrims fix not here their home,
 Strangers tarry but a night;
When the last dear morn is come,
 They'll rise to joyful light.

4 Cease, ye pilgrims, cease to mourn,
 Press onward to the prize;
Soon the Saviour will return,
 Triumphant in the skies:
There we'll join the heav'nly train,
 Welcom'd to partake the bliss;
Fly from sorrow and from pain,
 To realms of endless peace.

127 HYMN. 8, 7, 4.

1 YES! we trust the day is breaking;
 Joyful times are near at hand:
God, the mighty God, is speaking
 By his word in ev'ry land:
  When he chooses,
 Darkness flies at his command.

2 Let us hail the joyful season;
 Let us hail the dawning ray:
When the Lord appears, there's reason
 To expect a glorious day:
  At his presence
 Gloom and darkness flee away

3 While the foe becomes more daring;
 While he enters like a flood;
God, the Saviour, is preparing
 Means to spread his truth abroad;
  Ev'ry language
 Soon shall tell the love of God.

4 God of Jacob, high and glorious,
   Let thy people see thy hand;
Let the gospel be victorious,
   Through the world in every land;
And the idols
   Perish, Lord, at thy command.

128   HYMN.   C. M.

Walking with God.   Gen. v. 24.

1 O FOR a closer walk with God,
   A calm and heav'nly frame,
And light to shine upon the road
   That leads me to the lamb.

2 Where is the blessedness I knew
   When first I saw the Lord!
Where is the soul-refreshing view
   Of Jesus and his word!

3 What peaceful hours I then enjoy'd!
   How sweet their mem'ry still!
But now I find an aching void,
   The world can never fill.

4 Return, O holy Dove, return,
   Sweet messenger of rest!
I hate the sins that made thee mourn,
   And drove thee from my breast.

5 The dearest idol I have known,
   Whate'er that idol be,
Help me to tear it from thy throne,
   And worship only thee.

6 So shall my walk be close with God,
   Calm and serene my frame!
And purer light shall mark the road
   That leads me to the Lamb.

129   HYMN.   C. M.

1 HOW vain are all things here below,
   How false and yet how fair!
Each pleasure has its poison too,
   And every sweet a snare.

2 The brightest things below the sky
   Give but a flattering light;
We should suspect some danger nigh,
   Where we possess delight.

3 Our dearest joys, and nearest friends,
  The partners of our blood,
How they divide our wav'ring minds,
  And leave but half for God!

4 The fondness of a creature's love,
  How strong it strikes the sense!
Thither the warm affections move,
  Nor can we call them thence.

5 Dear Saviour! let thy beauties be
  My soul's eternal food;
And grace command my heart away
  From all created good.

THE HOLY SCRIPTURES.

130 HYMN. C. M.

Revelation welcomed.

1 HAIL, sacred truth! whose piercing rays
  Dispel the shades of night;
Diffusing o'er the mental world,
  The healing beams of light.

2 Jesus, thy word, with friendly aid,
  Restores our wandering feet;
Converts the sorrows of the mind
  To joys divinely sweet.

3 Oh! send thy light and truth abroad,
  In all their radiant blaze;
And bid th' admiring world adore
  The glories of thy grace.

131 HYMN L. M.

Divine Authority of the Bible.

1 'TWAS by an order from the Lord,
The ancient prophets spoke his word;
His Spirit did their tongues inspire,
And warm their hearts with heav'nly fire.

2 Great God! mine eyes with pleasure look
On the dear volume of thy book;
There my Redeemer's face I see,
And read his name who died for me.

3 Let the false raptures of the mind
Be lost and vanish in the wind:
Here I can fix my hope secure;
This is thy word—and must endure.

132   HYMN. C. P. M

1 HOW precious, Lord, thy sacred word!
What light and joy those leaves afford
  To souls in deep distress!
Thy precepts guide our doubtful way,
Thy fear forbids our feet to stray,
  Thy promise leads to rest.

2 Thy threat'nings wake our slumb'ring eye.
And warn us where our danger lies;
  But 'tis thy gospel, Lord,
That makes the guilty conscience clean,
Converts the soul, and conquers sin,
  And gives a free reward.

133   HYMN. C. M.

1 OPPRESS'D with guilt, and full of fears,
  I come to thee, my Lord;
While not a ray of hope appears,
  But in thy holy word.

2 The volume of my Father's grace
  Does all my grief dispel;
Here I behold my Saviour's face,
  And learn to do his will.

3 Here living water freely flows,
  To cleanse me from my sin;
'Tis here the tree of knowledge grows,
  Nor danger dwells therein.

4 O! may thy counsels, mighty God,
  My roving feet command;
Nor I forsake the happy road,
  That leads to thy right hand.

THE HOLY SCRIPTURES.

134   HYMN. S. M.

1 BEHOLD, the morning sun
    Begins his glorious way;
  His beams through all the nations run,
    And life and light convey.

2 But where the gospel comes,
    It spreads diviner light,
  It calls dead sinners from their tombs,
    And gives the blind their sight.

3 How perfect is thy word!
    And all thy judgments just!
  Forever sure thy promise, Lord,
    And we securely trust.

4 My gracious God, how plain
    Are thy directions given!
  O! may I never read in vain,
    But find the path to heaven.

135   HYMN. C. M.

1 HOW shall the young secure their hearts,
    And guard their lives from sin?
  Thy word the choicest rules imparts,
    To keep the conscience clean.

2 'Tis like the sun—a heavenly light,
    That guides us all the day;
  And, through the dangers of the night,
    A lamp to lead our way.

3 Thy precepts make me truly wise,
    I hate the sinner's road;
  I hate my own vain thoughts that rise
    But love thy law, my God.

4 Thy word is everlasting truth,
    How pure is every page!—
  That holy book shall guide our youth,
    And well support our age.

AFFLICTIONS AND DEATH.

136 HYMN. 8's, and 7's.

Mourners comforted.

1 CEASE, ye mourners, cease to languish,
  O'er the grave of those you love;
Pain, and death, and night, and anguish,
  Enter not the world above.

2 While our silent steps are straying,
  Lonely, through night's deep'ning shade,
Glory's brightest beams are playing
  Round th' immortal spirit's head.

3 Light and peace at once deriving
  From the hand of God most high,
In his glorious presence living,
  They shall never—never die.

4 Endless pleasure, pain excluding,
  Sickness there, no more can come;
There no fear of wo, intruding,
  Sheds o'er heav'n a moment's gloom.

5 Now, ye mourners, cease to languish
  O'er the grave of those you love;
Far remov'd from pain and anguish,
  They are chanting hymns above.

137 HYMN. L. M.

Death of the Righteous.

1 HOW bless'd the righteous when he dies!
  When sinks a weary soul to rest,
How mildly beam the closing eyes,
  How gently heaves th' expiring breast!

2 So fades a summer cloud away,
  So sinks the gale when storms are o'er,
So gently shuts the eye of day,
  So dies a wave along the shore.

3 A holy quiet reigns around,
  A calm which life nor death destroys;
Nothing disturbs that peace profound
  Which his unfetter'd soul enjoys.

AFFLICTIONS AND DEATH.　341

4 Farewell, conflicting hopes and fears,
   Where lights and shades alternate dwell;
   How bright th' unchanging morn appears!
   Farewell, inconstant world, farewell.

138　　HYMN. C. M.
Dying in the Lord.

1 HEAR what the voice from heav'n proclaims,
   For all the pious dead;
   Sweet is the savour of their names,
   And soft their sleeping bed.

2 They die in Jesus, and are bless'd;
   How kind their slumbers are!
   From suff'rings, and from sins releas'd,
   And freed from ev'ry snare.

3 Far from this world of toil and strife,
   They're present with the Lord;
   The labours of their mortal life
   End in a large reward.

139　　HYMN. C. M.
Mourning with Hope.

1 THAT once-lov'd form, now cold and dead,
   Each mournful thought employs;
   And nature weeps, her comforts fled,
   And wither'd all her joys.

2 Hope looks beyond the bounds of time;
   When what we now deplore,
   Shall rise in full immortal prime,
   And bloom to fade no more.

3 Then cease, fond nature, cease thy tears,
   Religion points on high;
   There everlasting spring appears,
   And joys that cannot die.

140　　HYMN. C. M.
Prayer for Support in Death.

1 WHEN, bending o'er the brink of life,
   My trembling soul shall stand,
   And wait to pass death's awful flood,
   Great God, at thy command.

2 Thou source of life and joy supreme,
  Whose arm alone can save,
  Dispel the darkness that surrounds
  The entrance to the grave.

3 Lay thy supporting, gentle hand
  Beneath my sinking head,
  And let a beam of life divine
  Illume my dying bed.

141 HYMN. L. M.
The Grave. Job iii. 17.

1 THE grave is now a favour'd spot—
  To saints who sleep, in Jesus bless'd;
  For there the wicked trouble not,
  And there the weary are at rest.

2 At rest in Jesus' faithful arms;
  At rest as in a peaceful bed:
  Secure from all the dreadful storms,
  Which round this sinful world are spread.

3 Thrice happy souls, who're gone before
  To that inheritance divine!
  They labour, sorrow, sigh no more,
  But bright in endless glory shine.

4 Then let our mournful tears be dry,
  Or in a gentle measure flow;
  We hail them happy in the sky,
  And joyful wait our call to go.

142 HYMN. 8's.
Death of a Brother.

1 HOW blest is our brother, bereft
  Of all that could burden his mind;
  How easy the soul that has left
  This wearisome body behind!
  Of evil incapable thou,
  Whose relics with envy I see,
  No longer in misery now,
  No longer a sinner like me.

2 This earth is affected no more
  With sickness, or shaken with pain,
  The war in the members is o'er,
  And never shall vex him again:

    No anger henceforward, or shame,
      Shall redden his innocent clay;
    Extinct is the animal flame,
      And passion is vanish'd away.

3 The lids he so seldom could close,
      By sorrow forbidden to sleep,
    Seal'd up in eternal repose,
      Have strangely forgotten to weep;
    These fountains can yield no supplies—
      These hollows from water are free;
    The tears are all wiped from those eyes,
      And evil they never shall see.

4 To mourn and to suffer is mine,
      While bound in a prison I breathe,
    And still for deliverance pine,
      And press to the issues of death.
    What now with my tears I bedew,
      Oh, shall I not shortly become!
    My spirit created anew,
      Ere I am consigned to the tomb!

143   HYMN. 8's.

Death of a Sister.

1 'TIS finish'd! the conflict is past,
      The heav'n-born spirit is fled;
    Her wish is accomplish'd at last,
      And now she's entomb'd with the dead.
    The months of affliction are o'er,
      The days and the nights of distress,
    We see her in anguish no more—
      She's gained her happy release.

    No sickness, or sorrow, or pain,
      Shall ever disquiet her now;
    For death to her spirit was gain,
      Since Christ was her life when below.
    Her soul has now taken its flight
      To mansions of glory above,
    To mingle with angels of light,
      And dwell in the kingdom of love.

3 The victory now is obtain'd;
      She's gone her dear Saviour to see;
    Her wishes she fully has gain'd—
      She's now where she longed to be.

Then let us forbear to complain,
  That she has now gone from our sight;
We soon shall behold her again,
  With new and redoubled delight.

144   HYMN.   C. M.
Death of a Young Person.

1 WHEN blooming youth is snatch'd away
  By death's resistless hand,
Our hearts the mournful tribute pay,
  Which pity must demand.

2 While pity prompts the rising sigh,
  Oh, may this truth, imprest
With awful pow'r—"I too must die"—
  Sink deep in ev'ry breast.

3 The voice of this alarming scene
  May ev'ry heart obey;
Nor be the heav'nly warning vain,
  Which calls to watch and pray.

4 Oh, let us fly, to Jesus fly,
  Whose pow'rful arm can save;
Then shall our hopes ascend on high,
  And triumph o'er the grave.

145   HYMN   C. M.
Death and Burial of Christians.

1 WHY do we mourn departing friends,
  Or shake at death's alarms!
'Tis but the voice that Jesus sends
  To call them to his arms.

2 Are we not tending upward too,
  To heav'n's desired abode?
Why should we wish the hours more slow,
  Which keep us from our God!

3 Why should we tremble to convey
  Their bodies to the tomb?
'Twas there the Saviour's body lay,
  And left a long perfume.

4 The graves of all his saints he blest,
  And soften'd ev'ry bed:
Where should the dying members rest,
  But with their dying Head?

5 Thence he arose, ascending high,
  And show'd our feet the way:
 Up to the Lord his saints shall fly
  At the great rising day.
6 Then let the last loud trumpet sound,
  And bid our kindred rise;
 Awake, ye nations under ground!
  Ye saints! ascend the skies.

146   HYMN. L. M.
The peaceful Death of the Righteous.

1 SWEET is the scene when Christians die,
   When holy souls retire to rest:
  How mildly beams the closing eye!
   How gently heaves th' expiring breast!
2 So fades a summer cloud away;
   So sinks the gale when storms are o'er;
  So gently shuts the eye of day;
   So dies a wave along the shore.
3 Triumphant smiles the victor's brow,
   Fann'd by some guardian angel's wing:
  O grave! where is thy victory now!
   And where, O death! where is thy sting

147   HYMN. S. M.

1 O FOR the death of those
   Who slumber in the Lord!
  O be like theirs my last repose,
   Like theirs my last reward.
2 Their bodies, in the ground,
   In silent hope may lie,
  Till the last trumpet's joyful sound
   Shall call them to the sky.
3 Their ransom'd spirits soar
   On wings of faith and love,
  To meet the Saviour they adore,
   And reign with him above.
4 With us their names shall live
   Through long succeeding years,
  Embalm'd with all our hearts can give,
   Our praises and our tears.
5 O for the death of those
   Who slumber in the Lord:
  O be like theirs my last repose,
   Like theirs my last reward.
15*

TIME AND ETERNITY

148   HYMN. C. M.
Time short and misspent.

1 HOW short and hasty is our life!
   How vast our soul's affairs!
Yet senseless mortals vainly strive
   To lavish out their years.

2 Our days run thoughtlessly along,
   Without a moment's stay;
Just like a story, or a song,
   We pass our lives away.

3 God from on high invites us home,
   But we march heedless on,
And, ever hastening to the tomb,
   Stoop downward as we run.

4 How we deserve the deepest hell,
   That slight the joys above!
What chains of vengeance should we feel,
   That break such cords of love!

5 Draw us, O God, with sov'reign grace,
   And lift our thoughts on high,
That we may end this mortal race,
   And see salvation nigh.

149   HYMN. C. M.

1 THE time is short!—sinners, beware,
   Nor trifle time away:
The word of great salvation hear,
   While yet 'tis called to-day.

2 The time is short!—O sinners, now,
   To Christ the Lord submit;
To mercy's golden sceptre bow,
   And fall at Jesus' feet.

3 The time is short!—ye saints, rejoice—
   The Lord will quickly come;
Soon shall you hear the Saviour's voice,
   To call you to your home.

4 The time is short!—it swiftly flies—
   The hour is just at hand,
When we shall mount above the skies,
   And reach the wished-for land.

5 The time is short!—the moment near,
   When we shall dwell above;
And be forever happy there,
   With Jesus, whom we love.

150   HYMN. C. M.

Time the Period to prepare for Eternity.

1 THEE we adore, Eternal Name!
   And humbly own to thee,
How feeble is our mortal frame,
   What dying worms are we!

2 The year rolls round, and steals away
   The breath that first it gave;
Whate'er we do—where'er we be,
   We're travelling to the grave.

3 Great God! on what a slender thread
   Hang everlasting things!
Th' eternal state of all the dead
   Upon life's feeble strings!

4 Eternal joy—or endless wo
   Attends on every breath!
And yet how unconcern'd we go
   Upon the brink of death!

5 Awake, O Lord, our drowsy sense,
   To walk this dang'rous road;
And if our souls are hurried hence,
   May they be found with God.

151   HYMN. L. M.

1 LIFE is the time to serve the Lord,
The time t' insure the great reward;
And while the lamp holds out to burn,
The vilest sinner may return.

2 Life is the hour that God has given
T' escape from hell, and fly to heaven;
The day of grace—and mortals may
Secure the blessings of the day.

3 Then, what my thoughts design to do,
My hands, with all your might, pursue;
Since no device, nor work, is found,
Nor faith, nor hope, beneath the ground.

4 There are no acts of pardon pass'd
  In the cold grave to which we haste;
  But darkness, death, and long despair
  Reign in eternal silence there.

152   HYMN. S. M.

TO-MORROW, Lord, is thine,
  Lodg'd in thy sov'reign hand;
And if its sun arise and shine,
  It shines by thy command.

2 The present moment flies,
    And bears our life away;
  O make thy servants truly wise,
    That they may live to-day.

3 Since on this fleeting hour
    Eternity is hung,
  Awake, by thine Almighty pow'r,
    The aged and the young.

4 One thing demands our care;
    O! be that still pursu'd!
  Lest, slighted once, the season fair
    Should never be renew'd.

5 To Jesus may we fly,
    Swift as the morning light,
  Lest life's young golden beams should die
    In sudden endless night.

153   HYMN. C. M.

1 SHINE on our souls, eternal God,
    With rays of mercy shine:
  O let thy favour crown our days,
    And all their round be thine.

2 With thee let every week begin;
    With thee each day be spent;
  To thee each fleeting hour be given,
    Since each by thee is lent.

3 Thus cheer us through this desert road,
    Till all our labours cease;—
  Till heav'n refresh our weary souls
    With everlasting peace.

154 HYMN. L. M.
Eternity anticipated.

1 ETERNITY is just at hand,
And shall I waste my ebbing sand?
And careless view departing day,
And throw my inch of time away?

2 Eternity!—tremendous sound!—
To guilty souls a dreadful wound!
But O! if Christ and heav'n be mine,
How sweet the accents!—how divine!

3 Be this my chief, my only care—
My high pursuit—my ardent pray'r—
An interest in the Saviour's blood,
My pardon seal'd, and peace with God.

4 But should my brightest hopes be vain;
The rising doubts how sharp their pain;
My fears, O gracious God, remove,
Confirm my title to thy love.

5 Search, Lord—O search my inmost heart,
And light, and hope, and joy, impart;
From guilt and error set me free,
And guide me safe to heav'n and thee.

THE JUDGMENT.

155 HYMN. C. M.
Triumph over Death in Hope of the Resurrection.

1 GREAT God, I own thy sentence just,
And nature must decay;
I yield my body to the dust,
To dwell with fellow clay.

2 Yet faith may triumph o'er the grave,
And trample on the tombs;
My great Redeemer ever lives,
My God, my Saviour, comes.

3 The mighty Conqu'ror shall appear,
High on a royal seat;
And death, the last of all his foes,
Lie vanquish'd at his feet.

4 Then shall I see thy lovely face
  With strong, immortal eyes,
And feast upon thine unknown grace,
  With pleasure and surprise.

156   HYMN. S. M.

Hope of the Resurrection.

1 AND must this body die?
  This mortal frame decay?
And must these active limbs of mine
  Lie mould'ring in the clay?

2 God, my Redeemer, lives,
  And frequent from the skies,
Looks down and watches all my dust
  Till he shall bid it rise.

3 Array'd in glorious grace
  Shall these vile bodies shine,
And ev'ry shape, and ev'ry face
  Look heav'nly and divine.

4 These lively hopes we owe
  To Jesus' dying love—
We would adore his grace below,
  And sing his power above.

5 Accept, O Lord, the praise
  Of these our humble songs,
Till tunes of nobler sound we raise
  With our immortal tongues.

157   HYMN 8's, 7's, and 4's.

1 LO! He comes, with clouds descending
  Once for favour'd sinners slain!
Thousand, thousand saints, attending,
  Swell the triumph of his train:
    Hallelujah!
  Jesus comes—and comes to reign.

2 Every eye shall now behold him,
  Robed in dreadful majesty!
Those who set at nought and sold him,
  Pierced and nail'd him to the tree,
    Deeply wailing,
  Shall the true Messiah see!

THE JUDGMENT. 351

3 When the solemn trump has sounded,
   Heav'n and earth shall flee away;
All who hate him must, confounded,
   Hear the summons of that day—
    "Come to judgment!—
   Come to judgment—come away."

4 Yea, amen!—let all adore thee,
   High on thine eternal throne!
Saviour, take the pow'r and glory:
   Make thy righteous sentence known!
    O come quickly—
   Claim the kingdom for thine own!

158   HYMN. 7's.

1 HARK!—that shout of rapt'rous joy,
   Bursting forth from yonder cloud!
Jesus comes—and through the sky,
   Angels tell their joy aloud.

2 Hark! the trumpet's awful voice
   Sounds abroad through sea and land;
Let his people now rejoice!
   Their redemption is at hand.

3 See! the Lord appears in view;
   Heav'n and earth before him fly!
Rise, ye saints, he comes for you—
   Rise to meet him in the sky.

4 Go, and dwell with him above,
   Where no foe can e'er molest;
Happy in the Saviour's love!
   Ever blessing, ever blest.

159   HYMN. 8's, 7's, and 4's.

1 DAY of judgment—day of wonders!
   Hark!—the trumpet's awful sound,
Louder than a thousand thunders,
   Shakes the vast creation round!
    How the summons
   Will the sinner's heart confound!

2 See the Judge, our nature wearing,
   Clothed in majesty divine!
You who long for his appearing,
   Then shall say, "This God is mine!"
    Gracious Saviour,
   Own me in that day for thine!

3 At his call the dead awaken,
 Rise to life from earth and sea;
All the powers of nature, shaken
 By his looks, prepare to flee:
  Careless sinner,
 What will then become of thee?

4 But to those who have confessed,
 Loved and served the Lord below,
He will say, "Come near, ye blessed,
 See the kingdom I bestow;
  You forever
 Shall my love and glory know."

160　　　　HYMN. C. M.

Banishment from God intolerable.

1 THAT awful day will surely come,
 Th' appointed hour makes haste,
When I must stand before my Judge,
 And pass the solemn test.

2 Thou lovely Chief of all my joys—
 Thou Sov'reign of my heart—
How could I bear to hear thy voice
 Pronounce the word—"Depart!"

3 O! wretched state of deep despair,
 To see my God remove,
And fix my doleful station where
 I must not taste his love.

4 Oh! tell me that my worthless name
 Is graven on thy hands;
Show me some promise in thy book,
 Where my salvation stands.

HEAVEN.

161　　　　HYMN. S. M.

Rest in Heaven.

1 OH! where shall rest be found?
 Rest for the weary soul!
'Twere vain the ocean's depths to sound,
 Or search from pole to pole.

2 The world can never give
   The bliss for which we sigh;
'Tis not the whole of life to live,
   Nor all of death to die.

3 Beyond this vale of tears
   There is a life above,
Unmeasur'd by the flight of years—
   And all that life is love.

162   HYMN. C. M.
The Peace and Repose of Heaven.

1 THERE is an hour of hallow'd peace
   For those with cares opprest,
Where sighs and sorr'wing tears shall cease,
   And all be hush'd to rest:
'Tis then the soul is freed from fears
   And doubts, which here annoy;
Then they that oft had sown in tears,
   Shall reap again in joy.

2 There is a home of sweet repose,
   Where storms assail no more;
The stream of endless pleasure flows
   On that celestial shore:
There purity with love appears,
   And bliss without alloy;
There they that oft had sown in tears,
   Shall reap again in joy.

163   HYMN. L. M.
The Worship of Heaven.

1 O FOR a sweet inspiring ray,
To animate our feeble strains,
From the bright realms of endless day,
The blissful realms, where Jesus reigns!

2 There, low before his glorious throne,
Adoring saints and angels fall;
And with delightful worship own,
His smile their bliss, their heav'n, their all.

3 Immortal glories crown his head,
While tuneful hallelujahs rise,
And love, and joy, and triumph spread
Through all th' assemblies of the skies.

4 He smiles, and seraphs tune their songs
  To boundless rapture, while they gaze:
  Ten thousand, thousand joyful tongues
  Resound his everlasting praise.

5 There all the foll'wers of the Lamb
  Shall join at last the heav'nly choir:
  O may the joy inspiring theme
  Awake our faith and warm desire!

6 Dear Saviour, let thy spirit seal
  Our int'rest in that blissful place;
  Till death remove this mortal veil,
  And we behold thy lovely face.

164   HYMN.   8's and 6's.

The Everlasting Bliss of Heaven.

1 HEAV'N is the land where troubles cease,
    Where toils and tears are o'er;
  The blissful clime of rest and peace,
    Where cares distract no more,
  And not the shadow of distress
  Dims its unsullied blessedness.

2 Heav'n is the place where Jesus lives,
    To plead his dying blood;
  While to his pray'rs, his Father gives
    An unknown multitude,
  Whose harps and tongues, through endless d
  Shall crown his head with songs of praise.

3 Heav'n is the dwelling-place of joy,
    The home of light and love,
  Where faith and hope in rapture die,
    And ransom'd souls above
  Enjoy, before th' eternal throne,
  Bliss everlasting and unknown.

165   HYMN.   C. M.

1 WHEN I can read my title clear
    To mansions in the skies,
  I bid farewell to every fear,
    And wipe my weeping eyes.

2 Should earth against my soul engage,
   And hellish darts be hurl'd,
Then I can smile at Satan's rage,
   And face a frowning world.

3 Let cares like a wild deluge come,
   And storms of sorrow fall;
May I but safely reach my home,
   My God, my heav'n, my all:—

4 There shall I bathe my weary soul
   In seas of heav'nly rest,
And not a wave of trouble roll
   Across my peaceful breast.

166   HYMN. C. M.

1 THERE is a land of pure delight,
   Where saints immortal reign;
Infinite day excludes the night,
   And pleasures banish pain.

2 There everlasting spring abides,
   And never-with'ring flow'rs:
Death, like a narrow sea, divides
   This heav'nly land from ours.

3 Sweet fields beyond the swelling flood,
   Stand dress'd in living green;
So to the Jews old Canaan stood,
   While Jordan roll'd between.

4 But tim'rous mortals start and shrink,
   To cross this narrow sea;
And linger, shiv'ring on the brink,
   And fear to launch away.

5 O! could we make our doubts remove,
   Those gloomy doubts that rise,
And see the Canaan that we love
   With unbeclouded eyes!—

6 Could we but climb where Moses stood,
   And view the landscape o'er,
Not Jordan's stream, nor death's cold flood,
   Should fright us from the shore.

167 HYMN. S's, and 6's.

The Peace and Rest of Heaven.

1 THERE is an hour of peaceful rest,
   To mourning wand'rers giv'n;
There is a joy for souls distress'd,
A balm for ev'ry wounded breast—
   'Tis found above in heav'n.

2 There is a home for weary souls,
   By sin and sorrow driv'n,
When toss'd on life's tempestuous shoals,
Where storms arise, and ocean rolls,
   And all is drear but heav'n.

3 There faith lifts up her cheerful eye,
   To brighter prospects giv'n;
And views the tempest passing by,
The ev'ning shadows quickly fly,
   And all serene in heav'n!

4 There, fragrant flowers immortal, bloom,
   And joys supreme are given:
There, rays divine disperse the gloom:—
Beyond the confines of the tomb,
   Appears the dawn of heav'n.

168 HYMN. C. M.

1 JERUSALEM! my happy home!
   Name ever dear to me!
When shall my labours have an end,
   In joy, and peace, and thee!

2 When shall these eyes thy heav'n-built walls
   And pearly gates behold!
Thy bulwarks, with salvation strong,
   And streets of shining gold!

3 O, when, thou city of my God,
   Shall I thy courts ascend,
Where congregations ne'er break up,
   And Sabbaths have no end!

4 There happier bow'rs than Eden's bloom,
   Nor sin nor sorrow know;
Blest seats! through rude and stormy scenes
   I onward press to you.

5 Why should I shrink at pain and wo?
  Or feel at death, dismay!
I've Canaan's goodly land in view,
  And realms of endless day.

6 Apostles, martyrs, prophets there,
  Around my Saviour stand;
And soon my friends in Christ below,
  Will join the glorious band.

7 Jerusalem! my happy home!
  My soul still pants for thee!
Then shall my labours have an end,
  When I thy joys shall see.

169   HYMN. L. M.

1 "WE'VE no abiding city here"—
  'This may distress the worldly mind;
But should not cost the saint a tear,
  Who hopes a better rest to find.

2 "We've no abiding city here"—
  Sad truth, were this to be our home:
But let this thought our spirits cheer,
  "We seek a city yet to come."

3 "We've no abiding city here"—
  Then let us live as pilgrims do;
Let not the world our rest appear,
  But let us haste from all below.

4 "We've no abiding city here"—
  We seek a city out of sight;
Zion its name—the Lord is there,
  It shines with everlasting light.

170   HYMN. 8's.

Earnest Desire of Heaven.

1 I LONG to behold him array'd
  With glory and light from above,—
The King in his beauty display'd,
  His beauty of holiest love:
I languish and sigh to be there,
  Where Jesus has fix'd his abode:
Oh when shall we meet in the air,
  And fly to the mountain of God?

2 With him I on Zion shall stand,
  (For Jesus hath spoken the word,)
The breadth of Immanuel's land
  Survey by the light of my Lord;
But when on thy bosom reclined,
  Thy face I am strengthen'd to see,
My fulness of rapture I find,
  My heaven of heavens, in thee.

3 How happy the people that dwell
  Secure in the city above!
No pain the inhabitants feel,
  No sickness or sorrow shall prove
Physician of souls, unto me
  Forgiveness and holiness give;
And then from the body set free,
  And then to the city receive.

171   HYMN. 7's.

The Redeemed in Heaven.

1 WHAT are these in bright array,
  This innumerable throng
Round the altar night and day,
  Hymning one triumphant song:
"Worthy is the Lamb once slain,
  Blessing, honour, glory, power,
Wisdom, riches, to obtain,
  New dominion, every hour,

2 These through fiery trials trod,
  These from great affliction came;
Now before the throne of God,
  Seal'd with his Almighty name;
Clad in raiment pure and white,
  Victor-palms in every hand,
Through their dear Redeemer's might,
  More than conquerors they stand.

3 Hunger, thirst, disease unknown
  On immortal fruits they feed;
Them, the Lamb amidst the throne,
  Shall to living fountains lead:
Joy and gladness banish sighs,
  Perfect love dispels all fears,
And for ever from their eyes,
  God shall wipe away the tears.

172 HYMN. L. M

Vanity of the World, and Happiness of Heaven.

1 HOW vain is all beneath the skies!
   How transient every earthly bliss!
How slender all the fondest ties,
   That bind us to a world like this!

2 The ev'ning cloud, the morning dew,
   The with'ring grass, the fading flower,
Of earthly hopes are emblems true—
   The glory of a passing hour!

3 But, though earth's fairest blossoms die,
   And all beneath the skies is vain,
There is a land whose confines lie
   Beyond the reach of care and pain.

4 Then let the hope of joys to come
   Dispel our cares, and chase our fears,
If God be ours, we're trav'ling home,
   Though passing through a vale of tears.

173 HYMN. C. M

1 O HAPPY soul, that lives on high,
   While men lie grov'ling here!
His hopes are fixed above the sky,
   And faith forbids his fear.

2 His conscience knows no secret stings,
   While grace and joy combine
To form a life whose holy springs
   Are hidden and divine.

3 He waits in secret on his God,
   His God in secret sees;
Let earth be all in arms abroad,
   He dwells in heavenly peace.

4 His pleasures rise from things unseen,
   Beyond this world of time,
Where neither eyes nor ears have been
   Nor thoughts of mortals climb.

5 He wants no pomp nor royal throne,
   To raise his figure here;
Content and pleased to live alone,
   Till Christ his life appear.

174   HYMN.   10 and 11.

View of Heaven.

1 ON wings of faith, mount up, my soul, and rise,
  View thine inheritance beyond the skies;
  Nor heart can think, nor mortal tongue can tell,
  What endless pleasures in those mansions dwell:
There my Redeemer lives, all bright and glorious,
O'er sin, and death, and hell, he reigns victorious.

2 No gnawing grief, no sad heart-rending pain
  In that bless'd country can admission gain;
  No sorrow there, no soul-tormenting fear,
  For God's own hand shall wipe the falling tear:
There my Redeemer lives, &c.

3 Before the throne a crystal river glides,
  Immortal verdure decks its cheerful sides;
  There the fair tree of life majestic rears
  Its blooming head, and sovereign virtue bears:
There my Redeemer lives, &c.

4 No rising sun his transient beam displays,
  No sickly moon emits her feeble rays;
  The Godhead there celestial glory sheds,
  Th' exalted Lamb eternal radiance spreads:
There my Redeemer lives, &c.

5 One distant glimpse my eager passion fires
  Jesus, to thee my longing soul aspires!
  When shall I at my heav'nly home arrive—
  When leave this earth, and when begin to live!
For there my Saviour is all bright and glorious,
O'er sin, and death, and hell, he reigns victorious.

THE END.

STANDARD SPEAKERS,

PUBLISHED BY CHARLES DESILVER.

CHESTNUT STREET, PHILADELPHIA.

SARGENT'S SERIES OF STANDARD SPEAKERS.

THE STANDARD SPEAKER;

CONTAINING

Exercises in Prose and Poetry,

FOR DECLAMATION IN SCHOOLS, ACADEMIES, LYCEUMS, AND COLLEGES.

NEWLY TRANSLATED OR COMPILED FROM CELEBRATED ORATORS, AUTHORS, AND POPULAR DEBATERS, ANCIENT AND MODERN.

A TREATISE ON ORATORY AND ELOCUTION.

WITH NOTES EXPLANATORY AND BIOGRAPHICAL.

BY EPES SARGENT.

In one demi-octavo volume, of 538 pages, half-roan binding. Price, $

This SPEAKER has undoubtedly acquired a higher reputation throughout the United States than any other similar work. In its production there has been a great expenditure of original labor, it contains all the great master-pieces of eloquence, and it abounds in original translations from the Greek, Latin, and French.

SARGENT'S SERIES OF STANDARD SPEAKERS.

THE
INTERMEDIATE STANDARD SPEAKER,
CONTAINING
PIECES FOR DECLAMATION, DIALOGUES, ETC., IN SCHOOLS AND COLLEGES.
INTRODUCTORY OR SUPPLEMENTARY TO THE STANDARD SPEAKER.

In one volume, 12mo., of 432 pages, half Turkey binding. Price, $`

This SPEAKER contains a capital collection of Dialogues, and short, spirited pieces for declamation; and the original *Debates* have acquired for it a well merited and wide-spread reputation. The pieces are quite distinct from those contained in the larger STANDARD SPEAKER.

For beginners in Declamation, this is the most attractive and serviceable work in the language; the selections being admirable, the original pieces skilfully adapted to their purpose, and the whole style of the book of a superior character.

All the above works are models of taste in typography, &c.; they are printed upon fine paper, and great care has been taken to render them fully equal to the requirements of the present progressive age.

Sargent's Series of Standard Speakers.

OPINIONS OF CRITICS AND TEACHERS

We have no hesitation in saying that the "Standard Speaker" is the best compilation of the kind, in the variety and in the comprehensiveness of its selections, which has yet been made on either side of the Atlantic. The various pieces are selected with great judgment from a long array of celebrated orators and writers, and not only is the volume admirably adapted to serve its primal purposes as a Speaker, but the general reader will find it to be a most stimulating and attractive book, far excelling any work of "elegant extracts" we have seen. — *E. P. Whipple, the well-known Essayist and Critic.*

I pronounce "Sargent's Series of Speakers" to be decidedly superior to any I have yet seen; and I will spare no pains in endeavoring to introduce them, not only into the schools of which I have charge, but also, into others, as far as my acquaintance extends. — *Giles Hathaway, Principal of Taylorsville Seminary, Taylorsville, Ky.*

Beside the old standard pieces, Mr. Sargent has given us a great many new ones, and, to my surprise, has put a new vigor into some of the old translations, which makes them quite new and redolent of their originals. — *E. S. Dixwell, Esq., late Principal of the Public Latin School, Boston.*

I trust that the improvement of the pupils of the old Latin School in elocution, will soon afford the most gratifying proofs of the good service rendered them by putting into their hands a collection of pieces so admirably adapted to their purposes. — *Francis Gardner, Principal of the Public Latin School, Boston.*

I have been using "Sargent's Standard Speaker" as a text-book in my class in Elocution, and I am highly pleased with it. It is the best work I have met with. My students are themselves delighted with it, which I consider a better recommendation than any I might offer. — *Jasper Packard, La Porte, Ind.*

I consider the "Standard Speaker" an invaluable companion in the school-room, and that for beauty of arrangement and the taste evinced in the collection of the several pieces, it holds a position pre-eminently superior to that of any other work of the kind I have ever examined. — *W. Hamilton Myers, Johnstown, Pa.*

Having given "Sargent's Standard and Primary Speakers" a thorough perusal, I speak advisedly when I say that they are the best works of the kind ever issued from the American press. I have adopted them in the Institute, and am now using them with great satisfaction. — *J. D. H. Corwine, Principal of Institute, Crittenden, Ky.*

Sargent's "Intermediate Standard Speaker" needs but to be known to be appreciated. We shall use the work, thankful to the author for the valuable selection he has given us, and to the publisher for the attractive mechanical dress in which he has presented it. — *M. L Hofford, Beverly, N. J.*

I am very much pleased with "Sargent's Standard Speakers," and have no hesitation in saying that I regard them, in several important particulars, as the best works of the kind that have come under my observation. — *L. A. Spencer, Principal of Swansboro' Academy, Swansboro', North Carolina.*

The "Standard Speaker" furnishes by far the best storehouse of oratorical matter with which I am acquainted — probably superior to any other in the language. — *G. F. Thayer, President of the American Institute, and Principal of the Chauncey Place School, Boston.*

The "Standard Speaker" contains the choicest selections of oratorical literature in the English language. No man of any literary taste can call his library complete without it. — *W. H. Boies, Hennepin, Ill.*

I have used the "Standard Speaker" for a number of years, and I am very happy to say that it is unrivalled in the number and excellence of its selections. — *Geo. P. Butler, East Island, Maine.*

The "Intermediate Standard Speaker" pleases me so much, that I shall recommend it to the booksellers in my vicinity. — *O. O. Wheeler, South Hero, Vt.*

I am using "Sargent's Standard Speakers" in my school, and like them very much. — *W. E. Mitchell, Germantown, Tenn.*

Sargent's Series of Standard Speakers.

OPINIONS OF EMINENT MEN ETC.

Mr. Sargent has given new and improved translations of great merit from the most celebrated orations of antiquity, in Greek and Latin; from the most distinguished efforts of modern eloquence in the languages of civilized Europe; and side by side with these, amid the masterpieces of a Chatham and Burke, and Sheridan and Fox, he has placed many specimens of our cis-Atlantic eloquence, which have no reason to shun the proximity and comparison. The material and mechanical execution of the work, and especially the accuracy of punctuation, are worthy of the highest commendation; and while, with great pleasure, we recommend this compilation to those institutions for the especial use of which it was designed, we venture to say that the desultory reader will not peruse it without profit and satisfaction. — *Professor Whitwell, Farmers' College, Ohio.*

"Sargent's Standard Speaker" embraces a fair representation of specimens of the eloquence of all nations and languages. It is remarkably complete in all the departments of modern eloquence, and yet, after a diligent scrutiny, we find that the editor has judiciously retained nearly all of those old standard favorite pieces, whether in prose or poetry, which we hope may always be perpetuated in the pages of speaking-books and the memories of youth. — *Charles Hale.*

"Sargent's Standard Speaker" presents an unexampled range of well-systematized productions of the most distinguished orators and writers of the world, from which the favored student who possesses it may, during his whole course preparatory to an active and earnest participation in public affairs, derive the best examples of eloquence of various styles, and in its various departments. — *Alfred Stebbins, Principal of High School, Northampton, Mass.*

I have seen no work which contains so complete and judicious a collection of pieces for declamation as "Sargent's Standard Speaker." The introductory treatise contains many valuable directions to the student; the original translations are rendered into excellent English; and the whole deserves to be regarded as a highly important contribution to the wants of our literary institutions. — *Thomas Sherwin, Principal of High School, Boston, Mass.*

The arrangement of "Sargent's Standard Speaker" appears to me to be an excellent one, and the selections are, in all respects, unexceptionable. I cannot doubt that the book must be extensively useful. — *Millard Fillmore.*

"Sargent's Standard Speaker" is a work which cannot fail to be useful, and to be well received by the public. — *Lewis Cass.*

OPINIONS OF THE PRESS.

"Sargent's Standard Speaker" is manifestly the most comprehensive collection of the kind, and we doubt if ever so much labor was given to one before. Besides the many new and spirited translations from the ancient languages and from the French which are given, the editor seems to have carefully studied the works of all the great orators, from Demosthenes to Chatham, and from Patrick Henry to Henry Clay, for appropriate extracts, now for the first time adopted as elocutionary exercises. This work should be in the possession of every teacher and pupil. — *Louisville Journal.*

"The Standard Speaker," by Mr. Epes Sargent, is the most comprehensive collection of exercises for declamation and elocution which has ever been published in this country. It comprises several hundred articles in prose and verse, gleaned from the best writers and orators, ancient and modern. — *National Intelligencer, Washington, D. C.*

"Sargent's Standard Speaker" is a very artist-like book. It eclipses every previous collection of the kind, the editor having evidently bestowed upon it a degree of labor which has been given to no similar production. A capital introductory treatise on elocution, and a full index, give completeness to the volume. — *New Orleans Picayune.*

Sargent's Series of Standard Speakers.

OPINIONS OF THE PRESS.

"Sargent's Standard Speaker" is one of the best books of the kind yet presented to the public. It shows common sense and good sense in its introduction, is judicious in its extracts, copious in those departments of the Senate and the Bar, where Americans should be best informed, and is free throughout from the prevailing preference—in school-books of this class—for expediency before classicality. Mr. Sargent's taste accepts nothing that is not worthy, and omits little that is desirable. We commend his "Standard Speaker" to the attention of teachers. — *Literary World.*

"Sargent's Standard Speaker" is the most thorough and comprehensive collection of elocutionary exercises that we remember to have seen. As a compendium of the eloquence of all nations and times, it is well deserving of a place in every library; while as a repository of pieces admirably adapted in their length and general character for declamation and recitation in schools, it cannot fail to be widely introduced into our seminaries of learning.—*Democratic Review.*

"Sargent's Standard Speaker" is an admirable collection for the purposes of school declamation, and is introduced with a valuable treatise upon the principles of the art. The selections, varied, copious, and directed by excellent taste, are from English and American orators, and translations from foreign writers. We do what we very seldom do in regard to a school-book — heartily endorse it. — *Providence, (R. I.) Journal.*

No Speaker extant — none ever published — contains so many gems of oratory, so large an amount and splendid variety of pieces, as "Sargent's Standard Speaker." In the case of selections, care has been taken to collect them from the latest and most authentic editions of the works from which they are extracted; and thus many current errors and mutilations have been avoided. — *Troy (N. Y.) Daily Times.*

The "Standard Speaker," by Mr. Epes Sargent, brother of our fellow-citizen, supplies a desideratum long needed in our schools and colleges, and which we hope, for the sake of the hitherto neglected and highly important branch of education of which it treats, may at once be adopted into the educational institutions throughout the land.—*Davenport (Iowa) Gazette.*

It is not merely as a judicious manual for educational purposes that we recommend "Sargent's Standard Speaker" to our readers. It is, in fact, a collection of many of the rarest and brightest gems in English literature, no less adapted to family reading and literary reference than to use in the classes of a school. — *New York Tribune.*

The pulpit, the bench, the bar, the legislative hall, and the lecture-room of our own and even foreign countries, have each furnished their contributions, and the book has high claims to its title of being the "Standard Speaker." We commend it to the attention of professors and students of oratory everywhere. — *Cincinnati Christian Herald.*

From a somewhat familiar acquaintance with Speakers of this description, we feel qualified to pronounce the opinion that "Sargent's Standard Speaker" is the best work of the kind extant. We have no doubt but it will readily be adopted as a standard in all our schools and colleges. — *New York Mirror.*

Such is Sargent's Standard Speaker," that, while it will be found to justify its title in the retention of all the standard specimens of rhetoric suitable for its purposes, it presents, in its large proportion of new exercises of a high character, fresh and enduring claims to popularity. — *International Magazine.*

As a book to be used in instruction, "Sargent's Standard Speaker" is excellent, the pieces being well adapted for declamation, and the introductory essay full, judicious, and instructive. We commend it to the special attention of young speakers — *Cincinnati Gazette.*

Sargent's Series of Standard Speakers.

OPINIONS OF THE PRESS.

The celebrated speeches of Robespierre, "Against War," and "Morality the Basis of Civilized Society," and the speeches of Mirabeau and Victor Hugo, are now for the first time placed before the American student of oratory; and "Sargent's Standard Speaker" as a whole — its unusual variety, methodical arrangement, and comprehensive grouping, constitutes the most valuable collection of literary gems that can be imagined. — *Cincinnati Daily Atlas.*

The collection is an admirable one, eminently judicious in the length of its articles, as well as in the great variety of the schools and styles of eloquence; and the fine taste of the compiler has left nothing to be wished for in the tone, moral or intellectual, of his book. We think "Sargent's Standard Speaker" will supply a desideratum long existing in our public seminaries. — *New Bedford Mercury.*

The selections in "Sargent's Standard Speaker" are from the most celebrated authors and orators, ancient and modern, and the translations from foreign languages are new. It is adapted in all respects for high schools, academies, colleges, and public schools of the higher grades, and will meet with the heartiest approbation of teachers in these educational institutions. — *New Haven Palladium.*

In comparing "Sargent's Standard Speaker" with its predecessors of the same genus, we find it of so distinct a species, that we may call it original. It is a great step in advance of them in idea and in fact. The whole collection may be called *living* specimens. The essay on oratory is an excellent production, and the notes a rich addition. — *Cincinnati Times.*

We recommend "Sargent's Standard Speaker" to the attention of teachers, students, and others, who will find it a depository of the true and beautiful in the world of thought, which have enchained senates, swayed the popular mind, and exercised such an influence on the destinies of nations. — *Bangor (Me.) Daily Mercury.*

"Sargent's Standard Speaker" is evidently a work of much labor, and has been prepared with great taste and excellent discretion. Not only is it adapted to serve its primal purpose as a Speaker, but to the general reader it will be found to be a most stimulating and attractive book. — *Boston Daily Journal.*

"Sargent's Standard Speaker" is the largest, most varied, and best collection of pieces for declamation that we have seen. It will prove a great acquisition to the youth whose duty it is "to appear in public on the stage." — *Utica (N. Y.) Daily Gazette.*

"Sargent's Standard Speaker" will prove a decided acquisition. While it evinces the judgment of the author, it also indicates an extensive and familiar acquaintance with the best writers and speakers, ancient and modern. — *Baltimore American.*

In the combination of many excellencies, "Sargent's Standard Speaker" seems to us the most complete and valuable of the many works of the kind which have issued from the press during the last dozen years. — *Boston Courier.*

The merits of Epes Sargent's work on Oratory and Elocution have been attested by its general adoption in our schools and colleges as a standard book in these branches of instruction. — *Charleston Evening News.*

We commend "Sargent's Standard Speaker" to aspirants in elocution, for the great variety of excellent examples and exercises in prose and poetry for declamation which it contains. — *London Athenæum.*

The "Standard Speaker" is the best book of the kind we have yet seen, and we have examined with some care every similar publication that we could find. — *Cambridge Chronicle.*

The exercises are prefaced by an able treatise on oratory, which will prove most valuable to all who wish to acquire the facility of speaking well in public. — *Indiana Daily Sentinel.*

Sargent's Series of Standard Speakers.

OPINIONS OF THE PRESS.

It is the paramount duty of him who prepares a work like the "Standard Speaker" to exclude every sentiment whose tendency is mischievous, however eloquently uttered, and to suffer nothing there *unfit to be treasured through life, and remembered in a dying hour.* We have examined this work with attention, and are happy to perceive that Mr. Sargent has exercised a sound discretion in this important particular. This work may well claim precedency, *longo intervallo,* of all similar productions with which we are acquainted. — *Boston Christian Observer.*

The value of the "Standard Speaker" is much enhanced by an introductory treatise on Oratory and Elocution, in which the author has manifested his good sense and judgment by rejecting the customary humbug of a tiresome series of artificial rules for reading, by written formulas and rhetorical notation, which, *during several years of experience as a teacher,* we have found productive of no other result than to weary and disgust the young pupil, with, to him, an incomprehensible jargon, and a set of useless or cabalistic signs. — *Fitchburg Reveille.*

The great feature of "Sargent's Standard Speaker" is the completeness of the Senatorial Department, in which have been introduced not only passages of rare beauty and effect from Chatham, Burke, Grattan, Shiel, Macaulay, and many others, but also some translations from Mirabeau, Victor Hugo, and other great speakers of France, which will become especial favorites in schools and elocutionary classes. — *Graham's Magazine.*

While the compiler of the "Speaker" has retained all the indispensable masterpieces, and restored many that have been omitted from the collections the last twenty years, he has given an amount of fresh, new, and appropriate matter, that will astonish and delight the youthful prize-seeking orators of our academies and schools. — *Knickerbocker (N. Y.) Magazine.*

"Sargent's Standard Speaker" is the most thorough in its adaptation to its general purpose, and the most extended in its range, of any of the Speakers that have preceded it. The book is fresh, the pieces are of the right length, and are selected with most critical care. — *Springfield (Mass.) Republican.*

The most complete and valuable of the many works of the kind which have issued from the press during the last dozen years. All the old favorites of our boyish days are here, together with a large amount of matter which is wholly new. *It is not so much a "Speaker," as the "Speaker."* — *Boston Courier.*

We are disposed to believe this book will, in very deed, become the "Standard Speaker" for our schools, &c. We know not where the student can find so extensive and choice a collection of pieces for declamation. — *Boston Daily Traveller.*

This "Speaker" speaks as never Speaker spake before. * * * The work is executed with great discretion, to the careful exclusion of every sentiment, however eloquently expressed, not fit to be uttered by the most fastidious. — *Washington (D. C.) Republic.*

It deserves to become "the Standard Speaker" in the highest schools throughout the Union. We know no collection of specimens of remarkable orators heretofore published, that can be compared with it in variety or extent. — *New York Commercial Advertiser.*

The whole range of ancient and modern oratory, pulpit, forensic, or occasional, as well as of poetry, dramatic, lyrical, or epic, has been explored, and the choicest gems from each brought together into this literary casket. — *Lowell Courier.*

The volume deserves to be, what its title claims, a "Standard Speaker." — *Boston Daily Advertiser.*

The "Standard Speaker" has been prepared with care, industry, and good taste, and is no lazy gleaning from the labors of others. — *Boston Post.*

It may well be called a "Standard Speaker." *It eclipses everything of the kind hitherto published.* It is *as perfect* in every department as could be desired. — *Salem (Mass.) Register.*

Sargent's Series of Standard Speakers.

OPINIONS OF THE PRESS.

The "Intermediate Standard Speaker" is introductory, being the second in a series, of which the Primary Speaker is the first. Thus the different lessons in elocution are suitable to the ages of the pupils, and they proceed in their studies until they reach the highest example. The present volume contains an excellent preliminary treatise, and capital selections from the orations and writings of eminent Europeans and Americans. — *Sunday Dispatch.*

"Sargent's Standard Speaker" is an invaluable book, and is not likely to be soon superseded. This, with the Intermediate and Primary Speakers, forms a series admirably adapted to the wants of learners of all ages, as there is no repetition of pieces in these books; the three, collectively, containing all the choice masterpieces in ancient and modern history. — *Philadelphia North American.*

The "Standard Speaker" is one of the most superbly executed works that ever emanated from the American press, and is the best book for the purposes for which it was designed, ever issued in the language. It must become a standard school-book, wherever reading and elocution are taught. — *New York Express.*

The "Intermediate Standard Speaker" is another volume in Mr. Epes Sargent's fine series of exercises in elocution. This is graduated for pupils of an age between those to which the "Standard" and the "Primary Speakers" are severally adapted, and is withal beautifully printed. — *New York Independent.*

The "Primary Standard Speaker" is the title of an admirable book for the *little speakers*, filled with the most desirable matter, and beautiful illustrations. Those teachers familiar with the other works of Mr. Sargent will need no other recommendation than the name of the author. — *School Visitor, Spencerport, Monroe Co., N. Y.*

The "Intermediate Standard Speaker" is an extremely interesting publication, contains a number of excellent specimens of oratory, and will doubtless be a valuable acquisition to the student of elocution. — *Philadelphia Sunday Mercury.*

The "Intermediate Standard Speaker" is especially rich in spirited declamatory passages, dialogues, and humorous pieces. The arrangement throughout is judicious, and the mechanical execution is of the very best description. — *Philada. Pennsylvania Inquirer.*

The "Intermediate Standard Speaker" contains a very excellent solid collection of specimens of English literature (most of them from the old orators) well selected for the use of schools. — *Philadelphia Courier.*

The enormous sales of Sargent's Speakers are the best guarantees of their excellence, and we are happy to say that a careful examination of the "Primary Standard Speaker" has convinced us that its merits correspond to this great demand. — *Philada. Evening Bulletin.*

The "Intermediate Standard Speaker" will make a sensation among the school-boys. With some familiar and indispensable pieces for declamation, it contains a great variety of new and spirited pieces in prose and verse. — *Boston Daily Courier.*

The "Primary Speaker" is designed for children, and every piece in the book is suitable to be committed to memory, and to be spoken by the young. — *Westminster Herald, New Wilmington, Pa.*

"Sargent's Intermediate Standard Speaker," published by Chas. Desilver, is one of the best works on declamation ever issued in the United States. — *Philada. Public Ledger.*

Considered strictly as a Speaker, and not as a Reader, we think the "Standard Speaker" is the best work of the kind we have seen. — *Philada. Saturday Evening Post.*

"Sargent's Standard Speaker" is adapted to the wants of the *whole* Union, and not of a section. — *New Orleans Picayune.*

Sargent's Series of Standard Speakers.

OPINIONS OF THE PRESS.

While the selections for the "Intermediate Standard Speaker" have been made with view chiefly to their effective declamatory character, they evince, as a whole, a clear perception of all the requirements of true eloquence, and effectiveness in public speaking, whether upon the rostrum, the floor of Congress, or the stage. In each and all of the departments is to be found a collection of gems of eloquence, and the whole work, including its typography, has been presented in a manner befitting its high literary ability.— *Phila. Evening Argus.*

At several recent school exhibitions, "the Congressional Debates," first published in Epes Sargent's new "Intermediate Standard Speaker," have been presented by the pupils with great applause. We have received from the publisher a circular announcing the issue of the last and smallest volume of Mr. Sargent's "Series of Speakers." It is entitled "the Primary Standard Speaker," and a good part of the contents are original.— *Boston Transcript.*

The introductory matter of the "Intermediate Standard Speaker" has been compiled from the best authorities, while the selections have been made with great care; the translations from the Greek, Latin, and French having been, with two or three exceptions, prepared expressly for this work.— *New York Courier and Enquirer.*

In the "Primary Standard Speaker" the selections have been made with great care, and with good taste. We are greatly pleased with the book, as the pieces are of moderate length, and present the most inspiring portions of the speeches of the best orators.— *Lutheran Observer, Baltimore, Md.*

The "Intermediate" is the second of the series of "Sargent's Standard Speakers." The selections are very judiciously made, and the introduction, containing practical and illustrated lessons in rhetoric from the pen of Mr. Sargent, will be found extremely useful both to pupil and teacher.— *New Orleans Picayune.*

The chimerical "systems," through which a short cut to the attainment of good elocution is promised, are set down at their true value. All the available information on the subject is summed up in "Sargent's Standard Speaker."— *New York Home Journal.*

The "Primary Standard Speaker" is embellished with spirited wood-cuts, and is just the book to delight the young pupil, who is looking for pieces to commit to memory and declaim.—*Philadelphia Inquirer.*

"Sargent's Primary Standard Speaker" is especially valuable to young people, as it contains a fine variety of original and selected pieces, adapted to the declamatory powers of the youngest pupils. It is beautifully illustrated.— *Philada. Sunday Mercury.*

The "Primary Standard Speaker," made up of original and selected pieces, especially adapted to declamation, for the youngest pupils in schools, is well illustrated, and appears to be an excellent book in other respects.— *New Orleans Daily Crescent.*

There is much in the "Primary Speaker" for its size, and it contains several original translations from French and German, together with many English pieces, not to be found in any similar work. Another pleasing feature is the illustrations.— *Boston Post.*

For declamation the "Standard Speaker" is one of the best books ever published, and is full of the richest gems of ancient and modern eloquence.— *Advertiser, St. Paul, Minnesota.*

The selections in Sargent's "Intermediate and Primary Speakers" are remarkably discriminating, and, as far as we have observed, free from all sectional bias.—*New Orleans Bee.*

The selections in the "Primary Standard Speaker" are well adapted to their purpose. Such a work was needed.— *News Letter.*

SARGENT'S SERIES OF STANDARD SPEAKERS.

SELECTIONS IN POETRY,
for Exercises at School and at Home.

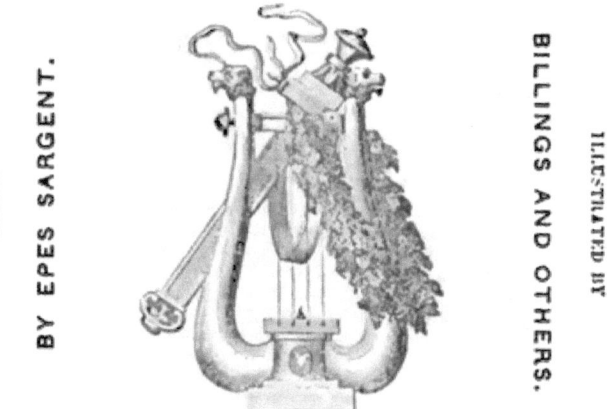

EDITED BY EPES SARGENT.

ILLUSTRATED BY BILLINGS AND OTHERS.

In one volume, 12mo., containing 336 pages, half-morocco binding. Price, .

This choice collection has been welcomed by both teachers and pupils with scarcely less cordiality than the well-known STANDARD SPEAKER, compiled by the same author.

OPINIONS OF THE PRESS.

"Sargent's Selections in Poetry" have been made by a man of true taste, and himself a genuine poet. He has culled these pieces from the entire range of English literature, and afforded specimens from writings not commonly accessible. Such a selection may be used with great profit, both in the family and in the school. — *Christian Times, Chicago, Ill.*

"Sargent's Selections in Poetry" are an admirable collection of gems culled by an editor who is unrivalled in that particular line of literature. It is beautifully illustrated, and the illustrations are worthy of the subjects, as well as of the very handsome style in which they are encased. — *Bedford Sentinel, Liberty, Va.*

The editor, with an observant and practised eye, seems to have ranged the whole field of periodical literature, and to have culled therefrom a rare collection of unfading flowers. The volume is an excellent one for the use of schools, and no less valuable as a table and literary companion. — *Boston Traveller.*

Many a school will be enlightened, and many a fireside enlivened by the perusal of these pure and beautiful effusions of the muse. — *Home Journal.*

Every piece in the book is a gem. British and American collections of poetry have been rifled of their choicest sweets, to make up the contents. — *Boston Journal.*

The selections are most judicious, chaste and numerous, and the illustrations beautiful — *Godey's Lady's Book.*

The artists, in the illustrations that adorn this book, have shown a fine appreciation of the thoughts of the poets. — *Boston Commonwealth.*

We believe this to be the best collection of English poetry that can be found in any single volume, of similar size. — *Cambridge (Mass.) Chronicle.*

14

STANDARD SPEAKERS.

FLOWERS OF ELOCUTION,

CONSISTING OF

POEMS ESSAYS, TALES, DIALOGUES, AND DRAMATIC SKETCHES.

ARRANGED FOR

A CLASS-BOOK.

BY MRS. CAROLINE LEE HENTZ,

AUTHOR OF "LINDA," "RENA," THE "PLANTER'S NORTHERN BRIDE," ETC.

In one 12mo. volume, comprising 322 pages, half-morocco binding. Price,

---

"Brave youth! thy words are kindling — they have waked
Ardors I deemed despair had quench'd forever!
I rushed with desperate purpose to this wild;
Driven to the verge of madness! Thou hast come
Like a redeeming spirit 'mid the storm,
And brought the wanderer back to reason's goal.
Ask not my name or rank. The sounding blasts
May bear them far as their wild wings extend.
Give me no name; but when in these free vales
Rumor is busy o'er the stranger's relics,
Say that thou found'st him prostrate in despair,
And that thy hand the fallen pillar raised,
To prop awhile fair Freedom's glorious dome."

OPINIONS OF THE PRESS.

The "Flowers of Elocution" is the name of a volume from the pen of a lady too well known in the literary world to need further commendation. Suffice it to say that, like everything else from her elegant pen, it abounds with the most beautiful gems. — *Bedford Sentinel, Liberty, Va.*

We need not say one word to prepossess the public in favor of this charming volume, this casket of literary and poetic pearls. The authoress has long since secured a sympathy in the hearts of both old and young, for the lovely offspring of her head and heart. — *Philadelphia Saturday Courier.*

The "Flowers of Elocution" only differs from "Sargent's Selections" in being entirely the production of one writer, instead of comprising a selection from different authors. With few exceptions, we find the pieces in this book well suited to their purpose. — *Christian Times, Chicago, Ill.*

The dramatic scenes, founded on Revolutionary events, are the most striking portion of the volume, and appear well adapted for representation in private circles. — Designed for a class-book, it seems to be every way suited to the purpose. — *N. Y. Daily Times.*

There is a purity of matter, and excellence of aim in this book, which recommends it to our favor. It is specially adapted for advanced classes of young ladies, and furnishes some pleasant, well-sustained dialogues. — *N. Y. Sun.*

This volume bears the bright impress of the authoress' mind, "is a fit offering to innocence and youth, and deserves the kindest reception from all hearts that hold congeniality with what is fair, and lovely, and of good report." — *Culpepper Weekly (Va.) Observer.*

The "Flowers of Elocution" is the title of a pleasant volume of prose and poetry, composed as a class-book, by the late Caroline Lee Hentz. — *New Orleans Bee.*

15

STANDARD SPEAKERS.

FROST'S AMERICAN SPEAKER,

COMPRISING A

COMPREHENSIVE TREATISE ON ELOCUTION,

AND

AN EXTENSIVE SELECTION OF SPECIMENS OF AMERICAN AND FOREIGN ELOQUENCE

EMBELLISHED WITH

Portraits of Distinguished American Orators,

ENGRAVED ON STEEL.

BY JOHN FROST, LL.D.,

AUTHOR OF THE 12MO. HISTORY OF THE UNITED STATES.

In one 12mo. volume, containing 448 pages, half-roan binding. **Price,**

This work furnishes, within a small space, a correct and satisfactory Treatise on the Principles of Elocution; and a very rich and copious collection of specimens of Deliberative, Forensic, Academic, and Popular Eloquence fills up the greater portion of the volume. It has met with a very rapid sale, and the estimation in which it is held by intelligent teachers has been attested by **numerous recommendations.**

EXTRACT FROM THE PREFACE.

"Eloquence is one of the chief elements of political distinction, as well as one of the most efficient aids in advancing the cause of moral and religious improvement. How necessary a correct and tasteful elocution is to the education of an orator, is obvious on the slightest reflection. If it is true that some remarkable men have won their way to distinction as orators, without carefully studying the principles of elocution, it is not less true that their way would have been smoother, and their difficulties fewer, if they had afforded themselves this auxiliary; while, with the great mass of aspirants for this sort of eminence, a course of instruction in elocution is a matter of absolute necessity."

OPINIONS OF EMINENT TEACHERS.

The "American Speaker," edited by Mr. Frost, is, I think, one of the best volumes for practical exercises in elocution that instructors or students can find. The numerous rules on the manner of reading the *series*—so termed by elocutionists—may be differently viewed by instructors, according to the extent to which they follow Walker's authority. But there can be no diversity of opinion as to the utility of the other parts of the work, and, particularly, the many pieces in which the inflections of the voice are marked throughout by appropriate accents.—*William Russell, Teacher of Elocution, and first Editor of the Journal of Education.*

I consider "Frost's American Speaker" to be the best compilation of the kind that has ever met my eye. The principles of elocution therein laid down are excellent, and well calculated to promote eloquence in every youthful American freeman. The extracts are of a high order, and, in general, breathe the spirit of liberty and independence.—*William Alexander.*

STANDARD SCHOOL HISTORIES,
PUBLISHED BY CHARLES DESILVER.
714 CHESTNUT STREET, PHILADELPHIA.

LORD'S HISTORY OF THE UNITED STATES.

A NEW HISTORY OF THE UNITED STATES OF AMERICA,
For the Use of Schools.
BY JOHN LORD, A.M.,
AUTHOR OF A MODERN HISTORY FROM THE TIME OF LUTHER TO THE FALL OF NAPOLEON.

One volume, 12mo., 508 pages, half-morocco binding. Price,

This work, written in the attractive style for which the author is so noted, is admirably calculated to produce a love for the study in the minds of those pupils who use it. It is beautifully illustrated with numerous fine Engravings, and contains an excellent colored Map of the United States, beside several maps showing the position of various battle fields and places noted in our history.

Lord's History of the United States.

OPINIONS OF TEACHERS AND OF THE PRESS.

I have carefully examined "Lord's History of the United States," and am free to say that, for the use of schools, I consider it the best history with which I am acquainted. — *James Rhoads, Professor of Belles Lettres, Central High School, Philadelphia.*

I consider "Lord's History of the United States" far superior to any work of the kind yet published, as he seems to strike a medium between the extremes of dry skeleton and diffuse composition. It is just the thing needed for schools. — *J. J. Havener, Allendale, S. C.*

To be brief, but not uninteresting, entertaining but impartial, is a rare gift in a historian; and this school history, excellent for its declared purpose, is well worth a place in the family library as well as in the school-room. — *Philadelphia North American.*

As far as I am able to judge, "Lord's History of the United States" is a most efficient school book, and should be in the hands of all the youth who have had a sufficient training in easier reading lessons. — *H. Freeman, Mount Ephraim, Ohio.*

We shall be mistaken if this work is not at once hailed with acclamation as by far the best school history in the United States yet published. It should at once be introduced into our Public Schools. — *Philadelphia City Item.*

The facts given in "Lord's History of the United States" are well chosen, and set forth in a manner well calculated to fix them in the memory of the learner. — *Phila. Evening Bulletin.*

It is not only an excellent School History, but an excellent general history, that may be perused with profit by readers of all ages and acquirements. — *New York Evening Mirror.*

LORD'S MODERN HISTORY.

A HISTORY OF MODERN EUROPE.

FROM THE TIME OF LUTHER TO THE FALL OF NAPOLEON.
FOR THE USE OF SCHOOLS AND COLLEGES.
BY JOHN LORD, A.M.,
LECTURER ON HISTORY, AND AUTHOR OF A NEW HISTORY OF THE UNITED STATES.

One volume, 12mo., 544 pages, half-morocco binding. Price,

OPINIONS OF EMINENT EDUCATIONISTS.

The narrative is clear, the style is animated and perspicuous, the estimate of the characters and motives of the prominent actors is discriminating and judicious, and, above all, there is an enlarged and generous spirit running through the whole, which produces the conviction that the author everywhere aims at truth, impartiality, and strict justice. — *Jared Sparks, President of Harvard College.*

I am satisfied that "Lord's History" is one of the most valuable books which has been issued from the press in this country or in England. It unites the qualities of brevity and clearness, with a power to interest which is rarely found in works of this class. — *Rev. Dr Tappan, formerly Professor of History and Philosophy in the University of New York.*

I scarcely know any work on history as interesting, or better calculated to answer a most valuable purpose in the cause of education; besides being especially useful as a text book, it may be read to advantage by almost any person in any walk of life. — *Prof. H. Webster, Principal of the New York Free Academy.*

"Lord's Modern History" is a living book, and presents the great events of an age in an attractive manner. Its style is beautifully simple and graphic. It is remarkable for its condensation and clearness. — *Professor West, Principal of Rutger's Institute, New York.*

I have carefully examined "Lord's History of Modern Europe," and am free to say that, for the use of schools, I consider it the best history with which I am acquainted. — *James Rhoads, Professor of Belles Lettres, Central High School, Philadelphia.*

Lord's Modern History.

OPINIONS OF EDUCATIONISTS, ETC.

I have examined "Lord's Modern History" with satisfaction and interest, and most cheerfully commend it to favorable attention, hoping that it may secure the very liberal patronage which it certainly deserves. — *M. L. Stoever, Professor of History in Pennsylvania College Gettysburg, Pennsylvania.*

I have sufficiently examined "Lord's Modern History" to be satisfied that he has made a valuable contribution to this important branch of the literature of our country. For the period embraced in it, I should give it the preference to any other book in the same department. — *Stephen Taylor, Richmond, Va.*

Lord's Modern History" marks the extraordinary events of the period on which it treats with precision, and as much candor as is usually the case with authors who have favored the world with works treating of the wonders which have transpired, and of the good which has been done by paper and type, genius and gunpowder. — *Pennsylvanian, Philadelphia.*

The author of the "Modern History" has handled his subjects with great ability. His style is nervous and graphic, and often strikingly eloquent; and the work will prove to be an interesting reading-book for schools, besides forming an interesting text-book for the student of history. — *Washington Union.*

All know what important events have occurred in the world's history since the time of Luther. Mr. Lord narrates them in a clear, concise, and vigorous manner, treating each subject in the true philosophical spirit which should always animate the historian. — *Philadelphia Evening Bulletin.*

"Lord's Modern History" abounds in animated and interesting sketches of character, brief yet judicious criticisms upon artists and men of letters, and well-timed reflections upon the different reforms and agitations which have revolutionized society. — *Boston Evening Transcript.*

"Lord's Modern History" may well be adopted in our schools as a text-book, and would accomplish a most happy result in inviting its students to something of the zeal for historical studies and acquirements which characterizes its author. — *Columbia (S.C.) Telegraph.*

As a compendious history of the times from "Luther to the Fall of Napoleon" we regard "Lord's Modern History" as an excellent text-book for schools and colleges, and also as worthy the attention of the general reader. — *Richmond (Va.) Christian Advocate.*

Mr. Lord does not sacrifice truth to effect, nor simplicity to ornament, as is the modern fashion of romancing history; but gleans from the apparent chaos of dates and names, some great truths, as the living pictures of the way of life. — *Rutland Co. (Vt.) Herald.*

The style of "Lord's Modern History" is clear and vigorous, and the arrangement throughout judicious. The work is indeed one of a very high character, and furnishes, within comparatively brief limits, an immense mass of valuable information. — *Philad. Inquirer.*

Mr. Lord has compiled this book with considerable judgment, passing over long wastes of comparatively unimportant history, and commenting with force upon points of acknowledged interest. — *Richmond (Va.) Daily Whig.*

"Lord's Modern History" may be read with advantage as a manual of instruction for the young, or be consulted by more mature readers as an authentic book of reference. — *New York Tribune.*

Lord's Modern History.

OPINIONS OF THE PRESS.

The field explored by Mr. Lord embraces the most important portion of English history, with which, however, it is somewhat remarkable, that young people, generally, are but little acquainted. The style, too, has its charms. Mr. Lord writes with grace, and with the ease of one who is perfectly familiar with his subject, and the reader feels confidence in the author's statements and opinions. We know no volume which we should so heartily commend to young people, either for domestic reading, or for use in the higher classes in collegiate and academic institutions. — *New York Commercial Advertiser.*

The narrative and descriptive portions of "Lord's Modern History" are graphic, and the occasional portraitures are life-like and correct. There is less imagination than in Abbott, but far more comprehension and correctness; less of the picturesque than in Macauley, less power of arresting and enchaining all the faculties of the mind; while, at the same time, for practical scientific purposes, for actual study, as a text-book and guide in our higher schools, we should give it the preference — *Congregationalist.*

The same kind of attraction that characterizes Mr. Lord's lectures, making them so universally popular, both with the masses and with the learned, pervades his "Modern History." He states his own opinions with great independence and candor, and appends his authorities and references to each chapter — a great help to those who may desire more minute information. — *Brattleboro (Vt.) Eagle.*

The task of the historian has been accomplished with singular fidelity. The plan of the work is simple, and has been well filled up; and the style is not only lucid and vigorous, but happily adapted to the highly dramatic character of the events he unfolds. To the reader or student, as a source of information, or as a book of reference, it is invaluable. — *Ohio School Friend, Cincinnati.*

The author of this book is well known by his popular lectures upon History, delivered in the United States and in Great Britain, and though, in the volume before us, he makes no pretensions to original and profound investigations, yet, in the arrangement, style, and sentiment, it is entirely his own. — *Congre. Journal, Concord, N. H.*

Mr. Lord combines, in an uncommon degree, brilliancy with accuracy, vivid dramatic representation with profound philosophic analysis and generalization. He aims, very successfully we think, at that high historic virtue, impartiality; and the tone of his opinions is decidedly, though not excessively, conservative. — *New York Presbyterian.*

We have not before been acquainted with Mr. Lord as a writer; but this book, we think, will perfectly sustain his high reputation won in the desk. His style is pleasant and perspicuous, while terse and compact, and he is eminently fortunate in the selection of his subjects, as well as in the grouping of his characters. — *New York Home Journal.*

"Lord's Modern History" is especially adapted to supply the exigencies of students of history, while to readers of maturer years, who lack time for more extended treatises, it supplies a lucid and connected sketch of the great events that have transpired since the Protestant Reformation. — *New York Journal of Commerce.*

The author of "Lord's Modern History" has been well known as a public lecturer on history, both in this country and in Europe, and in that capacity has received very favorable testimonials from the most competent judges. — *Daily Telegraph, Columbia, S. C.*

We commend "Lord's Modern History" both to the general reader, and to those who select and examine books for our higher seminaries of learning. — *Philadelphia Christian Observer*

Lord's Modern History.

OPINIONS OF THE PRESS.

Mr. Lord has furnished in a somewhat moderate compass, for the use of students and young persons generally, a substitute for those wretched, lifeless skeletons, with which publishers and paid book-makers are flooding us, under the name of abridgments, or histories for the use of schools. The most conspicuous characteristic of Mr. Lord, as a historian, is enthusiasm in his favorite subject; and, like all genuine enthusiasm, it imparts itself to his reader. — *Biblical Repository and Princeton Review.*

To condense the great and varied subjects extending over the exciting period of the last three hundred years, so as to furnish a connected narrative of all that is most interesting and vital in its history, has been the object of this work. This has been so successfully accomplished that the three centuries of which it treats are clearly and distinctly brought before the mind of the student and general reader. — *Banner and Advocate, Pittsburg, Pa.*

It is rather late in the day to produce a "Modern History" which can lay claim to much of originality or research, but Mr. Lord's aim is not to compete on these grounds with his predecessors on the same field, but to simplify and concentrate, according to his own system of arrangement, the facts and data which go to make up the sum and substance of the many histories already before the world. — *New York Literary World.*

"Lord's Modern History" is a volume of very attractive appearance, prepared by a well-read and warm-hearted man, full of his subject, full of matter, and full of scholar-like enthusiasm. Though professedly written "for the use of schools and colleges," it is admirably fitted for the instruction of that best of all schools — the domestic circle. — *Boston Puritan and Recorder.*

It would be difficult to imagine how a volume like the present could be used as a class-book in a public institution without imparting benefits rarely experienced in kindred studies. Indeed we know no other compend covering the same ground equal to it; and it will be found as interesting and instructive in the family as in schools. — *Newark (N.J.) Advertiser.*

Mr. Lord has woven into his work all the leading features and events of the last three centuries, and clothed the whole in his own happy and agreeable style of thought. He merits the scholar's thanks for so instructive a book, and we hope it may meet with an extensive circulation. — *New York Protestant Churchman.*

The book is well and boldly written; great thoughts worthily clothe great facts; and the latter aptly suggest the former. The style of the work is a model of historical writing. The chronological tables and questions are full, useful, and good. — *English Journal of Education.*

In this excellent History the author has given a connected narrative of the most vital events of the last three hundred years, avoiding all those minute details, and elaborate disquisitions, which are calculated to embarrass young students. — *Educational Expositor.*

"Lord's Modern History" should be possessed by every one who has not the leisure to read extensive works, but who desires to be informed regarding all the notable events which have transpired since the Reformation. — *Westminster Herald, Wilmington, Del.*

"Lord's History" contains a vast amount of valuable information on subjects of which no one should be ignorant. It betrays no spirit of political prejudice or religious bigotry; and its general correctness cannot be impeached. — *Southern Christian Advocate, Charleston, S. C.*

The best recommendation which can be given to "Lord's History" is that it recognizes a God in history, and assigns Him His proper agency in the government of this world. — *Christian Secretary, Hartford, Ct.*

Such a book as this has been long wanted for schools, and here we find the essential facts well and correctly set forth in a small volume. — *Church of England Quarterly Review.*

The sketches of character presented in "Lord's Modern History" are excellent portraits and drawn with a free, bold touch. — *London Athenæum.*

The divisions of "Lord's Modern History" are broad and distinctive, and the style clear. — *London Spectator.*

FROST'S SCHOOL HISTORIES.

HISTORY OF THE UNITED STATES,

FROM THE DISCOVERY OF AMERICA BY COLUMBUS TO THE PRESENT TIME.

For the Use of Schools and Academies.

BY JOHN FROST, LL. D.

ILLUSTRATED WITH FORTY ENGRAVINGS.

In one volume, 12mo., containing 479 pages, half-roan binding. Price,

The design of the author in this, his larger history, has been to furnish a text-book sufficiently full and complete for the use of colleges, academies, and the higher seminaries. It begins with the discovery of the New World, and presenting the series of events in a clear and connected narrative, rejecting whatever was considered irrelevant or unimportant, and dwelling chiefly on those striking features of the subject which give it vividness and character; the history is brought down to the present day. The numerous testimonials to the merit of this work, and its popularity, evinced quite unequivocally by the sale of ten thousand copies within a few months after its first publication, afford a strong presumption that the author has succeeded in his purpose of making it a first-rate school history.

EXTRACT FROM THE PREFACE.

"Although the considerable period embraced, the multitude of characters and events delineated, and the extent of the field in which they figure, have rendered the preservation of historical unity no easy task, the author has labored to give the work such a degree of compactness as would enable the student to perceive the relation of all its parts, and to grasp the whole without any very difficult exercise of comprehension."

FROST'S SCHOOL HISTORIES.

HISTORY OF THE UNITED STATES,
For the Use of Common Schools.
BY JOHN FROST, LL. D.
CONDENSED FROM THE AUTHOR'S LARGE HISTORY OF THE UNITED STATES,

AND

BROUGHT DOWN TO THE PRESENT TIME.
ILLUSTRATED WITH FORTY ENGRAVINGS ON WOOD.
One volume, 18mo., containing 375 pages, neat half-roan binding. Price, cents.

This smaller history is abridged very judiciously from the larger one, and can be recommended confidently to general use. Many interesting and important facts relative to American affairs, omitted in other works of the kind, are herein skilfully introduced. The simplicity of the style cannot fail to please every attentive reader. The appendix, containing the Constitution of our country, as also a useful Chronological Table, will render the work doubly valuable.

These invaluable Histories are extensively used in the schools of Philadelphia, New York, Baltimore, Pittsburg, Cincinnati, St. Louis, New Orleans, and are daily being introduced into all the best schools throughout the Union.

OPINIONS OF TEACHERS.

The style is clear, concise, and spirited; free, on the one hand, from the ambitions and rhetorical character, and on the other, from the negligence and inaccuracy into which most of our popular compends have fallen. As a History of the United States, it is, in my opinion more full and more exact than any of the same size, and in all other respects preferable, as a book intended to aid the business of instruction.—*William Russell, Editor of the American Journal of Education, First Series.*

I cheerfully recommend "Frost's History of the United States" to the attention of teachers as a very superior work. In style, a most important point in works of this character, it is decidedly superior to some of the most popular historical compends now used in our schools and academies.— *R. Connolly, Teacher, Baltimore.*

I am so much pleased with the elegance of language, neat arrangement, copious questions, and style of getting up, exhibited in "Frost's History of the United States," that I shall at once introduce it into my school, and use my influence to give it a wide circulation.— *E. B Hurney, Teacher, Baltimore.*

PINNOCK'S HISTORICAL SERIES.

HISTORY OF ENGLAND.

Pinnock's Improved Edition of Dr. Goldsmith's History of England,
FROM THE INVASION OF JULIUS CÆSAR
TO THE DEATH OF GEORGE THE SECOND;
WITH A CONTINUATION TO THE PRESENT TIME,
AND
QUESTIONS FOR EXAMINATION AT THE END OF EACH SECTION;

BESIDES A VARIETY OF VALUABLE INFORMATION ADDED THROUGHOUT THE WORK, CONSISTING OF

Tables of Contemporary Sovereigns and Eminent Persons, copious Explanatory Notes, Remarks on the Politics, Manners, and Literature of the Age, and an Outline of the British Constitution.

BY W. C. TAYLOR, LL. D., OF TRINITY COLLEGE, DUBLIN,
AUTHOR OF A "MANUAL OF ANCIENT AND MODERN HISTORY," ETC., ETC.

Illustrated with numerous Engravings.
A NEW AND REVISED EDITION.
In one vol. 12mo., 512 pages, half-roan binding. Price

EXTRACT FROM THE PREFACE.

"Among all the histories of England which have been written, none has been so long and so deservedly popular as that of Dr. Goldsmith. Whether this be owing to its attractive and perfectly intelligible style, or to the vivid impression which his simple and clear narrative of the facts never fails to leave, it is not now important to inquire. The fact of its established classical character is sufficient to justify the publisher in selecting the most improved edition of this work, to be revised and adapted to the use of schools in our own country."

PINNOCK'S HISTORICAL SERIES.

HISTORY OF FRANCE AND NORMANDY

FROM THE EARLIEST TIMES TO THE PRESENT PERIOD;

TOGETHER WITH

QUESTIONS FOR EXAMINATION AT THE END OF EACH SECTION.

By W. C. TAYLOR, LL. D., OF TRINITY COLLEGE, DUBLIN,

AUTHOR OF A "MANUAL OF ANCIENT, MODERN HISTORY," ETC., ETC., AND EDITOR OF "PINNOCK'S IMPROVED EDITIONS OF GREECE, ROME, AND ENGLAND."

Illustrated with numerous Engravings.

A NEW AND REVISED EDITION.

One vol. 12mo., 500 pages, half-roan binding. Price

EXTRACT FROM THE PREFACE.

"France not only presents to the American a most profitable study in its history, but it advances a strong claim to the sympathy of our own happy country. To her we are in a great measure indebted for the successful assertion of our own claim to national independence. To her we are indebted for the Lafayettes, the Rochambeaus, the Armands, the De Grasses, and the D'Estaings of the Revolution; and to her great Napoleon we owe the easy acquisition of a most important portion of our national territory.

"In this history, written by the accomplished Dr. Taylor, the events are narrated clearly and forcibly; and justice is done to the great characters who have figured on that grand theatre of human affairs. The questions for examination of pupils, and mottoes at the heads of chapters, are the same as in the English edition. The American editor has made some few additions to the text, including the last chapter, which brings the history down to the present time. He has also inserted the numerous historical embellishments, consisting of portraits, costumes, historical pictures of battles and sieges, and views of important places. In editing the work, he has endeavored to conform to the active spirit of improvement in books for the education of youth, which is so marked a feature of the present age."

PINNOCK'S HISTORICAL SERIES.

HISTORY OF ROME.

PINNOCK'S IMPROVED EDITION
OF
DR. GOLDSMITH'S HISTORY OF ROME;

TO WHICH IS PREFIXED

AN INTRODUCTION TO THE STUDY OF ROMAN HISTORY,

A GREAT VARIETY OF INFORMATION IS GIVEN THROUGHOUT THE WORK,

CONCERNING THE

MANNERS, INSTITUTIONS, AND ANTIQUITIES OF THE ROMANS;

TOGETHER WITH

QUESTIONS FOR EXAMINATION AT THE END OF EACH SECTION.

BY W. C. TAYLOR, LL.D.

Illustrated with numerous Engravings,
BY ATHERTON AND OTHERS.

A New and Revised Edition.

One volume, 12mo., 390 pages, half-roan binding. Price,

EXTRACT FROM THE PREFACE.

"The researches of Niebuhr and several other distinguished German scholars have thrown a new light on Roman History, and enabled us to discover the true constitution, of that republic which once ruled the destinies of the known world, and the influence of whose literature and laws is still powerful in every civilized state, and will probably continue to be felt to the remotest posterity. These discoveries have, however, been hitherto useless to junior students in this country; the works of the German critics being unsuited to the purposes of schools, not only from their price, but also from the extensive learning requisite to follow them through their laborious disquisitions. The editor has, therefore, thought that it would be no unacceptable service to prefix a few Introductory Chapters, detailing such results from their inquiries as best elucidate the character and condition of the Roman people, and explain the most important portion of the history."

PINNOCK'S HISTORICAL SERIES.

HISTORY OF GREECE.

PINNOCK'S IMPROVED EDITION
OF
DR. GOLDSMITH'S HISTORY OF GREECE;

REVISED CORRECTED, AND GREATLY ENLARGED,

BY THE ADDITION OF

Several New Chapters, numerous Useful Notes,

AND

QUESTIONS FOR EXAMINATION AT THE END OF EACH SECTION.

BY W. C. TAYLOR, LL. D.

ILLUSTRATED WITH NUMEROUS ENGRAVINGS,
BY ATHERTON AND OTHERS.

One vol. 12mo., 305 pages, half-roan binding. Price

EXTRACT FROM THE PREFACE.

"The alterations that have been made in this new edition of the Grecian history are so numerous and extensive as almost to make it a new work. The original history of Dr. Goldsmith contains many anecdotes of questionable authority, and very doubtful interest, derived from Plutarch and Curtius; while such important matters as the Dorian migration and the sedition of Ceylon are wholly omitted. The compiler of the abridgment, following the same track, hurried over some of the most important periods with brief and scanty notice, while he assigned very disproportionate length to a few isolated incidents. The present editor has endeavored to remedy both evils, by abridging whatever appeared too diffuse, expanding those parts which were so brief as to be scarcely intelligible, and supplying the numerous omissions of the original work. The authorities to which he has principally had recourse are the histories of Gillies and Mitford in the earlier part of the work, and Leland and Gast for the period subsequent to the Peloponnesian war. A brief sketch of modern Grecian history is subjoined, in order that the student may have an opportunity of comparing the present prospects with the former fame of Greece."

"A brief sketch of the history of the minor states and of the Islands is subjoined to the Appendix, and references are given to the share they had in any of the transactions recorded in the body of the work."

Pinnock's Historical Series.

Pinnock's Series have been recommended by several State Superintendents for the school libraries of their respective States, and great numbers of them have been sold for that purpose. In fact, they have become school classics; and, in order to make the series more complete, the several volumes have been revised by that well-known historian, W. C. Taylor, LL. D., of Trinity College, Dublin. The popularity of these books is almost without a parallel. Teachers unacquainted with them, will on examination give them a decided preference to any other historical series published.

OPINIONS OF TEACHERS AND OF THE PRESS.

A well written and authentic History of France possesses unusual interest at the present time. It becomes especially valuable when, as in the present case, it has been prepared with questions, as a text-book for common schools and seminaries, by a scholar so accomplished as Dr. Taylor. The style is clear and forcible, and, from the compactness of the work, forming, as it does, a complete chain of events in a most important part of the history of Europe, it will be found interesting and valuable for general readers, or as a text-book in our schools. — *New York Evening Post.*

The popularity of these histories is almost without a parallel among our school books. Their use is co-extensive with the English language, and their names are familiar to all who have received an English education. — *Pennsylvania Inquirer, Philadelphia.*

I consider "Pinnock's edition of Goldsmith's History of England" as the best edition of that work which has as yet been published for the use of schools. — *John M. Keagy, Friends' Academy, Philadelphia.*

The style and elegance of the language, the arrangement of the chapters, and the questions for examination, render "Pinnock's improved edition of Goldsmith's Rome," in my estimation, a most valuable school book. — *J. F. Gould, Teacher, Baltimore.*

Pinnock's Historical Series.

OPINIONS OF THE PRESS.

Other histories as correct, other histories as full and learned have been written but no history has yet appeared which combines, as does Goldsmith's, simplicity of diction and clearness of style with classic elegance, and which compresses into a necessary compactness, without confounding and obscuring, so immense a mass of matter as is comprised in the annals of Old England. The edition which we have now to commend to our readers is the latest published, and contains all the additions, emendations, and improvements to the author's original work, which long experience and careful study have suggested.—*Quebec Mercury.*

"Taylor's History of France" is truly an attractive book for the family and the school, neatly printed, and illustrated with numerous engravings, which describe to the eye many historical characters and events of general interest. As an epitome of history, it is founded on the authority of French writers of high repute as historians. The style in which the writer has briefly narrated the great events of French history, is manly and vigorous, yet simple, and intelligible to the young.—*Christian Observer.*

"Pinnock's Goldsmith's Histories of Greece, Rome, and England," hold the rank of school classics, and are to be found in almost every school in England and America, in which history is studied. In the History of England, the last chapters, which were added since the time of Goldsmith, have been re-written, and so extended, as to include the nation's history, and a view of the progress of its arts, sciences, and literature, to the present time.—*Philada. North American and U. S. Gazette.*

Government is seen in its every form, and society in its every phase, in the History of France. The questions, tables, and engravings, add much to the value of the work. Of the last there are two or three hundred, illustrative of striking events; portraits of sovereigns and prominent characters; and illustrations of the manners, dress, and weapons of the people, in different periods of their national existence.—*Christian Watchman, Toronto, Canada W.*

"Pinnock's Goldsmith's England" is so well known and universally approved, that any commendation were superfluous. We need only remark that the tables of contemporary sovereigns and eminent persons at the close of each chapter, and the mass of illustrative matter, consisting of notes, numerous tables, and engravings, give to this edition a superiority over every other one not thus illustrated.—*Christian Watchman, Toronto, Canada W.*

"Taylor's France" is designed for the use of schools, and is a part of Pinnock's school series. It is admirably adapted to the purpose for which it is intended, and will give to pupils, in a brief space, much useful information in relation to the history of France. Such works ought to be introduced into all schools, as history is the most important study to which the mind of the young can be directed.—*Baltimore Clipper.*

"Goldsmith's Histories of Greece, Rome, and England," as now published, have been subjected to a most thorough revision, with a view to adapt them to the present state of historical learning. Numerous notes are appended, chapters have been added, to make the works more complete, and to each section, questions have been annexed for the use of schools.—*Worcester (Mass.) Palladium.*

"Taylor's History of France" is appropriately placed within the reach of American readers, and if it fails to satisfy those who have occasion to examine minutely the field over which the author has gone, it will at least lay a good foundation for further inquiries, and stimulate ingenious readers to a further study of the subject.—*American Courier.*

"Taylor's France" is designed for schools, and treats of the history of a country that has, in every age, exerted a great influence upon the character and destinies of man. We recommend this book as a correct, compendious, and useful history, and which, we doubt not, will be extensively used in our school.—*Gazette of the Union.*

"Taylor's History of France and Normandy" is an admirable work, not merely for children, but for the general reader, who may not have the time, or the opportunity afforded him of perusing works more in detail.—*Republican Banner, Nashville, Tenn.*

STANDARD WORKS
ON
NATURAL SCIENCES,
PUBLISHED BY CHARLES DESILVER,
1229 CHESTNUT STREET, PHILADELPHIA.

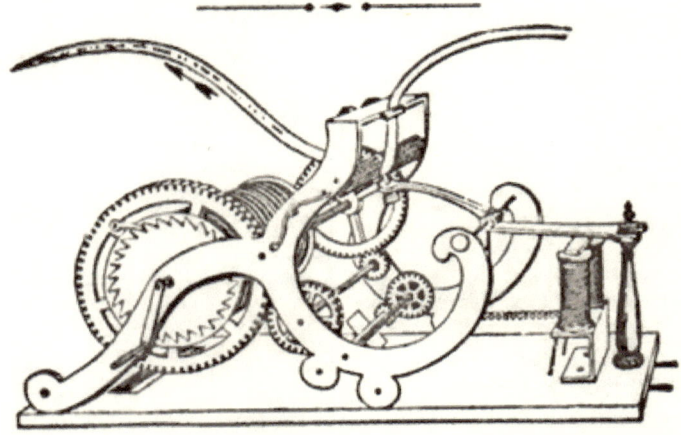

JOHNSTON'S TURNER'S CHEMISTRY

A MANUAL OF CHEMISTRY,
ON THE BASIS OF
DR. TURNER'S ELEMENTS OF CHEMISTRY;
CONTAINING, IN A CONDENSED FORM,
ALL THE MOST IMPORTANT FACTS AND PRINCIPLES OF THE SCIENCE, AND
DESIGNED AS A
TEXT-BOOK IN COLLEGES AND OTHER SEMINARIES OF LEARNING.
A New and Improved Edition.
BY JOHN JOHNSTON, LL. D.,
PROFESSOR OF NATURAL SCIENCE IN WESLEYAN UNIVERSITY.
ILLUSTRATED BY THREE HUNDRED AND EIGHTEEN ENGRAVINGS
In one volume, 12mo., 879 pages, half turkey-morocco binding. Price,

JOHNSTON'S TURNER'S ELEMENTS OF CHEMISTRY

ELEMENTS OF CHEMISTRY,
FOR THE USE OF COMMON SCHOOLS.
BY JOHN JOHNSTON, LL. D.,
PROFESSOR OF NATURAL SCIENCE IN THE WESLEYAN UNIVERSITY.
BEAUTIFULLY ILLUSTRATED WITH NUMEROUS ENGRAVINGS ON WOOD
A New and Improved Edition.
In one volume, 12mo., containing 383 pages, half-morocco binding. Price

"Johnston's Turner's Chemistry" is the standard text-book of many of the leading Colleges and prominent Medical Institutions of the United States; and the "Elementary Chemistry" is extensively used in the best Public Schools.

Johnston's Turner's Chemistries.

"Johnston's Turner's Manual of Chemistry" is now in use in the University of Pennsylvania, in the Central High School of Philadelphia, in the Girard College for Orphans, Philadelphia, in the Virginia Military Institute, Lexington, Va., in the University of Michigan, and in numerous other equally celebrated institutions, which want of space precludes mention of in this place. No better evidence can be adduced of the merit of these books, than the fact that they now are, as they have been for years, the standard text-books of renowned seminaries of learning.

OPINIONS OF EMINENT PROFESSORS, ETC.

Being familiar with "Johnston's Manual of Chemistry," I am glad to testify to its merits as a text-book for schools and colleges. Compiled upon the basis of the excellent work of Dr. Turner, the arrangement of its subjects is philosophical, and the method of treating them clear and instructive; which, aided by the numerous wood-cut illustrations in elucidation of the text, well adapt it to the purpose for which it is designed. — *R. E. Rogers, Professor of Chemistry in the University of Pennsylvania.*

I find "Johnston's Turner's Chemistry" to be a carefully compiled and well-digested treatise, and, as I believe, well adapted to serve the purposes of a text-book. It has been introduced into many academies and several colleges, and is held in high estimation — *John F. Frazer, formerly Professor of General Chemistry in the Franklin Institute, Philadelphia.*

I regard "Johnston's Turner's Chemistry" as an excellent text-book. Indeed, to most students in the higher seminaries of learning, I know of no book upon the subject which I could recommend in preference to it. — *F. Merrick, Professor of Chemistry in the Ohio Wesleyan University and Starling Medical College, Columbus, Ohio.*

As a text-book, I regard "Johnston's Manual of Chemistry" as far superior to "Turner's Chemistry," on which it is based; being more condensed and practical, and yet sufficiently and equally presenting the late rapid advancement of the science. — *Professor Booth, formerly of the High School, Philadelphia.*

I have examined "Johnston's Turner's Chemistry," and can recommend it as an excellent elementary work on that subject. — *B. Howard Rand, Professor of Chemistry in the Central High School, Philadelphia.*

Johnston's Turner's Chemistries.

OPINIONS OF EMINENT PROFESSORS, ETC.

I like "Johnston's Turner's Chemistry" now much better than before. The arrangement of questions at the foot of each page, with numbers referring to the paragraphs, is a great help to students; and the new illustrations, with the new experiments, which I see in all parts of the work, are also additional recommendations. There is also a very manifest improvement in the style; which is more concise, and, if I may use the word, more pointed.—*Professor Aaron White, Oneida Conference Seminary, Cazenovia, N. B.*

Having carefully examined "Johnston's Turner's Elements of Chemistry, for the use of Schools," I take pleasure in expressing the opinion that it is what it professes to be,—"a faithful compendium of the science in its present state,"—and that it is admirably suited to elementary instruction in male and female academies.—*R. T. Brumly, Professor of Chemistry in South Carolina College, Columbia. S. C.*

The arrangement of the book is judicious, and the principles of chemical science are developed in a style remarkable for its clearness and precision. I never before met with a treatise on chemistry in which the subject was so thoroughly treated within narrow limits.—*J. Simmons, Principal of the Locust Street Institute for Young Ladies, Philadelphia.*

"Johnston's Turner's Chemistry" is fully up to the times in recent improvements and discoveries; and I think every teacher will be pleased with the author's method, as well as with the mechanical execution of the work.—*C. C. Olds, Professor of Natural Sciences, Wesleyan Seminary, Albion, Michigan.*

Professor Johnston has done well in selecting Turner as a basis; and, by a careful and skilful revision of that excellent work, he has given us a book admirably adapted to the higher classes in our best institutions.—*Samuel Randall, Principal of Young Ladies' School, Walnut Street, Philadelphia.*

At a meeting of the Board of Visitors of the Natchez (Miss.) Institute, "Johnston's Elements of Chemistry" was unanimously adopted as a text-book for the use of pupils.—*L. M. Patterson, Secretary.*

It affords me great pleasure to say that I am much gratified with the appearance, plan, and mechanical execution of "Johnston's Turner's Chemistry," and I shall immediately introduce this edition into my classes.—*Professor A. Davis, Emory and Henry College, Virginia.*

I must say that "Johnston's Turner's Chemistry" presents, both internally and externally, everything that one can desire.—*Henry S. Noyes, Professor of Mathematics in the North-Western University, Evanston, Illinois.*

Johnston's Turner's Chemistries.

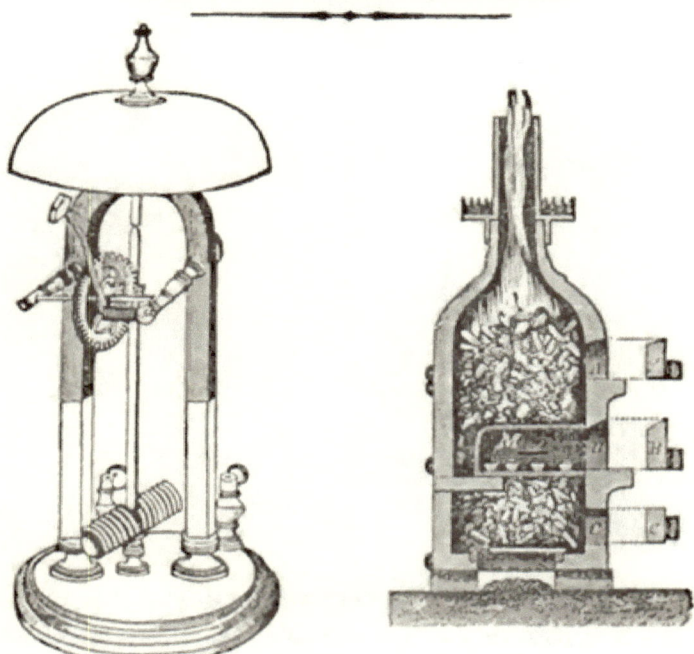

OPINIONS OF THE PRESS.

Dr. Johnston enjoys the high satisfaction of a professor whose ambition and ability have enabled him to dispense instruction from text-books stamped with his own imprint and shaped to his own views. The issue of the sixth edition of "Johnston's Turner's Chemistry" gives ample assurance of success. The revisions are important and valuable, and the work may be safely recommended, with additional credentials of its high excellence for the purposes of collegiate and academic instruction. — *Methodist Quarterly Review.*

"Johnston's Elementary Chemistry" is an abridgment of a larger work by the author on the same subject, which has a well-established reputation. He was induced to prepare this volume to supply a lack that was felt for a long time; the text-books in use being either too large and full, or else of too juvenile a character. It is admirably adapted to the wants of youth in our public and private schools. — *Newport (R. I.) Daily News.*

The present edition of "Johnston's Turner's Chemistry" has been in part re-written, entirely re-stereotyped, and new illustrations prepared for it, some of which have been taken from the popular work of *M. Regnault*. The work is thus presented as substantially an original manual, complete in its design, and containing all which could be gleaned from the most prominent works on the subject. — *New York Sun.*

The best elementary work on Chemistry ever written is that of Turner; and the various editions through which it has passed are satisfactory proofs of its excellence. The volume before us has been revised by Professor Johnston, and such additions made as to embrace the very latest discoveries in the science. It is an admirable work for schools and colleges. — *New Orleans Bee.*

The volume before us is most tastefully gotten up, and, without reserve or qualification, we pronounce it, after a careful examination, the best treatise on chemistry, for schools and colleges, now before the American or English public. — *Washington Christian Advocate, Cincinnati, Ohio.*

Johnston's Turner's Chemistries.

OPINIONS OF THE PRESS.

We consider "Johnston's Turner's Chemistry" one of the best manuals on the subject with which we are acquainted. The author treats of the various subjects in a plain, familiar style; the description of each element is prefaced by an epitome of its history; all the formulæ are given necessary to exhibit the changes that take place in the formation of new compounds from several existing elements; and the directions for performing experiments are, of themselves, sufficient to recommend the work to any one desirous of obtaining an experimental knowledge of chemistry. — *Westminster Herald, New Wilming'on, Pa.*

"Johnston's Turner's Chemistry" leads the pupil on very gradually from the simplest elements of the science to its higher departments. Its arrangement is natural, its statements perspicuous, and its illustrations amply sufficient. All the more recent and important discoveries in the science are introduced; for Professor Johnston, with the spirit of a true student, keeping fully up with the march of the science, has almost re-written the present edition. — *Maine Evangelist.*

The two points of excellence in a work on chemistry are, firstly, the ability and intelligence of the writer, and secondly, its novelty; and we have the assurance of an ex-student of Gmelin (whose works have been used in preparing this edition of "Johnston's Turner's Chemistry"), that, as a complete compendium for the use of schools, there is at present no work published which can be compared with this. — *Philadelphia Evening Bulletin.*

In chemistry, continually improving as the science is by new discoveries, the latest book must be sought; and when, as in this, an approved standard is taken as the basis, and the work is re-written from time to time, to keep pace with the advance of discovery, every requisite to a complete manual is embraced in it. — *Philadelphia North American.*

"Johnston's Turner's Chemistry" is formed upon the basis of "Turner's Elements of Chemistry," and contains, in a condensed form, all the most important facts and principles of the science. — *New Orleans Bulletin.*

JOHNSTON'S NATURAL PHILOSOPHIES

JOHNSTON'S NATURAL PHILOSOPHY.

A MANUAL OF NATURAL PHILOSOPHY,
COMPILED FROM VARIOUS SOURCES, AND DESIGNED AS A
TEXT-BOOK IN HIGH SCHOOLS AND ACADEMIES

BY JOHN JOHNSTON, LL. D.
PROFESSOR OF NATURAL SCIENCE IN THE WESLEYAN UNIVERSITY.

Illustrated with Three Hundred and Thirty-Two Engravings on Wood
A New and Revised Edition,
ENLARGED AND IMPROVED.

In one volume, 12mo., 379 pages, half turkey-morocco binding. Price,

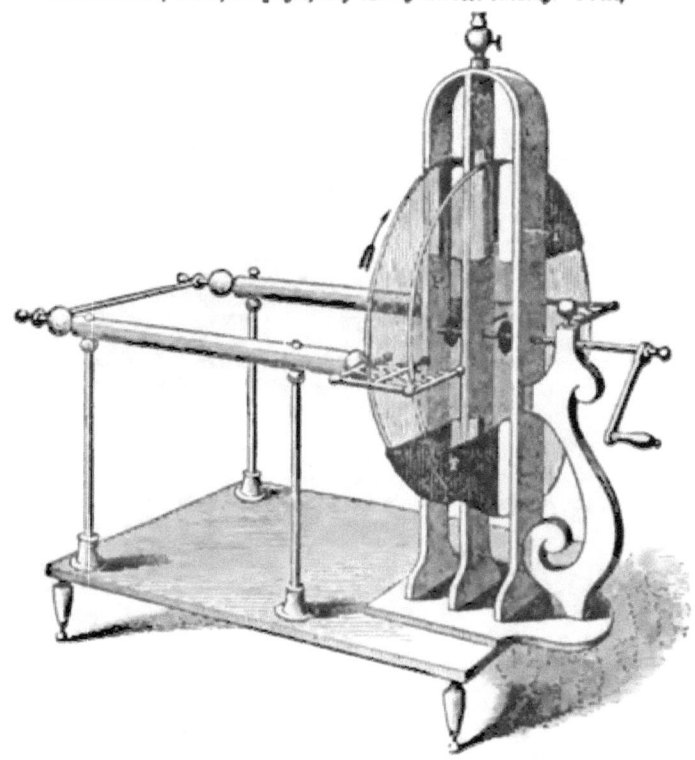

The present edition of this work will be found much enlarged and greatly improved. Exact in its definitions, original in its illustrations, full and familiar in explanations, the publisher feels confident that an examination of the work cannot fail to result in its decided approval. Recently it has been recommended for use in the common schools by the Board of Education of the State of New Hampshire. It has also been adopted in the High School of Cambridge, Massachusetts, and in Girard College, Philadelphia, as well as in many Academies and Schools in various sections of the Union.

JOHNSTON'S NATURAL PHILOSOPHIES.

PRIMARY NATURAL PHILOSOPHY,

DESIGNED FOR

THE USE OF THE YOUNGER CLASS OF LEARNERS.

BY JOHN JOHNSTON, LL. D.

PROFESSOR OF NATURAL SCIENCE IN THE WESLEYAN UNIVERSITY, AUTHOR OF "JOHNSTON'S TURNER'S CHEMISTRY," "JOHNSTON'S TURNER'S ELEMENTS OF CHEMISTRY," AND "JOHNSTON'S NATURAL PHILOSOPHY."

Illustrated by One Hundred and Seventy-Two Engravings.

One vol. 18mo., 184 pages, half-roan binding. Price   cents.

This little volume is intended to aid the younger class of learners in acquiring a knowledge of some of the fundamental principles of Natural Philosophy, and to give them such a taste for the study as will lead to the examination of more

advanced works on the science. Though but a short time before the public, it has met with such decided success, that it is now used in a large number of schools in all sections of the Union.

Johnston's Natural Philosophies.

ENDORSEMENTS BY PROFESSORS, ETC.

A class of young ladies in my school having recently finished the study of Professor Johnston's "Natural Philosophy" with great satisfaction to both them and myself, I cannot refrain from bestowing upon the work my decided approbation. It would require too much space to enumerate its merits. I would merely say that, in my judgment, it is the best book of its kind at present before the public. — *Samuel Randall, Young Ladies' School, Walnut Street, Philadelphia.*

At a meeting of the Commissioners of Common Schools for the State of New Hampshire, held in Concord, on motion of Mr. Whidden, of Lancaster, Coos County, "Johnston's Natural Philosophy" was recommended to be used in the common schools of the State. — *Extract from the Minutes of the Board.*

I consider "Johnston's Manual of Natural Philosophy" as an excellent text-book for instruction in schools and academies. — *M. J. Williams, Professor of Mathematics and Natural Philosophy in South Carolina College.*

At a meeting of the Board of Visitors of the Natchez (Miss.) Institute, "Johnston's Natural Philosophy" was unanimously adopted as a text-book for the use of the pupils. — *L. M. Patterson, Secretary.*

Johnston's Natural Philosophies.

OPINIONS OF THE PRESS.

A new and revised edition of this extensively used text-book has been issued. The explanations of the natural phenomena are full and intelligible, and illustrated by numerous engravings, while the work combines the merits of simplicity and brevity.—*Boston Daily Journal.*

We know no better text-book of the physical sciences than this. As a manual for schools, it is worthy of all praise; and the information it embraces is of a character that every intelligent reader should refresh his mind with occasionally.—*Boston Transcript.*

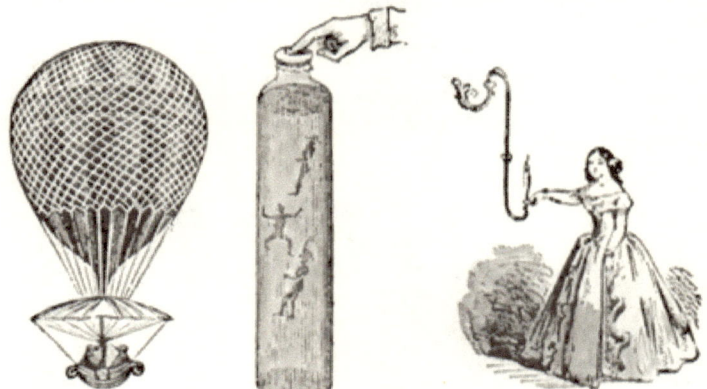

"Johnston's Natural Philosophy" is a compilation from the most able writers on Natural Science, condensed into a work bearing an original impress, by an experienced teacher. We commend it to the attention of professors and principals of schools.—*Phil. North American.*

"Johnston's Natural Philosophy," designed for the use of high schools and academies, has been prepared in a very able and judicious manner for the comprehension of the student.—*Philadelphia Advertiser.*

Johnston's Natural Philosophies.

OPINIONS OF THE PRESS.

This book belongs to a rare species. It is better than its design, and performs more than it promises. It was prepared expressly for the tyro of science in our high schools and academies, and, while we commend its admirable adaptation to that end, we also believe it to be equally suited to the wants of a numerous class of general readers, who desire information upon physical subjects, but are deterred from seeking it in larger and more abstruse treatises. — *Literary Record.*

This excellent and standard work on Natural Philosophy was very thoroughly revised a few years ago, and brought, in every respect, up to the modern standard. But the science advances very rapidly; and it is only very recently that the Foucault experiment with the pendulum, the gyroscope, and the stereoscope have been invented. All of these are added to this edition, making it in every respect a very desirable book for schools. — *Philadelphia Evening Bulletin.*

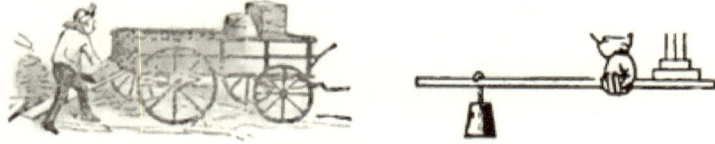

"Johnston's Primary Natural Philosophy," intended for the use of young beginners, has been very happily designed by Professor Johnston. The lessons in Philosophy are very plainly told, and neatly illustrated; and the book is well worthy of a place in our schools. — *Philadelphia Sunday Dispatch.*

In the preparation of "The Manual of Natural Philosophy," the author has made use of the latest and best independent treatises on the subjects considered; and his work is deserving of a careful examination by teachers and school committees. — *Boston Traveller.*

The "Primary Natural Philosophy," designed for the use of the younger class of learners is an admirable work, from the pen of Professor Johnston, author of several works on Chemistry and Natural Philosophy. It is copiously illustrated. — *Constitution, Middletown, Conn.*

The "Manual of Natural Philosophy" is an excellent work, and should be introduced into all our schools. — *Newport (R. I.) Daily News.*

ELEMENTARY PHYSIOLOGY—ANIMATED NATURE.

(In Preparation.)

ELEMENTARY PHYSIOLOGY:

A CONCISE DESCRIPTION

OF

THE FUNCTIONS OF ORGANIZED BODIES,

AND

Especially of Man.

ADAPTED TO THE USE OF COLLEGES, ACADEMIES, AND SCHOOLS GENERALLY

WITH NUMEROUS ILLUSTRATIONS.

BY RICHARD J. DUNGLISON, M.D.

One vol., royal 12mo., half-morocco binding. Price $

This work will be a comprehensive and accurate text-book on the interesting and important subject of which it treats, and will be found well adapted to the purposes of Colleges, Academies, and Schools, as well as of great utility to the general reader. It will embrace, so far as may be deemed necessary, the applications of Descriptive Anatomy, Microscopy, and Organic Chemistry to the elucidation of the various subjects.

(In Preparation.)

GLIMPSES

OF

ANIMATED NATURE;

COMPRISING DESCRIPTIONS OF

Birds, Animals, Fishes, Reptiles, Insects, Etc.:

WITH

SKETCHES OF THEIR PECULIAR HABITS AND CHARACTERISTICS;

COMPILED FROM THE WRITINGS OF

Cuvier, Buffon, Goldsmith, Bigland, Wood, Godwin, Audubon, Cassin,

AND OTHER EMINENT NATURALISTS,

AND

ADAPTED TO THE CAPACITIES OF ALL READERS.

BY J. W. O'NEILL.

𝕮𝖔𝖕𝖎𝖔𝖚𝖘𝖑𝖞 𝖆𝖓𝖉 𝕭𝖊𝖆𝖚𝖙𝖎𝖋𝖚𝖑𝖑𝖞 𝕴𝖑𝖑𝖚𝖘𝖙𝖗𝖆𝖙𝖊𝖉.

In one royal 12mo. volume, half morocco binding. Price $

In this volume will be presented accurate descriptions of every variety of Bird, Animal, Reptile, Insect, Fish, etc., written in plain and familiar language, and divested of those technicalities which are calculated rather to embarrass than to inform the ordinary reader. It will be so arranged as to fill equally well a place in the family library, or a vacuum on the school-desk; for which it will be adapted by judicious Questions appended at the close of the volume. The Illustrations will be true to Nature, and engraved in the very highest style of the art.

GUY ON ASTRONOMY, AND KEITH ON THE GLOBES.

GUY'S ELEMENTS OF ASTRONOMY,

AND AN ABRIDGMENT OF

KEITH'S NEW TREATISE

ON

THE USE OF THE GLOBES.

THIRTIETH AMERICAN EDITION, WITH ADDITIONS AND IMPROVEMENTS,

AND AN

EXPLANATION OF THE ASTRONOMICAL PART OF THE AMERICAN ALMANAC.

ILLUSTRATED WITH EIGHTEEN BEAUTIFUL PLATES,

DRAWN AND ENGRAVED ON STEEL, IN THE BEST MANNER.

In one royal 18mo. volume, containing 309 pages, half-roan binding. Price $1.00.

As an elementary work, "Guy's Astronomy" is free from two very common objections — extreme brevity on the one hand, and excessive prolixity on the other; but a just medium has been observed between these two extremes. Every one is aware not only of the impropriety, but also of the positive injury, effected by an attempt to overload the yet unexpanded faculties of the mind by filling it with a too great redundancy of ideas, during a first course in any science; and, therefore, the work has been so arranged as to make it suit the purposes of scholars of different classes, capacities, and ages, while, at the same time, it is rendered more accommodating to instructors.

The extensive and clear definitions of "Keith on the Globes" include everything which is necessary for a thorough knowledge of the structure, design, and uses of the globes. The present abridgment has been prepared to meet a demand which has been frequently made by teachers who, though desirous of giving their pupils thorough instruction on the globes, yet think the larger work of Keith contains a great deal more than is necessary for the purpose.

ENDORSEMENTS OF EDUCATIONISTS.

A volume containing Guy's popular "Treatise on Astronomy" and "Keith on the Globes" having been submitted to us for examination, we can, without any hesitation, recommend it to the notice and patronage of parents and teachers. The work on Astronomy is clear, intelligible, and suited to the comprehension of young persons. It comprises a great amount of information, and is well illustrated with steel engravings. "Keith on the Globes" has long been recognised as a standard school-book. The present edition, comprised in the same volume with the "Astronomy," is improved by the omission of much extraneous matter, and the reduction of size and price. On the whole, we know of no school-book which contains so much in so little space as the new edition of Guy and Keith.—*Thomas Eustace, John Haslam, W. Curran, Samuel Clendenin, Charles Mead, Benjamin Mayo, Hugh Morrow, J. H. Black.*

The subjoined, teachers in the city of Baltimore, Maryland, concur in the opinion above expressed — *E. Bennett, C. F. Banaemar, E. R. Harney, Robert O'Neill, N. Spelman, O. W. Treadwell, James Shanley, David King, Robert Walker, D. W. McClelan.*

STANDARD WORKS
ON
MATHEMATICS, ETC.,
PUBLISHED BY CHARLES DESILVER,
714 CHESTNUT STREET, PHILADELPHIA.

SMITH'S MATHEMATICAL SERIES.

AMERICAN STATISTICAL ARITHMETIC,
DESIGNED FOR ACADEMIES AND SCHOOLS.

BY FRANCIS H. SMITH, A.M.,
SUPERINTENDENT AND PROFESSOR OF MATHEMATICS IN THE VIRGINIA MILITARY INSTITUTE, LATE PROFESSOR OF MATHEMATICS IN HAMPDEN SIDNEY COLLEGE, AND FORMERLY ASSISTANT PROFESSOR IN THE UNITED STATES MILITARY ACADEMY, WEST POINT,

AND

R. T. W. DUKE,
ASSISTANT PROFESSOR OF MATHEMATICS IN THE VIRGINIA MILITARY INSTITUTE.

Fourth Edition.

In one volume, royal 18mo., containing 282 pages, half-roan binding. Price, 38 cents.

INTRODUCTION
TO
SMITH AND DUKE'S ARITHMETIC.

BY FRANCIS H. SMITH, A.M.,
SUPERINTENDENT AND PROFESSOR OF MATHEMATICS IN THE VIRGINIA MILITARY INSTITUTE.

One vol., 18mo., 93 pages, half-roan binding. Price 20 cents.

A KEY
TO
SMITH AND DUKE'S ARITHMETIC.

PREPARED BY WILLIAM FORBES,
ASSISTANT PROFESSOR OF MATHEMATICS IN THE VIRGINIA MILITARY INSTITUTE.

One volume, 18mo., 112 pages, half-roan binding. Price, 30 cents.

The design of the author of the "Statistical Arithmetic" has been to illustrate the various rules by examples selected, whenever practicable, from the most prominent facts connected with the history, geography, and statistics of the United States. Arithmetic thus becomes a medium for communicating much important information, which will readily be apprehended by the youthful mind, and be impressed upon it throughout life.

Standard Works on Mathematics, Etc.

ENDORSEMENTS OF SMITH'S ARITHMETICS.

The Board of Directors of the Literary Fund Board having examined the Introduction to Smith and Duke's American Statistical Arithmetic, take pleasure in recommending the work especially for the purpose for which it is designed, "to prepare beginners for the study of the more advanced parts of the science." The plan of inculcating valuable statistical information in the illustration of arithmetical rules is not only novel and attractive, but useful, and is doubtless calculated to make a strong impression on the minds of youth. — *J. Brown, Jr., Second Auditor Literary Fund Board, Va.*

The character of this work is simplicity, and the rules are given in plain and brief language. It is the only Arithmetic we have ever seen which can truly be called American, and as all the illustrations are drawn from the most prominent facts connected with the history, geography, and statistics of our country, it will be seen that while the pupil is advancing in arithmetic, he is also acquiring valuable statistical information which will be useful at all periods of life. — *Saturday Evening News, Washington, D. C.*

"Smith and Duke's American Statistical Arithmetic" evidently simplifies the process of calculation, while it lets the pupil into the *rationale* or science of its rules of computation — and as might be expected, from the practical sphere in which its authors have been operating, much of the redundancy of former publications on Arithmetic has been made to give place to rules and illustrations more laconic, while more accessible to the general minds of students. — *Norfolk Daily Courier.*

The American Statistical Arithmetic, and an Introduction to the same, are works of more than ordinary merit. With clear and definite Rules, they convey a large amount of valuable information not usually within the reach of students of Arithmetic. Their general introduction will aid the cause of sound instruction in the schools and academies of our country. — *J. H. Brown, A. M., late Principal of Zane Street School, Philadelphia.*

I consider it decidedly the best Arithmetic I have seen, not only as regards the valuable statistical information it contains, but also in the arrangement, and the very clear and simple explanations of the rules which it gives. — *Professor Pike Powers, late of Virginia University*

SMITH'S BIOT.

AN ELEMENTARY TREATISE
ON
ANALYTICAL GEOMETRY.

TRANSLATED FROM THE FRENCH OF J. B. BIOT,

BY FRANCIS H. SMITH, A.M.,

SUPERINTENDENT AND PROFESSOR OF MATHEMATICS IN THE VIRGINIA MILITARY INSTITUTE.

A New and Revised Edition,

In one volume, 8vo, containing 302 pages, full-bound in sheep. Price $1.50.

OPINIONS OF EDUCATIONSTS.

I have long lamented the defect in logical arrangement of most of the principal treatises on the subject of Analytical Geometry, with regard to one of its most important applications — Conic Sections. The treatise of *Biot* comes precisely up to my idea of the proper arrangement in this respect. — *Professor Saunders, of William and Mary College.*

It gives the definitions and some of the most abstruse parts of the science with greater clearness and perspicuity than any similar work with which I am acquainted — and I also think the copious examples given a great desideratum. — *A. W. Millspaugh, Principal of the Classical School, Farmville.*

I have your Geometry, and, after a careful examination of it, I do not hesitate to pronounce it an excellent work — the best on the subject that I have seen. I shall therefore adopt it immediately in the academy. — *Professor John B. Strange, Norfolk Academy.*

STANDARD WORKS ON MATHEMATICS, ETC.

SMITH'S ALGEBRA.

AN ELEMENTARY TREATISE ON ALGEBRA,
PREPARED FOR THE USE OF
THE CADETS OF THE VIRGINIA MILITARY INSTITUTE
AND ADAPTED TO
THE PRESENT STATE OF MATHEMATICAL INSTRUCTION
IN THE
SCHOOLS AND COLLEGES OF THE UNITED STATES.
BY FRANCIS H. SMITH, A. M.,
SUPERINTENDENT AND PROFESSOR OF MATHEMATICS IN THE VIRGINIA MILITARY INSTITUTE;

TOGETHER WITH
A LARGE SELECTION OF PROMISCUOUS EXAMPLES,
CAREFULLY SELECTED FROM THE MOST APPROVED AUTHORITY,
BY S. CRUTCHFIELD,
ADJUNCT PROFESSOR OF MATHEMATICS IN THE VIRGINIA MILITARY UNIVERSITY.
NEW EDITION, ENLARGED.

In one volume, demi-octavo, containing 379 pages, half turkey-morocco binding. Price $1.

This work is designed to present as complete an elementary course of Algebra as the time devoted to the study of Mathematics in the Colleges of the United States will allow, while it will be equally within the comprehension of the pupil of the High School or the Academy.

The author has adopted those explanations and demonstrations which an experience of many years in teaching, and a careful comparison of standard authors, have shown to be best. Without following the system of any other writer, he has derived important aid from the works of *Garnier, Bézout, Reynaud, Bourdon, Lacroix, Francœur, Euler, Hutton, Thomson, Goodwyn, Scott,* and the *Encyclopedia Metropolitana.* Many of his examples have been selected from the valuable edition of Hutton's Mathematics, by Professor Rutherford, of the Royal Military Academy, Woolwich.

This Algebra covers the full course of Davies' Bourdon, and contains a new and beautiful demonstration of the Binomial Theorem in the case of an Exponent, by Professor Pike Powers, late of the University of Virginia.

ENDORSEMENTS BY PROFESSORS, ETC.

I have been using "Smith's Algebra" for nearly twelve months, and can truly say it answers my purpose better than any other I am acquainted with. It presents the leading principles of the science in a concise and simple form, and especially those higher principles which give beginners most trouble, so that I have never had my classes master them before with so little difficulty. — *Prof. P. Powers, late of Virginia University.*

This very excellent Algebra has been prepared with the greatest possible care, on an eclectic basis, from the best authorities. As an introduction it contains a very interesting history of algebra. — *Philadelphia Evening Bulletin.*

Standard Works on Mathematics, Etc.

ENDORSEMENTS OF SMITH'S ALGEBRA.

I have, ever since becoming familiar with "Smith's Algebra," regarded it as a masterpiece in that department of mathematical science — indeed, my feelings respecting it have always partaken much of the enthusiastic. It bears the evident stamp of genius, and embodies more of the beauties of ingenuity, simplicity, and generalization, than any other work of that class of subjects with which my mathematical studies have made me acquainted. — *Professor W. N. Pendleton.*

A new Algebra, by Col. Francis A. Smith, the highly efficient and esteemed Superintendent of our Military Institute at Lexington, will require no eulogy of ours, in view of the rapid and entire success of the author's previous work, the Statistical Arithmetic. No Virginia school-boy will lose much by being *minus* Bonnycastle and *plus* Smith. — *Virginian, Winchester, Va.*

Mr. Smith has had long experience in the absorbing pursuit of mathematics. This treatise, eminently adapted to the purposes of elementary instruction, has attractions also for advanced students, who have the enthusiasm of adepts for the science. — *Philadelphia North American.*

This is an ably composed work, fitted for the use of High-schools and Colleges. The author's design is to present as complete an elementary course of algebra as the time devoted to the study of mathematics in our academies will allow. — *Saturday Evening Post.*

Originally prepared for the use of the cadets of the Virginia Military Institute, it has since been adapted to the present state of mathematical instruction in the schools, academies, and colleges of the United States. — *Pennsylvania Inquirer.*

BRIDGE'S ALGEBRA.

A TREATISE
ON
THE ELEMENTS OF ALGEBRA.

BY THE

REV. B. BRIDGE, B. D., F. R. S.,

FELLOW OF ST. PETER'S COLLEGE, CAMBRIDGE, AND LATE PROFESSOR OF MATHEMATICS IN THE EAST INDIA COLLEGE, HERTS.

THE FIFTY-SECOND AMERICAN,

REVISED AND CORRECTED FROM THE SEVENTH LONDON EDITION.

In one vol. 12mo., 224 pages, half-roan binding. Price 67 cents.

EXTRACT FROM THE PREFACE.

"The favorable reception which this treatise has met with from the public, has induced the author, in this edition, to make some considerable additions and alterations. The whole has also been revised, and the press corrected, by a friend on whose judgment and accuracy the author has the greatest reliance. It is hoped, therefore, that it may still retain its character as a useful elementary work on this branch of mathematical science."

KERL'S ARITHMETIC.

A SYSTEM OF ARITHMETIC,
On an Original Plan;
DESIGNED AS
AN IMPROVEMENT ON THE SYSTEMS IN COMMON USE.
BY SIMON KERL, A. M.,
WASHINGTON UNIVERSITY, ST. LOUIS, MO.

One vol. 18mo, containing 162 pages, half-roan binding. Price 30 cents.

OPINIONS OF EDUCATIONISTS.

"Kerl's Primary Arithmetic" is just the thing wanted to fill a vacancy among the school-books now used, which had not been adequately supplied before. We shall adopt it in the Preparatory Department of the University; and we recommend it to all Primary schools, confidently believing that they will find it a most valuable auxiliary in laying the foundation of mathematical knowledge. N. D. THRALL, } *Prins. of Ac. Depart. Washington Univer* J. D. LOW,

All parts of Kerl's Primary Arithmetic are illustrated by an unusually large number of examples; and I believe that any student, with ordinary attention, will be almost compelled to understand it. I therefore commend it highly, and hazard the opinion that it will be approved by every teacher who will give it a fair trial.—*W. W. Hudson, Pres. Missouri Univ.*

I concur in the above recommendation of Mr. Simon Kerl's Arithmetic.—*B. S. Head, Professor of Mathematics in Missouri University.*

I consider "Kerl's Primary Arithmetic" not only a practical and analytical work, but eminently adapted to the speedy and successful acquisition of a thorough knowledge of the great and fundamental principles which are the very foundation upon which alone can be built the sublime structure of mathematical knowledge.—*James J. Searcy, Principal of Primary Department, Missouri University.*

In simplicity, scientific arrangement, comprehensiveness, practical utility, and adaptation to the taste and capacity of the young, I consider Kerl's Arithmetic, Part I., superior to any similar book now used in this State. I therefore recommend its adoption by the Common Schools of our State, and should be pleased to see it brought into general use by the teachers.—*H. B. Stark, Superintendent of Common Schools, Jefferson, Mo.*

I have examined Kerl's Elementary Arithmetic sufficiently to satisfy myself that the work is admirably well calculated to attain the end which the author has in view. The child that has been carefully drilled in the manner prescribed, will make an expert accountant.—*Francis P. O'Loughlen, S. J., Professor of Mathematics in St. Louis University.*

I am delighted with the simplicity and clearness with which you have presented the fundamental principles of Arithmetic, and hope that you will receive sufficient encouragement to give us a complete series of Mathematics. I am inclined to adopt it as a text-book as soon as convenient, and encourage others to do likewise.—*J. A. Hollis, Baptist Fem. Col. Columbia, Mo.*

OPINIONS OF THE PRESS.

"Kerl's System of Arithmetic" aims to furnish such a series of mental exercises as will enable the pupil to acquire in the easiest and most direct manner all the knowledge requisite for undertaking and prosecuting with rapidity and accuracy the study of written Arithmetic. We recommend it as a very good introduction to the more abstract and difficult branches of Mathematics.—*Missouri Republican.*

I am fully satisfied that if the plan of Kerl's Elementary Arithmetic were fully carried out by teachers, written arithmetic would be better understood, and each pupil would perform his calculations in a more satisfactory manner than heretofore.—*Charles Stewart, formerly Teacher of Mathematics in St. Louis, Missouri.*

We think well of its plan and design, and commend the work to the attention of instructors of youth.—*Missouri Statesman.*

We believe it will answer admirably the purpose for which it was intended.—*Mo. Argus*

STANDARD WORKS
ON THE
MODERN LANGUAGES,
PUBLISHED BY CHARLES DESILVER,
714 CHESTNUT STREET, PHILADELPHIA.

CHANDLER'S
COMMON SCHOOL GRAMMAR.

A GRAMMAR
OF
THE ENGLISH LANGUAGE,
Adapted to the Use of the Schools of America.
BY JOSEPH R. CHANDLER,
LATE EDITOR OF THE UNITED STATES GAZETTE.

In one volume, 12mo., 208 pages, half-roan binding. Price 38 cents.

ENDORSEMENTS OF TEACHERS, ETC.

The undersigned, having examined Chandler's English Grammar with a view to ascertain its adaptation to the purpose of teaching, take great pleasure in recommending the same as a work of superior merit. The prominent features which seem to recommend the book strongly to the undersigned, are, first, the system of commencing the study with the business of inductive parsing; the introduction of the different parts of speech progressively; with a correct reference to definitions, together with the uniform simplicity of explanation. It is the only text-book on this subject now in use in Ward School No. 19, New York, containing over twelve hundred pupils.

W. C. KING, *Principal Male Department,*   G. W. PETIT, *Assistant,*
J. D. DEWITT, *Assistant,*   HARRIET N. GOLDEY, *Prin. Female Depart.*

The Book Committee of the Ward School Teachers' Association of New York city, to whom was referred a Grammar of the English Language, by Joseph R. Chandler, of Philadelphia, beg leave to report that they have carefully and critically examined it, and have compared it with several other recent books of the same class, and have no hesitation in expressing the opinion that it is, in many respects, and on the whole, decidedly superior. We therefore submit the following resolution:—"*Resolved,* That Chandler's Grammar be adopted by this Association, and that it be introduced into our schools as soon as it can be done conveniently."

E. McILROY,   WM. KENNEDY,   } *Committee.*   JOHN WALSH, *Chairman.*
D. HAYNES,   J. BLACKMAR,

The Book Committee of the Albany Co. Teachers' Institute, having carefully examined Chandler's Grammar, would cheerfully recommend it to teachers and friends of education.

Prof. HENRY GALLUP,   Dr. PLATT WICKES,   W. D. PALMER,
H. S. M'CALL, *Ch. Sup't,*   Dr. Z. W. SAY,   HENRY W. SPAWN,   } *Committee.*
Rev. MARCUS SMITH,   GIDEON CORNELL,   JEREMIAH C. SNYDER,
                                                         WILLETT MACKEY,

The thorough acquaintance of the author with the subject renders it unnecessary for us to do more than to endorse his views, and to commend the work as one to be relied on.— *New Orleans Commercial Times.*

Chandler's Common School Grammar.

The undersigned, Commissioners and Inspectors of Common Schools of the 13th Ward, N. Y., having, with much care and deliberation, examined Chandler's Grammar of the English language, are of the opinion that for scientific arrangement, happy illustration, and judicious application of the principles of Grammar to language, it is unequalled by any work of the kind extant. We have, therefore, adopted it to be used in the Ward Schools under our charge. WILLIAM A. WALTERS, JAMES H. COOK, *Commissioners.* CHAS. D. FIELD, *Inspector.*

For lucid explanations and familiar examples, Chandler's Grammar is not surpassed by any other work of a similar character heretofore issued. As the hand-book of the scholar who wishes to commence the study of English Grammar, and feels the need of simple and familiar explanations and illustrations of oft-repeated rules, this work will be found to be one of the most useful ever issued. — *Cincinnati Daily Advertiser.*

The chief merit of this work is the great simplicity of explanation which characterizes it throughout. It is a decided improvement upon the old and obscure books so long used in most of our schools. — *Springfield (Ill.) State Register.*

This seems to be a good, sensible Grammar, and it would be well if we all, including "children of a larger growth," studied it or some other; for every day shows instances of great need of such attention. — *N. Y. Christian Inquirer.*

The "Grammar King" is sufficient guarantee to us for the excellency of the work, particularly on that subject. — *Official Journal, 2d Municipality, New Orleans.*

Its explanations are clear and comprehensive, simplifying the intricacies of Grammar to the level of the humblest intellect. — *New Orleans Daily Bee.*

Decidedly the best English Grammar that we have ever seen. — *Cincinnati Daily Atlas.*

(*In Preparation.*)
THE MODEL SPELLER;

IN WHICH,

By a Progressive Gradation,

THE JUVENILE LEARNER PASSES FROM THE SIMPLE MONOSYLLABLE TO THE MOST DIFFICULT WORDS IN THE ENGLISH LANGUAGE, AND ALSO BECOMES CONVERSANT WITH THE DERIVATIONS OF WORDS, AND THE MODES OF GROUPING THEM INTO SENTENCES.

In one royal 18mo volume, bound in boards. Price

McROBERTS' GRAMMAR.

THE SELF-INSTRUCTING
MODEL ENGLISH GRAMMAR;

EMBRACING

EXERCISES IN ORTHOGRAPHY, ETYMOLOGY, SYNTAX, AND PROSODY,

AND

A COMPLETE KEY TO THE METHOD OF ANALYZING AND PARSING:

INTENDED TO AID TEACHERS AND PRIVATE STUDENTS.

BY JOHN A. McROBERTS,

TEACHER OF ENGLISH GRAMMAR, TENNESSEE.

In one volume, 12mo, 262 *pages, half-roan binding. Price* 50 *cents.*

LAIDLAW'S PRONOUNCING DICTIONARY.

AN
AMERICAN PRONOUNCING DICTIONARY
OF
THE ENGLISH LANGUAGE;

IN WHICH

VARIABLE, CONTESTED, AND DIFFICULT SPELLINGS ARE DESIGNATED; AND IRREGULAR INFLECTIONS, PRIMARY AND SECONDARY ACCENTS, APPROPRIATE PREPOSITIONS, CORRESPONDING CONJUNCTIONS AND ADVERBS, AND NUMEROUS REFERENCES TO WRITINGS OF STANDARD MERIT ARE INSERTED;

AND TO WHICH ARE APPENDED

DEFINITIONS OF GEOGRAPHICAL NAMES, AND PROPER NAMES OF PERSONS, TRANSLATIONS OF FOREIGN PHRASES, RULES FOR SPELLING, LISTS CONTAINING THE CONSERVATIVE AND WEBSTERIAN ORTHOGRAPHIES, AND A COLLECTION OF PROVERBS AND MAXIMS.

BY ALEXANDER H. LAIDLAW, A.M.

In one volume, square 8vo., containing 600 pages, half-roan binding. Price, $1.25.

OPINIONS OF EDUCATIONISTS, ETC.

If this book had been entirely anonymous, a very cursory examination would have been sufficient to show that it was the work of a practical teacher. Avoiding, with wise moderation, the attempt to make a large and ambitious book, Mr. Laidlaw has contented himself with the more useful purpose of making a Dictionary which should meet, directly and explicitly, the wants that he has himself experienced as a teacher. Every one who knows much of the public schools of Philadelphia knows that Mr. Laidlaw has been for years one of her most successful teachers. His own eminent and marked success of itself creates a presumption in favor of a work in which he has embodied the fruits of his own experience, growing out of his own professional wants. The mechanical arrangement and execution of the work, as a specimen of book manufacture, deserves the highest commendation.—*John S. Hart, late Principal of the Central High School of Philadelphia.*

To keep up with the language is the duty of the Dictionary. New and enlarged editions must appear as a matter of necessity. One of the very latest is the work now under notice. Its scope is fully set forth in the title-page. We believe it has peculiarities which constitute a claim to public patronage. The volume is much smaller than Webster, owing mainly to the abridgment of the definitions, and the exclusion of words entirely obsolete; and not to its being less comprehensive in its range.—*The Catholic Mirror.*

This is a work of unusual merit. In all of its parts it shows that it has been undertaken by a teacher who has felt the want of a dictionary at the same time compact and comprehensive, and by one, too, who has well known how to supply that want. It is the first Dictionary which contrasts Websterian and conservative spellings; and for terse completeness of definitions it has no superior in the language.—*Philadelphia Sunday Dispatch.*

At a meeting of the "Controllers of the Public Schools, First District, Pennsylvania," held at the Controllers' Chamber, on Tuesday, June 14, 1859, the following resolution was adopted: *Resolved*, That "The American Pronouncing Dictionary," by Alexander H. Laidlaw, A.M., be introduced to be used in the Public Schools of this District.—*Robert J. Hemphill, Secretary of the Board of Controllers.*

We have long felt that such a book should be prepared, but did not expect to find it so well done, and in such a comparatively small space. Mr. Laidlaw's definitions are plain and sensible. The Dictionary, we suppose, will become a much-used school-book, but every one who reads and writes may advantageously consult it.—*Philadelphia Press.*

As a school-book it is invaluable; serving not only as a certain and reliable guide in the spelling of all words in the English language, but also affording a full insight into the art of English composition. We heartily commend this Dictionary to the public.—*Pennsylvanian.*

Laidlaw's Pronouncing Dictionary.

OPINIONS OF THE PRESS.

The volume is distinguished for a masterly treatment of the powers and properties of our tongue, for a judicious extension of the uses of a dictionary, for a display of nice discrimination in discarding as well as in inserting words, and for choice and cultivated diction. The definitions of geographical names, and of the proper names of persons, give it additional interest and value. The rules for spelling contain much that is new and useful, and the contrast of Websterian and conservative orthographies constitutes the only full exhibition of the differences, advantages, and disadvantages of both systems, that has yet been offered to the public.— *Daily Argus, Philadelphia.*

Mr. Laidlaw's Dictionary is intended to be a manual for all who speak and write, or, at least, for such as desire to do this kind of work with precision and elegance. It contains, in a volume of very moderate size, all the living words in common use in our language, and many of their inflections, especially those which are irregular and consequently most like to cause embarrassment to a writer; variable and contested spellings and pronunciations are carefully designated, and accents marked. The work is prepared with a good deal of care, and we believe it to be a perfectly reliable standard of pronunciation and definition.—*Catholic Herald and Visitor.*

Besides the comprehensive catalogue of words contained in this *vade mecum* of the English language, there is much additional matter of a very useful character. The "hints to spellers" are invaluable to those who have not quite mastered the language. Laidlaw's Dictionary should be at the elbow of every man who writes, and its substance on the tongue of every one who speaks. We cannot recommend it too highly, and we feel a pride in saying that it is a Philadelphia production.— *Daily News, Philadelphia.*

Besides its school purposes, this dictionary will be found very useful for ordinary reference in families. It is certainly one of the most comprehensive volumes for its size which we have ever examined, containing among its tables and lists many things very useful and convenient. The excellence of the larger dictionaries now in use demanded an improvement in the school abridgments, and the author of this work has responded to the call.— *North American, Philadelphia.*

This work contains nearly 40,000 classified words, their pronunciations and primary and secondary accents, variable, contested and difficult spellings designated, appropriate prepositions, references to writings of standard merit, definitions of geographical names, and proper names of persons; translations of foreign phrases, rules for spelling, lists contrasting the conservative and Websterian orthographies, &c., making it an excellent school Dictionary — *Public Ledger, Philadelphia.*

A book like this deserves a place upon the household shelf of every man, whether he be laborer, mechanic, or professional. It will be a matter of reference every day, to settle those vexed little questions "gramatically" which are constantly occurring, and the scholar will find it an invaluable companion in his studies, when a ponderous Webster might prove an incubus.— *Philadelphia Sunday Mercury.*

This is a carefully compiled, well-arranged, and eminently useful work. It embraces a large collection of words, to which brief but clear definitions are affixed, and is well calculated to become a welcome visitor in the schools and homes of America, in both of which it will be found a useful companion.— *Sunday Atlas.*

At a time when all the world is quarrelling as to which is the correct system, that of Webster or Worcester, a neat, practical and carefully compiled work like the present, giving both readings is much needed. As a school book it is one of great merit.—*Evening Bulletin.*

For those who would have a Dictionary of a tolerable size, this one is a consideration: and so far as we have examined it, it is in all respects reliable. We commend the work to schools and private families, as a ready resolver of many a difficulty. — *Philada. Evening Journal.*

Laidlaw's Dictionary — Jaudon's Expositor.

OPINIONS OF THE PRESS.

The pronunciation is carefully marked, the vocabulary full without, as was the case with Walker, being overburdened. In the spelling the author, who is Principal of the Monroe Grammar School, Philadelphia, has sought to provide "a bridge on which the advocates of both ideas may meet to compromise," by supplying both the Worcester and Websterian modes of writing. The different words are given in the body of the work, and specially at the end We observe the first place is given to the "Websterian," the second to the "conservative." There is some other tabular matter at the end, lists of foreign words, and a collection of proverbs. — *The Century, New York.*

A peculiarity of this Dictionary, which the title page does not set forth, consists of a large number of "starred" words, of peculiar spelling, and which of themselves render it valuable as a first class spelling-book. In other respects, the best commendation that we can possibly give it, is the assertion, that the contents entirely and faithfully fulfil what the title page promises. — *Philadelphia Sunday Transcript.*

This is really a very useful work of reference, in which the true pronunciation of every word in the language is given in the clearest and most familiar manner. Not only is the accentuation perfect, but contested and difficult spellings are designated, while the definitions are concise and correct. — *Philadelphia Inquirer.*

JAUDON'S EXPOSITOR.

THE
ENGLISH ORTHOGRAPHICAL EXPOSITOR;
BEING
A COMPENDIOUS SELECTION
OF THE
MOST USEFUL WORDS IN THE ENGLISH LANGUAGE,
ALPHABETICALLY ARRANGED, DIVIDED, ACCENTED, AND EXPLAINED,
ACCORDING TO THE MOST APPROVED MODERN AUTHORS.
ALSO
A LIST OF MORE THAN EIGHT HUNDRED WORDS,
SIMILAR, OR NEARLY SIMILAR IN SOUND, BUT OF DIFFERENT SPELLING AND IMPORT.

BY DANIEL JAUDON,
THOMAS WATSON, AND STEPHEN ADDINGTON.

One vol., 12mo., 93 pages, half-roan binding. Price 38 cents.

OPINIONS OF THE PRESS.

We cordially commend "Jaudon's Expositor" to all teachers, and to those desirous of having at hand a compendious and useful spelling-book; and there are few persons so carefully educated that they do not at times need some aid in this particular. — *Evening Bulletin, Philadelphia.*

"Jaudon's Expositor" is a comprehensive manual, fully supporting its title, so far as the common purposes of rudimentary instruction require. — *Phila. North American.*

www.ingramcontent.com/pod-product-compliance
Lightning Source LLC
Chambersburg PA
CBHW020100020526
44112CB00032B/681